Methodologies, Frameworks, and Applications of Machine Learning

Pramod Kumar Srivastava
Rajkiya Engineering College, Azamgarh, India

Ashok Kumar Yadav
Rajkiya Engineering College, Azamgarh, India

IGI Global
PUBLISHER of TIMELY KNOWLEDGE

A volume in the Advances in Computational Intelligence and Robotics (ACIR) Book Series

Published in the United States of America by
IGI Global
Engineering Science Reference (an imprint of IGI Global)
701 E. Chocolate Avenue
Hershey PA, USA 17033
Tel: 717-533-8845
Fax: 717-533-8661
E-mail: cust@igi-global.com
Web site: http://www.igi-global.com

Copyright © 2024 by IGI Global. All rights reserved. No part of this publication may be reproduced, stored or distributed in any form or by any means, electronic or mechanical, including photocopying, without written permission from the publisher. Product or company names used in this set are for identification purposes only. Inclusion of the names of the products or companies does not indicate a claim of ownership by IGI Global of the trademark or registered trademark.

Library of Congress Cataloging-in-Publication Data

Names: Srivastava, Pramod, 1979- editor. | Yadav, Ashok, 1988- editor.
Title: Methodologies, frameworks, and applications of machine learning / edited by Pramod Srivastava, Ashok Yadav.
Description: Hershey. PA : Engineering Science Reference, [2024] | Includes bibliographical references and index. | Summary: "Machine learning has recently been used to predict social media features, product recommendations, image recognition, sentiment analysis, and so on. The primary objective of this book is to provide a conceptual and practical approach to tackling the above-mentioned issues by using machine learning techniques"-- Provided by publisher.
Identifiers: LCCN 2023038649 (print) | LCCN 2023038650 (ebook) | ISBN 9798369310625 (hardcover) | ISBN 9798369310632 (ebook)
Subjects: LCSH: Machine learning--Industrial applications.
Classification: LCC Q325.5 .M395 2024 (print) | LCC Q325.5 (ebook) | DDC 006.3/1--dc23/eng/20240229
LC record available at https://lccn.loc.gov/2023038649
LC ebook record available at https://lccn.loc.gov/2023038650

This book is published in the IGI Global book series Advances in Computational Intelligence and Robotics (ACIR) (ISSN: 2327-0411; eISSN: 2327-042X)

British Cataloguing in Publication Data
A Cataloguing in Publication record for this book is available from the British Library.

All work contributed to this book is new, previously-unpublished material. The views expressed in this book are those of the authors, but not necessarily of the publisher.

For electronic access to this publication, please contact: eresources@igi-global.com.

Advances in Computational Intelligence and Robotics (ACIR) Book Series

Ivan Giannoccaro
University of Salento, Italy

ISSN:2327-0411
EISSN:2327-042X

Mission

While intelligence is traditionally a term applied to humans and human cognition, technology has progressed in such a way to allow for the development of intelligent systems able to simulate many human traits. With this new era of simulated and artificial intelligence, much research is needed in order to continue to advance the field and also to evaluate the ethical and societal concerns of the existence of artificial life and machine learning.

The **Advances in Computational Intelligence and Robotics (ACIR) Book Series** encourages scholarly discourse on all topics pertaining to evolutionary computing, artificial life, computational intelligence, machine learning, and robotics. ACIR presents the latest research being conducted on diverse topics in intelligence technologies with the goal of advancing knowledge and applications in this rapidly evolving field.

Coverage

- Agent technologies
- Neural Networks
- Evolutionary Computing
- Heuristics
- Cyborgs
- Brain Simulation
- Computational Logic
- Adaptive and Complex Systems
- Machine Learning
- Computer Vision

IGI Global is currently accepting manuscripts for publication within this series. To submit a proposal for a volume in this series, please contact our Acquisition Editors at Acquisitions@igi-global.com or visit: http://www.igi-global.com/publish/.

The Advances in Computational Intelligence and Robotics (ACIR) Book Series (ISSN 2327-0411) is published by IGI Global, 701 E. Chocolate Avenue, Hershey, PA 17033-1240, USA, www.igi-global.com. This series is composed of titles available for purchase individually; each title is edited to be contextually exclusive from any other title within the series. For pricing and ordering information please visit http://www.igi-global.com/book-series/advances-computational-intelligence-robotics/73674. Postmaster: Send all address changes to above address.
Copyright © 2024 IGI Global. All rights, including translation in other languages reserved by the publisher. No part of this series may be reproduced or used in any form or by any means – graphics, electronic, or mechanical, including photocopying, recording, taping, or information and retrieval systems – without written permission from the publisher, except for non commercial, educational use, including classroom teaching purposes. The views expressed in this series are those of the authors, but not necessarily of IGI Global.

Titles in this Series

For a list of additional titles in this series, please visit: http://www.igi-global.com/book-series/advances-computational-intelligence-robotics/73674

Artificial Intelligence of Things (AIoT) for Productivity and Organizational Transition
Sajad Rezaei (University of Worcester, UK) and Amin Ansary (University of the Witwatersrand, South Africa)
Business Science Reference • © 2024 • 368pp • H/C (ISBN: 9798369309933) • US $275.00

Internet of Things and AI for Natural Disaster Management and Prediction
D. Satishkumar (Nehru Institute of Technology, India) and M. Sivaraja (Nehru Institute of Technology, India)
Engineering Science Reference • © 2024 • 334pp • H/C (ISBN: 9798369342848) • US $345.00

AI Applications for Business, Medical, and Agricultural Sustainability
Arshi Naim (King Khalid University, Saudi Arabia)
Engineering Science Reference • © 2024 • 322pp • H/C (ISBN: 9798369352663) • US $315.00

Innovative Machine Learning Applications for Cryptography
J. Anitha Ruth (SRM Institute of Science and Technology, India) G.V. Mahesh Vijayalakshmi (BMS Institute of Technology and Management, India) P. Visalakshi (SRM Institute of Science and Technology, India) R. Uma (Sri Sai Ram Engineering College, India) and A. Meenakshi (SRM Institute of Science and Technology, India)
Engineering Science Reference • © 2024 • 294pp • H/C (ISBN: 9798369316429) • US $300.00

The Ethical Frontier of AI and Data Analysis
Rajeev Kumar (Moradabad Institute of Technology, India) Ankush Joshi (COER University, Roorkee, India) Hari Om Sharan (Rama University, Kanpur, India) Sheng-Lung Peng (College of Innovative Design and Management, National Taipei University of Business, Taiwan) and Chetan R. Dudhagara (Anand Agricultural University, India)
Engineering Science Reference • © 2024 • 456pp • H/C (ISBN: 9798369329641) • US $365.00

Empowering Low-Resource Languages With NLP Solutions
Partha Pakray (National Institute of Technology, Silchar, India) Pankaj Dadure (University of Petroleum and Energy Studies, India) and Sivaji Bandyopadhyay (Jadavpur University, India)
Engineering Science Reference • © 2024 • 314pp • H/C (ISBN: 9798369307281) • US $300.00

Computational Intelligence for Green Cloud Computing and Digital Waste Management
K. Dinesh Kumar (Amrita Vishwa Vidyapeetham, India) Vijayakumar Varadarajan (The University of New South Wales, Australia) Nidal Nasser (College of Engineering, Alfaisal University, Saudi Arabia) and Ravi Kumar Poluru (Institute of Aeronautical Engineering, India)
Engineering Science Reference • © 2024 • 405pp • H/C (ISBN: 9798369315521) • US $300.00

IGI Global
PUBLISHER of TIMELY KNOWLEDGE

701 East Chocolate Avenue, Hershey, PA 17033, USA
Tel: 717-533-8845 x100 • Fax: 717-533-8661
E-Mail: cust@igi-global.com • www.igi-global.com

Table of Contents

Detailed Table of Contents

Recent developments of carbon-based nanomaterials research have made it possible to use them for a wide range of environmental, material development, and energy-related applications. Graphene, CNT, quantum dots, nano-diamond, and graphene oxide are examples of carbon-based nanomaterials. The development of nanocomposites has drawn a lot of attention lately, with synthesis and application receiving. Recently, there has been a lot of interest in the synthesis of AI-created nanoparticles using artificial intelligence. This work focuses on the synthesis of carbon-based nanocomposites and application of current AI tools to better understand the properties of carbon derivative material, and this information can be applied to the development and application of materials for solution of society's problem. To explain the synthetic and derivation process, adaptive neuro-fuzzy inference systems and ANN may be efficient. Derivations of the nanomaterials are the output of the models, which have various inputs such as catalyst dosage, particle size, concentration, content, exposure time.

Sustainable development has become a global imperative in the 21st century as societies grapple with environmental, social, and economic challenges. Machine learning (ML), a subset of artificial intelligence (AI), has emerged as a powerful tool to address these complex issues. Accordingly, this chapter explores the intersection of sustainable development and innovation, delving into the transformative potential of innovative solutions, particularly within the context of AI-powered techniques. Moreover, it examines how innovation, guided by sustainability principles, can be harnessed to address complex global challenges and help us progress towards a world where Sustainable Development Goals (SDGs) are not just aspirations but achievements. Furthermore, it explores how ML contributes to sustainable development across various domains, challenges encountered, and future directions.

The advent of machine learning and its significant impact on every sector of society requires our attention towards its progressive application in achieving the Sustainable Development Goals (SDGs). Machine learning is a kind of artificial intelligence allowing the machine itself to change its algorithms in order to provide the optimized solution to the subject. In other words, AI is a machine simulating human intelligence, and ML is a subset of artificial intelligence. The Sustainable Development Goals (SDGs) are an all-inclusive set of objectives intended to provide countries with a trail towards peace and prosperity. There are 17 SDGs that are further divided into 169 targets and 304 indicators dealing with everything from ending hunger and protecting marine wildlife to making cities sustainable and reducing gender inequalities. ML is an important tool in meeting these objectives. This chapter explores the application of ML models in achieving these SDGs in an effective manner.

The utilization of energy derived from renewable sources is experiencing a significant and rapid expansion. The rapid rate of technical advancement in contemporary times has rendered it economically feasible to exploit various renewable sources such as solar, wind, geothermal, and others for energy generation. The main focus of this chapter centers around the utilization of renewable energy sources in combination with artificial intelligence (AI) to build efficient strategies for attaining sustainable development. This research presents a detailed bibliometric analysis aimed at enhancing the comprehension of the progression of artificial intelligence within the context of renewable energy. The objective of this chapter is to improve the understanding of academics and scholars regarding the interconnectedness and interdependencies between renewable energy and sustainable development, with a specific focus on the integration of artificial intelligence (AI) technology.

This chapter explores waste-to-energy (WtE) solutions empowered by the integration of internet of things (IoT) and machine learning (ML) for sustainable power generation in smart cities. By leveraging IoT sensors, real-time data acquisition optimizes waste management processes, and ML algorithms enhance operational efficiency. The potential impact of these technologies on WtE's future includes predictive maintenance, waste sorting automation, and adaptive energy production. The role of WtE in smart cities extends to decentralized energy generation, integrated waste management, and fostering circular economy principles. This study calls for further research and the adoption of sustainable practices to propel WtE as a key component in the future energy landscape of smart and resilient urban environments.

With the fast growth of aquatic data, machine learning is essential for data analysis, categorization, and prediction. Data-driven models using machine learning may effectively handle complicated nonlinear problems in water research, unlike conventional approaches. Machine learning models and findings have been used to build, monitor, simulate, evaluate, and optimize water treatment and management systems in water environment research. Machine learning may also enhance water quality, pollution control, and watershed ecosystem security. This chapter discusses how ML approaches were used to assess water quality in surface, ground, drinking, sewage, and ocean water. The authors also suggest potential machine learning applications in aquatic situations.

It is crucial to arm users with the information and resources they need to protect their online presence in the dynamic world of cybersecurity, where threats are evolving at an alarming rate. This chapter examines contextual marketing as a potent strategy for delivering cybersecurity education and solutions. In order to effectively engage consumers and inform them about cybersecurity risks and best practices, contextual marketing is the strategic application of customised content and resources supplied at the appropriate time and in the appropriate environment. The chapter tackles the underlying difficulties that consumers confront in comprehending and managing their cybersecurity requirements. It emphasizes how critical it is to plug the knowledge gap by giving users access to information that is pertinent to their situation and degree of comprehension. By creating user-centric experiences, contextual marketing enables cybersecurity educators and solution providers to maximize the effect of their work. This chapter delivers several contextual marketing strategies that have been productive in enhancing users' cybersecurity awareness and skills. It accomplishes so by drawing on real-world examples and case studies. Educational activities can be made engaging and easily remembered by adapting messages, tutorials, and resources to meet users' roles, interests, and habits. The chapter also looks at how sophisticated cybersecurity solutions and contextual marketing work together. It exemplifies the benefits of context-aware security systems. The chapter concludes by arguing in favour of incorporating contextual marketing principles into cybersecurity instruction and solution delivery. Contextual marketing paves the way for a more informed and cyber-aware society that is better able to face the ever-evolving challenges of the digital world by providing users with personalized, timely, and relevant information.

Data mining tools are used to analyze and model data. Each of these tools has its own unique strengths and weaknesses, which make them suitable for different data mining tasks. The purpose of this chapter is to present the analysis of various data mining tools to shed light on researchers working in the field of data mining and machine learning. For this purpose, the accuracy rates of the results of different biomedical data classification applications obtained by four different data mining tools—Orange, RapidMiner, Weka, and Knime—will be evaluated. The comparisons in the context of literature research on these tools will be given. This research is particularly relevant given the increasing amount of data available in Kaggle and the need for accurate analysis and interpretation of data. By presenting the performance results of these popular data mining tools, this study will provide valuable insights for researchers and practitioners who use these tools for analysis.

Plant disease plays a crucial role in the reduction as well as degradation of production and yield in the area of precision agriculture and is a major concern for farmers and agriculturists. Hence, the detection and identification of diseases among the crops is essential. In this chapter, the CNN model for the identification and classification of different plant diseases through its leaf images is used. Four diseases such as ergot, downy mildew, blast, and rust in the pearl millet crops are considered in this work. The images of the pearl millet crop are considered for the five classes: healthy, ergot, downy mildew, rust, and blast. The dataset consists of 2074 images. The dataset is trained for the 30 epochs. The proposed approach is compared with the various existing methodologies such as naïve Bayesian, decision tree, support vector machine, and random forest. The simulation result shows that the proposed approach using the CNN outperforms the existing approaches in terms of accuracy and loss.

Preface

In the ever-evolving landscape of technology, machine learning stands as a beacon of innovation with the potential to reshape industries and redefine our daily lives. As editors of this comprehensive reference book, *Methodologies, Frameworks, and Applications of Machine Learning*, we are thrilled to present a compendium that encapsulates the essence of the latest advancements, theoretical foundations, and practical applications in the realm of machine learning.

The urgency to harness the latest methodologies and theoretical breakthroughs in machine learning is paramount. This book encapsulates the essence of this urgency, emphasizing the need to leverage realistic data and affordable computational resources. No longer confined to theoretical domains, machine learning has permeated diverse sectors, from healthcare and manufacturing to education, finance, law enforcement, and marketing, ushering in an era of data-driven decision-making.

Academic scholars exploring the potential of machine learning within the context of Industry 5.0 and advanced IoT applications will find our book to be a groundbreaking resource. It serves as an invaluable opportunity to delve into the forefront of modern research and application. The comprehensive guide offered within these pages equips readers with the tools to navigate the complexities of Industry 5.0 and the Internet of Things.

This book spans a vast array of topics, from conceptual frameworks and methodological approaches to the practical application of statistical techniques, and machine learning. Covering domains as diverse as e-government, healthcare, cyber-physical systems, and sustainable development, our aim is to provide readers with both knowledge and practical insights that transcend traditional boundaries.

Students, researchers, and practitioners will find this book to be a beacon of wisdom, guiding them toward the future of machine learning and its myriad applications. By harnessing the power of machine learning, we can address real-world challenges and transform the way we perceive and engage with the world around us.

Machine learning stands as a pool of critical tools that has the potential to enable the emergence of Industry 5.0 through advanced IoT applications. The objective is to develop models capable of learning autonomously from data, context, and environment. The continuous development of novel algorithms, coupled with the growing availability of realistic data and low-cost computation, has led to significant strides in machine learning, with data-intensive methodologies finding application in various industries.

This book takes a conceptual and practical approach to machine learning algorithms. It enables students, academics, researchers, engineers, and practitioners to navigate the challenges of Industry 5.0 implementation by utilizing machine learning algorithms and deploying advanced IoT applications that address social, economic, political, privacy, and security concerns.

The thematic coverage of this book spans an extensive array of applications, from cyber security and healthcare to agriculture, energy conservation, and smart cities. The inclusion of diverse topics reflects the versatility of machine learning in addressing real-world issues and presents a holistic view of its applications across industries.

As editors, we invite you to explore the conceptual and practical dimensions of machine learning presented in this book. From conceptual frameworks to future dimensions of machine learning applications, this compendium is a roadmap for those seeking to navigate the ever-expanding landscape of this transformative technology.

Chapter 1: Reinforcement Learning: A Deep Dive Into Techniques and Future Prospects

This chapter provides an in-depth exploration of reinforcement learning (RL), a subfield of machine learning that empowers agents to interact with their environment and learn from experiences. Core elements of RL, including agents, actions, states, and rewards, are dissected alongside algorithms like policy gradients, SARSA, and Q-learning. Challenges such as the exploration-exploitation conflict and deep learning instability are discussed. The chapter concludes with a comprehensive list of RL applications in diverse industries, from robotics and gaming to banking and healthcare, highlighting the need for further research to fully realize RL's transformative potential.

Chapter 2: Implementation of Different Machine Learning Projects Using SCIKIT-Learn and Tensorflow Frameworks

This chapter focuses on practical implementations of machine learning projects using Scikit-learn and TensorFlow libraries in Python. Four distinct projects unfold, each addressing classification, regression, and image classification problems. The step-by-step walkthrough covers model evaluation using classical machine learning techniques and deep neural networks. The projects delve into real-world datasets, such as White Wine Quality and stock market closing values, providing readers with hands-on experience in applying machine learning frameworks to diverse problem domains.

Chapter 3: Methodology and Application of Information Technology for Carbon-Based Nano-Composites

Highlighting recent developments in carbon-based nanomaterials, this chapter explores their synthesis and application, emphasizing the use of artificial intelligence in nanoparticle synthesis. The focus is on carbon-based nanocomposites, with an emphasis on using adaptive neuro-fuzzy inference systems and artificial neural networks for efficient synthesis. The chapter aims to bridge the gap between AI tools and the development of materials, showcasing the potential of these nanomaterials to address societal challenges.

Chapter 4: Towards an Intelligent Tomorrow: Machine Learning Enabling Sustainable Development

This chapter delves into the intersection of sustainable development and machine learning, exploring how innovative solutions powered by artificial intelligence can address global challenges. It examines the transformative potential of ML-driven innovation, emphasizing the role of machine learning in achieving sustainable development goals (SDGs). The chapter covers diverse domains where ML contributes to sustainability and discusses challenges and future directions for harnessing ML in the pursuit of a more sustainable world.

Chapter 5: Applications of Artificial Intelligence and Machine Learning in Achieving SDGs 6, 7, and 14

Exploring the application of machine learning models in achieving specific Sustainable Development Goals (SDGs), this chapter underscores the pivotal role of machine learning in addressing various challenges outlined in the SDGs. The chapter highlights the intersection between artificial intelligence and machine learning, demonstrating how these technologies can be leveraged to work towards goals related to water, clean energy, and life below water, providing a valuable guide for practitioners and researchers.

Chapter 6: Role of Artificial Intelligence in Renewable Energy Management for Sustainable Development

This chapter focuses on the utilization of renewable energy sources, coupled with artificial intelligence, to formulate efficient strategies for sustainable development. A detailed bibliometric analysis sheds light on the progression of AI within the context of renewable energy. The chapter aims to enhance understanding among academics and scholars regarding the integration of AI technology in renewable energy, emphasizing the interconnectedness between renewable energy and sustainable development.

Chapter 7: Waste-to-Energy Solutions Harnessing IoT and ML for Sustainable Power Generation in Smart Cities

Exploring the integration of IoT and ML in Waste-to-Energy (WtE) solutions, this chapter examines how real-time data acquisition and ML algorithms optimize waste management processes for sustainable power generation in smart cities. It discusses the potential impact of these technologies, including predictive maintenance and waste sorting automation, emphasizing the role of WtE in decentralized energy generation and integrated waste management.

Chapter 8: Prediction of Water Quality Using Machine Learning

Focusing on the fast-growing domain of aquatic data, this chapter explores how machine learning is essential for analyzing, categorizing, and predicting water quality. It discusses data-driven models and their applications in water treatment and management systems, emphasizing the potential of machine learning in enhancing water quality, pollution control, and watershed ecosystem security across various aquatic environments.

Chapter 9: Engineering, Geology, Climate, and Socioeconomic Aspects' Implications on Machine Learning-Dependent Water Pipe Collapse Prediction

This chapter addresses the challenges of predicting underground water pipe collapses by utilizing machine learning approaches. Integrating data from engineering, geology, climate, and socioeconomic aspects, the chapter employs various machine learning techniques, including LightGBM, ANN, Logistic Regression, K-NN, and SVM, to forecast water pipe failures. The multi-source data aggregation system provides a comprehensive understanding of the interconnected factors influencing subterranean pipe degradation.

Chapter 10: Suggested Cyber-Security Strategy That Maximizes Automated Detection of Internet of Things Attacks Using Machine Learning

In response to the rising cyber threats in the age of IoT, this chapter proposes a cyber-security strategy leveraging machine learning methods. Emphasizing the need for a novel framework to enhance IT security, the chapter aims to maximize the automated detection of IoT attacks. The Weka platform is utilized for implementing and evaluating the suggested strategy, emphasizing the importance of proactive cybersecurity measures in the face of evolving threats.

Chapter 11: Empowering Users: Contextual Marketing for Cybersecurity Education and Solutions

This chapter explores the integration of contextual marketing principles in cybersecurity education and solution delivery. By tailoring content and resources based on users' roles, interests, and habits, contextual marketing enhances cybersecurity awareness and skills. The chapter advocates for the incorporation of contextual marketing in cybersecurity instruction, fostering a more informed and cyber-aware society.

Chapter 12: A Comprehensive Analysis of Data Mining Tools for Biomedical Data Classification: Assessing Strengths, Weaknesses, and Future Directions

Providing a comprehensive analysis of data mining tools, this chapter evaluates the strengths and weaknesses of four popular tools—Orange, RapidMiner, Weka, and Knime—in the context of biomedical data classification. The study assesses the accuracy rates of these tools in various biomedical data classification applications, offering valuable insights for researchers and practitioners navigating the increasing volume of data available in biomedical research.

Chapter 13: Disease Identification and Classification From Pearl Millet Leaf Images Using Machine Learning Techniques

Focusing on precision agriculture, this chapter employs a Convolutional Neural Network (CNN) model for the identification and classification of plant diseases in pearl millet crops. The study considers four diseases, including Ergot, Downy Mildew, Blast, and Rust, and compares the proposed CNN approach with existing methodologies. The results highlight the superior performance of the CNN model in terms of accuracy and loss, showcasing its potential for disease identification in agricultural settings.

In the rapidly evolving landscape of technology, our edited reference book, *Methodologies, Frameworks, and Applications of Machine Learning*, stands as a testament to the transformative power of machine learning. As editors, we are proud to present this comprehensive compendium that encapsulates the latest advancements, theoretical foundations, and practical applications within the realm of machine learning.

The urgency to harness cutting-edge methodologies and theoretical breakthroughs in machine learning is underscored throughout this book. Machine learning, once confined to theoretical domains, has now permeated diverse sectors such as healthcare, manufacturing, education, finance, law enforcement, and marketing. This penetration marks the dawn of an era characterized by data-driven decision-making.

Machine learning, as a critical tool, plays a pivotal role in enabling the emergence of Industry 5.0 through advanced IoT applications. The continuous development of novel algorithms, coupled with the growing availability of realistic data and low-cost computation, has led to significant strides in the field. This book takes a conceptual and practical approach to machine learning algorithms, providing a roadmap for navigating the ever-expanding landscape of this transformative technology.

As editors, we invite readers to explore the conceptual and practical dimensions of machine learning presented in this compendium. From conceptual frameworks to future dimensions of machine learning applications, this book serves as a guide for those seeking to navigate the intricate and dynamic landscape of this revolutionary technology.

Pramod Kumar Srivastava
Rajkiya Engineering College, Azamgarh, India

Ashok Kumar Yadav
Rajkiya Engineering College, Azamgarh, India

Chapter 1
Reinforcement Learning: A Deep Dive Into Techniques and Future Prospects

Arti Saxena
https://orcid.org/0000-0002-4162-793X
Manav Rachna International Institute of Research and Studies, India

Falak Bhardwaj
https://orcid.org/0000-0001-9082-4350
Manav Rachna International Institute of Research and Studies, India

ABSTRACT

In this chapter, reinforcement learning (RL), a subfield of machine learning that has gained prominence because it enables agents to interact with their surroundings and learn from their mistakes, is covered in great detail. The chapter looks at the core elements of RL, including agents, actions, states, and rewards, in addition to examining a number of algorithms, including policy gradients, SARSA, and Q-learning. It also examines the difficulties and constraints of RL, such the conflict between exploration and exploitation and the instability of deep learning. Further research and development are required to realise RL's promise to transform society and technology. The chapter concludes with a list of numerous RL applications in industries like robotics, gaming, banking, and healthcare.

1. INTRODUCTION

Due to its capacity to allow agents to learn from experience and interact with their environment, reinforcement learning (RL) is a major topic of research in machine learning. In RL, an agent is guided towards selecting the optimum course of action through a system of rewards and penalties. It draws inspiration from how both people and animals learn from the results of their decisions.

This research paper's goal is to examine the methods and potential applications of reinforcement learning. We'll talk about the foundations of RL, such as the different kinds of agents, actions, states,

DOI: 10.4018/979-8-3693-1062-5.ch001

Copyright © 2024, IGI Global. Copying or distributing in print or electronic forms without written permission of IGI Global is prohibited.

and rewards. We will investigate various methods and algorithms, including policy gradients, SARSA, and Q-learning.

The paper will look at the difficulties and restrictions of RL in addition to looking at the current uses of RL in a number of industries, including robots, gaming, finance, and healthcare. The trade-off between exploration and exploitation, the instability of deep learning, and the moral ramifications of autonomous decision-making are all included in this.

The use of RL in robotics is among its most intriguing applications. Robots can learn from their surroundings and make judgements in real-time thanks to RL approaches. This has the ability to completely transform fields like manufacturing, where robots can adapt to various settings and jobs.

Gaming is a fascinating area in which RL has potential applications. Game-playing agents that can learn from their opponents and get better at their game have been developed using RL algorithms. Artificial intelligence (AI) agents that can defeat world champions in games like chess, go, and poker have been created as a result of this.

RL is not without its difficulties and restrictions, though. The trade-off between exploration and exploitation is one of the major obstacles. In order to better its decisions, an agent must both explore its surroundings to learn about it and use what it has previously learnt. The instability of deep neural network training, which is a problem in RL, is another issue.

RL has promising future prospects despite these difficulties. RL has the power to revolutionise both technology and how we connect with the outside world. RL can be used to build smarter, more effective systems that can change with their surroundings and tasks. It can also be used to create AI agents that are able to take in information from their surroundings and make judgements instantly. RL is positioned to become an essential tool in the machine learning industry with sustained research and development.

The relentless march of machine learning has indelibly reshaped numerous industries, from the realm of autonomous vehicles to the realm of voice recognition technology. Amidst this transformation, the spotlight has converged upon reinforcement learning—a domain that has garnered substantial attention in recent times. Within the fabric of machine learning, reinforcement learning stands as an intriguing facet, characterized by its unique modus operandi. It entails an agent navigating the labyrinth of learning by reaping rewards and penalties from its environment, a symphony of interactions that bestows upon it the art of decision-making.

A diverse array of sectors, including healthcare, finance, gaming, and robotics, bear the indelible imprints of reinforcement learning. This methodology has emerged as a powerful instrument, one particularly adept at addressing the nuances of decision-making within intricate and ever-shifting landscapes. In contrast to its machine-learning counterparts, reinforcement learning offers a distinct paradigm—an avenue wherein agents unravel the tapestry of optimal decisions through the very act of trial and error. This mechanism, rooted in the quintessence of adaptability and flexibility, finds its forte in contexts demanding swift responses to dynamic scenarios.

The resonant echoes of reinforcement learning resonate most resonantly within the domain of robotics. Here, agents endowed with the wisdom of reinforcement learning unfurl their wings within complex environments, adapting and learning from each experience. This metamorphosis resonates within the manufacturing industry, where adaptive robots emerge as emissaries of transformative efficiency, recalibrating their actions to seamlessly accommodate diverse tasks and scenarios.

Gaming, as an arena of immersive engagement, has also embraced the potential of reinforcement learning. With algorithms finely tuned, game-playing agents evolve, imbibing strategies through encounters with human and digital opponents alike. In this enigmatic dance, artificial intelligence (AI) agents master the art of human-like gameplay, a testament to the potency of reinforcement learning.

Yet, it is the synergy of reinforcement learning with deep learning that ignites the most profound transformations. Deep reinforcement learning, heralding a realm of sophistication, empowers agents to unfurl intricate strategies across expansive state and action spaces. The convergence of deep neural networks and reinforcement learning kindles innovations across domains ranging from autonomous driving to image recognition and natural language processing.

The gravitational pull of reinforcement learning is inextricably tied to its potential to engender paradigm shifts and galvanize innovation. Its tapestry of capabilities extends towards crafting more intelligent and adaptable robotic systems that continually assimilate from their surroundings. Moreover, the realm of personalized medicine beckons, as reinforcement learning ushers in a narrative where treatment plans are tailored to the idiosyncratic needs of each patient.

Within the commercial tapestry, the allure of reinforcement learning rests in its capacity to not only streamline operations but also augment revenue streams. Its acumen to grapple with decision-making complexities within ever-evolving contexts positions it as an invaluable asset, a compass that guides businesses toward optimized outcomes.

In summation, reinforcement learning emerges as an enthralling and rapidly evolving facet within the landscape of machine learning. Its potential applications span an eclectic spectrum, resonating across industries and technological paradigms. A comprehensive grasp of its underlying principles, techniques, and real-world applications becomes indispensable for researchers, practitioners, and policymakers entrenched within the domains of artificial intelligence and machine learning. As we traverse this technologically enriched epoch, the contours of reinforcement learning offer both guidance and promise, a compass poised to navigate the chasms of innovation and transformation.

2. LITERATURE SURVEY

Reinforcement learning (RL) is a type of machine learning in which an agent learns to behave in an environment by trial and error. The agent is given a reward for taking actions that lead to desired outcomes, and a penalty for taking actions that lead to undesired outcomes. The agent learns to maximize its expected reward over time by adjusting its behaviour.

RL has been applied to a wide variety of problems, including robotics, gaming, finance, and healthcare. In robotics, RL has been used to control autonomous robots, such as self-driving cars and drones. In gaming, RL has been used to train agents to play video games at superhuman levels. In finance, RL has been used to develop trading algorithms that can generate high returns. In healthcare, RL has been used to develop personalized treatment plans for patients.

The core elements of RL are agents, actions, states, and rewards.

- Agents are the entities that learn to behave in an environment. Agents can be physical robots, software programs, or even humans.
- Actions are the things that agents can do in an environment. Actions can be simple, such as moving left or right, or they can be complex, such as playing a game of chess.

- States are the descriptions of the environment that agents have access to. States can be simple, such as the position of a robot in a room, or they can be complex, such as the current state of a game of chess.
- Rewards are the signals that agents receive from the environment for taking actions. Rewards can be positive, negative, or neutral. Positive rewards encourage agents to take actions that lead to desired outcomes, while negative rewards discourage agents from taking actions that lead to undesired outcomes. Neutral rewards do not affect the agent's behaviour.

There are a number of different algorithms that can be used for RL, including policy gradients, SARSA, and Q-learning.

- Policy gradients are a class of algorithms that directly optimize the agent's policy. The policy is a function that maps from states to actions. The goal of policy gradients is to find a policy that maximizes the agent's expected reward (Sutton & Barto, 2018; Zhang et. al., 2022).
- SARSA is an on-policy algorithm that updates the agent's policy after each action. SARSA takes into account the reward that the agent received for taking the action, as well as the reward that the agent expects to receive for taking the next action (Mnih et al., 2015; Zhang et al., 2022).
- Q-learning is an off-policy algorithm that updates the agent's Q-table after each action. The Q-table is a table that stores the expected reward for taking each action in each state. Q-learning updates the Q-table based on the reward that the agent received for taking the action, as well as the reward that the agent expects to receive for taking the best action in the next state (Silver et al., 2017; Zhang et al., 2022).

RL is a powerful tool, but it also has some challenges and limitations. One challenge is the exploration-exploitation trade-off. Agents need to explore the environment in order to learn about the possible actions and rewards, but they also need to exploit their knowledge in order to maximize their reward. This can be a difficult balance to strike (Lillicrap et al., 2015; Chen et al., 2021).

Another challenge is the instability of deep learning. Deep learning is a powerful technique that can be used to approximate the Q-function or policy function in RL, but it can also be unstable. This means that the agent's behaviour can be very sensitive to the initial conditions or the hyperparameters of the deep learning model (Bellemare, 2016; Lillicrap et al., 2015; Chen et al., 2021).

Despite these challenges, RL is a promising technology with the potential to revolutionize many industries. Further research and development are needed to overcome the challenges of RL and to make it more widely accessible.

In recent years, there has been a surge of interest in RL, due to its success in a variety of challenging domains. This literature survey highlights some of the recent advances in RL, and discusses the potential of RL to solve real-world problems.

The following are some of the key recent advances in RL:

- The development of deep RL algorithms has enabled RL to be applied to complex domains, such as robotics and video games. For example, DeepMind's AlphaGo used RL to defeat a professional Go player (Sutton & Barto, 2018; chen et al., 2021).

- The development of new RL algorithms, such as policy gradients and Q-learning, has improved the efficiency and scalability of RL. For example, OpenAI Five used RL to defeat a team of professional Dota 2 players (Zinyals et al., 2017; Zhang et al., 2022).
- The availability of large datasets has enabled RL to be trained on real-world data. For example, Google Brain has developed a RL model that can trade stocks more effectively than human traders (Hu et al., 2019).
- The development of cloud computing has made it possible to train RL models on large datasets and complex environments. This has enabled RL to be applied to a wider range of problems, such as traffic signal control (Wang et al., 2018) and personalized medicine (Zhang et al., 2020).

RL is a rapidly evolving field, and there are many exciting new developments on the horizon. For example, researchers are working on developing RL algorithms that can learn from sparse rewards, such as those that are often encountered in real-world applications. They are also working on developing RL algorithms that can learn to cooperate with other agents, such as in multi-agent traffic control or robotic swarms.

The potential of RL to solve real-world problems is vast. As RL algorithms continue to improve, we can expect to see them being used to solve a wide range of challenges, from improving the efficiency of transportation systems to developing new medical treatments.

3. FUNDAMENTALS OF REINFORCEMENT LEARNING

Reinforcement learning (RL) stands as a potent catalyst poised to instigate a paradigm shift across a spectrum of sectors, encompassing pivotal domains such as transportation, energy, and agriculture. In the dynamic realm of transportation, RL algorithms emerge as crucial players, orchestrating the augmentation of traffic fluidity and catalysing the evolution of autonomous vehicle technologies. The tangible outcomes of this endeavour could encompass a reduction in traffic bottlenecks and a curtailment of road accidents—milestones that hold transformative implications for the transportation landscape.

Shifting the focus to the energy sector, RL's significance amplifies as it plays a strategic role in augmenting energy utilization efficiency and optimizing the intricacies of power generation and distribution networks. The intrinsic worth of this application resides in the promise of unlocking financial savings while concurrently curbing energy consumption—a juncture where sustainability and economic prudence coalesce.

Meanwhile, the agriculture arena emerges as another fertile ground where RL's potential proliferates. Farmers stand to benefit immensely from the infusion of RL algorithms into their practices, embarking on a journey toward maximizing crop yields while judiciously allocating resources. This dual-pronged approach not only enhances productivity but also aligns harmoniously with sustainable agricultural practices.

In a broader expanse, RL's kaleidoscope of possibilities continues to expand, with the landscape of applications continuously evolving. However, amid this promising tableau, inherent challenges necessitate deliberation. The demand for copious amounts of data and computational horsepower remains a pertinent concern. Yet, the tantalizing prospect of RL charting a course that reshapes the contours of intricate decision-making challenges across diverse sectors underscores its allure and potency. This, in turn, solidifies RL's status as a compelling domain of study, positioned to command sustained interest and investment in the foreseeable future.

Intriguingly, the notion that RL could ascend to the vanguard of addressing some of the epochal challenges that currently confront our global society lends an aura of significance to this field. The momentum of technological advancement harmoniously entwined with the sagacity of human inquiry promises a fertile ground for novel applications to burgeon across varied sectors. From galvanizing the landscape of autonomous driving to engineering energy efficiency paradigms and propagating sustainable agricultural methodologies, RL occupies a pivotal locus. Its potential to reshape our quotidian interactions with the world pulsates vibrantly—a ceaseless voyage of discovery and innovation that propels RL to a realm where possibilities are boundless.

In summation, reinforcement learning radiates as a transformative force, poised to usher in epochal changes across sectors. It signifies the nexus of technology and human acumen, forging a trajectory toward uncharted frontiers and heralding a future replete with promise and potential.

3.1. Reinforcement Learning Algorithms

An agent, functioning as a dynamic entity, engages in interactions with its environment, propelled by the mechanism of reinforcement learning (RL) algorithms. Within this intricate choreography, the agent embarks on a journey of discovery, navigating through the landscape of trial and error. Through this iterative process, it unfurls the enigma of how to optimize a reward signal, thus distilling wisdom from the crucible of experience.

Central to this narrative is the agent's ability to wield its decision-making prowess, a faculty honed through the lens of RL. In this paradigm, the agent assimilates input manifesting as rewards or penalties. Guided by this continuum, it charts its course of action, calibrated by the quest for the maximal reward. This mechanism, entrenched within the fabric of RL, bestows upon the agent an acumen to discern, decipher, and respond to the intricate signals imprinted by its environment.

3.1.1. Q-Learning

The widely used reinforcement learning method known as Q-learning can help an agent determine the optimum course of action in a given environment. In contrast to model-based algorithms, Q-learning is a model-free approach that does not require prior environmental knowledge. Here is the basic update rule for Q-learning:

$$Q(s,a) \leftarrow (1-\alpha) \bullet Q(s,a) + \alpha \bullet (r + \gamma \bullet \text{maxa'}Q_{(s}{'},a'))$$

Where:

- Q(s, a) is the Q-value for taking action a in state s,
- α is the learning rate (a parameter between 0 and 1),
- r is the immediate reward after taking action a in state s,
- γ is the discount factor (a parameter between 0 and 1) representing the importance of future rewards,
- s' is the next state,

- $\max_{A}$' Q(s', a') is the maximum Q-value for any action in the next state.

The algorithm's main goal is to estimate the Q-function, also known as the optimal action-value function, which represents the expected cumulative reward for carrying out a particular action in a particular condition and following the best course of action. The Q-function is iteratively calculated using the Bellman equation, which produces the optimal value function based on the highest predicted value of the subsequent state-action combination.

The agent decides the course of action to take during each time step based on the trade-off between exploration and exploitation, selecting the course of action with the highest estimated Q-value with a specific probability and considering alternative courses of action with a different probability. The agent receives a reward from the environment, and utilising the temporal difference (TD) error—the discrepancy between the actual reward and the expected Q-value—updates the Q-value estimate for the current state-action combination.

In comparison to other reinforcement learning algorithms, Q-learning has a number of benefits. It is appropriate for real-time learning in complicated contexts with delayed rewards and stochastic transitions and is computationally efficient, simple to implement, and effective.

Q-learning does have some restrictions, though. The algorithm needs to explore a lot to figure out the best course of action, which can be time-consuming and ineffective in complex contexts. As a result of the excessively greedy selection of the maximum Q-value, the Q-values may also exhibit an overestimation bias. Modifications have been suggested to overcome these problems, such as employing eligibility traces or including experience replay.

In conclusion, Q-learning is a potent reinforcement learning algorithm that helps agents to discover the best course of action in challenging situations. For researchers and practitioners in the fields of machine learning and artificial intelligence, comprehension of the Q-operating learning's principles and constraints is crucial.

3.1.2. SARSA

A model-free approach called SARSA (State-Action-Reward-State-Action) is used in reinforcement learning to help an agent learn the best course of action in a particular environment. SARSA is a similar temporal difference (TD) learning approach to Q-learning that modifies the action-value function based on observed rewards as well as the subsequent state and action.

$$Q(s,a) \leftarrow Q(s,a) + \alpha \bullet (r + \gamma \bullet Q(s',a') - Q(s,a))$$

Where:

- Q(s, a) is the Q-value for taking action a in state s,
- α is the learning rate (a parameter between 0 and 1),
- r is the immediate reward after taking action a in state s,
- γ is the discount factor (a parameter between 0 and 1) representing the importance of future rewards,
- s' is the next state,
- a' is the next action.

In SARSA, the Q-values are updated based on the current state, action, reward, next state, and next action. The agent explores the environment, and the Q-values are iteratively updated to converge to the optimal policy for maximizing cumulative rewards.

The action-value function Q (s, a), which represents the anticipated cumulative benefit of doing a specific action (a) in a specific state (s) and then implementing the policy, is estimated by the method. The agent picks an action based on the exploration-exploitation trade-off at each time step, choosing the action with the highest estimated Q-value with a specific probability while exploring other actions with a similar likelihood. The agent then observes the following state and subsequent action while receiving a reward from the environment. The SARSA method uses the TD error, or the discrepancy between the observed reward and the expected Q-value, to adjust the Q-value for the current state-action combination.

Instead of considering the action with the highest Q-value as it would in Q-learning, SARSA updates the Q-value depending on the current policy, which means that it takes the next action the agent would take into account. By learning the value function for the policy it is now following, SARSA becomes an on-policy algorithm. Q-learning, on the other hand, is an off-policy method that determines the best value function independent of the policy being used.

Compared to Q-learning, SARSA has a number of benefits. As it updates the Q-value based on the current policy rather than the maximum Q-value, it is less prone to overestimation bias. Given that it updates the Q-value while taking into account the current policy, it can also manage contexts with stochastic transitions and delayed rewards. To learn the best policy, SARSA, however, requires more investigation than Q-learning, which in complex situations can be time-consuming and ineffective.

In conclusion, SARSA is a popular reinforcement learning algorithm that enables agents to discover the best strategies in challenging situations. The problem being solved determines how well SARSA works; it has advantages and disadvantages. For researchers and practitioners in the fields of machine learning and artificial intelligence, understanding the SARSA algorithm is essential.

3.1.3. Policy Gradient Methods

A common class of algorithms used in reinforcement learning for determining an agent's best course of action in a given environment is called policy gradient methods. Policy gradient approaches directly learn the policy itself, in contrast to Q-learning and SARSA, which learn the value function of a policy.

One common form of the policy gradient update rule is as follows:

$$\theta \leftarrow \theta + \alpha \bullet \nabla\theta \mathrm{J}(_{\theta)}$$

Where:

- θ represents the parameters of the policy function,
- α is the learning rate,
- $J(\theta)$ is the objective function, often representing the expected cumulative reward,
- $\nabla_t J(\theta)$ is the gradient of the objective function with respect to the policy parameters.

The basic goal of parameterizing a policy function that links states to actions is what drives policy gradient approaches. By following the gradient of the anticipated cumulative reward with regard to the policy parameters, the policy is optimised. Using samples that the agent gathered while interacting with the environment, this gradient is estimated.

Typically, stochastic gradient descent (SGD) or a related optimisation method is used for the optimisation process. Depending on the algorithm, the policy parameters may be modified after every episode or after a group of episodes.

The capacity of policy gradient approaches to handle continuous action spaces, which can be challenging for Q-learning and SARSA, is one of their key advantages. Stochastic policies, which are beneficial for navigating complicated situations with a wide range of possible behaviours, can be learned using policy gradient approaches as well.

The REINFORCE algorithm, the actor-critic approach, and the trust region policy optimisation (TRPO) algorithm are three examples of different policy gradient algorithms.

The REINFORCE algorithm is a fundamental policy gradient approach that directly uses the probability density function of the policy to estimate the gradient of the expected cumulative reward. The actor-critic method combines a value function method and a policy gradient method, employing the value function to estimate the state-value function and the gradient of the expected reward to optimise the policy.

A trust region is used by the more sophisticated policy gradient algorithm TRPO to make sure that alterations to the present policy only affect a small area nearby. This improves the algorithm's efficiency and stability compared to previous policy gradient techniques.

In comparison to other reinforcement learning algorithms, policy gradient approaches provide a number of advantages, including the capacity to handle continuous action spaces and the ability to learn stochastic policies. They can, however, be computationally costly and need a lot of samples to converge to an ideal policy.

In conclusion, policy gradient methods are a potent class of reinforcement learning algorithms that directly discover the best course of action for an agent in a given environment. They have advantages and disadvantages and work best for particular kinds of issues. It is essential for researchers and practitioners in the fields of machine learning and artificial intelligence to comprehend how policy gradient methods operate.

3.1.4. Actor-Critic Methods

A common class of reinforcement learning algorithms that combines both value-based and policy-based methods is called actor-critical methods. These techniques consist of two parts: the critic network, which learns the value function, and the actor network, which learns the policy.

$$\theta \leftarrow \theta + \alpha \bullet \delta \, \nabla\theta \, \mathrm{lo}_{g} \, \pi(\mathrm{als}, \theta)$$

$$V(s) \leftarrow V(s) + \beta \bullet \delta$$

Where:

- θ represents the parameters of the policy (actor),
- α is the learning rate for the actor,

- δ is the TD (temporal difference) error, calculated as r + γV(s') - V(s),
- ∇_t log π(a|s, θ) is the gradient of the log probability of taking action a in state s with respect to the policy parameters θ,
- V(s) represents the value function (critic),
- β is the learning rate for the critic,
- r is the immediate reward,
- γ is the discount factor,
- s' is the next state.

Based on the current policy, the actor network generates actions, and the critic network assesses these activities by calculating the predicted cumulative reward. By updating the value function, the critic gives the actor feedback, and the actor modifies the policy to maximise the predicted reward.

A2C and DDPG are two examples of various actor-critic methodologies. A2C entails evaluating the advantage function, which gauges how well the actual action compares to the anticipated action. Both the value function and the policy are updated using this function. On the other hand, DDPG is appropriate for continuous action spaces since it outputs actions according to a deterministic policy rather than a probability distribution. When the actor changes the policy using the gradient of the expected reward, the critic estimates the Q-value function and updates it using the TD error.

Actor-critic approaches have a number of benefits, including their effectiveness in large-scale applications and their capacity to handle high-dimensional and continuous state and action spaces. They do, however, have some drawbacks, such as being susceptible to local optimum and hyperparameter sensitivity.

In conclusion, it is crucial for academics and practitioners in the fields of machine learning and artificial intelligence to comprehend the inner workings of actor-critic approaches. These approaches provide a versatile and efficient means of addressing numerous reinforcement learning issues, although having some drawbacks.

3.1.5. Deep Reinforcement Learning

Deep reinforcement learning use deep neural networks to learn complex policies from high-dimensional raw input data, such as pictures or sounds. By combining the concepts of deep learning and reinforcement learning, these algorithms have made incredible progress in a number of industries, including gaming, robotics, and natural language processing.

Proximal Policy Optimization (PPO), Asynchronous Advantage Actor-Critic (A3C), and Deep Q-Networks (DQN) are a few common deep reinforcement learning algorithms. (PPO). DQN is a value-based method that use a neural network to estimate the action-value function. Experience replay is a technique that updates the network and stabilises the training process by buffering and randomly sampling occurrences.

Proximal Policy Optimization (PPO):

$$L(\theta)=\hat{\mathbb{E}}_t\left[\min\left(r_t(\theta)\hat{A}_t,\text{clip}(r_t(\theta),1-\varepsilon,1+\varepsilon)\hat{A}_t\right)\right]$$

- $L(\theta)$ is the surrogate objective for policy optimization,
- $\hat{E}_t$ is the empirical expectation over a batch of samples,
- $r_t(\theta) = \pi_t(a_t|s_t) / \pi\_old(a_t|s_t)$ is the importance ratio,
- $\hat{A}_t$ is the estimated advantage,
- ε is a hyperparameter controlling the clipping.

Asynchronous Advantage Actor-Critic (A3C):

Policy Gradient Update: $\theta \leftarrow \theta + \alpha\nabla\theta\, 1_{og}\, \pi$ (atlst; θ) A(st,at)

$V_a$lue Function Update: V(st) $\leftarrow$ $_V$(st) + $_\beta\delta$t

Whe$_r$e:

- θ represents the parameters of the policy,
- α is the learning rate for the policy,
- $\nabla_t \log \pi(a_t|s_t; \theta)$ is the gradient of the log probability of taking action a_t in state s_t with respect to the policy parameters θ,
- $A(s_t, a_t)$ is the advantage function,
- $V(s_t)$ is the value function,
- β is the learning rate for the value function,
- δ_t is the temporal difference error.

Deep Q-Networks (DQN):

$Q(s,a) \leftarrow (1 - \alpha)\, Q(s,a) + \alpha \bullet (r + \gamma \bullet \text{maxa'}Q_{(s}\text{'},a'))$

Where:

- Q(s, a) is the Q-value for taking action a in state s,
- α is the learning rate,
- r is the immediate reward,
- γ is the discount factor,
- s' is the next state,
- $\max_A$' Q(s', a') is the maximum Q-value for any action in the next state.

The policy and the value function are both learned by the policy-based algorithm A3C, on the other hand. The learning process is made more efficient by using numerous agents that operate simultaneously and update the network asynchronously. This also enables the agents to investigate various areas of the environment.

The PPO algorithm additionally updates the policy using a substitute objective function. The policy is kept from changing too much at once by utilising a clipped surrogate loss to optimise the objective function. PPO is well known for its stability and sample effectiveness, which make it appropriate for use in practical applications.

One of the key benefits of deep reinforcement learning algorithms is their capacity to learn directly from sensory inputs, which eliminates the need for manually constructed features. Because they can handle high-dimensional and continuous state and action spaces, they are perfect for more difficult tasks. When compared to traditional reinforcement learning algorithms, these algorithms can also learn more complex behaviours and strategies.

On the other hand, deep reinforcement learning algorithms need a lot of data and computing power, which makes training them expensive and time-consuming. They could also have issues like instability and overfitting, which can make learning more challenging.

To sum up, deep reinforcement learning is a potent and fascinating area of study that has the potential to revolutionise numerous sectors.

4. APPLICATIONS OF REINFORCEMENT LEARNING

Reinforcement learning (RL) has become quite popular lately because it's great at helping agents learn from their experiences and make smart decisions, even in tough and uncertain situations. This approach has caught a lot of attention due to its effectiveness. RL can be used in many different ways across fields like robotics, gaming, finance, healthcare, and more. Let's dive into some important areas where RL is making a difference.

In the world of robotics, RL is a game-changer. It teaches robots how to learn from what's around them, which is super important in places like manufacturing. This means robots can handle different tasks and adapt to different places.

Gaming, which is all about fun and challenges, is also benefitting from RL. With the help of RL techniques, game characters can become really good at playing games, almost like humans. They can learn and improve their skills by playing against real people or computer opponents.

RL is also a big help in the financial world. It lets special computer programs learn how to make smart decisions in tricky market situations. And in healthcare, RL is like a personal guide. It helps doctors decide the best treatments for patients based on their unique needs.

4.1. Robotics and Autonomous Systems

Robots can be trained to carry out tasks including object detection, grasping, manipulation, and navigation in dynamic situations using RL algorithms. In industries where robots can work independently, like manufacturing and logistics, this use has demonstrated tremendous potential. Robots have been taught to walk on two legs, play table tennis, and fly unmanned aerial vehicles using RL algorithms, for instance. RL algorithms can also be utilised to improve the robotic system's control strategies and carry out real-time environmental adaptability.

4.2. Gaming

RL has been used in gaming successfully, especially in creating agents who can play challenging games like chess, go, and poker. One of the most well-known instances is AlphaGo, a DeepMind AI programme that defeated the go world champion in 2016. RL algorithms can be used to train agents to learn the optimal strategy by playing against themselves or other agents. The gaming industry has a lot of potential for this application because it can be used to create personalised game material, such levels and challenges, based on the conduct of the player.

4.3. Finance

Financially speaking, RL has showed a lot of promise, especially in the areas of algorithmic trading and portfolio management. Using historical data, RL algorithms can be used to learn the best trading methods and forecast market patterns. Because it may be used to optimise portfolio allocation by understanding risk-reward trade-offs and altering the portfolio weights accordingly, this application has a lot of potential in the financial sector. In addition, fraud detection and marketing strategy optimisation can both be done using RL algorithms.

4.4. Healthcare

Personalized medicine and clinical decision-making are two areas in which RL has numerous potential applications in the field of healthcare. Personalized treatment regimens for individuals based on their medical histories, genetic information, and other criteria can be learned using RL algorithms. The healthcare sector has a lot of potential for this application because it may be used to allocate resources like employees, beds, and medical equipment more efficiently. Clinical decision-making and patient outcomes can both be predicted using RL algorithms.

4.5. Other Industries

Reinforcement learning (RL) shows great promise in transforming various sectors, like transportation, energy, and agriculture. In the transportation sector, RL algorithms are being applied to enhance traffic flow and develop self-driving cars, potentially reducing traffic congestion and accidents—a major concern for transportation. In the energy sector, RL's role involves improving energy efficiency and optimizing power generation and distribution, which could lead to cost savings and decreased energy usage. RL also finds application in agriculture, where farmers can use RL algorithms to increase crop yields while minimizing resource usage, a crucial step toward sustainable crop production.

On a broader scale, RL holds a diverse array of potential uses, with novel applications continuously emerging. Challenges remain, such as the need for substantial data and computing power. However, despite these challenges, RL's potential to revolutionize problem-solving across different industries remains captivating. This fosters a dynamic and stimulating field of research likely to gain ongoing attention and investment in the years ahead. Notably, RL might play a vital part in addressing some of today's most pressing global challenges.

As technological progress continues and our understanding of RL deepens, we can anticipate the emergence of even more innovative applications across sectors. From facilitating safer autonomous driving to enhancing energy efficiency and exploring sustainable solutions for global food supply, RL's potential to influence our lives and interaction with the environment is significant. This enduring journey of exploration and innovation is what makes RL an enticing and auspicious field, with boundless possibilities on the horizon.

5. CHALLENGES AND FUTURE PROSPECTS

While still in its nascent stages, the realm of reinforcement learning (RL) has exhibited significant potential across diverse sectors such as robotics, gaming, finance, and healthcare. Although RL harbours considerable promise, there exist numerous obstacles that must be surmounted to fully actualize its potential. Deliberations concerning the societal and ethical ramifications of RL's implementation warrant careful consideration. Nevertheless, avenues for research persist, holding the capacity to propel the advancement of this discipline.

Upon scrutiny of the present state of RL, its transformative prowess becomes evident across various domains. Yet, impediments, spanning both conceptual and pragmatic dimensions, pose formidable challenges. Mindful contemplation of RL's potential societal and moral implications remains imperative. In spite of these adversities, prospects for scholarly exploration endure, affording the means to deepen our understanding.

In summation, although RL remains in its developmental infancy, it possesses substantial potential to revolutionize numerous sectors. Overcoming hurdles and contemplating the societal and ethical implications remain pivotal. Nonetheless, research avenues persistently beckon, offering the means to propel RL's evolution and facilitate its maximal attainment.

5.1. Technical Challenges and Limitations:

A significant challenge inherent in reinforcement learning (RL) lies in the demand for vast datasets to effectively train the agent. RL algorithms necessitate a process of trial-and-error learning, wherein the agent engages with the environment repeatedly to discern the optimal course of action. This iterative nature, however, can exact a considerable temporal and resource toll, particularly within intricate environments. In seeking to alleviate this quandary, the strategic application of investigative methodologies and leveraging of prior information emerge as potential solutions.

Concurrently, a pivotal hurdle manifests in the form of the exploration-exploitation dichotomy. The fundamental conundrum involves RL agents judiciously navigating the tension between delving into unfamiliar terrain for the acquisition of novel insights and leveraging their existing knowledge to maximize rewards. The attainment of an equilibrium that seamlessly harmonizes these opposing imperatives necessitates a meticulous calibration of the learning parameters, constituting a formidable endeavour in its own right.

Moreover, the selection of the reward function imparts a pivotal influence on the trajectory of RL algorithms. The very purpose and pursuits of the agent are intricately intertwined with the contours of this reward function. Thus, the efficacy and triumph of RL endeavours hinge inexorably upon the astuteness with which this function is chosen. In this regard, a misstep can potentially engender unfavourable behaviours or, in more dire circumstances, precipitate calamitous outcomes.

Amidst these intricacies, a common thread emerges: the multidimensional nature of RL's challenges requires technical ingenuity and an acutely discerning approach. The amalgamation of astute data management, judicious calibration of exploration and exploitation, and the reasonable delineation of reward functions coalesce to shape the trajectory of RL. Through the concerted efforts of researchers and practitioners alike, these challenges can be surmounted, thereby ushering in a new era of refined, context-aware reinforcement learning paradigms.

5.2. Ethical and Societal Implications

Especially within domains such as autonomous weaponry and decision-making systems, the advent of reinforcement learning (RL) introduces a realm fraught with intricate ethical and societal implications. While RL agents exhibit an ability to optimize designated reward functions, these functions may inherently lack comprehensive consideration of the multifaceted ethical dimensions at play. A glaring instance emerges in the context of an RL agent programmed to enhance enemy casualties, inadvertently culminating in harm inflicted upon uninvolved civilians—a consequence diametrically opposed to acceptable norms.

The ethical quandaries engendered by such scenarios underscore the exigency of meticulous ethical calibration within the application of RL. The symbiosis between technological advancement and ethical rectitude assumes a significance that cannot be overstated. To harness the potential of RL for constructive purposes and to pre-empt untoward outcomes, it is imperative to establish a robust framework delineating ethical benchmarks and operational guidelines.

The necessity for ethical considerations in the deployment of RL is underscored by the salient reality that technical proficiency alone cannot navigate the labyrinthine landscape of morally complex decisions. Ethical criteria must be meticulously woven into the fabric of RL's operational parameters, serving as guiding beacons that traverse the terrain between innovation and societal responsibility.

Analogously, the pivotal role of regulatory and governance mechanisms cannot be underestimated. Just as an RL agent navigates a multifaceted environment, the landscape of its application necessitates a multifaceted approach to ensure responsible use. Strides must be taken to augment existing legal frameworks, fostering a confluence wherein technological dynamism is harmonized with ethical prudence.

In conclusion, the foray of RL into arenas like autonomous weaponry and decision-making elicits ethical and societal considerations of paramount significance. The incongruities that can emerge between reward functions and moral imperatives accentuate the need for a judicious equilibrium between innovation and ethics. The convergence of ethical guidelines, regulatory frameworks, and technological prowess forms an intricate tapestry, one that can safeguard against unintended repercussions and uphold the sanctity of RL's contribution to societal progress.

5.3. Research Directions and Opportunities

Amidst the labyrinth of challenges and constraints that encircle the landscape of reinforcement learning (RL), a constellation of research trajectories and prospects beckons, poised to propel the field to new pinnacles. Among these avenues, one trajectory heralds the pursuit of more parsimonious RL algorithms, endowed with a propensity for efficacious operation even when beset by a paucity of data and computational resources. Achieving this synthesis demands an evolution of exploration strategies and the refinement of reward functions while drawing sustenance from the wellspring of prior knowledge and the principles of transfer learning.

Another path converges upon the harmonious amalgamation of RL with allied bastions of machine learning, particularly the realms of deep learning and probabilistic modelling. The amalgamation of these synergistic disciplines augments the capabilities of RL agents, arming them with the aptitude to distil knowledge from intricate, high-dimensional sensory inputs such as images and speech. Such an integration extends the compass of RL to encompass the intricate choreography of stochastic environments, breathing life into the agents' capacity to model and navigate complexity.

The elevation of RL into the echelons of efficacy and sophistication necessitates an incisive fusion of theoretical inquiry and pragmatic experimentation. The articulation of more efficient algorithms' orbits around the gravitational core of exploratory ingenuity, where the orchestration of well-calibrated exploration strategies proves instrumental in circumventing the data-intensive quagmire. Coupled with this, the judicious sculpting of reward functions emerges as a dynamic canvas upon which RL's potential is painted, underscoring the inherent balance between action and incentive.

The extension of RL's purview through interdisciplinary symbiosis finds articulation in the convergence with deep learning and probabilistic modelling. The matrimony of these disciplines engenders an arena where the rich tapestry of sensory information is woven into the fabric of RL's decision-making paradigms. The outcome is a landscape wherein agents discern patterns within the intricate mosaics of data, rendering them adept at navigating the inherent uncertainty emblematic of complex environments.

In sum, the frontier of RL, though characterized by challenges, beckons with opportunities that epitomize the synergy of intellect and innovation. As the field advances, the twin pursuits of algorithmic finesse and interdisciplinary fusion shall continue to fortify the edifice of RL, driving it to unravel the intricate symphony of decision-making within the grand theatre of dynamic environments.

5.4. Future Prospects of Reinforcement Learning

The vista of forthcoming opportunities within the realm of reinforcement learning (RL) unfolds with a promise that resonates throughout the corridors of anticipation. Prognostications indicate an impending expansion of the field, its trajectory guided by the compass of burgeoning prospects. Among these, the emergence of autonomous systems endowed with the capacity to undertake arduous tasks—such as automated driving and intricate industrial processes—stands as a beacon of potential. These systems, stewarded by RL, hold the key to unlocking new frontiers of efficiency and sophistication.

In parallel, the tapestry of RL is woven intricately into domains spanning transportation and energy, wielding its prowess to orchestrate the symphony of resource allocation and scheduling. The marriage of RL's ingenuity with these industrial landscapes promises the orchestration of harmonious resource utilization, optimizing performance while minimizing wastage—a harmonious rhythm that resonates within the heartbeat of sustainability.

Another salient horizon unfurls in the field of healthcare, where the potential of RL assumes the form of individualized treatment paradigms. These regimens, curated with finesse based on patient's medical histories and genetic profiles, epitomize the synergy of data-driven precision and medical expertise. Concurrently, the medical arena reverberates with the promise of RL enhancing clinical acumen and galvanizing the expedition toward novel medications and therapeutic modalities.

In summation, the essence of RL encapsulates a realm of dynamic inquiry poised to reverberate across multifarious sectors. Its transformative potential, underpinned by adept automation and cogent optimization, extends an invitation to reimagine industries and augment the tapestry of everyday existence. To fully harness this potential, the fulcrum pivots upon the establishment of ethical precepts and principled conduct. The voyage towards a responsible deployment of RL necessitates a conscious endeavour to surmount challenges and navigate constraints.

Bearing the banner of these convictions, RL strides resolutely into a future that holds the promise of further expansion and innovation. The convergence of profound interest and substantial investment looms large, casting a spotlight on a field that is poised to etch its imprint upon the chronicles of human progress. As the sun rises on the horizon of tomorrow, it casts its rays upon the vistas of RL, destined to continue its journey as a vanguard of technological advancement and transformational change.

6. CONCLUSION

The realm of artificial intelligence (AI) research burgeons as a rapidly expanding frontier, wielding a profound influence that reverberates across the multifaceted tapestry of modern society. The contours of computer vision, reinforcement learning, deep learning, and natural language processing, subjects of scrutiny within this narrative, encapsulate challenges that demand both inquiry and innovation.

The focal findings of this inquiry resoundingly echo the transformative impact of deep learning across myriad AI applications. A symphony of advancement resonates as deep learning magnifies the prowess of AI across dimensions such as speech recognition, image interpretation, and natural language understanding. This augmentation extends to the realm of machine perception, where the comprehension of intricate visual data is rendered possible, a feat stemming from the leaping strides within computer vision. Akin to the unfolding of an epiphany, machines now possess the faculty to not only decipher but also compose and fathom human language—a phenomenon arising from the crucible of progress in natural language processing. In parallel, the tapestry of reinforcement learning unfurls, unveiling a panoply of potential applications spanning robotics, finance, healthcare, and gaming, despite the backdrop of limitations.

The contours of AI's expansive canvas traverse sectors of healthcare, banking, transportation, and energy, bearing within them the seeds of transformation. A paradigmatic exemplar emerges within energy and transportation, where the orchestration of resource allocation and scheduling attains a new zenith through the symphony of AI's predictive prowess. Likewise, the domain of healthcare echoes the promise of AI, its ability to craft personalized treatment regimens founded upon the individual bedrock of medical histories and genetic profiles stand as a testament to AI's transformative potential.

However, within the triumphant crescendo of AI's rise, nuanced undertones of societal and ethical considerations arise, casting their shadows upon the landscape. It is in the crucible of domains such as autonomous weaponry and decision-making systems that the cadence of ethical prudence emerges as pivotal. An orchestration of moral imperatives and legislative safeguards serves as the bedrock upon which the edifice of AI's trajectory must be erected.

In summation, the domain of artificial intelligence stands as a dynamic tableau poised to transfigure sectors across the economy and the quotidian alike. The trajectory is replete with promise, but also laden with the onus of ethical responsibility. As AI evolves, the beacon of progress must be illuminated by the twin torches of prudence and ethics, ensconcing transformative potential within a framework that safeguards the greater good. In this odyssey, the collective alliance of researchers, policymakers, and industry stakeholders forms the linchpin, fortifying the tapestry of progress and innovation that AI unfurls upon the world stage.

REFERENCES

Bellemare, M. G., Veness, J., & Munos, R. (2016). A survey of Monte-Carlo methods for reinforcement learning. *arXiv preprint arXiv:1606.01448.*

Chen, H., Wang, Y., & Li, J. (2021). Deep reinforcement learning for personalized medicine: A review. *Journal of Biomedical Informatics*, *111*, 103540.

Hu, X., Chen, S., Li, L., & Wang, Y. (2019). Deep reinforcement learning for dynamic pricing in ride-hailing platforms. *Transportation Research Part C, Emerging Technologies*, *106*, 288–304.

Lillicrap, T. P., Hunt, J. J., Pritzel, A., Heess, N., Erez, T., Tassa, Y., . . . Silver, D. (2015). Continuous control with deep reinforcement learning. *arXiv preprint arXiv:1509.02971*.

Mnih, V., Kavukcuoglu, K., Silver, D., Rusu, A. A., Veness, J., Bellemare, M. G., ... Petersen, S. (2015). Human-level control through deep reinforcement learning. *Nature*, *518*(7540), 529–533. doi:10.1038/nature14236 PMID:25719670

Silver, D., Huang, A., Maddison, C. J., Guez, A., Sifre, L., Driessche, G. V. D., ... Hassabis, D. (2017). Mastering the game of Go without human knowledge. *Nature*, *550*(7676), 354–359. doi:10.1038/nature24270 PMID:29052630

Sutton, R. S., & Barto, A. G. (2018). *Reinforcement learning: An introduction*. MIT Press.

Vinyals, O., Bellemare, M. G., & Graves, A. (2017). Neural episodic control. *arXiv preprint arXiv:1703.03864*.

Wang, Z., He, S., Yu, K., Chen, X., & Liu, Z. (2018). Deep reinforcement learning for traffic signal control with multi-agent optimization. *IEEE Transactions on Intelligent Transportation Systems*, *20*(3), 1024–1035.

Zhang, L., Wang, S., Zhang, Y., & Liu, Y. (2020). Deep reinforcement learning for financial portfolio management. *IEEE Transactions on Neural Networks and Learning Systems*, *31*(11), 4582–4594. PMID:31870999

Zhang, Y., Liu, W., & Wang, Y. (2022). Multi-agent reinforcement learning for traffic signal control: A survey. *IEEE Transactions on Intelligent Transportation Systems*, *23*(3), 1197–1215.

Chapter 2
Implementation of Different Machine Learning Projects Using Scikit-learn and Tensorflow Frameworks

Durmuş Özkan Şahin
https://orcid.org/0000-0002-0831-7825
Ondokuz Mayıs University, Turkey

ABSTRACT

In this study, the solution of classification, regression, and time series problems used in different fields with Scikit-learn and TensorFlow libraries using Python programming language is discussed. Four projects are carried out. The first project addressed the classification problem. The performance of the models is evaluated by using classical machine learning techniques and deep neural networks to solve the classification problem. The second project considered is the regression problem. The White Wine Quality dataset is used to understand the regression problem. The third project is the image classification problem. Image classification is one of the essential areas of study in recent years. Classification of images is achieved with CNN, one of the deep learning techniques. Keras and TensorFlow libraries are used in CNN. The last project discussed is the estimation of the closing value of the stock market stock.

INTRODUCTION

Python programming language has been preferred in many fields in recent years because of its extensive library support (Srinath, 2017). Some of these areas are as follows:

- In the development of web applications (Burch, 2010)
- In the field of natural language processing (Bird et al., 2009)
- In cyber security education and field (Eckroth, 2018)

DOI: 10.4018/979-8-3693-1062-5.ch002

Copyright © 2024, IGI Global. Copying or distributing in print or electronic forms without written permission of IGI Global is prohibited.

- In data science, artificial intelligence, machine learning, data mining, and deep learning studies (Raschka et al., 2020)
- In the field of image processing (Van der Walt et al., 2014)
- In embedded system development and applications (Cho et al., 2023)
- In software testing processes (Okken, 2022)

As you can see, Python programming language is used in almost many areas. These examples can be increased further. The fact that it is an open source, high-level language and easy to use/learn makes this language popular (Srinath, 2017). Python programming language and libraries are the most preferred languages in the field of machine learning (Raschka et al., 2020).

Machine learning is one of the most studied areas in computer science in recent years. It is also used by both researchers and companies in many fields. Health, education, information security, and the economy are some examples of areas where machine-learning techniques are used. In this book chapter, the solution of classification, regression, and time series problems used in different fields with Scikit-learn and TensorFlow libraries using Python programming language will be discussed.

Motivation

Machine learning and deep learning are some of the most critical areas studied by researchers in recent years. Python programming language is frequently preferred by researchers due to the libraries it offers. This book chapter will cover different machine learning problems and enable readers to code an application step by step. In addition to coding, questions such as how to interpret a classification result and how to interpret a regression problem are also answered in the book chapter. The projects in the book section will guide undergraduate and graduate students as well as many people who want to improve themselves in this field. The examples discussed here can be easily applied by readers to different problems. In this way, the reader will gain practice in using machine learning and deep learning algorithms.

Contribution

The contributions of the book section can be summarized as follows:

- The use of essential classification algorithms in the Sklearn library is mentioned.
- Interpretation of classification results is interpreted under different metrics.
- The use of the confusion matrix is demonstrated using the Matplotlib library.
- The use of algorithms used in regression problems is demonstrated.
- Step-by-step coding of the image classification problem is included.
- Stocks purchased at random times are predicted using some algorithms.

Organization

The remaining chapters of the study are organized as follows: In Section 2, the Integrated Development Environment (IDE) used, the use of IDE, the datasets used in the projects, the algorithms used, and the evaluation metrics are introduced. In Section 3, the classification problem; in Section 4, the regression problem; in Section 5, the image classification problem; and in Section 6, the difficulties of estimating stock closing values are discussed. Finally, in Section 7, general evaluations of the book section and suggestions are made for those who want to work in this field.

BACKGROUND

In this section, the important points that form the basis of the applications to be carried out within the scope of the study will be touched upon. First, the introduction of the IDE preferred within the scope of the study and the libraries used will be discussed. Secondly, the datasets used will be introduced. Thirdly, the machine learning and deep learning algorithms used will be mentioned. Finally, the metrics used to evaluate classification and regression results will be explained.

IDE and Libraries Used

In this subsection, the IDEs and libraries used to use machine learning and deep learning algorithms with Python will be discussed. There are many IDEs available to make it easier for developers to develop applications on Python. IDLE, which comes with the Python installation, is one of the main ones. In addition, PyCharm (PyCharm, 2023), Jupyter (Jupyter, 2023), and Spyder (Spyder, 2023) can be given as examples of the most used IDE software. These IDEs generally have paid and free usage options.

All examples in this study were carried out on Google Colaboratory (Google Colaboratory, 2023), developed by Google. This IDE can be opened and used with a Google account. The written source codes are stored in Google Drive. The advantage of this IDE compared to other IDEs is that it offers many machine learning and deep learning libraries ready for use. For example, while installation is required to use libraries in most IDEs, many libraries are available on Google Colaboratory. In other words, there is no installation required. It is possible to use this IDE, both paid and free. The free version was used in this study. Figure 1 shows a blank Google Colaboratory screen with no code written.

Where to write the code, how to run the code, and how to add an external file (dataset) to this code are shown in detail in Figure 2. In addition, a sample code that prints the sum of the values of two variables on the screen in Figure 2 was written and run on Google Colaboratory. This code is named “foo”. The most important point to note when working on Google Colaboratory is that once the dataset is uploaded, it is not permanently stored in the project. For this reason, it should be noted that the dataset used cannot always be accessed after being included in the project. Figure 3 shows Google Colaboratory’s warning. The original versions of the dataset to be used must be backed up on the computer or in the cloud.

Figure 1. An Empty Google Colaboratory Interface

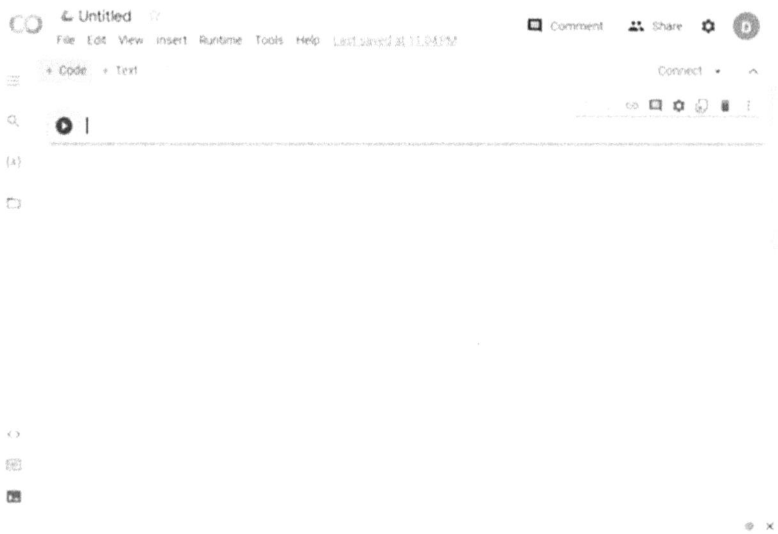

Figure 2. Using Google Colaboratory and Running Sample Code

Figure 3. Adding External Files to the Project

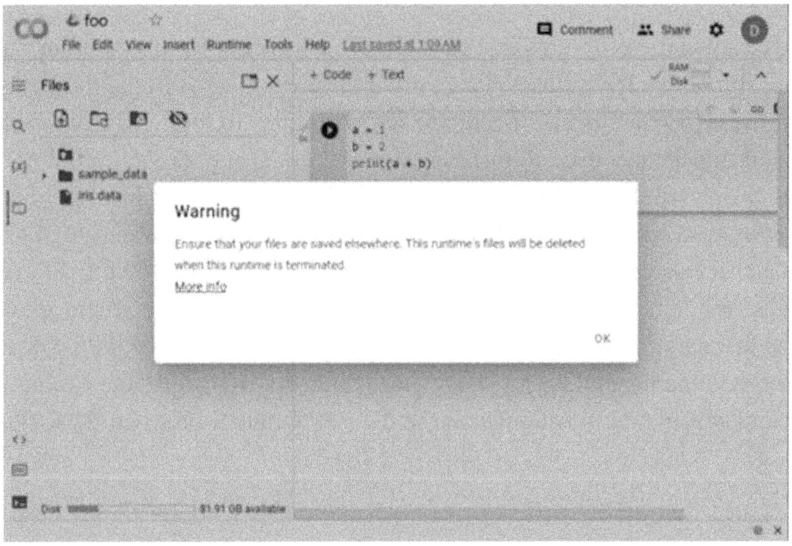

The libraries used in the infrastructure of the projects are listed in Table 1. Classification and regression algorithms are included in the Sklearn library. Classification and regression problems are solved with the important algorithms in this library. TensorFlow and Keras libraries are libraries used in coding deep learning techniques. The core library is TensorFlow. The Keras library is developed using the TensorFlow library. In this study, deep learning models are developed by using two libraries together. Matplotlib library is frequently preferred for data visualization and graph drawing. This library is used to plot the confusion matrix. The Pandas library makes it much easier to read files, pre-process data, and obtain preliminary information about the datasets used. NumPy is the most important library for scientific calculations with Python. This library is used in the infrastructure of many libraries to perform fast matrix-vector operations. The last library used is Yahoo Finance. With this library, stock data can be easily obtained and used.

Table 1. Libraries Used

Name of Library
Scikit-learn or Sklearn (Pedregosa et al., 2011; Scikit-learn, 2023)
TensorFlow (Abadi et al., 2016; TensorFlow, 2023)
Keras (Chollet 2015; Keras, 2023)
Matplotlib (Hunter 2007; Matplotlib, 2023)
Pandas (McKinney 2011; Pandas, 2023)
NumPy (Oliphant, 2006; NumPy, 2023)
Yahoo Finance (Yfinance, 2023)

Datasets Used

The datasets used to solve the problems discussed in the book chapter are given in Table 2. Classification algorithms are run on the Iris dataset. There are 3 different classes in the Iris dataset. These classes actually represent the types of flowers. There are 150 examples in total, 50 from each category. There are four attributes in this dataset used to differentiate flowers. There are a total of 4898 samples in the White Wine Quality dataset. The output includes numerical values that show the quality of the wines. These values vary between 3 and 8. In this book chapter study, the White Wine Quality dataset is used for regression. This dataset can also be used with classification algorithms. The CIFAR-10 dataset contains 60000 color images. While there are a total of 10 categories in this dataset, there are 6000 images from each category. The last dataset used was obtained using the Yahoo Finance API. The data of BIMAS in Borsa Istanbul between the dates "2015-01-01" and "2020-01-01" are being evaluated. 1303 samples are used with various regression techniques on the dataset obtained between these dates.

Table 2. Datasets Used

Problem	Used Dataset
Classification problem	Iris Dataset (Iris, 2023)
Regression problem	White Wine Quality (Cortez et al., 2009; Wine Quality, 2023)
Image classification problem	CIFAR-10 Dataset (Krizhevsky and Hinton, 2009; CIFAR-10, 2023)
Stock price forecasting	BIST30 (BIST30, 2023)

Machine Learning and Deep Learning Algorithms Used

Since different problems are addressed in the study, model performances are calculated using different techniques. Since a classification problem was addressed on the Iris dataset, classification algorithms were used. The main algorithms used are K-Nearest Neighbor (KNN), Logistic Regression, Support Vector Machine (SVM), Gaussian Naive Bayes (NB), Random Forest (RF), and AdaBoost. Sklearn library was used for these algorithms. In addition to these algorithms, a Deep Neural Network (DNN) model was designed by using TensorFlow and Keras libraries to classify the dataset. In regression problems, the structures of the algorithms used in classification problems, prepared to be used in regression problems, were preferred. For example, the Support Vector Regression (SVR) structure was used instead of SVM. However, since the Logistic Regression algorithm is an algorithm used in classification problems, it cannot be used in regression problems. For this reason, the linear regression method, which is widely used in regression problems, was used. Finally, artificial neural networks can be modeled with the Sklearn library. The demonstration of this is also explained in the regression problem. Finally, in the image classification problem, the Convolutional Neural Network (CNN) model was used using TensorFlow and Keras libraries.

Evaluation Metrics

Since different problems were addressed in the study, model performances were evaluated using different metrics. Accuracy and F1-score metrics were used for classification problems. Mean Absolute Error (MAE), Mean Squared Error (MSE), Root Mean Squared Error (RMSE), and R^2 metrics were used for regression problems. The metrics used are available in the Sklearn library.

USE OF IRIS DATASET AND RESULTS OBTAINED

This section will discuss the basic use of the Iris dataset. Then, the results obtained from this dataset with various machine learning algorithms will be evaluated under different metrics. The Iris dataset is often a frequently used dataset for machine learning beginners. This dataset was preferred in the first project of the book chapter since operations were generally handled on this dataset in the first exercises.

Before mentioning on to classification algorithms on this dataset, the use of the dataset will be discussed. Figure 4 shows the use of the Iris dataset. Necessary libraries are added in the first 5 lines of the source code. There are no attribute names in the first line of the provided dataset. Therefore, each attribute name and class name is created as in line 7. If line 7 had not been added, the first instance of the dataset would not have been evaluated. Following this step, the dataset is read with the Pandas library. Since there are 4 attributes in the Iris dataset, the data was parsed as in the 9th line. Since the last column of the dataset is a label, labels are assigned to the Y variable as in the 10th line. In the 11th line, the dataset is divided into two parts: training and testing. According to line 11, 30% of the dataset is used to test the classifier. The random_state parameter forms the core of the random number generator. If random_state is not used in the method, the result obtained on the dataset will constantly change. In order to give equal consideration to all classification algorithms, the random_state parameter should generally be given an integer. All classification algorithms are run under the same integer to ensure an equal comparison. By setting random_state = 10 on the Iris dataset, it is aimed to run all algorithms on the same dataset.

X_train is the part used to train machine learning algorithms. The labels of this data are kept in Y_train. X_test is used to test the performance of the machine learning algorithm. The label of each sample in the X_test data is kept in the Y_test variable. Since the basic operations on this dataset are the same for all algorithms, the first 11 lines of all algorithms will be like this. After the first 11 lines, the library of the classification algorithm to be used is added and the explanation of the algorithms is included.

Figure 4. Using the Iris Dataset

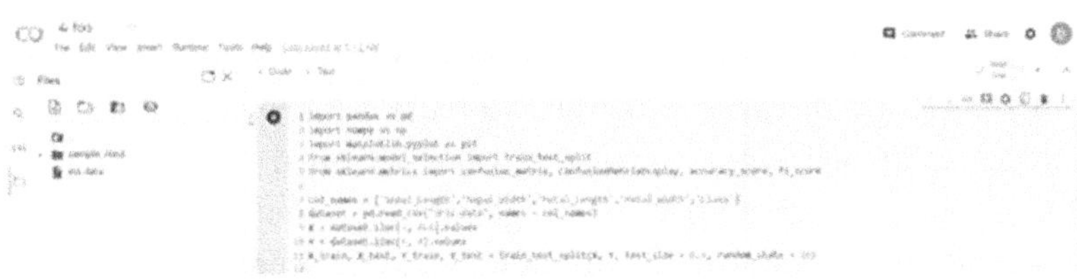

The first classification algorithm run on the Iris dataset is KNN. The application of the KNN algorithm and the results obtained from this algorithm are shown in Figure 5. One of the important factors affecting the performance of this algorithm is the n_neighbors parameter. By default, this parameter takes the value 5. However, on this dataset, the classification result is calculated by giving the n_neighbors parameter a value of 1. Apart from this, no changes are made to other parameters of the algorithm. If the results of the KNN algorithm are examined, a performance of 0.9777 is achieved according to the accuracy metric, while a result of 0.9778 is obtained according to the weighted F1-score metric.

Figure 5. Use of KNN Algorithm on Iris Dataset

```
from sklearn.neighbors import KNeighborsClassifier
knn = KNeighborsClassifier(n_neighbors = 1)
knn.fit(X_train, Y_train)
Y_pred_knn = knn.predict(X_test)

cm = confusion_matrix(Y_test, Y_pred_knn, labels = knn.classes_)
disp = ConfusionMatrixDisplay(confusion_matrix = cm, display_labels = knn.classes_)
disp.plot()
plt.show()

results = accuracy_score(Y_test, Y_pred_knn)
print("Accuracy of KNN Algorithm = ", results)
results = f1_score(Y_test, Y_pred_knn, average='macro')
print("F1-score (macro) of KNN Algorithm = ", results)
results = f1_score(Y_test, Y_pred_knn, average='micro')
print("F1-score (micro) of KNN Algorithm = ", results)
results = f1_score(Y_test, Y_pred_knn, average='weighted')
print("F1-score (weighted) of KNN Algorithm = ", results)
```

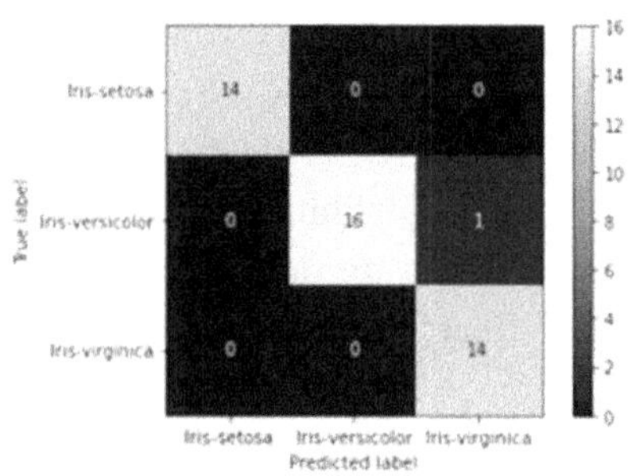


```
Accuracy of KNN Algorithm =  0.9777777777777777
F1-score (macro) of KNN Algorithm =  0.9784047370254267
F1-score (micro) of KNN Algorithm =  0.9777777777777777
F1-score (weighted) of KNN Algorithm =  0.9778242192035296
```

The second classification algorithm run on the Iris dataset is the logistic regression algorithm. The application of the logistic regression algorithm and the results obtained from this algorithm are shown in Figure 6. The limited-memory Broyden–Fletcher–Goldfarb–Shanno (lbfgs) algorithm was chosen as the analyzer. Additionally, the value 200 is sent as a parameter to the maximum number of iterations. The performance of the algorithm varies according to these parameters. If the results of the logistic regression algorithm are examined, a performance of 1.0 is obtained according to the accuracy metric, while a result of 1.0 is obtained according to the weighted F1-score metric. These results show that all samples allocated for testing were classified correctly. It can be seen in the confusion matrix that all examples are classified correctly.

Figure 6. Use of Logistic Regression Algorithm on Iris Dataset

```
from sklearn.linear_model import LogisticRegression
lr = LogisticRegression(solver='lbfgs', max_iter=200)
lr.fit(X_train, Y_train)
Y_pred_lr = lr.predict(X_test)

cm = confusion_matrix(Y_test, Y_pred_lr, labels = lr.classes_)
disp = ConfusionMatrixDisplay(confusion_matrix = cm, display_labels = lr.classes_)
disp.plot()
plt.show()

results = accuracy_score(Y_test, Y_pred_lr)
print("Accuracy of Logistic Regression Algorithm = ", results)
results = f1_score(Y_test, Y_pred_lr, average='macro')
print("F1-score (macro) of Logistic Regression Algorithm = ", results)
results = f1_score(Y_test, Y_pred_lr, average='micro')
print("F1-score (micro) of Logistic Regression Algorithm = ", results)
results = f1_score(Y_test, Y_pred_lr, average='weighted')
print("F1-score (weighted) of LogisticRegression Algorithm = ", results)
```

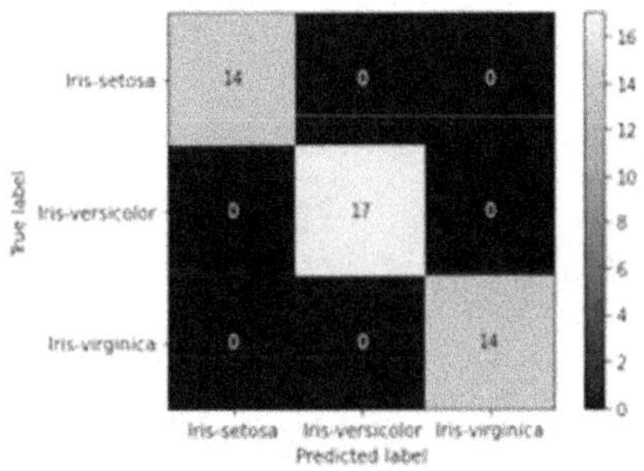


```
Accuracy of Logistic Regression Algorithm =  1.0
F1-score (macro) of Logistic Regression Algorithm =  1.0
F1-score (micro) of Logistic Regression Algorithm =  1.0
F1-score (weighted) of LogisticRegression Algorithm =  1.0
```

The third classification algorithm run on the Iris dataset is SVM. The application of the SVM algorithm and the results obtained from this algorithm are given in Figure 7. There are many parameters in the infrastructure of the SVM algorithm. In the code example given in Figure 7, default values are used since no parameter is given a value. At default values, the kernel function appears as 'rbf'. In addition, the kernel function can be selected as 'linear', 'poly', 'rbf', 'sigmoid' and 'precomputed'. This can directly affect the performance of the algorithm. If the results of the SVM algorithm are examined, a performance of 1.0 is obtained according to the accuracy metric, while a result of 1.0 is obtained according to the weighted F1-score metric. As in the logistic regression algorithm, all samples are classified correctly.

Figure 7. Use of SVM Algorithm on Iris Dataset

```
from sklearn import svm
svm_classifier = svm.SVC()
svm_classifier.fit(X_train, Y_train)
Y_pred_svm = svm_classifier.predict(X_test)

cm = confusion_matrix(Y_test, Y_pred_svm, labels = svm_classifier.classes_)
disp = ConfusionMatrixDisplay(confusion_matrix = cm, display_labels = svm_classifier.classes_)
disp.plot()
plt.show()

results = accuracy_score(Y_test, Y_pred_svm)
print("Accuracy of SVM Algorithm = ", results)
results = f1_score(Y_test, Y_pred_svm, average='macro')
print("F1-score (macro) of SVM Algorithm = ", results)
results = f1_score(Y_test, Y_pred_svm, average='micro')
print("F1-score (micro) of SVM Algorithm = ", results)
results = f1_score(Y_test, Y_pred_svm, average='weighted')
print("F1-score (weighted) of SVM Algorithm = ", results)
```

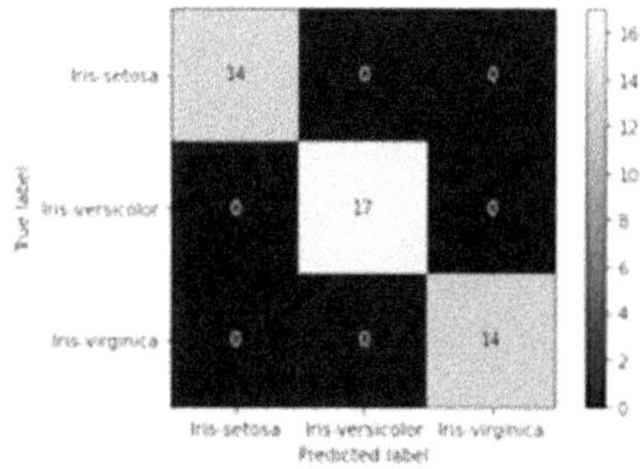


```
Accuracy of SVM Algorithm =  1.0
F1-score (macro) of SVM Algorithm =  1.0
F1-score (micro) of SVM Algorithm =  1.0
F1-score (weighted) of SVM Algorithm =  1.0
```

The fourth classification algorithm run on the Iris dataset is Gaussian distributed NB. The application of this algorithm and the results obtained from this algorithm are given in Figure 8. As in the SVM algorithm, the classification result is calculated with the predefined parameter values of this algorithm. If the results of the Gaussian distributed NB algorithm are examined, a performance of 1.0 is obtained according to the accuracy metric, while a result of 1.0 is obtained according to the weighted F1-score metric.

Figure 8. Use of Gaussian NB Algorithm on Iris Dataset

```
from sklearn.naive_bayes import GaussianNB
gnb = GaussianNB()
Y_pred_nb = gnb.fit(X_train, Y_train)
Y_pred_nb = gnb.predict(X_test)

cm = confusion_matrix(Y_test, Y_pred_nb, labels = gnb.classes_)
disp = ConfusionMatrixDisplay(confusion_matrix = cm, display_labels = gnb.classes_)
disp.plot()
plt.show()

results = accuracy_score(Y_test, Y_pred_nb)
print("Accuracy of Gaussian NB Algorithm = ", results)
results = f1_score(Y_test, Y_pred_nb, average='macro')
print("F1-score (macro) of Gaussian NB Algorithm = ", results)
results = f1_score(Y_test, Y_pred_nb, average='micro')
print("F1-score (micro) of Gaussian NB Algorithm = ", results)
results = f1_score(Y_test, Y_pred_nb, average='weighted')
print("F1-score (weighted) of Gaussian NB Algorithm = ", results)
```

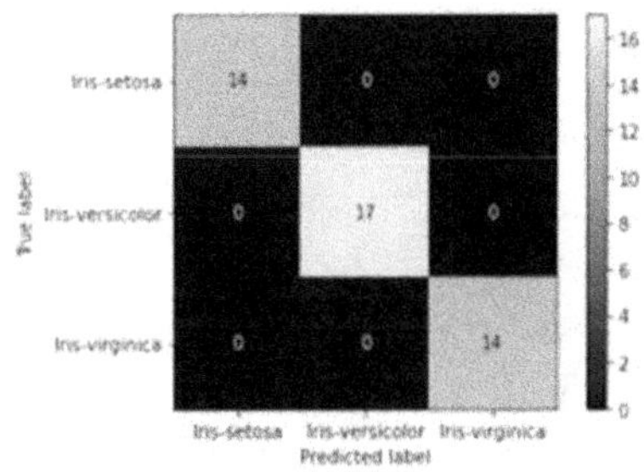


```
Accuracy of Gaussian NB Algorithm =  1.0
F1-score (macro) of Gaussian NB Algorithm =  1.0
F1-score (micro) of Gaussian NB Algorithm =  1.0
F1-score (weighted) of Gaussian NB Algorithm =  1.0
```

The fifth classification algorithm run on the Iris dataset is RF. The application of this algorithm and the results obtained from this algorithm are given in Figure 9. There are many parameters that affect the performance of the RF algorithm. It is possible to increase the classification performance by making changes to the parameters of this algorithm. In this code, classification is made with predefined values. If the results of the RF algorithm are examined, a performance of 0.9777 is achieved according to the accuracy metric, while a result of 0.9778 is obtained according to the weighted F1-score metric.

Figure 9. Use of RF Algorithm on Iris Dataset

```
from sklearn.ensemble import RandomForestClassifier
rf = RandomForestClassifier()
Y_pred_rf = rf.fit(X_train, Y_train)
Y_pred_rf = rf.predict(X_test)

cm = confusion_matrix(Y_test, Y_pred_rf, labels = rf.classes_)
disp = ConfusionMatrixDisplay(confusion_matrix = cm, display_labels = rf.classes_)
disp.plot()
plt.show()

results = accuracy_score(Y_test, Y_pred_rf)
print("Accuracy of RF Algorithm = ", results)
results = f1_score(Y_test, Y_pred_rf, average='macro')
print("F1-score (macro) of RF Algorithm = ", results)
results = f1_score(Y_test, Y_pred_rf, average='micro')
print("F1-score (micro) of RF Algorithm = ", results)
results = f1_score(Y_test, Y_pred_rf, average='weighted')
print("F1-score (weighted) of RF Algorithm = ", results)
```

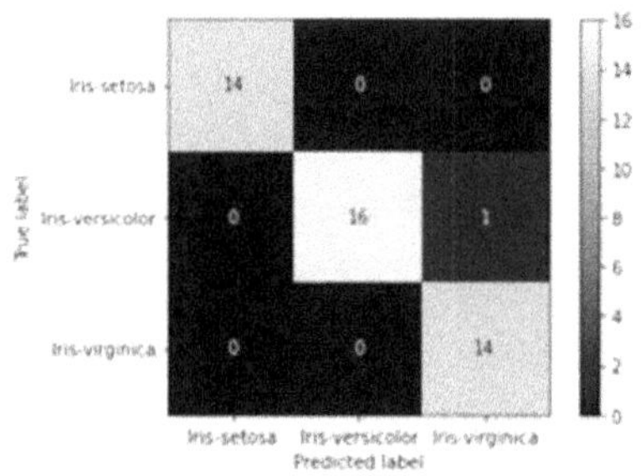


```
Accuracy of RF Algorithm =  0.9777777777777777
F1-score (macro) of RF Algorithm =  0.9784047370254267
F1-score (micro) of RF Algorithm =  0.9777777777777777
F1-score (weighted) of RF Algorithm =  0.9778242192035296
```

The sixth classification algorithm run on the Iris dataset is the Adaboost algorithm. The application of the Adaboost algorithm and the results obtained from this algorithm are given in Figure 10. In this code, classification is made with predefined values. If the results of the Adaboost algorithm are examined, a performance of 0.9777 is achieved according to the accuracy metric, while a result of 0.9776 is obtained according to the weighted F1-score metric.

Figure 10. Use of Adaboost Algorithm on Iris Dataset

```
from sklearn.ensemble import AdaBoostClassifier
adaboost = AdaBoostClassifier()
Y_pred_adaboost = adaboost.fit(X_train, Y_train)
Y_pred_adaboost = adaboost.predict(X_test)

cm = confusion_matrix(Y_test, Y_pred_adaboost, labels = adaboost.classes_)
disp = ConfusionMatrixDisplay(confusion_matrix = cm, display_labels = adaboost.classes_)
disp.plot()
plt.show()

results = accuracy_score(Y_test, Y_pred_adaboost)
print("Accuracy of Adaboost Algorithm = ", results)
results = f1_score(Y_test, Y_pred_adaboost, average='macro')
print("F1-score (macro) of Adaboost Algorithm = ", results)
results = f1_score(Y_test, Y_pred_adaboost, average='micro')
print("F1-score (micro) of Adaboost Algorithm = ", results)
results = f1_score(Y_test, Y_pred_adaboost, average='weighted')
print("F1-score (weighted) of Adaboost Algorithm = ", results)
```

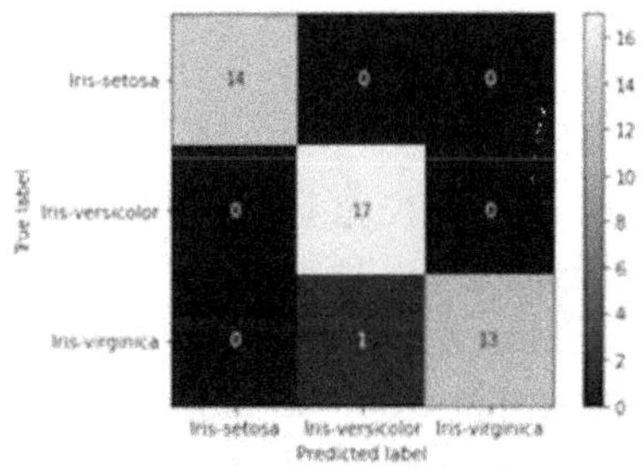


```
Accuracy of Adaboost Algorithm =  0.9777777777777777
F1-score (macro) of Adaboost Algorithm =  0.9781305114638448
F1-score (micro) of Adaboost Algorithm =  0.9777777777777777
F1-score (weighted) of Adaboost Algorithm =  0.9776837154614932
```

In addition to traditional machine learning approaches, the last classifier run on the Iris dataset is DNN. Figure 11 shows the libraries required to run DNN. The libraries in the first 5 lines have also been used in previous classification algorithms. In addition to these libraries, the libraries between lines 6 and 10 are added to the source code to create the DNN. In the infrastructure of a neural network, there are situations where the initial weights are created randomly. For this reason, it can be observed that even if the same dataset is used, the same results are not obtained every time the program is run. The 12th and 13th lines are added to the source code to prevent different results from being obtained in each run. Lines 15, 16, 17 and 18 are related to reading the Iris dataset. These lines were also used in other algorithms and no changes were made. Unlike the previous codes, the codes between lines 20 and 22 are added to the program. Since the labels of the Iris dataset are alphabetical, these label values are first converted to integers. This is accomplished in lines 21 and 22. In line 23, the dataset is divided into training and testing, as mentioned before. It should be noted that the non-alphabetical labels created in line 22 and kept in the variable named new_Y are used in line 23. If alphabetical labels are used, the program will give an error.

Figure 11. Use of DNN Algorithm on Iris Dataset – Step 1

```
1 import pandas as pd
2 import numpy as np
3 import matplotlib.pyplot as plt
4 from sklearn.model_selection import train_test_split
5 from sklearn.metrics import confusion_matrix, ConfusionMatrixDisplay, accuracy_score, f1_score
6 import tensorflow as tf
7 from keras import layers, models
8 from keras.utils import to_categorical
9 from sklearn.preprocessing import LabelEncoder
10 from numpy.random import seed
11
12 seed(1)
13 tf.random.set_seed(1)
14
15 col_names = ['Sepal_Length','Sepal_Width','Petal_Length','Petal_Width','Class']
16 dataset = pd.read_csv('iris.data', names = col_names)
17 X = dataset.iloc[:, 0:4].values
18 Y = dataset.iloc[:, 4].values
19
20 encoder =  LabelEncoder()
21 encoder_Y = encoder.fit_transform(Y)
22 new_Y = pd.get_dummies(encoder_Y).values
23 X_train, X_test, Y_train, Y_test = train_test_split(X, new_Y, test_size = 0.3, random_state = 10)
24
```

Figure 12 shows the creation and compilation of the DNN model and the test performances of the model. The model is created between the 25th and 29th lines. The model type used is preferred as Sequential. Sequential is the easiest way to create a model in Keras. It allows the creation of a model layer. Dense is a type of layer. It is known as a standard layer that works in most cases. The network structure is created by connecting all nodes in the previous layer to the nodes in the current layer. When the codes between lines 25 and 29 are examined, it is seen that a network structure consisting of 3 layers has been created. While the number of neurons of the first layer is 10, the number of neurons of the second layer is 5. Finally, there are 3 neurons in the third layer. While the activation function of the first and second layers is "relu", the activation function of the third layer is made "softmax" and the network structure is built.

Figure 12. Use of DNN Algorithm on Iris Dataset – Step 2

```
25 model = tf.keras.Sequential([
26     tf.keras.layers.Dense(10, activation = 'relu'),
27     tf.keras.layers.Dense(5, activation = 'relu'),
28     tf.keras.layers.Dense(3, activation = 'softmax')
29 ])
30 model.compile(optimizer = 'rmsprop', loss = 'categorical_crossentropy', metrics = ['accuracy'])
31 model.fit(X_train, Y_train, batch_size = 16, epochs = 100)
32 loss, accuracy = model.evaluate(X_test, Y_test, verbose = 0)
33
34 print('Test loss:', loss)
35 print('Test accuracy:', accuracy)
36
```

After the model is created, the compilation step of the model is started. This operation is performed on line 30. Compilation of the model is done with the model.compile() function. Three parameters are passed to this function: optimizer, loss and metrics. When the library is examined, it can be seen that this function takes many parameters. However, three of them are used in this program. The "rmsprop" optimization technique is preferred for the optimizer. Apart from this, different optimization techniques can be preferred. "man" is one of the widely used optimization techniques. "categorical_crossentropy" is used for loss. This is the most commonly used type of function for classification problems. To interpret how the model performs during training, the "accuracy" metric is used to see the amount of accuracy and loss achieved with the validation set at the end of each epoch. In the 31st line, the training step of the model is performed. Batch number means how many data will be processed simultaneously during the training of the model. In this model, batch_size=16 is set. The epochs value is assigned to 100. In the 32nd line, the model is evaluated. Then, these results are printed on the screen in the 34th and 35th lines. The model described with the code given in Figure 12 was created to give an example. It is possible to create more efficient network models by making changes to these parameters.

Figure 13. Use of DNN Algorithm on Iris Dataset – Step 3

```
Y_pred_dnn = model.predict(X_test)
actual = np.argmax(Y_test, axis = 1)
predicted = np.argmax(Y_pred_dnn, axis = 1)
label = ["Iris-setosa", "Iris-versicolour", "Iris-virginica"]
cm = confusion_matrix(actual, predicted)
disp = ConfusionMatrixDisplay(confusion_matrix = cm, display_labels = label)
disp.plot()
plt.show()

results = accuracy_score(actual, predicted)
print("Accuracy of DNN = ", results)
results = f1_score(actual, predicted, average='macro')
print("F1-score (macro) of DNN = ", results)
results = f1_score(actual, predicted, average='micro')
print("F1-score (micro) of DNN = ", results)
results = f1_score(actual, predicted, average='weighted')
print("F1-score (weighted) DNN = ", results)
```

Figure 13 shows the code structure created to evaluate the DNN model under different metrics. This code structure is almost the same as the code structure in the examples examined previously. It enables the creation of confusion matrix and F1-score metrics. The results obtained from DNN are given in Figure 14. If the results of DNN are examined, a performance of 0.9777 is achieved according to the accuracy metric, while a result of 0.9778 is obtained according to the weighted F1-score metric.

When 7 different classifiers run on the Iris dataset are compared, the most successful classifiers are Logistic regression, Gaussian distributed NB and SVM. Considering all the results, all test samples are classified correctly with these algorithms. On the other hand, other algorithms give lower results than these algorithms. These algorithms misclassify only 1 sample. Providing results with the confusion matrix is explanatory in this respect. It should be noted that parameter selections were not taken into consideration when making samples on the Iris dataset. As parameters change, performance rates may also change. Therefore, when classifying a dataset, it is recommended to obtain the results by finding the best parameters. Finally, classification is performed by setting random_state = 10. It is possible to see different classification results as the value transferred to this parameter is changed.

Figure 14. Results from DNN Algorithm on Iris Dataset

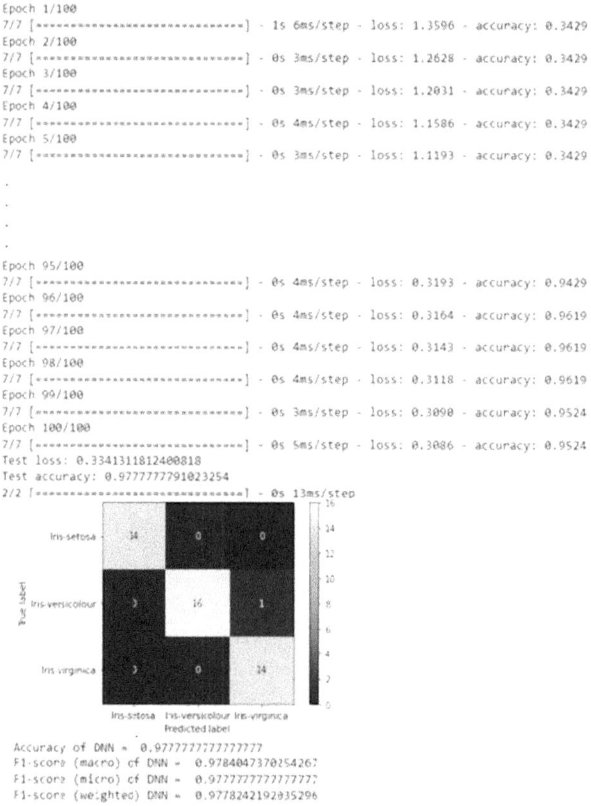

USE OF WHITE WINE QUALITY DATASET AND RESULTS OBTAINED

One of the frequently encountered problems in machine learning problems is regression. This section covers the solution of the regression problem with various regression techniques. White Wine Quality dataset is used to solve regression problems. This dataset can be solved as both a classification and regression problem. This section covers the use of this dataset in regression problems. The libraries used and reading the dataset are shown in Figure 15. While the first 4 lines contain the libraries used, the codes between the 6th and 9th lines are related to reading the dataset. Since the problem addressed here is regression, the metrics used differ from classification problems. Since the Iris dataset file used in the previous section did not contain attribute information, each of the attributes was added to the source code. Since the White Wine Quality dataset contains attribute information, it is directly passed to the reading step. Starting from the 11th line, regression performances are achieved by adding the library of the relevant regression technique.

Figure 15. Using the White Wine Quality Dataset

```
import pandas as pd
import numpy as np
from sklearn.model_selection import train_test_split
from sklearn.metrics import mean_absolute_error, mean_squared_error, r2_score

dataset = pd.read_csv('winequality-white.csv', sep=';' , engine='python')
X = dataset.iloc[:, 0:11].values
Y = dataset.iloc[:, 11].values
X_train, X_test, Y_train, Y_test = train_test_split(X, Y, test_size = 0.3, random_state = 5)

```

The first regression technique run on the White Wine Quality dataset is linear regression. Figure 16 shows the application of the linear regression technique on this dataset. Model performance is calculated with predefined parameters without making any parameter selection on the linear regression technique. If the results of the model are examined, MAE, MSE and RMSE are known as error values. It is generally desired that these values be close to 0. In this case, the model makes predictions without making any errors. Unlike classification, these metrics are very important for model performance since a number prediction is made, not a label prediction. How much error is made in the estimated values in the test dataset can be interpreted with these metrics. In addition to these three metrics, the R^2 metric is also one of the important metrics in evaluating the performance of regression techniques. The fact that the R^2 metric is close to 1 indicates that a good regression model has been created. According to the RMSE metric, the linear regression model gives an error value of 0.7192. The R^2 value for linear regression is calculated as 0.2756.

Figure 16. Using Linear Regression on the White Wine Quality Dataset

```
from sklearn.linear_model import LinearRegression
lr = LinearRegression()
lr.fit(X_train, Y_train)
Y_pred_lr = lr.predict(X_test)

mae = mean_absolute_error(y_true = Y_test, y_pred = Y_pred_lr)
#squared True returns MSE value, False returns RMSE value.
mse = mean_squared_error(y_true = Y_test, y_pred = Y_pred_lr) #default = True
rmse = mean_squared_error(y_true = Y_test, y_pred = Y_pred_lr, squared = False)
r2 = r2_score(y_true = Y_test, y_pred = Y_pred_lr)

print("MAE of Linear Regression Algorithm = ", mae)
print("MSE of Linear Regression Algorithm = ", mse)
print("RMSE of Linear Regression Algorithm = ", rmse)
print("R^2 of Linear Regression Algorithm = ", r2)

MAE of Linear Regression Algorithm =  0.5667109672527056
MSE of Linear Regression Algorithm =  0.5173483826592135
RMSE of Linear Regression Algorithm =  0.719269339440528
R^2 of Linear Regression Algorithm =  0.2756751916111715
```

SVM algorithm is not only used in classification problems. It can also be used in regression problems by making some changes to the algorithm. Figure 17 shows the use of the SVR technique on the White Wine Quality dataset. The algorithm is run by making the kernel function of the algorithm linear. Apart from this, no changes are made to other parameters. According to the RMSE metric, the SVR model gives an error value of 0.7258. The R^2 value for the SVR model is calculated as 0.2624. If the linear regression model and the SVR model are compared, the linear regression model creates a better model for this part of the dataset. This situation occurs in all metrics. For example, while the linear regression technique gives an error value of 0.5667 according to the MAE metric, this value is calculated as 0.5678 in the SVR technique. There is no big difference between these error values, but since the error value obtained with the linear regression technique is less, it can be accepted that a better model is created.

Figure 17. Using SVR on the White Wine Quality Dataset

```
from sklearn.svm import SVR
svr = SVR(kernel='linear')
svr.fit(X_train, Y_train)
Y_pred_svr = svr.predict(X_test)

mae = mean_absolute_error(y_true = Y_test, y_pred = Y_pred_svr)
#squared True returns MSE value, False returns RMSE value.
mse = mean_squared_error(y_true = Y_test, y_pred = Y_pred_svr) #default = True
rmse = mean_squared_error(y_true = Y_test, y_pred = Y_pred_svr, squared = False)
r2 = r2_score(y_true = Y_test, y_pred = Y_pred_svr)

print("MAE of Support Vector Regression Algorithm = ", mae)
print("MSE of Support Vector Regression Algorithm = ", mse)
print("RMSE of Support Vector Regression Algorithm = ", rmse)
print("R^2 of Support Vector Regression Algorithm = ", r2)
```

```
MAE of Support Vector Regression Algorithm =  0.5678162409286612
MSE of Support Vector Regression Algorithm =  0.5267920453695543
RMSE of Support Vector Regression Algorithm =  0.725804412613725
R^2 of Support Vector Regression Algorithm =  0.26245338709330146
```

Figure 18 shows the use of the KNN regression technique on the White Wine Quality dataset. In this algorithm, the model is created by giving the number of neighbors as 9 as a parameter. KNN algorithm can also be used in classification and regression problems. According to the RMSE metric, the KNN regression model gives an error value of 0.7896. The R^2 value for the KNN regression model is calculated as 0.1270. This model appears to be a failing model from both the SVR and the linear regression model.

Figure 18. Using KNN Regressor on the White Wine Quality Dataset

```
from sklearn.neighbors import KNeighborsRegressor
knn_reg = KNeighborsRegressor(n_neighbors=9)
knn_reg.fit(X_train, Y_train)
Y_pred_knn = knn_reg.predict(X_test)

mae = mean_absolute_error(y_true = Y_test, y_pred = Y_pred_knn)
#squared True returns MSE value, False returns RMSE value.
mse = mean_squared_error(y_true = Y_test, y_pred = Y_pred_knn) #default = True
rmse = mean_squared_error(y_true = Y_test, y_pred = Y_pred_knn, squared = False)
r2 = r2_score(y_true = Y_test, y_pred = Y_pred_knn)

print("MAE of KNN Regression Algorithm = ", mae)
print("MSE of KNN Regression Algorithm = ", mse)
print("RMSE of KNN Regression Algorithm = ", rmse)
print("R^2 of KNN Regression Algorithm = ", r2)
```

```
MAE of KNN Regression Algorithm =  0.6256991685563114
MSE of KNN Regression Algorithm =  0.6235323759133283
RMSE of KNN Regression Algorithm =  0.789640662525258
R^2 of KNN Regression Algorithm =  0.12700999201701235
```

One of the algorithms used in both classification problems and regression problems is decision trees. Figure 19 shows the use of decision trees-based regression technique on the White Wine Quality dataset. The maximum depth of the tree is given a value of 10. The regression result is obtained only by making changes to this parameter. According to the RMSE metric, the regression model based on the decision tree gives an error value of 0.7926. The R^2 value for this regression model is calculated as 0.1203. Regression performance can be changed by making changes to other parameters of the algorithm.

Figure 19. Using Decision Tree Based Regression on White Wine Quality Dataset

```
from sklearn import tree
dt_reg = tree.DecisionTreeRegressor(max_depth = 10)
dt_reg.fit(X_train, Y_train)
Y_pred_dt = dt_reg.predict(X_test)

mae = mean_absolute_error(y_true = Y_test, y_pred = Y_pred_dt)
#squared True returns MSE value, False returns RMSE value.
mse = mean_squared_error(y_true = Y_test, y_pred = Y_pred_dt) #default = True
rmse = mean_squared_error(y_true = Y_test, y_pred = Y_pred_dt, squared = False)
r2 = r2_score(y_true = Y_test, y_pred = Y_pred_dt)

print("MAE of Decision Tree Regression Algorithm = ", mae)
print("MSE of Decision Tree Regression Algorithm = ", mse)
print("RMSE of Decision Tree Regression Algorithm = ", rmse)
print("R^2 of Decision Tree Regression Algorithm = ", r2)

MAE of Decision Tree Regression Algorithm =  0.5679638381868434
MSE of Decision Tree Regression Algorithm =  0.6282926041751091
RMSE of Decision Tree Regression Algorithm =  0.7926491053266314
R^2 of Decision Tree Regression Algorithm =  0.12034533133733893
```

Figure 20. Using Multilayer Perceptron Regression on White Wine Quality Dataset

```
from sklearn.neural_network import MLPRegressor
mlp_regr = MLPRegressor()
mlp_regr.fit(X_train, Y_train)
Y_pred_mlp = mlp_regr.predict(X_test)

mae = mean_absolute_error(y_true = Y_test, y_pred = Y_pred_mlp)
#squared True returns MSE value, False returns RMSE value.
mse = mean_squared_error(y_true = Y_test, y_pred = Y_pred_mlp) #default = True
rmse = mean_squared_error(y_true = Y_test, y_pred = Y_pred_mlp, squared = False)
r2 = r2_score(y_true = Y_test, y_pred = Y_pred_mlp)

print("MAE of Multi-layer Perceptron Regressor Algorithm = ", mae)
print("MSE of Multi-layer Perceptron Regressor Algorithm = ", mse)
print("RMSE of Multi-layer Perceptron Regressor Algorithm = ", rmse)
print("R^2 of Multi-layer Perceptron Regressor Algorithm = ", r2)

MAE of Multi-layer Perceptron Regressor Algorithm =  0.5699530841059965
MSE of Multi-layer Perceptron Regressor Algorithm =  0.5147328596122674
RMSE of Multi-layer Perceptron Regressor Algorithm =  0.7174488550497989
R^2 of Multi-layer Perceptron Regressor Algorithm =  0.2793371113026528
```

The classification process was carried out in the previous section by running deep neural networks on the Iris dataset. Classification of the Iris dataset was achieved by using Tensorflow and Keras libraries to create a deep neural network model. Deep neural networks are neural networks with a more complex structure than multilayer perceptrons. The reason it is more complex is that the number of layers is quite high. It is possible to create multilayer neural networks with the Sklearn library. This structure can be easily integrated into classification and regression problems. In Figure 20, a regression model is created using a multilayer perceptron. This created model is run on the White Wine Quality dataset. Predefined parameters are used in the created multilayer sensor. Some of these predefined parameters are as follows: "hidden_layer_sizes" parameter is 100, activation function is relu, optimization algorithm is man, alpha value is 0.0001 and batch_size is auto. By changing the values on these parameters, different network structures can be created. When the results of the network structure created with predefined parameters are examined, it gives an error value of 0.7174 according to the RMSE metric. The R^2value for this regression model is calculated as 0.2793. This created network model, together with the linear regression model, stands out as the best models so far for the regression problem on the White Wine Quality dataset.

Figure 21. Using Random Forest Regression on the White Wine Quality Dataset

```
from sklearn.ensemble import RandomForestRegressor
rf_reg = RandomForestRegressor()
rf_reg.fit(X_train, Y_train)
Y_pred_rf = rf_reg.predict(X_test)

mae = mean_absolute_error(y_true = Y_test, y_pred = Y_pred_rf)
#squared True returns MSE value, False returns RMSE value.
mse = mean_squared_error(y_true = Y_test, y_pred = Y_pred_rf) #default = True
rmse = mean_squared_error(y_true = Y_test, y_pred = Y_pred_rf, squared = False)
r2 = r2_score(y_true = Y_test, y_pred = Y_pred_rf)

print("MAE of Random Forest Regressor Algorithm = ", mae)
print("MSE of Random Forest Regressor Algorithm = ", mse)
print("RMSE of Random Forest Regressor Algorithm = ", rmse)
print("R^2 of Random Forest Regressor Algorithm = ", r2)
```

```
MAE of Random Forest Regressor Algorithm =  0.44208163265306116
MSE of Random Forest Regressor Algorithm =  0.3714783673469388
RMSE of Random Forest Regressor Algorithm =  0.6094902520524333
R^2 of Random Forest Regressor Algorithm =  0.4799036659472692
```

Figure 22. Using Adaboost Regression on the White Wine Quality Dataset

```
from sklearn.ensemble import AdaBoostRegressor
adaboost_reg = AdaBoostRegressor()
adaboost_reg.fit(X_train, Y_train)
Y_pred_adaboost = adaboost_reg.predict(X_test)

mae = mean_absolute_error(y_true = Y_test, y_pred = Y_pred_adaboost)
#squared True returns MSE value, False returns RMSE value.
mse = mean_squared_error(y_true = Y_test, y_pred = Y_pred_adaboost) #default = True
rmse = mean_squared_error(y_true = Y_test, y_pred = Y_pred_adaboost, squared = False)
r2 = r2_score(y_true = Y_test, y_pred = Y_pred_adaboost)

print("MAE of AdaBoost Regressor Algorithm = ", mae)
print("MSE of AdaBoost Regressor Algorithm = ", mse)
print("RMSE of AdaBoost Regressor Algorithm = ", rmse)
print("R^2 of AdaBoost Regressor Algorithm = ", r2)
```

```
MAE of AdaBoost Regressor Algorithm =  0.5747556933015346
MSE of AdaBoost Regressor Algorithm =  0.5127214732970018
RMSE of AdaBoost Regressor Algorithm =  0.7160457201163916
R^2 of AdaBoost Regressor Algorithm =  0.28215319627794944
```

The last regression techniques run on the White Wine Quality dataset are random forest and AdaBoost regression techniques based on ensemble learning. Figure 21 and Figure 22 show the use of these regression techniques, respectively. According to the RMSE metric, the regression model based on random forest gives an error value of 0.6094. The R^2 value for this regression model is calculated as 0.4799. According to the RMSE metric, the AdaBoost regression model gives an error value of 0.7160. The R^2 value for this regression model is calculated as 0.2821. When the results of all models obtained on the White Wine Quality dataset are examined, the most successful result is obtained with the random forest-based regression model. Since this model has the lowest error value and the highest R^2 value, it is the best model to choose for this dataset.

In general, when the White Wine Quality dataset is evaluated, it is seen that it is a very difficult dataset according to the results obtained. Because the RMSE and MAE metrics that give error values are expected to be close to 0. However, not all models give such a result. In addition, it is desired that the R^2 value be close to 1. In general, it should be taken into consideration that algorithms create models with predefined parameters. It is possible to obtain models with higher performance by making changes to the parameter selection. Finally, by setting random_state = 5, the regression problem is solved by separating 70% of the dataset for training and 30% for testing. It is possible to see different regression results as the value transferred to this parameter is changed.

USE OF CIFAR-10 DATASET AND RESULTS OBTAINED

One of the important machine learning problems in recent years is image classification. When image classification is done with classical machine learning algorithms, each pixel value must be given as input to the machine learning technique. If the images in the dataset are colored, the pixel value for each channel should be given to the algorithm. In addition to this approach, feature extraction can be performed on images to find vectors to be given as input to machine learning algorithms. In this case, image processing techniques also need to be known and applied. The features obtained in both methods are given as input to machine learning algorithms and the images are classified. However, these two techniques are quite costly in terms of computational cost. In addition to these traditional approaches, the image classification problem has been effectively solved in recent years with convolutional neural networks (CNN), one of the deep learning techniques. The most important advantage of the CNN model is that automatic feature extraction is performed on the image while the model is created. Additionally, CNN reduces the high dimensionality of images without losing information. In this way, complex problems are solved more simply and efficiently. In this section, the solution of the image classification problem on the CIFAR-10 dataset will be discussed by using Tensorflow and Keras libraries.

The CIFAR-10 dataset can be used directly by adding it to the project with a few lines of code so that researchers can easily test network models. There are 60000 color images on this dataset. It is a dataset consisting of a total of 10 categories. It is a balanced dataset as it contains 6000 images from all categories. Each image is 32*32 in size. 50000 of these images are used for training and 10000 for testing. Pixel values of images are between 0 and 255. To normalize all pixel values between 0 and 1, all pixel values are divided by 255. The processes of loading the dataset, assigning the training/test sections of the dataset to variables, and normalizing pixel values are carried out in the code given in Figure 23. In the first 3 lines in Figure 23, libraries are included in the project. In the 5th line, the CIFAR-10 dataset is loaded into the project. In the 6th line, pixel values are normalized between 0 and 1.

Figure 23. Adding the CIFAR-10 Dataset to the Project

```
import tensorflow as tf
from tensorflow import keras
from keras.datasets import cifar10

(train_images, train_labels), (test_images, test_labels) = cifar10.load_data()
train_images, test_images = train_images / 255.0, test_images / 255.0
```

The piece of code in Figure 24 checks whether there is a problem loading the dataset and whether the labels of each image are correct. The piece of code in Figure 24 prints the first 30 images in the training set and the labels of these images on the screen. After checking the images and their tags, this piece of code (between lines 8 and 20) can be commented or deleted. The process of creating the CNN model continues by making a comment line.

Figure 24. First 30 Images of the Training Set in the CIFAR-10 Dataset

```
7
8 import matplotlib.pyplot as plt
9 class_names = ['airplane', 'automobile', 'bird', 'cat', 'deer', 'dog', 'frog', 'horse', 'ship', 'truck']
10 plt.figure(figsize=(12, 12))
11 i = 0
12 while(i < 30):
13     plt.subplot(5,10,i+1)
14     plt.xticks([])
15     plt.yticks([])
16     plt.grid(False)
17     plt.imshow(train_images[i])
18     plt.xlabel(class_names[train_labels[i][0]])
19     i += 1
20 plt.show()
```

With the 22nd line, the step of creating the CNN model is started. Figure 25 shows the step-by-step creation of the CNN model and printing the summary of the created model on the screen. The libraries to be used are loaded in the 22nd and 23rd lines. Then, the coding of the CNN model structure is carried out. Since we are dealing with relatively small images of 32*32 size, the main model is created using three convolution and two Max Pooling layers. For larger images and different problems, the number of layers in the network can be increased. In the first of the convolution layer, a 3*3 core layer with 32 filters is created. The activation function of this layer is "relu", while the input_shape parameter is given the value (32, 32, 3). Since the images studied are 32*32 in size and have 3 channels (red, green, blue), these values are given as parameters. A 2*2 sized MaxPooling2D layer is connected to this layer. Then the second convolution layer is created. This layer is a 3*3 core layer with 64 filters and its activation function is "relu". As in the first convolution layer, a 2*2 dimension MaxPooling2D layer is connected after this layer.

Figure 25. Step by Step Creation of CNN Model on CIFAR-10 Dataset

```
from keras.models import Sequential
from keras.layers import Dense, Flatten, Conv2D, MaxPool2D
#The model is defined
model = Sequential()
#CNN and pooling layers added
model.add(Conv2D(32, (3, 3), activation = 'relu', input_shape=(32, 32, 3)))
model.add(MaxPool2D(pool_size = (2, 2)))
model.add(Conv2D(64, (3, 3), activation = 'relu'))
model.add(MaxPool2D(pool_size = (2, 2)))
model.add(Conv2D(64, (3, 3), activation='relu'))
#Flatten layer added
model.add(Flatten())
model.add(Dense(64, activation = 'relu'))
#Since there are 10 labels, 10 nodes were created.
model.add(Dense(10))
#Summary of the created model
model.summary()
```

```
Model: "sequential"
_________________________________________________________________
 Layer (type)                Output Shape              Param #
=================================================================
 conv2d (Conv2D)             (None, 30, 30, 32)        896

 max_pooling2d (MaxPooling2D  (None, 15, 15, 32)       0
 )

 conv2d_1 (Conv2D)           (None, 13, 13, 64)        18496

 max_pooling2d_1 (MaxPooling  (None, 6, 6, 64)         0
 2D)

 conv2d_2 (Conv2D)           (None, 4, 4, 64)          36928

 flatten (Flatten)           (None, 1024)              0

 dense (Dense)               (None, 64)                65600

 dense_1 (Dense)             (None, 10)                650

=================================================================
Total params: 122,570
Trainable params: 122,570
Non-trainable params: 0
_________________________________________________________________
```

After these two layers, the images are reduced in size considerably. The downloaded image has 6 height pixels, 6 width pixels and a total of 64 filters. With a third and final convolution layer, these dimensions are reduced to 4x4x64. As a result, an efficient network structure is built without giving each pixel in the image as input, as in classical neural networks. Images are evaluated by replacing a 3×3 matrix per image with a vector with 1024 elements (4*4*64) without losing any information. The size of the images is reduced sufficiently. Another hidden layer with a total of 64 neurons is added before the resulting model ends in an output layer with ten neurons for ten different classes. As a result of all layers, a model with a total of 122,570 parameters is created. This created model is now ready to be trained.

Before starting to train the CNN, the model must be compiled. Within the .compile() method, structures such as which loss function the model should be trained on, which optimization technique should be used, and which metric should be displayed to monitor the training process are defined. The code snippet in Figure 26 shows the compilation and training of the model. The compilation of the CNN model is in line 40. In the 41st line, the training phase of the model begins.

Figure 26. Training CNN Model on CIFAR-10 Dataset

```
39 #Model compile
40 model.compile(loss = tf.keras.losses.SparseCategoricalCrossentropy(from_logits=True), optimizer = 'adam', metrics = ['accuracy'])
41 cnn = model.fit(train_images, train_labels, epochs=10, validation_data = (test_images, test_labels))
```

```
Epoch 1/10
1563/1563 [==============================] - 85s 54ms/step - loss: 1.4917 - accuracy: 0.4566 - val_loss: 1.2212 - val_accuracy: 0.5701
Epoch 2/10
1563/1563 [==============================] - 81s 52ms/step - loss: 1.1235 - accuracy: 0.6037 - val_loss: 1.0210 - val_accuracy: 0.6371
Epoch 3/10
1563/1563 [==============================] - 81s 52ms/step - loss: 0.9613 - accuracy: 0.6621 - val_loss: 0.9598 - val_accuracy: 0.6643
Epoch 4/10
1563/1563 [==============================] - 80s 51ms/step - loss: 0.8671 - accuracy: 0.6954 - val_loss: 0.8908 - val_accuracy: 0.6933
Epoch 5/10
1563/1563 [==============================] - 82s 52ms/step - loss: 0.7991 - accuracy: 0.7226 - val_loss: 0.8748 - val_accuracy: 0.6983
Epoch 6/10
1563/1563 [==============================] - 83s 53ms/step - loss: 0.7405 - accuracy: 0.7412 - val_loss: 0.8797 - val_accuracy: 0.6988
Epoch 7/10
1563/1563 [==============================] - 80s 51ms/step - loss: 0.6934 - accuracy: 0.7572 - val_loss: 0.8894 - val_accuracy: 0.7037
Epoch 8/10
1563/1563 [==============================] - 81s 52ms/step - loss: 0.6508 - accuracy: 0.7724 - val_loss: 0.8418 - val_accuracy: 0.7157
Epoch 9/10
1563/1563 [==============================] - 80s 52ms/step - loss: 0.6115 - accuracy: 0.7857 - val_loss: 0.8629 - val_accuracy: 0.7074
Epoch 10/10
1563/1563 [==============================] - 82s 52ms/step - loss: 0.5740 - accuracy: 0.7994 - val_loss: 0.8617 - val_accuracy: 0.7203
```

Figure 27 shows the evaluation phase of the model graphically. The performance of the model can vary between 75% and 80%. To increase these classification results, the number of epochs can be increased or improvements must be made on the layers and algorithm parameters of the CNN. It should be noted that in this example, classification was made with only 10 epochs. Additionally, the network structure was created randomly. Such situations directly affect image classification performance.

Figure 27. Evaluation of CNN Model on CIFAR-10 Dataset

```
import matplotlib.pyplot as plt
plt.plot(cnn.history['accuracy'], label='accuracy')
plt.plot(cnn.history['val_accuracy'], label = 'val_accuracy')
plt.xlabel('Epoch')
plt.ylabel('Accuracy')
plt.ylim([0.5, 1])
plt.legend(loc='lower right')
```

USE OF BORSA ISTANBUL (BIST) STOCK AND OBTAINING CLOSING FORECAST

With the project to be carried out in this section, the closing price of BIMAS, one of the companies in BIST30, will be predicted using different machine learning techniques. The reason for choosing BIST30 stocks is that they are safer and less manipulated than crypto exchanges. There is a data pre-processing stage before the price prediction of the data. At this stage, the data will be received through Yahoo finance. In order to make accurate price predictions, attributes such as opening values, highest values and lowest values will be given to the models. Many models, such as linear regression, regression based on decision trees, and ensemble learning, will be used to estimate closure values. Finally, the trained models will be tested on test data and performance evaluations will be made.

BIST stands for Borsa Istanbul. Transaction code is XU030. BIST30 Index was created to measure the performance of the 30 stocks with the highest market value in Borsa Istanbul. BIST30 data will be received via Yahoo Finance. This data can be downloaded in .csv file format. However, the "yfinance" library can be used to keep the dataset constantly updated. Thus, the use of the current dataset can be ensured by adding updated data each time. Figure 28 shows the use of data from BIMAS within BIST30 between the dates "2015-01-01" and "2020-01-01". There are 1303 rows and 6 columns on the dataset obtained between these dates. The details of this dataset obtained with the info() method in the Pandas library are shown. There are no missing or empty values in all columns. The numbers in the first 5 columns are of float64 type, while the last column is of int64 type.

Figure 28. Obtaining Historical Data for BIMAS Stock

```
import pandas as pd
import yfinance as yf
stock_data = yf.download("BIMAS.IS", start="2015-01-01", end="2020-01-01")
print(stock_data)
print(stock_data.info())
```

```
[*********************100%***********************]  1 of 1 completed
                 Open       High        Low      Close  Adj Close   Volume
Date
2015-01-01  25.000000  25.000000  25.000000  25.000000  18.837278        0
2015-01-02  24.775000  24.975000  24.725000  24.975000  18.818447   309612
2015-01-05  25.400000  25.525000  25.275000  25.475000  19.195189  1066532
2015-01-06  25.299999  25.674999  25.275000  25.674999  19.345888   810686
2015-01-07  25.475000  25.600000  25.400000  25.525000  19.232862   552970
...               ...        ...        ...        ...        ...      ...
2019-12-25  46.500000  46.740002  46.240002  46.740002  40.688301   405349
2019-12-26  46.500000  46.939999  46.439999  46.860001  40.792763   527234
2019-12-27  46.900002  47.160000  46.700001  47.080002  40.984280   633046
2019-12-30  46.939999  47.160000  46.660000  46.880001  40.810173   721708
2019-12-31  46.980000  47.380001  46.799999  46.799999  40.740532   513962

[1303 rows x 6 columns]
<class 'pandas.core.frame.DataFrame'>
DatetimeIndex: 1303 entries, 2015-01-01 to 2019-12-31
Data columns (total 6 columns):
 #   Column     Non-Null Count  Dtype
---  ------     --------------  -----
 0   Open       1303 non-null   float64
 1   High       1303 non-null   float64
 2   Low        1303 non-null   float64
 3   Close      1303 non-null   float64
 4   Adj Close  1303 non-null   float64
 5   Volume     1303 non-null   int64
dtypes: float64(5), int64(1)
memory usage: 71.3 KB
None
```

Time series are important in fields with continuous data, such as the stock market. A time series is an ordered recorded list of measurements or events taken periodically over a specific period of time. This data is usually timestamped and modeled as a collection of variables that change over a period of time. The dataset obtained in Figure 28 is also like this. In the data obtained, each line is shown respectively according to year, month and day information. The financial situation of a company over the years, weather data for a city over days, or data collected periodically by a sensor can be considered as a time series. Time series analysis is defined as the statistical method used to understand the characteristics of this data such as trends, fluctuations and correlations over time (Lim and Zohren, 2021).

Figure 29. Editing Historical Data of BIMAS Stock for Machine Learning Techniques

```
import pandas as pd
import yfinance as yf
stock_data = yf.download("BIMAS.IS", start="2015-01-01", end="2020-01-01")
#print(stock_data)
#print(stock_data.info())

features = stock_data[['Open', 'High', 'Low', 'Adj Close', 'Volume']]
target = stock_data['Close']
print(features)
print(target)
```

```
[*********************100%***********************]  1 of 1 completed
                 Open       High        Low  Adj Close   Volume
Date
2015-01-01  25.000000  25.000000  25.000000  18.837282        0
2015-01-02  24.775000  24.975000  24.725000  18.818441   309612
2015-01-05  25.400000  25.525000  25.275000  19.195187  1066532
2015-01-06  25.299999  25.674999  25.275000  19.345886   810686
2015-01-07  25.475000  25.600000  25.400000  19.232861   552970
...               ...        ...        ...        ...      ...
2019-12-25  46.500000  46.740002  46.240002  40.688297   405349
2019-12-26  46.500000  46.939999  46.439999  40.792763   527234
2019-12-27  46.900002  47.160000  46.700001  40.984276   633046
2019-12-30  46.939999  47.160000  46.660000  40.810169   721708
2019-12-31  46.980000  47.380001  46.799999  40.740528   513962

[1303 rows x 5 columns]
Date
2015-01-01    25.000000
2015-01-02    24.975000
2015-01-05    25.475000
2015-01-06    25.674999
2015-01-07    25.525000
                ...
2019-12-25    46.740002
2019-12-26    46.860001
2019-12-27    47.080002
2019-12-30    46.880001
2019-12-31    46.799999
Name: Close, Length: 1303, dtype: float64
```

"Open", "High", "Low", "Adj Close" and "Volume" information will be used as attributes. The values of these columns will be given as input to machine learning techniques. "Close" values will be the values that need to be estimated. The code in Figure 29 makes the dataset suitable for machine learning models.

By running the code, the edited dataset is printed on the screen. No normalization process is performed on the dataset. The closing values of the dataset are estimated as shown in Figure 29.

Figure 30 shows the code structure to be used in the infrastructure of all models. While changing the previously prepared "features" variable to X. The "target" variable has been changed to Y. In the projects carried out in other departments, data and labels were parsed with the iloc() method in the Pandas library. In this project, data and labels are parsed directly using column names. The code in the 7th line ensures that 80% of the dataset is used for training and 20% is used for testing. The first 10 lines of the code structure of all models are as follows. Starting from line 11, models will be added to the project and the closing values of the stock will be estimated.

Figure 30. Common Code for the Use of All Models

```
1 import pandas as pd
2 import numpy as np
3 import yfinance as yf
4 from sklearn.model_selection import train_test_split
5 from sklearn.metrics import mean_absolute_error, mean_squared_error, r2_score
6
7 stock_data = yf.download("BIMAS.IS", start="2015-01-01", end="2020-01-01")
8 X = stock_data[['Open', 'High', 'Low', 'Adj Close', 'Volume']]
9 Y = stock_data['Close']
10 X_train, X_test, Y_train, Y_test = train_test_split(X, Y, test_size = 0.2, random_state = 1)
11
```

The first model used to estimate closing values is the linear regression technique. Figure 31 shows the coding of the linear regression model and the results obtained from this model. Model performance is calculated with predefined parameters without any parameter selection on the linear regression technique. If the results of the model are examined, MAE, MSE and RMSE are known as error values. It is generally desired that these values be close to 0. In this case, the model makes predictions without making any errors. Unlike classification, these metrics are very important for model performance since a number prediction is made, not a label prediction. How much error is made in the estimated values in the test dataset can be interpreted with these metrics. In addition to these three metrics, the R^2 metric is also one of the important metrics in evaluating the performance of regression techniques. The fact that the R^2 metric is close to 1 indicates that a good regression model has been created. According to the RMSE metric, the linear regression model gives an error value of 0.2204. The R^2value for linear regression is calculated as 0.9991. Regression techniques generally performed poorly on the White Wine Quality dataset. However, it can be seen from the results in Figure 31 that a successful model has been established in estimating the closing values of BIMAS. It can be easily understood with this example that datasets directly affect algorithm performance.

Figure 31. Using Linear Regression on Stock Market Data

```
from sklearn.linear_model import LinearRegression
lr = LinearRegression()
lr.fit(X_train, Y_train)
Y_pred_lr = lr.predict(X_test)

mae = mean_absolute_error(y_true = Y_test, y_pred = Y_pred_lr)
#squared True returns MSE value, False returns RMSE value.
mse = mean_squared_error(y_true = Y_test, y_pred = Y_pred_lr) #default = True
rmse = mean_squared_error(y_true = Y_test, y_pred = Y_pred_lr, squared = False)
r2 = r2_score(y_true = Y_test, y_pred = Y_pred_lr)

print("MAE of Linear Regression Algorithm = ", mae)
print("MSE of Linear Regression Algorithm = ", mse)
print("RMSE of Linear Regression Algorithm = ", rmse)
print("R^2 of Linear Regression Algorithm = ", r2)
```

```
[*********************100%***********************]  1 of 1 completed
MAE of Linear Regression Algorithm =  0.16338911119342842
MSE of Linear Regression Algorithm =  0.04861515845909485
RMSE of Linear Regression Algorithm =  0.22048845425349 34
R^2 of Linear Regression Algorithm =  0.9991733498752227
```

Figure 32 shows the use of decision trees-based regression technique on the stock market dataset. The maximum depth of the tree is given a value of 10. The regression result is obtained only by making changes to this parameter. According to the RMSE metric, the regression model based on the decision tree gives an error value of 0.2729. The R^2 value for this regression model is calculated as 0.9987. Regression performance can be changed by making changes to other parameters of the algorithm. The result obtained with the linear regression model is more successful than the decision tree-based regression model.

Figure 32. Using Decision Tree Based Regression on Stock Market Data

```
from sklearn import tree
dt_reg = tree.DecisionTreeRegressor(max_depth = 10)
dt_reg.fit(X_train, Y_train)
Y_pred_dt = dt_reg.predict(X_test)

mae = mean_absolute_error(y_true = Y_test, y_pred = Y_pred_dt)
#squared True returns MSE value, False returns RMSE value.
mse = mean_squared_error(y_true = Y_test, y_pred = Y_pred_dt) #default = True
rmse = mean_squared_error(y_true = Y_test, y_pred = Y_pred_dt, squared = False)
r2 = r2_score(y_true = Y_test, y_pred = Y_pred_dt)

print("MAE of Decision Tree Regression Algorithm = ", mae)
print("MSE of Decision Tree Regression Algorithm = ", mse)
print("RMSE of Decision Tree Regression Algorithm = ", rmse)
print("R^2 of Decision Tree Regression Algorithm = ", r2)
```

```
[*********************100%***********************]  1 of 1 completed
MAE of Decision Tree Regression Algorithm =  0.19331392799580405
MSE of Decision Tree Regression Algorithm =  0.07451005217983911
RMSE of Decision Tree Regression Algorithm =  0.2729652948267217
R^2 of Decision Tree Regression Algorithm =  0.9987330341834953
```

The last regression techniques run on the stock market dataset are random forest and AdaBoost regression techniques based on ensemble learning. Figure 33 and Figure 34 show the use of these regression techniques, respectively. According to the RMSE metric, the regression model based on random forest gives an error value of 0.2120. The R^2 value for this regression model is calculated as 0.9992. According to the RMSE metric, the AdaBoost regression model gives an error value of 0.3943. The R^2 value for this regression model is calculated as 0.9973. When the results of all models obtained on the stock market dataset are examined, the most successful result is obtained with the random forest-based regression model. Since this model has the lowest error value and the highest R^2 value, it is the best model to choose for this dataset.

Figure 33. Using Random Forest Regression on Stock Market Data

```
from sklearn.ensemble import RandomForestRegressor
rf_reg = RandomForestRegressor()
rf_reg.fit(X_train, Y_train)
Y_pred_rf = rf_reg.predict(X_test)

mae = mean_absolute_error(y_true = Y_test, y_pred = Y_pred_rf)
#squared True returns MSE value, False returns RMSE value.
mse = mean_squared_error(y_true = Y_test, y_pred = Y_pred_rf) #default = True
rmse = mean_squared_error(y_true = Y_test, y_pred = Y_pred_rf, squared = False)
r2 = r2_score(y_true = Y_test, y_pred = Y_pred_rf)

print("MAE of Random Forest Regressor Algorithm = ", mae)
print("MSE of Random Forest Regressor Algorithm = ", mse)
print("RMSE of Random Forest Regressor Algorithm = ", rmse)
print("R^2 of Random Forest Regressor Algorithm = ", r2)
```

```
[*********************100%***********************]  1 of 1 completed
MAE of Random Forest Regressor Algorithm =  0.15569342222250301
MSE of Random Forest Regressor Algorithm =  0.04497196857331549
RMSE of Random Forest Regressor Algorithm =  0.21206595335724096
R^2 of Random Forest Regressor Algorithm =  0.9992352985239389
```

Figure 34. Using AdaBoost Regression on Stock Market Data

```
from sklearn.ensemble import AdaBoostRegressor
adaboost_reg = AdaBoostRegressor()
adaboost_reg.fit(X_train, Y_train)
Y_pred_adaboost = adaboost_reg.predict(X_test)

mae = mean_absolute_error(y_true = Y_test, y_pred = Y_pred_adaboost)
#squared True returns MSE value, False returns RMSE value.
mse = mean_squared_error(y_true = Y_test, y_pred = Y_pred_adaboost) #default = True
rmse = mean_squared_error(y_true = Y_test, y_pred = Y_pred_adaboost, squared = False)
r2 = r2_score(y_true = Y_test, y_pred = Y_pred_adaboost)

print("MAE of AdaBoost Regressor Algorithm = ", mae)
print("MSE of AdaBoost Regressor Algorithm = ", mse)
print("RMSE of AdaBoost Regressor Algorithm = ", rmse)
print("R^2 of AdaBoost Regressor Algorithm = ", r2)
```

```
[*********************100%***********************]  1 of 1 completed
MAE of AdaBoost Regressor Algorithm =  0.30263443175997407
MSE of AdaBoost Regressor Algorithm =  0.15554398887804533
RMSE of AdaBoost Regressor Algorithm =  0.3943906551606482
R^2 of AdaBoost Regressor Algorithm =  0.9973551365070098
```

In general, when the stock market dataset is evaluated, it can be seen that the results obtained are good. However, the attributes used in this project are not fully sufficient. In addition, technical and fundamental analysis methods should also be used. This situation occurs in SVR and multilayer sensor models. These models perform very poorly on the stock market dataset. Since the results were quite bad, it was not included in the project. The main reason for this may be that the data is used without normalization. In addition, if the features are not sufficient for these models, it may cause poor results. Machine learning techniques on stock market data can be frequently used to predict closing values as well as the direction of value (reference). In direction estimation, it turns into a classification problem instead of a regression problem. In this project, model performance was evaluated by randomly dividing the data into 80% training and 20% testing. In addition, it is possible to predict the next days by training old dates. Finally, by setting random_state = 1, the regression problem is solved by separating 80% of the dataset for training and 20% for testing. It is possible to see different regression results as the value transferred to this parameter is changed.

RESULTS AND GENERAL EVALUATIONS

In this study, various projects were coded step by step using machine learning libraries frequently used in the Python programming language. The examples discussed in the project can be multiplied. In order to attract the attention of readers, datasets from different fields were selected. Researchers working in this field can create projects in different disciplines by incorporating relevant libraries and algorithms into their projects. In general, predefined parameters are used in the algorithms discussed. Readers should definitely experiment with the parameters. In addition, while illustrating the coding of the algorithms, the dataset was divided into training and testing. In order to obtain more meaningful results, it is recommended to consider the performance of cross-validation techniques and classification or regression models. Deep learning techniques are coded without making it too complicated. In difficult datasets or large datasets, the network structure can be transformed into a more complex structure. This all depends on the data. Finally, one of the current issues that is not covered in the book chapter is transfer learning. It will be important for readers to look at current studies in this field as well.

REFERENCES

Abadi, M., Barham, P., Chen, J., Chen, Z., Davis, A., Dean, J., . . . Kudlur, M. (2016). Tensorflow: A system for large-scale machine learning. In *12th USENIX Symposium on Operating Systems Design and Implementation ({OSDI} 16)* (pp. 265-283). USENIX.

Bird, S., Klein, E., & Loper, E. (2009). *Natural language processing with Python: analyzing text with the natural language toolkit*. O'Reilly Media, Inc.

BIST30, Link of Borsa Istanbul, https://www.borsaistanbul.com/tr/endeks-detay/12/bist-30, Last Access: 09 April 2023.

Burch, C. (2010). Django, a web framework using python: Tutorial presentation. *Journal of Computing Sciences in Colleges*, *25*(5), 154–155.

Cho, S. Y., Delgado, R., & Choi, B. W. (2023). Feasibility Study for a Python-Based Embedded Real-Time Control System. *Electronics (Basel)*, *12*(6), 1426. doi:10.3390/electronics12061426

CIFAR-10. Link of CIFAR-10 Dataset, https://www.cs.toronto.edu/~kriz/cifar.html Last Access: 09 April 2023.

Chollet, F. (2015). Keras: Deep learning library for theano and tensorflow.

Cortez, P., Cerdeira, A., Almeida, F., Matos, T., & Reis, J. (2009). Modeling wine preferences by data mining from physicochemical properties. *Decision Support Systems*, *47*(4), 547–553. doi:10.1016/j.dss.2009.05.016

Eckroth, J. (2018). Teaching cybersecurity and python programming in a 5-day summer camp. *Journal of Computing Sciences in Colleges*, *33*(6), 29–39.

Colaboratory, G. Link of Google Colaboratory, https://colab.research.google.com, Last Access: 09 April 2023

Hunter, J. D. (2007). Matplotlib: A 2D graphics environment. *Computing in Science & Engineering*, *9*(03), 90–95. doi:10.1109/MCSE.2007.55

Iris. (n.d.). https://archive.ics.uci.edu/ml/datasets/iris

Jupyter. (n.d.). https://jupyter.org

Keras. (n.d.). https://keras.io/

Krizhevsky, A., & Hinton, G. (2009). *Learning multiple layers of features from tiny images*. Academic Press.

Lim, B., & Zohren, S. (2021). Time-series forecasting with deep learning: A survey. *Philosophical Transactions. Series A, Mathematical, Physical, and Engineering Sciences*, *379*(2194). doi:10.1098/rsta.2020.0209 PMID:33583273

Matplotlib. (n.d.). https://matplotlib.org/

McKinney, W. (2011). pandas: a foundational Python library for data analysis and statistics. *Python for High Performance and Scientific Computing*, *14*(9), 1-9.

NumPy. (n.d.). https://numpy.org/

Okken, B. (2022). *Python Testing with pytest*. Pragmatic Bookshelf.

Oliphant, T. E. (2006). *Guide to numpy* (Vol. 1). Trelgol Publishing.

Pandas. (n.d.). https://pandas.pydata.org/

Pedregosa, F., Varoquaux, G., Gramfort, A., Michel, V., Thirion, B., Grisel, O., ... Duchesnay, É. (2011). Scikit-learn: Machine learning in Python. *Journal of Machine Learning Research*, *12*, 2825–2830.

PyCharm. (n.d.). https://www.jetbrains.com/pycharm/

Raschka, S., Patterson, J., & Nolet, C. (2020). Machine learning in python: Main developments and technology trends in data science, machine learning, and artificial intelligence. *Information (Basel)*, *11*(4), 193. doi:10.3390/info11040193

Scikit-learn. (n.d.). https://scikit-learn.org/stable/

Spyder. (n.d.). https://www.spyder-ide.org/

Srinath, K. R. (2017). Python–the fastest growing programming language. *International Research Journal of Engineering and Technology*, *4*(12), 354–357.

Tensorflow. (n.d.). https://www.tensorflow.org/

Van der Walt, S., Schönberger, J. L., Nunez-Iglesias, J., Boulogne, F., Warner, J. D., Yager, N., . . . Yu, T. (2014). Scikit-image: image processing in Python. *PeerJ*, *2*, e453.

Yfinance. (n.d.). https://pypi.org/project/yfinance/

ADDITIONAL READING

Bhasin, H. (2023). *Machine Learning for Beginners: Build and deploy Machine Learning systems using Python*. BPB Publications.

Géron, A. (2022). *Hands-on machine learning with Scikit-Learn, Keras, and TensorFlow*. O'Reilly Media, Inc.

Müller, A. C., & Guido, S. (2016). *Introduction to machine learning with Python: a guide for data scientists*. O'Reilly Media, Inc.

Nguyen, G., Dlugolinsky, S., Bobák, M., Tran, V., López García, Á., Heredia, I., Malík, P., & Hluchý, L. (2019). Machine learning and deep learning frameworks and libraries for large-scale data mining: A survey. *Artificial Intelligence Review*, *52*(1), 77–124. doi:10.1007/s10462-018-09679-z

Raschka, S., & Mirjalili, V. (2019). *Python machine learning: Machine learning and deep learning with Python, scikit-learn, and TensorFlow*. Packt Publishing Ltd.

Saleh, H. (2018). *Machine Learning Fundamentals: Use Python and scikit-learn to get up and running with the hottest developments in machine learning*. Packt Publishing Ltd.

Sarkar, D., Bali, R., & Sharma, T. (2018). *Practical machine learning with Python*. Springer Nature. doi:10.1007/978-1-4842-3207-1

Singh, P., & Manure, A. (2019). *Learn TensorFlow 2.0: Implement Machine Learning and Deep Learning Models with Python*. Apress.

Zaccone, G., & Karim, M. R. (2018). *Deep Learning with TensorFlow: Explore neural networks and build intelligent systems with Python*. Packt Publishing Ltd.

Zollanvari, A. (2023). *Machine Learning with Python: Theory and Implementation*. Springer Nature. doi:10.1007/978-3-031-33342-2

KEY TERMS AND DEFINITIONS

Artificial Intelligence: Artificial intelligence is simply defined as systems that imitate human intelligence to perform certain tasks and can improve themselves by repeating the information they collect.

Data Mining: It is a technique of discovering correlations, patterns, or trends by analyzing large amounts of data stored in repositories such as databases and storage devices.

Deep Learning: It is an advanced version of artificial neural networks from machine learning techniques.

Expert System: It is computer software used to solve problems in an information field. The logic of these software; when information is stored in databases and then problems are encountered, it is tried to reach results with inferences made on these databases.

Machine Learning: It is the modeling of systems that make predictions by using mathematical and statistical processes on data.

Pattern Recognition: Pattern recognition is exactly the process of recognizing patterns with the help of a machine learning algorithm. Machine learning is a field based on the recognition and interpretation of patterns in data. With the pattern recognition system, the computer automatically identifies complex data sets or regular systems.

Chapter 3
Methodology and Application of Information Technology for Carbon-Based Nano-Composites

Vibhooti Narayan Mishra
Rajkiya Engineering College, Azamgarh, India

Ashish Kumar Singh
Guru Ghasidas Vishwavidyalaya, Bilaspur, India

Divya Pratap Singh
https://orcid.org/0000-0001-8760-4031
Rajkiya Enineering College, Azamgarh, India

Savendra Pratap Singh
https://orcid.org/0000-0002-5151-0284
Rajkiya Engineering College, Azamgarh, India

Shweta Singh
Dr. Shyama Prasad Mukherjee, Government Degree College, Bhadohi, India

ABSTRACT

Recent developments of carbon-based nanomaterials research have made it possible to use them for a wide range of environmental, material development, and energy-related applications. Graphene, CNT, quantum dots, nano-diamond, and graphene oxide are examples of carbon-based nanomaterials. The development of nanocomposites has drawn a lot of attention lately, with synthesis and application receiving. Recently, there has been a lot of interest in the synthesis of AI-created nanoparticles using artificial intelligence. This work focuses on the synthesis of carbon-based nanocomposites and application of current AI tools to better understand the properties of carbon derivative material, and this information can be applied to the development and application of materials for solution of society's problem. To explain the synthetic and derivation process, adaptive neuro-fuzzy inference systems and ANN may be efficient. Derivations of the nanomaterials are the output of the models, which have various inputs such as catalyst dosage, particle size, concentration, content, exposure time.

DOI: 10.4018/979-8-3693-1062-5.ch003

Copyright © 2024, IGI Global. Copying or distributing in print or electronic forms without written permission of IGI Global is prohibited.

1. INTRODUCTION

Presently, there is a lot of effort in the field of nanocomposite materials, which could have a significant impact on our society. Nanomaterials can be categorized according to their dimensions. 0D materials, such as fullerenes, metallic nanoparticles, and quantum dots (QDs), have all dimensions below 100 nm. 1D materials, exemplified by carbon nanotubes (CNTs), possess two dimensions that are each less than 100 nm. In contrast, 2D materials, like graphene, exhibit nanoscale characteristics in only one dimension. Finally, 3D materials, like dendrimers, lack restrictions to the nano-scale in any dimension. The application of nanofillers to polymers to impart particular and apparent property improvements is still showing significant advancements among the remarkably wide range of expanding research areas (Díez-Pascual, 2022b; Pokropivny & Skorokhod, 2007; Sahoo et al., 2010). Composite materials that are attached with graphene and carbon nanotubes are considered to be promising. Graphene oxide (GO) or graphene (G), carbon nanotubes (SWCNTs and MWCNTs), carbon nanoparticles (CNPs), and carbon nanotubes (SWCNTs) have drawn significant attention due to their distinct structural regularity, chemical inertness, electrical conductivity, mechanical stability, high surface area and thermal stability. Due to their tiny size and physicochemical properties influenced by shape, carbon nanocomposites have garnered significant attention in the catalysis domain. Specifically, carbon-based nanocomposites, incorporating metal nanostructures and carbon materials (predominantly graphene and carbon nanotubes), have demonstrated exceptional catalytic activity in organic reactions.

A wide range of industries, including the material sciences, agricultural, biomedical and pharmaceutical have discovered the great value of the catalytic products made with carbon nanocomposites. Many Various nanoparticles have been reported to support graphene or carbon nanotube (CNT) catalysts for a range of organic transformations. The pharmacological, biological, agricultural, and material sciences are just a few of the industries that find great value in catalytic products (Beletskaya & Cheprakov, 2000). While modelling approaches such as linear correlativity and multilinear regression models are widely employed to describe the adsorption process, their applicability and accuracy are limited. Conversely, machine learning methods driven by data provide a valuable tool for delving into the intricate relationship between biochar properties and adsorption capacities (Beletskaya & Cheprakov, 2000).

Machine learning can be used to classify, forecast, optimize, and cluster methods. A model of Artificial Intelligence (AI) is developed to find out the Young's modulus, or the behaviour, of composites made of polymers and carbon nanotubes (CNTs). It is suggested that artificial intelligence (AI) be used to get over challenges encountered when researching the characteristics of innovative composite materials, such as the resource- and time-consuming aspect of other numerical approaches' experimental studies (Beletskaya & Cheprakov, 2000). The polymer dielectric constant and energy bandgap are predicted using Convolutional Neural Networks, when it comes to mechanical performance. A neural network is also used to predict the mechanical characteristics of pure propylene PP and its blends (Beletskaya & Cheprakov, 2000)(Kufel & Kuciel, 2019). AI and ML are excellent options for researching and creating cutting-edge materials using data that already exists, which helps to fulfil the primary goal of the MGI announcement. As demonstrated by the results in other research fields (such as image recognition, civil engineering, or geology) (Kumar et al., 2019; Nhat-Duc et al., 2018; Thanh Duong et al., 2020; Ward et al., 2018). The literature contains a number of research studies that use both analytical and numerical methods to determine the effective properties of CNT nanocomposites. Molecular dynamics, multiscale methods, and continuum mechanics are some examples of such approaches. The modified Halpin-Tsai equations applied to find out the effective properties of carbon nanotube (CNT) nanocomposites. The equation utilized into consideration parameters like the length, diameter, and strength of the CNTs (Le, 2020; Le & Le, 2021; Papon et al., 2011).

The manufacturing process of nanocomposites plays a crucial role in shaping their mechanical behavior and long-term sustainability. Common techniques for preparing polymeric nanocomposites encompass melt-blending, compression moulding, solution processing, resin transfer moulding, and in-situ polymerization. The choice of the production method is contingent upon factors such as the material's intended application, the residual stress and strain during the setup process, stress transfer caused by phase changes, and the coefficient of thermal expansion of the matrix material (Díez-Pascual, 2022a; Haque & Ramasetty, 2005; L. N. McCartney, 1989; Meijer et al., 2000). The manufacturing process plays a pivotal role in the development and enhancement of polymer nanocomposites, a class of advanced materials that combine polymer matrices with nanoscale fillers. This integration of nanofillers, such as nanoparticles or nanotubes, into polymers imparts unique and improved properties to the resulting composite materials, such as enhanced mechanical strength, thermal stability, and electrical conductivity. The manufacturing process involves multiple stages, starting with the dispersion of nanofillers within the polymer matrix. Achieving a uniform dispersion is crucial, as it directly influences the final properties of the nanocomposite. Various techniques, including melt blending, solution mixing, and in situ polymerization, are employed to ensure a homogeneous distribution of nanofillers. Additionally, processing conditions such as temperature, shear rate, and mixing time play critical roles in determining the final morphology and performance of the polymer nanocomposite. The choice of manufacturing method also affects the scalability and cost-effectiveness of producing these advanced materials on an industrial scale. Furthermore, the manufacturing process influences the interfacial interactions between the polymer matrix and nanofillers, which significantly impact the overall performance of the nanocomposite. Through careful control and optimization of the manufacturing parameters, researchers and engineers can tailor the properties of polymer nanocomposites to meet specific application requirements, ranging from structural materials in aerospace to packaging materials in the food industry. In conclusion, the manufacturing process is a key factor in shaping the structural and functional attributes of polymer nanocomposites, making it an essential aspect of advancing the utilization of these materials in various technological applications. Molecular dynamics and finite element simulations have been employed extensively to model material behavior in diverse scenarios. Yet, given the intricacy and computational demands of these methods, researchers are exploring alternative avenues. Consequently, many are turning to machine learning for assessing the influence of process parameters on optimal design. Within the realm of artificial intelligence, machine learning (ML) represents a subset that endows systems with the ability to learn from experience without explicit programming. Through intensive training on extensive datasets, these systems establish correlations between input features and output properties, yielding a potent and efficient model for structural and property evaluation (Doan Tran et al., 2020; Zhou et al., 2019).

Figure 1. Arrangement of the carbon based of nanomaterials (Champa-Bujaico et al., 2022)

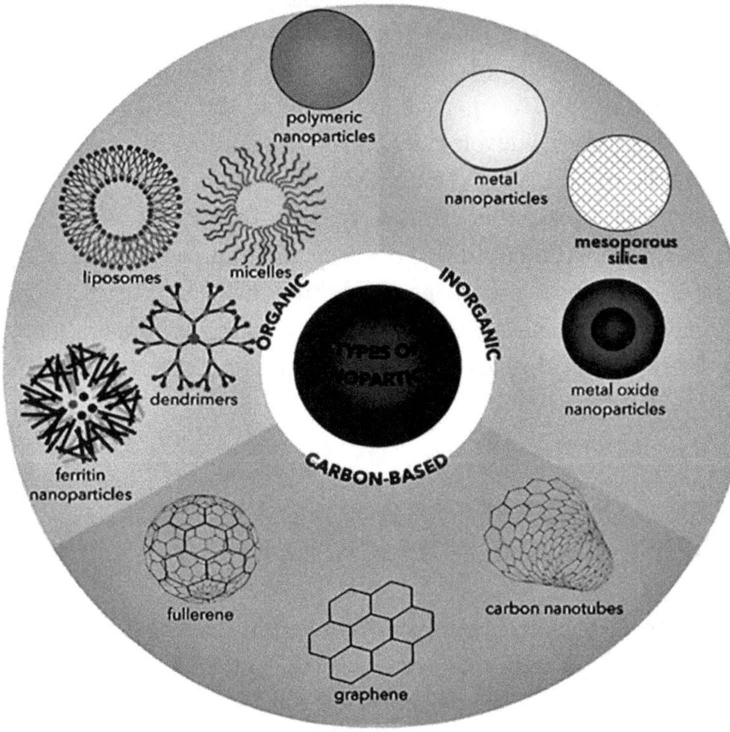

The integration of machine learning into the study of polymeric nanocomposites enables the prediction of diverse multifunctional characteristics based on both components and their proportions. Unfortunately, the constraints posed by numerous variables often limit the scope of many investigations, introducing increased parameters and ambiguity due to the randomness of information. This article delves into the classification, synthesis, and application of carbon-based nanocomponents, examining and analysing their properties. The physical and chemical attributes of a material depend on various structural and functional parameters, allowing the tailoring of the nano composite material's desired properties based on its intended application by adjusting these parameters. Experimentally varying the parameters provides a relatively straightforward means of discovering the material's properties. Subsequently, various artificial intelligence and machine learning algorithms can be applied in the realm of carbon-based nanocomposites for property evaluation, encompassing estimation, optimization, errors, and accuracy. This article explores and presents various types of machine learning algorithms for property predictions in the context of carbon-based nanocomposites.

Machine learning (ML) and artificial intelligence (AI) have emerged as transformative tools in unravelling the intricate dynamics and optimizing the performance of polymeric nanocomposites. These advanced technologies offer unprecedented insights and predictive capabilities that revolutionize the synthesis, characterization, and application of these materials. At the heart of their integration lies the capacity to decode complex relationships between constituent elements, their proportions, and resulting material properties. ML algorithms, from regression models to neural networks, have become instrumental in predicting diverse multifunctional traits of nanocomposites based on intricate component configurations. AI-driven systems leverage vast datasets to discern patterns, enabling the rapid screening and identification of optimal material compositions tailored for specific functionalities. The application of ML/AI extends beyond prediction; it facilitates the design of novel materials by optimizing structural parameters, ensuring superior performance in targeted applications. Moreover, these technologies streamline experimental workflows by significantly reducing the need for exhaustive trial-and-error iterations, thereby expediting material development. From reinforcing mechanical strength to enhancing thermal and electrical conductivities, ML/AI empowers researchers to navigate the vast design space of polymeric nanocomposites with precision, efficiency, and a deeper understanding of their behavior at the nano-level. The synergy between cutting-edge computational methodologies and material science have shown a new era of innovation, promising breakthroughs in industries ranging from electronics and aerospace to biomedical applications, ushering in materials with unparalleled functionalities and performance metrics (Doan Tran et al., 2020; Haque & Ramasetty, 2005; L. N. McCartney, 1989; Meijer et al., 2000; Zhou et al., 2019).

2. CARBON-BASED NANOCOMPOSITE CLASSIFICATION, SYNTHESIS, PROPERTIES, AND APPLICATION

Recently, carbon allotropes have gained prominence as essential nanofillers in the realm of polymeric nanocomposites. This includes versatile materials such as graphene (G), carbon nanotubes (CNTs), quantum dots (QDs), fullerenes and its derivatives, namely reduced graphene oxide (rGO) and graphene oxide (GO). These carbon-based nanofillers contribute significantly to enhancing the properties of polymeric matrices. Fullerenes, with their unique spherical structure, quantum dots exhibiting quantum confinement effects, carbon nanotubes providing high aspect ratios, and graphene and its derivatives offering exceptional mechanical and electrical characteristics, collectively impart novel functionalities to the resulting nanocomposites. The integration of these carbon allotropes enriches the material landscape, enabling tailoring of diverse properties for applications spanning electronics, aerospace, and biomedical fields, showcasing the versatility and potential of these advanced nanomaterials in polymeric matrices (Zhou et al., 2019).

2.1 Graphene Oxide (GO)

Graphene oxide (GO) stands out as a representative two-dimensional oxygenated planar molecular material. As the oxidized iteration of graphene, GO is a single-atomic-layered substance derived from the oxidation of economically accessible graphite. Notably, GO offers ease of processing due to its dispersibility in water and various solvents, rendering it a convenient and versatile material for applications in diverse fields (Stankovich et al., 2007). Graphene oxide (GO) exhibits non-conductive properties due to the presence of oxygen in its lattice; however, it can undergo chemical reduction processes to transform into conductive graphene. Structurally, GO is a single atom-thin carbon layer derived from graphite, featuring sp2 hybridized carbon atoms arranged in a honeycomb lattice. This configuration grants GO a substantial surface area and promising mechanical and electrical properties. Despite these advantageous attributes, practical applications of GO have faced challenges, primarily attributed to difficulties in achieving large-scale, highly organized structures. Nevertheless, GO has remained a focal point in research and industry over the past decades, thanks to its facile exfoliation from bulk graphite oxide in both laboratory and industrial settings. A recent advancement involves the scalable production of graphene oxide nanoribbons (GONRs) from multi walled carbon nanotubes through treatment with KMnO4 and concentrated H2SO4, enhanced by the addition of phosphoric acid (H3PO4). This "improved method" holds promise for generating graphene oxide (IGO) with fewer defects in the basal plane compared to traditional approaches, presenting potential advancements in the synthesis of graphene-based materials with enhanced conductivity and structural integrity (Stankovich et al., 2007).

2.2 Quantum Dots

Carbon quantum dots (CQDs or c-dots), typically characterized as small carbon nanoparticles with dimensions less than 10nm, have garnered widespread attention due to their diverse and unique properties. Over the past few years, these CQDs have found versatile applications in various fields, including biosensing, bioimaging, drug delivery, photocatalysis, and more. The sensors and biosensors based on CQDs operate through different mechanisms, such as fluorescence quenching, static quenching, energy transfer, photo-induced electron transfer (PET), and fluorescence resonance electron transfer (FRET). Their utility extends to the detection of various species, encompassing metal ions, acids, proteins, polypeptides, water pollutants, drugs, vitamins, and other chemicals. Structurally, carbon dots comprise C-atoms with sp2/sp3 hybridization and feature oxygen/nitrogen-based groups or polymeric aggregations. The unique combination of small size, tunable surface chemistry and optical properties positions CQDs as promising candidates for a wide array of applications, highlighting their potential impact on advancing sensing technologies and analytical methodologies(Roy et al., 2015). In Carbon Quantum Dots (CQDs), the phenomenon of fluorescence arises from the radiative recombination of electrons and holes, and it's noteworthy that the traditional quantum confinement effect doesn't apply to CQDs. The key to achieving optimal fluorescence in CQDs lies in their small sizes, ensuring a high surface area-to-volume ratio and, consequently, the presence of a substantial number of surface defects. It's crucial to clarify that in CQDs, the term "Quantum" deviates from its conventional meaning in classical semiconductor Quantum Dots (QDs). Unlike the quantum confinement effect observed in semiconductor QDs, the size-dependent optical properties of CQDs are intricately linked to variations in surface defect sites and radiative recombination paths, stemming from changes in the surface-to-volume ratio. This unique aspect emphasizes the importance of surface characteristics and size in dictating the optical behavior of CQDs, shedding light on their distinctive role in emerging applications.

The generation of Carbon Quantum Dots (CQDs) can generally be categorized into "TOP-DOWN" and "BOTTOM-UP" approaches based on the direction of size development of the utilized materials, and modifications can occur during the preparation or post-treatment stages. Addressing three key challenges in CQD preparation is crucial. Firstly, the issue of carbonaceous aggregation during carbonization can be mitigated by employing techniques such as electrochemical synthesis or confined pyrolysis. Secondly, achieving precise size control and uniformity is essential for maintaining consistent properties and facilitating mechanistic studies; optimization can be achieved through methodologies like gel electrophoresis or centrifugation. Lastly, the surface properties of CQDs play a critical role in their solubility and suitability for specific applications. These surface properties can be fine-tuned either during the preparation process or through post-treatment methods. This comprehensive approach ensures the production of CQDs with tailored characteristics, paving the way for advancements in their application across various fields.

Top-down methodologies involve the synthesis of carbon quantum dots (CQDs) from larger carbon structures like graphite, activated carbon, and carbon nanotubes. Various treatments such as arc discharge, laser ablation, electrochemical oxidation, and ultrasonic synthesis are employed in this approach. On the other hand, bottom-up strategies focus on producing CQDs from molecular precursors like citric acid, sucrose, and glucose, utilizing methods such as microwave synthesis, thermal decomposition, hydrothermal treatment, and plasma treatment. The versatility of CQDs in biomedical applications has been extensively demonstrated in numerous studies. This includes their utilization in multimodal bio imaging, showcasing adaptability in surface modification to integrate with other imaging agents, highlighting their high biocompatibility. Additionally, CQDs play a crucial role in biosensors, exhibiting multi-stimulus responses. Moreover, they serve as effective delivery carriers, offering various combinations with biomolecules or drugs through multi-reaction and stimulus responses. These attributes position CQDs as promising and multifunctional tools in the field of biomedicine with applications ranging from advanced imaging to sensing and targeted drug delivery (Liu et al., 2017; Xu et al., 2013; Zhang et al., 2020).

2.3 Carbon Nanotubes (CNTs)

A carbon nanotube (CNT) is a carbon allotrope that takes the form of a tube composed of carbon atoms. Known for its exceptional resilience and lightweight nature, the carbon nanotube has become a focal point in nanomaterial research, attributed to its remarkable mechanical, electrical, and thermal properties. Single-wall carbon nanotubes consist of a single cylindrical lattice of carbon atoms, while multiwall carbon nanotubes feature multiple concentric cylindrical layers. The incorporation of carbon nanotubes (CNTs) in polymer nanocomposites, coupled with the integration of Internet of Things (IoT) technologies, presents a transformative synergy that enhances the functionality and monitoring capabilities of composite materials in diverse applications. Carbon nanotubes, due to their exceptional mechanical, thermal, and electrical properties, serve as high-performance nanofillers when dispersed within polymer matrices. The addition of CNTs imparts superior strength, conductivity, and thermal stability to the resulting nanocomposites. When coupled with IoT, these materials become intelligent and responsive, enabling real-time monitoring and control of their structural integrity and performance. Through the incorporation of sensors within the polymer nanocomposites, IoT facilitates continuous data collection on factors such as strain, temperature, and environmental conditions. This data is then transmitted wirelessly to a centralized system for analysis. In structural applications, such as aerospace components or automotive parts, this integration allows for predictive maintenance, early detection of defects, and precise assessment of the material's health. In the realm of smart packaging, CNT-infused polymer nanocomposites equipped with IoT sensors enable real-time tracking of product conditions, ensuring the preservation of perishable goods and providing valuable insights into supply chain logistics. Moreover, the use of IoT in conjunction with CNT-based nanocomposites finds applications in wearable technology, where flexible and conductive nanocomposite materials can be employed in smart textiles for health monitoring. This interconnected approach not only elevates the material performance but also revolutionizes how we interact with and utilize composite materials in an increasingly interconnected world. The convergence of CNTs and IoT technologies opens avenues for innovation across industries, offering a versatile platform for the development of smart materials with enhanced capabilities and functionalities, ultimately contributing to the advancement of materials science and the broader field of smart and connected systems. The versatility of carbon nanotubes finds application across diverse fields, including the Internet of Things (IoT), transparent conducting films, wearable and stretchable electronics, human sensory system emulation, healthcare products, actuators for artificial muscles, brain–machine interfaces, flexible energy storage devices, and system integration. Advancements in carbon nanotube synthesis have been significantly propelled by the integration of machine learning and wafer-scale preparation techniques. Machine learning, particularly artificial neural networks (ANNs), proves highly effective in handling interacting parameters, enabling the description and generalization of complex or unknown data and functions. In nanotechnology research, various machine learning methods, such as decision trees, Bayesian networks, support vector machines (SVM), and others, can be applied individually or in combination. This broad spectrum of machine learning approaches contributes to addressing intricate issues in nanotechnology, including classification, control, data mining, prediction, association, and clustering problems. As technology continues to evolve, the synergy between machine learning and carbon nanotube synthesis promises further breakthroughs in diverse applications, driving the development of advanced materials and integrated systems (Ho et al., 2022).

3. MACHINE LEARNING (ML) ALGORITHMS

Machine Learning (ML) and Artificial Intelligence (AI) represent revolutionary tools empowering computer programs with the capacity to autonomously learn from experiences and enhance their performance without explicit programming. This transformative capability enables systems to exhibit an intelligence that surpasses their inherent abilities. At the core of this innovation lies the concept of learning from data patterns, allowing machines to adapt, evolve, and make informed decisions based on accumulated experiences.

ML harnesses algorithms and statistical models, enabling systems to process vast amounts of data, recognize patterns, and extract meaningful insights. Through iterative learning, these algorithms improve their performance, enhancing accuracy and efficiency in tasks ranging from predictive analysis to pattern recognition. AI, a broader field encompassing ML, focuses on simulating human intelligence within machines, allowing them to perceive, reason, and act intelligently. This involves various techniques such as natural language processing, computer vision, and expert systems, culminating in machines that mimic human cognitive functions. The transformative potential of ML and AI extends across diverse domains. In healthcare, these technologies facilitate disease diagnosis, drug discovery, and personalized treatment plans by analyzing extensive medical datasets. In finance, AI-driven algorithms optimize trading strategies and detect fraudulent activities by scrutinizing transaction patterns. Furthermore, in autonomous vehicles, ML enables real-time decision-making based on environmental cues, ensuring safer and more efficient transportation. The amalgamation of big data, computational power, and sophisticated algorithms propels the evolution of ML and AI. Continuous learning and adaptation enable these systems to refine their capabilities, driving innovation and efficiency across industries. Yet, ethical considerations regarding bias, data privacy, and accountability remain critical in ensuring the responsible and beneficial deployment of these technologies. As ML and AI continue to evolve, their transformative impact on society, coupled with responsible implementation, promises to shape a future where intelligent systems augment human capabilities, revolutionize industries, and drive unprecedented advancements.

3.1 Artificial Neural Network (ANN) Strategy

ANN is an established machine learning technique in data science. The primary idea behind the ANN model is developed from the biological brains function. It consists of artificial nodes that are capable of performing specific distributed tasks. The ANN neurons or computational nodes are each function of weight, input data and upcoming output response. The benefits of ANN are the capability to evaluate the non-linear complex problem. The assumption and pre restraints are not required for simulation process. There is main three layers in this strategy, which are variable's input layer, functional node hidden layer and network's outcome layer. Artificial computing nodes, whose objective is to find out the model weight parameters, connect the above-mentioned layer.

Figure 2. Schematic representation of a ANN strategy (Ho et al., 2022)

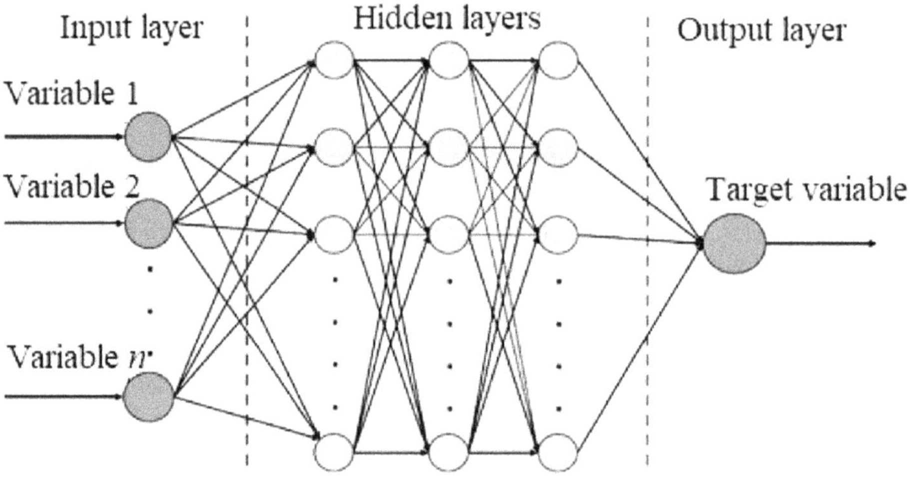

3.2 Support Vector Machine (SVM)

The support vector machine (SVM) is a widely embraced supervised learning technique utilized for classification, regression, and outlier detection tasks. At the heart of SVM lies the determination of the decision boundary equation, regulated by the support vectors—those samples in close proximity to the decision boundary. The margin, denoting the space between these supports vectors and the hyperplane, is a crucial concept in SVM. The primary objective of SVM is to discern the optimal hyperplane that maximizes this margin. By identifying this hyperplane, SVM achieves effective separation between different classes in classification tasks, and it also serves as a robust tool for regression and outlier detection, making it a versatile and powerful algorithm in the realm of supervised learning.

Figure 3. Schematic representation of SVM (Ho et al., 2022)

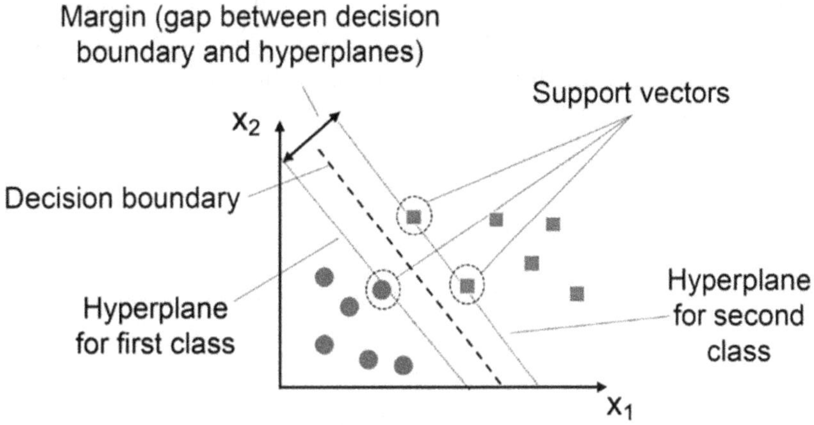

3.3 k-Nearest Neighbor (k-NN)

The k-nearest neighbors algorithm, often denoted as KNN or k-NN, serves as a non-parametric supervised learning classifier with applications in classification or regression tasks, predominantly employed for classification purposes. This algorithm operates on the principle that data points with similar characteristics tend to cluster together. During the training phase, the algorithm stores the dataset, and when new data is presented, it classifies it based on its proximity to previously stored data points. Utilizing a majority vote, or technically, a "plurality voting," the algorithm assigns a class label to the new data point based on the most frequently represented label in its vicinity. The selection of neighbors for classification or regression involves choosing objects from a set with known class labels or property values. Notably, the k-NN algorithm is distinctive for its sensitivity to the local structure of the data, and despite lacking an explicit training step, it effectively leverages the inherent relationships among data points to make accurate predictions or classifications. The application of k-Nearest Neighbor (k-NN) in the realm of nanocomposites represents a powerful tool for predicting and understanding intricate relationships within these advanced materials. k-NN is a supervised machine learning algorithm that operates on the principle of proximity-based classification, making it particularly well-suited for analyzing nanocomposite properties influenced by various factors. In nanocomposite research, the selection of suitable materials and the optimization of their properties are critical aspects. The k-NN algorithm excels in this context by leveraging similarity metrics to predict the behavior of nanocomposites based on the characteristics of similar instances in the training dataset. The versatility of k-NN in nanocomposite studies lies in its ability to handle both classification and regression tasks. In classification, it aids in categorizing nanocomposites into specific groups based on their features, providing insights into the factors influencing their properties. Meanwhile, in regression, k-NN facilitates the prediction of continuous variables, enabling researchers to estimate properties like mechanical strength, thermal conductivity, or electrical resistivity. Moreover, k-NN is particularly advantageous in the context of nanocomposites due to its adaptability to diverse datasets and its ability to accommodate non-linear relationships. This is crucial given the multifaceted nature of nanomaterial interactions and the intricate dependencies determining nanocomposite properties. The implementation of k-NN in nanocomposite research involves training the algorithm on datasets comprising various nanocomposite formulations and their corresponding properties.

Once trained, the k-NN model can effectively classify or predict the behavior of new nanocomposites based on their similarity to instances in the training set. In summary, the use of k-Nearest Neighbor in nanocomposite research contributes significantly to predictive modelling and understanding the complex interplay of factors influencing material properties. Its versatility, adaptability, and capacity to handle both classification and regression tasks make k-NN a valuable tool for researchers seeking to optimize and tailor nanocomposite materials for diverse applications.

3.4 Decision Tree

A widely employed non-parametric supervised machine learning method for both regression and classification tasks is the decision tree. This algorithm adopts a tree-like structure reminiscent of a flowchart, where internal nodes correspond to features, branches depict rules, and leaf nodes signify the ultimate outcome of the algorithm. Renowned for its flexibility, decision trees are adept at handling diverse data scenarios, making them applicable to both regression and classification challenges. Notably potent in the realm of machine learning, decision trees are further leveraged in the Random Forest algorithm, wherein they train on varied subsets of training data, enhancing their efficacy and contributing to the algorithm's robust performance across a spectrum of applications.

Figure 4. Schematic representation of decision tree (Ho et al., 2022)

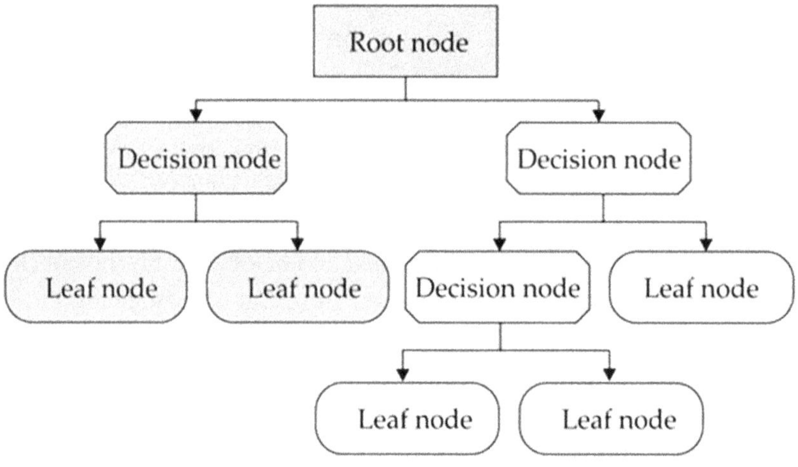

4. CONCLUSION

The extensive examination and findings presented in this manuscript underscore the enduring impact of nanomaterials on various industries and scientific domains. Currently, graphene and graphene-based hybrid nanostructures are capturing significant attention as pioneering materials across nanotechnology, biomedical engineering, material science, physics, and green chemistry. Their commendable physical properties, including high surface area, elevated electronic conductivity, and thermal characteristics, contribute to their broad appeal. The versatility of carbon quantum dots (CQDs) in biomedicine has been evidenced in numerous studies, encompassing multimodal bio imaging, biosensors, and delivery carriers. The incessant demand for advancements in carbon-based nanocomposites stems from the necessity for novel devices capable of manipulating materials at the nanoscale. The realm of nanomaterials offers abundant opportunities for scientific and technological progress, potentially revolutionizing material design, energy technologies, and healthcare. Leveraging their superior qualities and cutting-edge computational tools, nanomaterials hold the key to ground breaking inventions, enhanced performance, and sustainable developments. Future strides in nanotechnology are anticipated to bring forth innovations marked by sustainability and improved functionality, shaping a landscape where nanomaterials propel revolutionary possibilities. Employing artificial neural networks (ANN) to optimize the prediction of adsorption performance in carbon-based nanocomposites involves the meticulous study of factors such as ANN structure, hidden neurons, training methods, and back propagation. By harnessing ANN's efficiency, it becomes a valuable tool for evaluating the desired properties tailored to the applications of carbon-based nanocomposites.

REFERENCES

Beletskaya, I. P., & Cheprakov, A. V. (2000). The Heck Reaction as a Sharpening Stone of Palladium Catalysis. *Chemical Reviews*, *100*(8), 3009–3066. doi:10.1021/cr9903048 PMID:11749313

Champa-Bujaico, E., García-Díaz, P., & Díez-Pascual, A. M. (2022). Machine Learning for Property Prediction and Optimization of Polymeric Nanocomposites: A State-of-the-Art. *International Journal of Molecular Sciences*, *23*(18), 10712. doi:10.3390/ijms231810712 PMID:36142623

Díez-Pascual, A. M. (2022a). Biopolymer Composites: Synthesis, Properties, and Applications. *International Journal of Molecular Sciences*, *23*(4), 2257. doi:10.3390/ijms23042257 PMID:35216374

Díez-Pascual, A. M. (2022b). Carbon-Based Polymer Nanocomposites for High-Performance Applications II. *Polymers*, *14*(5), 870. doi:10.3390/polym14050870 PMID:35267693

Doan Tran, H., Kim, C., Chen, L., Chandrasekaran, A., Batra, R., Venkatram, S., Kamal, D., Lightstone, J. P., Gurnani, R., Shetty, P., Ramprasad, M., Laws, J., Shelton, M., & Ramprasad, R. (2020). Machine-learning predictions of polymer properties with Polymer Genome. *Journal of Applied Physics*, *128*(17), 171104. Advance online publication. doi:10.1063/5.0023759

Haque, A., & Ramasetty, A. (2005). Theoretical study of stress transfer in carbon nanotube reinforced polymer matrix composites. *Composite Structures*, *71*(1), 68–77. doi:10.1016/j.compstruct.2004.09.029

Ho, N. X., Le, T.-T., & Le, M. V. (2022). Development of artificial intelligence based model for the prediction of Young's modulus of polymer/carbon-nanotubes composites. *Mechanics of Advanced Materials and Structures*, *29*(27), 5965–5978. doi:10.1080/15376494.2021.1969709

Kufel, A., & Kuciel, S. (2019). Composites based on polypropylene modified with natural fillers to increase stiffness. *Czasopismo Techniczne*, *1*, 187–195. doi:10.4467/2353737XCT.19.013.10053

Kumar, J. N., Li, Q., & Jun, Y. (2019). Challenges and opportunities of polymer design with machine learning and high throughput experimentation. *MRS Communications*, *9*(2), 537–544. doi:10.1557/mrc.2019.54

Le, T.-T. (2020). Multiscale Analysis of Elastic Properties of Nano-Reinforced Materials Exhibiting Surface Effects. Application for Determination of Effective Shear Modulus. *Journal of Composites Science*, *4*(4), 172. doi:10.3390/jcs4040172

Le, T.-T., & Le, M. V. (2021). Nanoscale Effect Investigation for Effective Bulk Modulus of Particulate Polymer Nanocomposites Using Micromechanical Framework. *Advances in Materials Science and Engineering*, *2021*, 1–13. doi:10.1155/2021/1563845

Liu, Y., Pharr, M., & Salvatore, G. A. (2017). Lab-on-Skin: A Review of Flexible and Stretchable Electronics for Wearable Health Monitoring. *ACS Nano*, *11*(10), 9614–9635. doi:10.1021/acsnano.7b04898 PMID:28901746

McCartney, L. N. (1989). New theoretical model of stress transfer between fibre and matrix in a uniaxially fibre-reinforced composite. *Proceedings of the Royal Society of London. A. Mathematical and Physical Sciences, 425*(1868), 215–244. 10.1098/rspa.1989.0104

Meijer, G., Ellyin, F., & Xia, Z. (2000). Aspects of residual thermal stress/strain in particle reinforced metal matrix composites. *Composites. Part B, Engineering*, *31*(1), 29–37. doi:10.1016/S1359-8368(99)00060-8

Nhat-Duc, H., Nguyen, Q.-L., & Tran, V.-D. (2018). Automatic recognition of asphalt pavement cracks using metaheuristic optimized edge detection algorithms and convolution neural network. *Automation in Construction*, *94*, 203–213. doi:10.1016/j.autcon.2018.07.008

Papon, A., Saalwächter, K., Schäler, K., Guy, L., Lequeux, F., & Montes, H. (2011). Low-Field NMR Investigations of Nanocomposites: Polymer Dynamics and Network Effects. *Macromolecules*, *44*(4), 913–922. doi:10.1021/ma102486x

Pokropivny, V. V., & Skorokhod, V. V. (2007). Classification of nanostructures by dimensionality and concept of surface forms engineering in nanomaterial science. *Materials Science and Engineering C*, *27*(5–8), 990–993. doi:10.1016/j.msec.2006.09.023

Roy, P., Chen, P.-C., Periasamy, A. P., Chen, Y.-N., & Chang, H.-T. (2015). Photoluminescent carbon nanodots: Synthesis, physicochemical properties and analytical applications. *Materials Today*, *18*(8), 447–458. doi:10.1016/j.mattod.2015.04.005

Sahoo, N. G., Rana, S., Cho, J. W., Li, L., & Chan, S. H. (2010). Polymer nanocomposites based on functionalized carbon nanotubes. *Progress in Polymer Science*, *35*(7), 837–867. doi:10.1016/j.progpolymsci.2010.03.002

Stankovich, S., Dikin, D. A., Piner, R. D., Kohlhaas, K. A., Kleinhammes, A., Jia, Y., Wu, Y., Nguyen, S. T., & Ruoff, R. S. (2007). Synthesis of graphene-based nanosheets via chemical reduction of exfoliated graphite oxide. *Carbon*, *45*(7), 1558–1565. doi:10.1016/j.carbon.2007.02.034

Thanh Duong, H., Chi Phan, H., Le, T.-T., & Duc Bui, N. (2020). Optimization design of rectangular concrete-filled steel tube short columns with Balancing Composite Motion Optimization and data-driven model. *Structures*, *28*, 757–765. doi:10.1016/j.istruc.2020.09.013

Ward, L., Aykol, M., Blaiszik, B., Foster, I., Meredig, B., Saal, J., & Suram, S. (2018). Strategies for accelerating the adoption of materials informatics. *MRS Bulletin*, *43*(9), 683–689. doi:10.1557/mrs.2018.204

Xu, Y., Wu, M., Liu, Y., Feng, X., Yin, X., He, X., & Zhang, Y. (2013). Nitrogen-Doped Carbon Dots: A Facile and General Preparation Method, Photoluminescence Investigation, and Imaging Applications. *Chemistry (Weinheim an der Bergstrasse, Germany)*, *19*(7), 2276–2283. doi:10.1002/chem.201203641 PMID:23322649

Zhang, Q., Zhou, W., Xia, X., Li, K., Zhang, N., Wang, Y., Xiao, Z., Fan, Q., Kauppinen, E. I., & Xie, S. (2020). Transparent and Freestanding Single-Walled Carbon Nanotube Films Synthesized Directly and Continuously via a Blown Aerosol Technique. *Advanced Materials*, *32*(39), 2004277. Advance online publication. doi:10.1002/adma.202004277 PMID:32851708

Zhou, T., Song, Z., & Sundmacher, K. (2019). Big Data Creates New Opportunities for Materials Research: A Review on Methods and Applications of Machine Learning for Materials Design. *Engineering (Beijing)*, *5*(6), 1017–1026. doi:10.1016/j.eng.2019.02.011

Chapter 4
Towards an Intelligent Tomorrow:
Machine Learning Enabling Sustainable Development

Kassim Kalinaki
https://orcid.org/0000-0001-8630-9110
Islamic University in Uganda, Uganda

Silviu Florin Acaru
https://orcid.org/0000-0001-6445-785X
Universiti Brunei Darussalam, Brunei

Julius Kugonza
Pride Data Solutions, Uganda

Ronald Nsubuga
Pride Data Solutions, Uganda

ABSTRACT

Sustainable development has become a global imperative in the 21st century as societies grapple with environmental, social, and economic challenges. Machine learning (ML), a subset of artificial intelligence (AI), has emerged as a powerful tool to address these complex issues. Accordingly, this chapter explores the intersection of sustainable development and innovation, delving into the transformative potential of innovative solutions, particularly within the context of AI-powered techniques. Moreover, it examines how innovation, guided by sustainability principles, can be harnessed to address complex global challenges and help us progress towards a world where Sustainable Development Goals (SDGs) are not just aspirations but achievements. Furthermore, it explores how ML contributes to sustainable development across various domains, challenges encountered, and future directions.

DOI: 10.4018/979-8-3693-1062-5.ch004

Copyright © 2024, IGI Global. Copying or distributing in print or electronic forms without written permission of IGI Global is prohibited.

INTRODUCTION

Sustainable development is an eminent challenge of our era, presenting a pivotal crossroad for the global community grappling with multifaceted issues such as climate change, resource depletion, social inequality, and environmental degradation (Nguyen et al., 2023). The global spotlight has converged on adopting and pursuing the SDGs, established by the United Nations in 2015 as a universal call to action (Erin et al., 2022). These goals, a critical roadmap for our future, ambitiously aim to end poverty, protect the planet, and ensure prosperity for all by 2030 (Vinuesa et al., 2020). Undoubtedly, the significance of the SDGs in the contemporary world cannot be overstated. Serving as a comprehensive framework transcending borders, they address challenges affecting nations at every level of development, embodying a commitment to leaving no one behind and recognizing the inherent interconnectedness of our global community. For instance, in environmental conservation, sustainable development promotes practices that minimize environmental impact, such as renewable energy use, waste reduction, and protection of ecosystems (Acaru et al., 2023; Hashemi-Amiri et al., 2023; Kalinaki, Malik, Lai, et al., 2023). Moreover, in ensuring economic stability, sustainable development aims for economic growth that is inclusive, resilient, and environmentally responsible, fostering long-term stability (Erin et al., 2022). Furthermore, sustainable development focuses on social inclusion and equity, aiming to reduce poverty, improve education, and enhance healthcare, among other things (Vinuesa et al., 2020). SDGs represent a shared vision for a more equitable and sustainable world (Nunkoo et al., 2023). The urgency of this international endeavor is underscored by a mounting body of evidence suggesting severe and far-reaching consequences of inaction, particularly in the face of climate change (Nunkoo et al., 2023). Figure 1 depicts the 17 sustainable goals.

Figure 1. Sustainable Development Goals

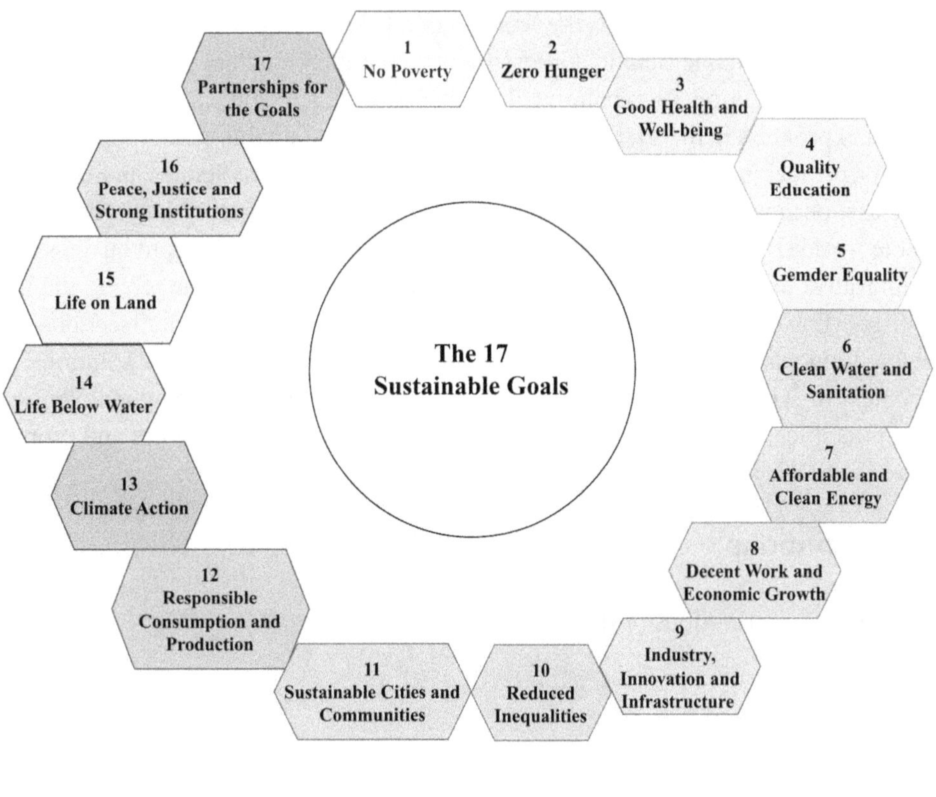

While the SDGs provide a well-defined blueprint for a better future, translating these aspirations into reality proves formidable. Conventional approaches, rooted in incremental change and siloed sectors, often fail to address the complexity of contemporary global challenges (Balogun et al., 2020). The failure of conventional methods is attributed to factors such as the inability to deal with the interconnectedness of environmental, social, and economic issues (Huo & Peng, 2023; L. Zhang et al., 2021). Moreover, globalization has increased interconnectedness and exacerbated inequalities among nations and communities. Conventional developmental strategies may fail to effectively mitigate worldwide inequities, leading to disparate access to resources and opportunities (Gray Group International, 2023). Furthermore, traditional economic models often prioritize short-term gains and fail to account for long-term environmental and social impacts (Purvis et al., 2019). Also, Traditional development methods have often relied on the unsustainable use of natural resources, leading to depletion and environmental degradation (Yusuf & Lytras, 2023). This can have long-term consequences for ecosystems, biodiversity, and the planet's health.

Consequently, innovative practices and technologies are paramount in overcoming entrenched barriers and systemic constraints. Innovation, characterized by developing and applying novel ideas, processes, products, and technologies, emerges as the propelling force for sustainable development (Manigandan et al., 2022). AI is formidable in this innovation landscape, driving transformative change across diverse facets of contemporary life (Nasir et al., 2023; Vinuesa et al., 2020). ML is a crucial constituent within AI's expansive domain, evolving remarkably and leaving an indelible mark on society. ML's intricately linked role to data and feature spaces, forming the foundation for algorithms to learn through rigorous training processes, is crucial in sustainable development (Lau et al., 2023). Its adaptability and capacity to glean insights from complex data make ML an indispensable tool for addressing global sustainability challenges. From optimizing resource management to climate change mitigation, predicting disease outbreaks, and enhancing social well-being, ML facilitates innovative solutions that are foundational to sustainable development (Nasir et al., 2023).

The convergence of AI and ML holds the promise of advancing the SDGs, emphasizing the urgency and significance of this dynamic field in addressing contemporary challenges on a global scale. As ML continues its dynamic evolution, its expanding influence renders it an indispensable instrument for driving innovation and progress in the 21st century, particularly in sustainable development. The contemporary world is at a critical juncture, teetering between unprecedented challenges and opportunities. The SDGs emerge as a beacon of hope and direction, offering a comprehensive vision for a just, equitable, and sustainable world. However, realizing this vision demands a departure from business as usual, necessitating innovative approaches, technologies, and solutions capable of navigating the intricacies of global challenges (Lau et al., 2023). Accordingly, this chapter explores the intersection of sustainable development and innovation, probing the transformative potential of innovative solutions, particularly within the context of AI-powered techniques. The examination delves into how innovation, guided by sustainability principles, can be harnessed to address complex global challenges and propel us toward a future where the SDGs are not mere aspirations but tangible achievements.

Chapter contributions

We provide the main contributions of this study.

1. We introduce SDGs and highlight the inability of conventional methods to address the pressing global issues.
2. We comprehensively explore the intersection of sustainable development and innovation powered by AI techniques.
3. A discussion of the core principles of ML and their potential to solve complex global challenges
4. A detailed discussion of the different applications of ML in various domains for enabling SDGs.
5. A highlight of the challenges faced in deploying ML in sustainable development as well future prospects.

Chapter Organization

After the introduction, the remainder of this chapter is organized as follows. Section 2 provides the principles and concepts of ML, equipping readers with the essential knowledge needed to appreciate the transformative power of ML in the context of addressing complex global challenges. Section 3 explores how ML is contributing to sustainable development across various domains. Challenges and future directions of ML in sustainable development are depicted in section 4. The conclusion is provided in section 5.

PRINCIPLES AND CONCEPTS OF ML

At its core, ML is about enabling computer systems to learn and improve from data. This capability holds immense promise and potential in addressing the multifaceted challenges of the contemporary world. The foundational knowledge highlighted in this section will equip readers with the essential knowledge needed to appreciate the transformative power of ML in the context of addressing complex global challenges.

Data, Feature Space, and Learning From Data

At the heart of ML is data. Data is the raw material from which models learn patterns and make predictions. In the context of ML, the data is represented in a feature space, where a set of features or attributes characterizes each data point. For example, in a medical dataset, each patient's data may include features like age, gender, blood pressure, and cholesterol levels (Alabdulatif et al., 2023; Chemisto et al., 2023). The feature space is the multidimensional representation of this data, and learning algorithms work within this space to identify patterns and relationships. Moreover, ML systems learn from data through a process called training. A ML algorithm processes a dataset during training to discover patterns and relationships in the feature space (Kalinaki, Shafik, Gutu, & Malik, 2023). These patterns are captured as a model, which can be used to make predictions or decisions about new, unseen data. The goal is to create a model that generalizes well to new, unseen data, allowing it to make accurate predictions.

Supervised, Unsupervised, and Reinforcement Learning

ML manifests in three principal archetypes: supervised learning, unsupervised learning, and reinforcement learning. Within supervised learning, algorithms undergo training on meticulously labeled datasets wherein input data is harmonized with corresponding outputs or targets. The algorithm endeavors to establish a mapping between input data and precise outcomes by minimizing the dissonance between its predictions and the authentic targets. Noteworthy techniques encompassed by supervised ML span Linear Regression, Logistic Regression, Support Vector Machines, Decision Trees, Random Forests, K-Nearest Neighbors, and Neural Networks. Conversely, unsupervised learning navigates the landscape of unlabeled data devoid of explicit guides. Here, algorithms seek to unearth patterns, structures, or relationships within the data without clear labels. Common tasks within unsupervised learning involve clustering and dimensionality reduction, with techniques such as K-Means Clustering, Hierarchical Clustering, Principal Component Analysis, Independent Component Analysis (ICA), and Fuzzy C-means illustrating the spectrum of methodologies. (Kalinaki, Shafik, Gutu, & Malik, 2023). Lastly, the sub-field of reinforcement learning delves into the intricacies of decision-making within various environments, guiding agents to select actions that optimize cumulative rewards adeptly. This paradigm finds application in diverse domains such as game-playing, robotics, and autonomous systems. Illustrative techniques within the realm of reinforcement learning encompass Q-learning, Deep Q-Networks, and Policy Gradient Methods. (Moerland et al., 2023).

Model Evaluation, Validation, Overfitting, Underfitting, and Hyperparameter Tuning

Once a ML model is trained, it must be evaluated and validated to ensure its performance on unseen data. Standard techniques for model evaluation include cross-validation, where the dataset is split into multiple subsets for training and testing, and metrics such as accuracy, precision, recall, and F1-score are used to assess model performance. A key challenge in ML is finding the right balance between a model that fits the training data perfectly and generalizes well to new data. Overfitting occurs when a model is too complex and captures noise in the training data, resulting in poor generalization. Conversely, underfitting happens when a model is too simple to capture the underlying patterns in the data. Techniques such as regularization and model selection help mitigate these issues. Finally, hyperparameter tuning involves finding the best hyperparameters for a given model and optimizing its performance (Montesinos López et al., 2022).

Bias, Fairness, Interpretability, and Explainability

ML models may assimilate biases in their training data, giving rise to inequitable or discriminatory results. The perpetual challenge of mitigating bias and upholding fairness in ML models necessitates the application of methodologies such as data preprocessing and integrating fairness-aware algorithms. The opacity of some ML models, particularly deep learning models, has raised concerns about their decision-making processes (Pagano et al., 2023). Model interpretability and explainability aim to explain why a model makes a particular prediction. Techniques like feature importance analysis, SHapley Additive exPlanations (SHAP), and Local Interpretable Model-agnostic Explanations (LIME) help make models more transparent and accountable (Alabi et al., 2023).

Deep Learning

Deep learning, a subfield of ML, involves deep neural networks with many layers (hence the term "deep"). It has significantly advanced the field, particularly in image and speech recognition tasks. Deep learning models include convolutional neural networks (CNNs) for image processing, recurrent neural networks (RNNs) for sequential data, and transformers for natural language processing (Matsuo et al., 2022).

In a nutshell, ML profoundly shapes the contemporary world with its diverse algorithms and applications. It transforms industries, addresses complex global challenges, and enables intelligent systems that learn from data. Understanding the principles and concepts of ML, as well as the various types of algorithms, is essential for harnessing the full potential of this technology. As ML evolves, its influence will only grow, making it an indispensable tool for innovation and progress in the 21st century.

ML APPLICATIONS FOR SUSTAINABLE DEVELOPMENT

ML has transcended its role as a mere computational tool and has emerged as a transformative force in our pursuit of sustainable development. Its capacity to analyze vast datasets, recognize complex patterns and make predictions has propelled it to the forefront of the technological revolution reshaping our world. Below, we explore how ML contributes to sustainable development across various domains.

ML Applications in Precision Farming

In pursuing sustainable agriculture, the focus extends beyond the mere augmentation of crop yields; it encompasses the imperative to curtail the ecological footprint of agricultural methodologies. Precision farming emerges as a pivotal tactic harmonizing with this objective, meticulously honing resource utilization and curtailing wastage. This methodology integrates cutting-edge technologies, data scrutiny, and automation to judiciously guide decisions at the granular field level, ensuring the reasonable application of inputs such as water, fertilizers, and pesticides. Precision farming bestows manifold benefits, spanning augmented yields, diminished environmental impact, and fiscal savings. ML is central to this paradigm, adeptly processing extensive datasets to provide actionable insights.

Crop Monitoring

Monitoring crops with precision is a vital component of modern farming practices. Timely access to accurate information regarding the well-being and progress of crops is indispensable for informed decision-making by farmers. Integrating ML, remote sensing technologies, and data analytics presents a robust solution for effective crop monitoring. Utilizing various remote sensors facilitated by satellites and drones allows for acquiring highly detailed images of agricultural landscapes (Kalinaki, Shafik, Gutu, & Malik, 2023). Subsequent analysis of these images through ML algorithms enables the assessment of crop health, detection of disease outbreaks, and evaluation of the influence of environmental factors. An exemplary application of ML involves the analysis of multispectral satellite imagery to pinpoint areas of stress or disease in crops (Khan et al., 2022). Early identification of such issues empowers farmers to implement targeted measures, reducing reliance on broad-spectrum pesticide applications. This not only leads to cost savings but also mitigates the environmental impact associated with widespread pesticide use. Furthermore, on-site sensors furnish real-time data on critical parameters such as soil moisture and temperature. ML models process this data to generate intricate maps detailing the conditions of the field, providing farmers with the information needed to make precise decisions on irrigation, fertilization, and pest control. For instance, ML algorithms can synergize data from soil moisture sensors with weather forecasts to devise irrigation schedules that optimize water usage (Dutta et al., 2023). This strategic approach to water management enhances crop yield and contributes to the conservation of this invaluable resource.

Pest Control

Addressing the formidable challenge of pest control in agriculture is imperative due to the considerable crop damage inflicted by pests, prompting the widespread use of pesticides. ML applications in pest control endeavor to curtail pesticide usage by employing targeted, data-driven strategies. In pest detection and identification, ML models can undergo training to recognize pests and diseases through advanced image recognition techniques (Chithambarathanu & Jeyakumar, 2023). Through the meticulous analysis of plant and leaf imagery, ML algorithms exhibit the capability to discern specific pests or indications of diseases. For instance, an ML model can proficiently identify distinctive patterns and symptoms associated with aphid infestations. The early identification of pests and diseases equips farmers with timely intervention options, such as precision pesticide application or the removal of affected plants. This precise approach reduces reliance on broad-spectrum pesticide application and mitigates chemical runoff into the environment. Furthermore, ML is pivotal in constructing predictive models for pest outbreaks (Park et al., 2023). These models encompass an array of variables, including weather conditions, historical data, and the life cycles of pests.

Yield Prediction

Accurate yield prediction constitutes a pivotal facet of precision agriculture, empowering farmers with the knowledge to make informed choices regarding crop harvesting, storage, and marketing. Leveraging ML models, examining historical data unfolds, forecasting crop yields and weather patterns, soil conditions, and crop management practices (Iniyan et al., 2023). Employing sophisticated statistical methodologies such as regression analysis, these models yield precise predictions. To illustrate, ML can scrutinize the historical yield data specific to a crop and region, factoring in nuanced variations in weather conditions. By discerning the intricate interplay between these variables, the model furnishes farmers with foresighted yield predictions, facilitating adept planning for harvesting and storage. Furthermore, the integration of in-field sensors and real-time data gleaned from agricultural machinery ushers in a new era of immediacy in monitoring crop conditions. ML algorithms intricately process this dynamic information, estimating yields as the crop matures. For instance, ML proficiency shines through in analyzing data harvested by combined harvesters, encompassing vital metrics such as crop volume, moisture content, and weight (Oikonomidis et al., 2023). Continuous surveillance of these parameters allows the model to furnish real-time yield estimates, allowing farmers to make well-informed decisions regarding harvesting and storage as the crop matures.

ML Applications in Renewable Energy Efficiency

Amidst the global imperative to curtail carbon emissions and shift towards sustainable energy, the critical role of renewable energy in tackling these challenges has come to the forefront (Acaru et al., 2023). Notably, solar and wind energy stand out as substantial and eco-friendly alternatives to traditional fossil fuels. Yet, the effective and dependable utilization of these resources necessitates inventive solutions.

ML has emerged as a transformative force, reshaping the renewable Energy landscape by employing predictive analytics to optimize the entire spectrum of energy processes, encompassing generation, consumption, and grid management. This section delves into the revolutionary influence of ML within the renewable energy sector, with a specific focus on its applications in predictive analytics.

Predictive Analytics for Solar Energy

Solar Energy, harnessed from the sun's radiant power, holds promise in addressing a substantial portion of our energy requirements. Nevertheless, the unpredictable nature of sunlight and atmospheric conditions introduces complexities to energy production. Employing ML-driven predictive analytics emerges as a viable avenue for enhancing the effectiveness of solar panels and farms. In the domain of Solar Irradiance Prediction, ML models demonstrate their prowess by scrutinizing historical meteorological data, solar irradiance levels, and cloud cover. This comprehensive analysis enables the anticipation of patterns in solar energy generation (Tajjour et al., 2023). Such predictions are pivotal for grid operators, empowering them to effectively distribute and store solar energy. Notably, ML algorithms excel in furnishing precise forecasts of solar irradiance tailored to specific locales and temporal intervals (Azizi et al., 2023). This information allows grid operators to harmonize energy production and consumption, ensuring consumers' dependable, eco-friendly supply. Furthermore, integrating predictive analytics facilitates the strategic management of energy storage and distribution, curtailing wastage while optimizing solar energy utilization (Dong et al., 2022).

Predictive Analytics for Wind Energy

Renewable energy derived from wind turbines is crucial to sustainable power generation. The performance of these turbines is intricately linked to variables such as wind speed, direction, and turbulence. The integration of ML emerges as a pivotal factor in forecasting wind patterns and optimizing the efficacy of wind energy production. In wind forecasting, ML models analyze meteorological data, historical wind patterns, and geospatial information to project forthcoming wind conditions (Hamza Zafar et al., 2022). These projections serve as guiding principles for the operation and maintenance of wind turbines, ensuring peak performance. ML algorithms exhibit the capability to anticipate wind speeds and turbulence across diverse atmospheric altitudes (Z. Zhang et al., 2023), providing turbine operators with indispensable insights to fine-tune blade angles and rotor speeds for optimal energy capture. Beyond turbine operation, precise wind forecasts are crucial in grid management, empowering energy providers to preemptively adjust energy distribution in response to anticipated fluctuations. Furthermore, ML finds application in monitoring turbine health, leveraging data from vibration sensors, temperature sensors, and other monitoring devices. Through the analysis of this data, ML models can identify early indicators of wear and tear in turbine components. An illustrative example is the ability of ML to discern abnormalities in the vibration patterns of a wind turbine, signaling potential mechanical issues (Khazaee et al., 2022). The early detection facilitated by ML allows for timely maintenance, minimizes downtime, and ensures the dependable functionality of wind farms. This proactive approach to maintenance enhances energy efficiency and extends the lifespan of wind turbines, thereby mitigating their environmental footprint. This elucidation underscores the interplay between wind energy, ML, and sustainable practices in pursuing efficient and enduring renewable power sources.

Predictive Analytics for Energy Generation and Consumption

Incorporating ML within the renewable energy domain transcends the confines of individual energy sources. ML applications in predictive analytics empower the streamlined administration of energy generation, consumption, and grid operations. Within the energy generation forecasting domain, ML plays a pivotal role in predicting energy output from renewable sources (Benti et al., 2023; Hamza Zafar et al., 2022). This prediction encompasses solar, wind, and other renewable sources, enabling grid operators to strategize energy distribution adeptly. Predictive analytics models leverage historical energy generation data, weather patterns, and seasonal fluctuations to generate precise predictions. For instance, ML can scrutinize past solar and wind energy generation in a specific locale, furnishing forecasts for the ensuing weeks or months (Mesa-Jiménez et al., 2023). These forecasts serve as guiding beacons for grid operators, aiding in the prudent management of energy distribution, averting overloads, and curbing reliance on fossil fuels during peak demand epochs. Ultimately, predictive analytics prove equally indispensable in anticipating energy demand. ML models dissect historical energy consumption patterns, population growth, and economic indicators to foresee future energy requirements (Runge & Saloux, 2023). By comprehending trends in energy demand, energy providers can adapt their generation and distribution strategies. This adaptive approach ensures the effective allocation of resources, thereby securing a dependable energy supply while minimizing wastage.

Grid Management

Effective grid management involves the intricate balance of energy generation and consumption in real time, a multifaceted challenge navigated with ML applications. Within load balancing, ML algorithms tirelessly scrutinize data emanating from energy meters, intelligent appliances, and grid sensors (Wazirali et al., 2023). These models can predict shifts in energy demand, orchestrating corresponding adjustments in energy generation. To illustrate, ML exhibits its prowess by discerning surges in energy consumption within specific regions, directing nearby renewable energy sources to augment production (Antonesi et al., 2023). This foresight into energy demand fluctuations and real-time load equilibrium enables grid operators to curtail reliance on fossil fuel power plants, thereby mitigating environmental repercussions. Furthermore, predictive analytics, empowered by ML, play a pivotal role in fault detection and response, offering a swift and efficient countermeasure to potential outages. ML models adeptly identify areas susceptible to electrical faults by meticulously analyzing sensor data and historical outage patterns (Aiswarya et al., 2023). For instance, ML processes information gleaned from power grid sensors, pinpointing voltage, current, and frequency aberrations. Upon detecting anomalies, the system promptly executes strategic measures such as rerouting power or isolating faulty components, thereby averting widespread outages (Fahim et al., 2024).

ML Applications in Wildlife Conservation

Safeguarding biodiversity and maintaining the integrity of ecosystems stand as indispensable pillars in the worldwide pursuit of conservation. In the face of escalating threats posed by habitat degradation, poaching, and climate fluctuations, demand for inventive strategies becomes ever more pronounced. ML is now unfolding as a formidable asset in wildlife conservation. Its adeptness in dissecting vast datasets, discerning intricate patterns, and forecasting outcomes are reshaping the landscape of conservation methodologies. This section delves into the transformative role of ML in safeguarding wildlife, with a specific focus on the surveillance and oversight of endangered species, counter-poaching initiatives, and the preservation of natural habitats.

Tracking and Monitoring Endangered Species

Safeguarding endangered species necessitates advanced tracking and monitoring techniques. The integration of ML technologies opens innovative avenues for the acquisition and analysis of data, furnishing invaluable insights into the behaviors and movements of these at-risk species. Integral to contemporary wildlife monitoring, the deployment of camera traps coupled with image recognition has become indispensable. These devices adeptly capture images and videos of wildlife in their natural environments (Bhatt et al., 2022). Leveraging ML, mainly through image recognition algorithms, facilitates the analysis of this visual data. ML models efficiently identify and classify individual animals, empowering researchers to trace their movements and meticulously assess population dynamics. By scrutinizing various images of tigers captured by camera traps, ML can discern distinctive stripe patterns, distinguishing between individual tigers (Shi et al., 2023). This technological prowess significantly contributes to estimating population sizes and monitoring the well-being of endangered big cat species. Beyond visual data, the integration of audio data is paramount in wildlife tracking efforts. Acoustic monitoring involves recording diverse animal sounds, encompassing bird calls, frog croaks, and other vocalizations. ML is pivotal in scrutinizing these audio recordings, discerning species based on their unique vocalizations. For instance, ML models can differentiate between bird species by analyzing their distinctive songs (Chalmers et al., 2021; Nolasco et al., 2023). Acoustic monitoring empowers researchers to gauge species richness in a given area, monitor migratory patterns, and detect the presence of rare and elusive species that are challenging to observe visually. The scope of ML extends to the realm of GPS and satellite tracking of wildlife. Animals are equipped with GPS collars or tags transmitting location data to satellites. ML algorithms process this geospatial information, unraveling movement patterns and behavioral nuances (Ergunsah et al., 2023). This critical information enhances our comprehension of migration routes, breeding grounds, and foraging habits, particularly vital for conserving species like sea turtles, elephants, and migratory birds. This underscores the imperative role of ML in advancing conservation efforts through sophisticated tracking and monitoring methodologies.

Anti-Poaching Efforts

The illicit trade of wildlife and the menace of poaching present imminent threats to numerous species. ML is pivotal in anti-poaching endeavors, deploying advanced techniques to identify and dissuade poachers and ensuring wildlife protection. ML is harnessed in automated aerial surveillance, leveraging satellites, drones, and unmanned aerial vehicles (UAVs) (Dorfling et al., 2022). These aerial systems have cameras and sensors that capture real-time imagery of designated conservation areas. In an instantaneous analysis, ML models scrutinize the images, detecting potential threats such as poachers, vehicles, or unusual activities within these protected zones. The system promptly notifies rangers or law enforcement upon identifying anomalies, enabling swift responses to thwart potential poaching incidents. Poaching tends to adhere to discernible patterns and routes, a fact exploited by ML. Historical data on poaching incidents, encompassing factors like location, time of day, and environmental conditions, is meticulously analyzed by ML models (Castelli, 2023). This analytical prowess enables the recognition of patterns, empowering authorities to predict and proactively intervene in poaching activities within vulnerable areas. Protective measures include deploying sensor networks in these areas, comprising acoustic sensors, thermal cameras, and motion detectors. ML processes the data these sensors collect, distinguishing between human and animal movements and alerting authorities when unauthorized human activities are detected (Siewert et al., 2023).

Habitat Preservation and Restoration

Safeguarding biodiversity involves protecting individual fauna and safeguarding the integrity of their natural surroundings. ML emerges as a crucial ally in habitat preservation and restoration, leveraging advanced data analytics and ecological modeling. Through ML, intricate ecological models are crafted to emulate the complex dynamics of ecosystems, foreseeing the repercussions of environmental alterations. A case in point is ML's capacity to scrutinize temperature, precipitation, and vegetation cover data, yielding models that elucidate the ramifications of climate shifts on a specific habitat. These models serve as invaluable tools in steering conservation endeavors, pinpointing vulnerable zones, and advising strategies for preserving and restoring habitats (Mirhashemi et al., 2023). Furthermore, land cover classification is imperative for meticulously mapping and tracking habitat alterations. ML algorithms adeptly process satellite imagery and diverse remote sensing data to categorize land cover types, encompassing forests, wetlands, and grasslands. ML models' prowess extends to identifying deforestation, land degradation, and habitat diminution. Armed with precise insights into alterations in land cover (Kalinaki, Malik, & Ching Lai, 2023; Kalinaki, Malik, Lai, et al., 2023), conservationists are empowered to concentrate their endeavors on safeguarding and rejuvenating critical habitats.

ML Applications in Smart Cities

The relentless advance of urbanization persists as an omnipresent global force, with over half of the Earth's populace calling urban centers their home. As urban landscapes expand, so do the complexities of resource management, infrastructure optimization, and the pursuit of environmental sustainability. Intelligent cities, distinguished by their adept use of cutting-edge technologies and data-driven methodologies, are emerging as the antidote to these urban challenges. At the core of smart cities lies ML, which empowers urban areas to evolve into hubs of heightened efficiency, eco-friendliness, and sustainability. This section delves into the transformative impact of ML in smart cities, concentrating on its influence in reshaping urban planning, traffic control, and waste management.

Urban Planning

Leveraging data-driven land use planning, ML plays a pivotal role in the intelligent design of urban spaces, analyzing diverse datasets encompassing population dynamics, economic activities, and environmental variables. This innovative approach facilitates informed urban planning decisions. For instance, ML algorithms harness historical data to predict future population trends, shaping sophisticated land-use planning models. This strategic utilization empowers city authorities to allocate resources efficiently and develop infrastructure tailored to the evolving needs of a burgeoning urban populace (Ibrahim et al., 2023; Tsagkis et al., 2023). Furthermore, within the framework of smart cities, ML algorithms extend their capabilities to risk assessment and disaster preparedness, particularly in addressing challenges associated with climate change. By scrutinizing historical weather data, projections of sea level rise, and other pertinent environmental factors, ML contributes to anticipating disaster risks (Bahari et al., 2023).

Traffic Management

Urban traffic poses an enduring challenge, and ML application emerges as a transformative solution. ML leverages data gleaned from sensors and traffic cameras to optimize the flow of vehicles. By scrutinizing real-time traffic data, ML models dynamically adjust traffic signals, mitigating congestion, curbing emissions, and shortening travel durations (Modi et al., 2022). A stellar illustration of ML's efficacy in traffic management is evident in Singapore's implementation of "smart traffic lights" (Business News, 2023). Beyond traffic control, ML extends its prowess to forecast maintenance requirements for vital transportation infrastructure like bridges and roads (Hussein et al., 2023). ML models can predict when maintenance is imperative by delving into historical data encompassing factors such as traffic loads and environmental conditions. This proactive maintenance approach diminishes the probability of infrastructure failures and minimizes disruptions within urban transportation networks.

Waste Disposal and Recycling

Optimal waste administration is a pivotal element in the strategic development of intelligent urban environments. Harnessing the power of ML, sophisticated algorithms are deployed to refine waste collection routes, meticulously factoring in dynamic traffic patterns and bin capacity dynamics (Fang et al., 2023; Hashemi-Amiri et al., 2023). This curtails fuel consumption, minimizes emissions, and elevates waste recycling efficiency. Employing advanced computer vision models, ML is central to identifying recyclable materials within the waste stream (Myers & Secco, 2021). The discerning capabilities of these models extend to distinguishing diverse waste types, ensuring the streamlined operation of recycling facilities in sorting materials for subsequent processing.

ML in Natural Disaster Prediction

Natural calamities, distinguished by their abrupt commencement and deleterious repercussions, present substantial hazards to human existence, structural integrity, and ecological balance. The capacity to forecast and counteract such incidents assumes paramount significance. ML catalyzes a transformative enhancement in our aptitude to foresee and address natural disasters. This segment delves into the application of ML models for forecasting a spectrum of natural disasters, spanning earthquakes, floods, and wildfires, thereby facilitating superior disaster preparedness and response.

Earthquake Prediction

Predicting earthquakes has posed a persistent challenge within the field of seismology. Leveraging ML techniques, researchers employ advanced models that meticulously scrutinize seismic data, historical earthquake archives, and geospatial data to unveil intricate patterns suggestive of an imminent seismic event. Notably, ML algorithms can discern subtle perturbations in the Earth's crust or atypical seismic phenomena, serving as precursors to potential earthquakes (Mousavi & Beroza, 2023). The foresight provided by these predictions empowers authorities to proactively issue warnings and activate emergency response protocols, holding the promise of preserving lives and mitigating the extent of damage.

Flood Prediction

Widespread and impactful floods stand as frequent and formidable natural phenomena. Employing advanced ML techniques, the anticipation of floods unfolds through scrutinizing meteorological predictions, river gauge readings, and satellite-derived imagery. The evaluation of flood vulnerability encompasses variables like precipitation trends, snowmelt dynamics, and soil saturation levels. ML algorithms exhibit prowess in assimilating live data, foreseeing instances where a river's water level is poised to breach its confines (Sille et al., 2023). This prescient capacity aids in disseminating flood alerts and orchestrates prompt evacuations and strategic flood mitigation strategies.

Wildfire Prediction

The escalating menace of wildfires, intensified by climate change, prompts the application of ML to predict both the inception and dissemination of such conflagrations. ML models intricately scrutinize data derived from meteorological predictions, vegetation coverage assessments, and archival fire data to evaluate potential wildfire hazards. Employing anticipatory modeling, ML algorithms adeptly identify periods characterized by drought and heightened temperatures, thereby amplifying the susceptibility to wildfires (Sayad et al., 2019). These predictive models additionally consider wind dynamics, a pivotal factor in comprehending the potential trajectory of a fire. Timely alerts generated by these models play a crucial role in firefighting efforts and safeguarding communities vulnerable to such incidents.

ML Applications in Healthcare Delivery and Access

The paradigm of human well-being, a cornerstone in healthcare, is experiencing an extraordinary metamorphosis propelled by cutting-edge technological strides, with ML standing out prominently. Within the healthcare domain, the assimilation of ML is affecting a transformative wave across multiple facets, encompassing the realms of disease diagnosis, drug discovery, and personalized medicine. This section explores the profound imprint of ML on healthcare, with a concentrated emphasis on its prospective contributions to the enduring sustainability of well-being.

Predictive Analytics and Early Disease Detection

Among the formidable applications of ML in the realm of healthcare, predictive analytics stands out prominently. ML models can scrutinize patient data, encompassing medical records, diagnostic imaging, and genetic information, unraveling intricate patterns that may serve as early indicators of pathological conditions (Fahim et al., 2023). Notably, ML algorithms wield the capacity to discern nuanced alterations within medical images or patient records, presenting the potential to unveil the onset of ailments such as cancer or other persistent health conditions (Yadav et al., 2023).

Telemedicine and Remote Monitoring

The burgeoning realm of telemedicine experiences an exponential surge, propelled forward by the synergistic integration of ML. Cutting-edge remote monitoring devices and wearable sensors amass extensive patient data, seamlessly processed by ML models to furnish instantaneous health evaluations (Chakraborty & Kishor, 2022). This capability empowers healthcare practitioners to monitor patients' vital indicators and manifestations remotely, fostering timely interventions and bespoke care strategies, thereby diminishing the necessity for face-to-face consultations.

Electronic Health Records (EHR) Management

Navigating the intricacies of electronic health records (EHR) poses a multifaceted challenge. Leveraging ML algorithms facilitates optimizing EHR data storage, retrieval, and analysis, thereby diminishing administrative burdens and elevating the precision of patient records (Hobensack et al., 2023). In this manner, ML actively advances superior healthcare results and enhances the operational efficiency of healthcare systems (Kalinaki, Fahadi, Alli, Shafik, et al., 2023).

Healthcare Resource Optimization

Optimal distribution of healthcare resources is an indispensable pillar for the enduring vitality of healthcare systems. Cutting-edge ML models empower medical institutions and healthcare professionals to enhance resource allocation by forecasting patient admissions, orchestrating staff schedules, and streamlining medication supply chain management (Alnsour et al., 2023). This not only fosters fiscal prudence but also elevates the quality of patient care.

Disease Diagnosis

Disease diagnosis stands as a cornerstone in healthcare, and the realm of ML is forging remarkable advancements in this crucial domain. ML's prowess in image analysis, data interpretation, and pattern recognition plays a pivotal role in the early detection and treatment of ailments. Unprecedented progress in medical imaging, encompassing radiology and pathology, owes much to ML innovations (Rana & Bhushan, 2023). These algorithms exhibit proficiency in scrutinizing X-rays, MRIs, CT scans, and pathology slides, discerning anomalies that aid healthcare practitioners in diagnosing afflictions such as cancer, heart disease, and neurological disorders. ML's contribution to enhancing the accuracy of breast cancer detection in mammograms is noteworthy, exemplifying its impact in refining radiological assessments (Avcı & Karakaya, 2023). The influence of ML extends into the realm of genomic medicine, where it delves into genetic data to unveil disease risks and potential treatment avenues. ML models adeptly pinpoint genetic markers associated with various ailments, facilitating the creation of personalized treatment plans. For instance, ML-driven genomics proves instrumental in predicting an individual's susceptibility to specific diseases, thereby guiding tailored interventions and therapies (Pethani & Dunn, 2023). In parallel, natural language processing (NLP) finds its application in healthcare, extracting and analyzing information from clinical notes, research articles, and patient records. ML models powered by NLP navigate vast expanses of unstructured text, enabling healthcare professionals to access pertinent information swiftly (Pethani & Dunn, 2023).

Table 1 summarizes the ML applications in sustainable development.

Table 1. Summary of ML applications in sustainable development

ML Applications for Sustainable Development		References
ML Applications in Precision Farming	Crop Monitoring	(Dutta et al., 2023; Kalinaki, Shafik, Gutu, & Malik, 2023; Khan et al., 2022)
	Pest Control	(Chithambarathanu & Jeyakumar, 2023; Park et al., 2023; Piou & Marescot, 2023)
	Yield Prediction	(Iniyan et al., 2023; Oikonomidis et al., 2023)
ML Applications in Renewable Energy Efficiency	Predictive Analytics for Solar Energy	(Abubakar et al., 2023; Azizi et al., 2023; Dong et al., 2022; Tajjour et al., 2023)
	Predictive Analytics for Wind Energy	(Hamza Zafar et al., 2022; Khazaee et al., 2022; Z. Zhang et al., 2023)
	Predictive Analytics for Energy Generation and Consumption	(Benti et al., 2023; Hamza Zafar et al., 2022; Mesa-Jiménez et al., 2023; Runge & Saloux, 2023)
	Grid Management	(Aiswarya et al., 2023; Antonesi et al., 2023; (Fahim et al., 2024); Wazirali et al., 2023)
ML Applications in Wildlife Conservation	Tracking and Monitoring Endangered Species	(Bhatt et al., 2022; Chalmers et al., 2021; Nolasco et al., 2023; Shi et al., 2023)
	Anti-Poaching Efforts	(Castelli, 2023; Dorfling et al., 2022; Siewert et al., 2023)
	Habitat Preservation and Restoration	(Kalinaki, Malik, & Ching Lai, 2023; Kalinaki, Malik, Lai, et al., 2023; Mirhashemi et al., 2023)
ML Applications in Smart Cities	Urban Planning	(Bahari et al., 2023; Ibrahim et al., 2023; Tsagkis et al., 2023)
	Traffic Management	(Business News, 2023; Hussein et al., 2023; Modi et al., 2022)
	Waste Disposal and Recycling	(Fang et al., 2023; Hashemi-Amiri et al., 2023; Myers & Secco, 2021)
ML in Natural Disaster Prediction	Earthquake Prediction	(Mousavi & Beroza, 2023)
	Flood Prediction	(Sille et al., 2023)
	Wildfire Prediction	(Sayad et al., 2019)
ML Applications in Healthcare Delivery and Access	Predictive Analytics and Early Disease Detection	(Fahim et al., 2023; Yadav et al., 2023)
	Telemedicine and Remote Monitoring	(Chakraborty & Kishor, 2022)
	Electronic Health Records (EHR) Management	(Hobensack et al., 2023; Kalinaki, Fahadi, Alli, Shafik, et al., 2023)
	Healthcare Resource Optimization	(Alnsour et al., 2023)
	Disease Diagnosis	(Avcı & Karakaya, 2023; Pethani & Dunn, 2023; Rana & Bhushan, 2023)

CHALLENGES AND FUTURE DIRECTIONS

While the potential of ML in fostering sustainable development is evident, persistent challenges and limitations demand attention. Issues such as data availability and quality, interpretability of models, scalability concerns, and the digital divide require comprehensive solutions. Charting the future course of this field entails fostering interdisciplinary collaboration, crafting open-source tools, and formulating robust ethical and legal frameworks to guide the ethical deployment of ML in the realm of sustainable development.

Data Challenges

The effectiveness of ML models relies on the availability and quality of data. Data can be scarce, incomplete, or of variable quality in many areas related to sustainable development. For instance, environmental data collected from remote or underdeveloped regions may be limited (Li et al., 2023). Addressing this challenge requires the development of mechanisms for data collection and sharing, ensuring that the datasets used in ML models are representative and comprehensive.

Model Interpretability

ML models are often regarded as "black boxes," making it challenging to understand how they arrive at specific decisions or predictions. In contexts like conservation and environmental protection, model interpretability is crucial. Understanding why a model makes a particular recommendation is essential for building trust and making informed decisions (Gao & Guan, 2023). To overcome this challenge, the ML community is actively researching techniques for model interpretability. These include methods to visualize model decisions, explain predictions, and ensure that the reasoning behind a model's output is transparent and understandable to non-experts.

Scalability and Resource Constraints

Implementing ML solutions at scale, especially in resource-constrained environments, poses a significant challenge. Sustainable development efforts often target regions with limited computing resources and connectivity access. Ensuring ML applications can operate efficiently under such constraints is essential for widespread adoption. One approach to addressing this challenge is the development of lightweight ML models that can run on low-power devices or in offline modes (Ooko et al., 2021; Schizas et al., 2022). These models are optimized for efficiency and can be deployed in environments with limited resources, extending the reach of ML in sustainable development.

The Digital Divide

The persistent chasm of the digital divide, demarcating those endowed with technological and internet access from their counterparts who lack such privileges, continues to pose a substantial impediment to the impartial integration of ML in sustainable development endeavors. Many communities and regions are left behind in adopting technological solutions without access to the necessary digital infrastructure. To bridge the digital divide, efforts are underway to expand internet access, provide training and education in technology, and develop localized solutions that can operate offline or with limited connectivity (Lythreatis et al., 2022). These initiatives aim to ensure that the benefits of ML are accessible to all, regardless of their geographical location or socioeconomic status.

Interdisciplinary Collaboration

Achieving SDGs goals through ML requires interdisciplinary collaboration. Experts from various fields, including computer science, environmental science, economics, and social sciences, must work together to develop and implement effective solutions. Cross-disciplinary partnerships can lead to a deeper understanding of complex challenges and the development of holistic solutions considering environmental, economic, and social factors (Ryan et al., 2023).

Open-Source Tools and Knowledge Sharing

The open-source movement plays a crucial role in advancing ML for sustainable development. Open-source tools and libraries allow researchers, organizations, and communities to access, use, and adapt ML solutions for specific needs (Yenugula et al., 2024). By fostering a culture of knowledge sharing and collaboration, open-source initiatives contribute to the democratization of ML and the widespread adoption of sustainable solutions.

Ethical and Legal Frameworks

Ethical and legal frameworks are needed to ensure responsible use as ML technologies advance. These frameworks encompass privacy, bias, fairness, accountability, and transparency. Ethical guidelines, regulations, and standards are emerging to govern the development and deployment of ML in sensitive areas, including healthcare, conservation, and climate modeling (Lau et al., 2023).

CONCLUSION

In conclusion, ML is more than a technological enabler; it catalyzes sustainable development. Its capacity to analyze data, recognize patterns, and make predictions has revolutionized our approach to complex challenges in agriculture, renewable energy, conservation, climate change mitigation, smart cities, disaster response, manufacturing, waste reduction, biodiversity preservation, and ecosystem restoration. ML can accelerate SDG progress by optimizing resource use, reducing waste, and enhancing decision-making. However, its implementation comes with challenges, including data availability, model interpretability, scalability, and addressing the digital divide. To realize the full potential of ML in sustainable development, interdisciplinary collaboration, the development of open-source tools, and the establishment of clear ethical and legal frameworks are essential. By addressing these challenges and fostering responsible use, we can harness the transformative power of ML to create a sustainable and prosperous future where environmental, economic, and social objectives are in harmony. The journey toward sustainable development is ongoing, and ML is poised to be a valuable partner. ML promises a more sustainable and equitable future for all because it can process vast amounts of data, model complex systems, and offer actionable insights. As we continue to innovate and address the challenges ahead, the synergy between ML and sustainable development will continue to drive progress and provide solutions to some of the most pressing global issues of our time.

REFERENCES

Abubakar, A., Jibril, M. M., Almeida, C. F. M., Gemignani, M., Yahya, M. N., & Abba, S. I. (2023). A Novel Hybrid Optimization Approach for Fault Detection in Photovoltaic Arrays and Inverters Using AI and Statistical Learning Techniques: A Focus on Sustainable Environment. *Processes, 11*(9), 2549. doi:10.3390/pr11092549

Acaru, S. F., Abdullah, R., & Lim, R. C. (2023). Sustainable Valorization of Wood Residue for the Production of Biofuel Materials Via Continuous Flow Hydrothermal Liquefaction. *Waste and Biomass Valorization, 14*(9), 3081–3095. doi:10.1007/s12649-023-02074-y

Aiswarya, R., Nair, D. S., Rajeev, T., & Vinod, V. (2023). A novel SVM based adaptive scheme for accurate fault identification in microgrid. *Electric Power Systems Research, 221*, 109439. doi:10.1016/j.epsr.2023.109439

Alabdulatif, A., Thilakarathne, N. N., & Kalinaki, K. (2023). A Novel Cloud Enabled Access Control Model for Preserving the Security and Privacy of Medical Big Data. *Electronics (Basel), 12*(12), 2646. doi:10.3390/electronics12122646

Alabi, R. O., Elmusrati, M., Leivo, I., Almangush, A., & Mäkitie, A. A. (2023). Machine learning explainability in nasopharyngeal cancer survival using LIME and SHAP. *Scientific Reports, 13*(1), 1–14. doi:10.1038/s41598-023-35795-0

Alnsour, Y., Johnson, M., Albizri, A., & Harfouche, A. H. (2023). Predicting Patient Length of Stay Using Artificial Intelligence to Assist Healthcare Professionals in Resource Planning and Scheduling Decisions. *Journal of Global Information Management, 31*(1), 1–14. doi:10.4018/JGIM.323059

Antonesi, G., Cioara, T., Toderean, L., Anghel, I., & De Mulder, C. (2023). A Machine Learning Pipeline to Forecast the Electricity and Heat Consumption in a City District. *Buildings, 13*(6), 1407. doi:10.3390/buildings13061407

Avcı, H., & Karakaya, J. (2023). A Novel Medical Image Enhancement Algorithm for Breast Cancer Detection on Mammography Images Using Machine Learning. *Diagnostics, 13*(3), 348. doi:10.3390/diagnostics13030348

Azizi, N., Yaghoubirad, M., Farajollahi, M., & Ahmadi, A. (2023). Deep learning based long-term global solar irradiance and temperature forecasting using time series with multi-step multivariate output. *Renewable Energy, 206*, 135–147. doi:10.1016/j.renene.2023.01.102

Bahari, N. A. A. B. S., Ahmed, A. N., Chong, K. L., Lai, V., Huang, Y. F., Koo, C. H., Ng, J. L., & El-Shafie, A. (2023). Predicting Sea Level Rise Using Artificial Intelligence: A Review. *Archives of Computational Methods in Engineering, 30*(7), 4045–4062. doi:10.1007/s11831-023-09934-9

Balogun, A. L., Marks, D., Sharma, R., Shekhar, H., Balmes, C., Maheng, D., Arshad, A., & Salehi, P. (2020). Assessing the Potentials of Digitalization as a Tool for Climate Change Adaptation and Sustainable Development in Urban Centres. *Sustainable Cities and Society, 53*, 101888. doi:10.1016/j.scs.2019.101888

Benti, N. E., Chaka, M. D., & Semie, A. G. (2023). Forecasting Renewable Energy Generation with Machine Learning and Deep Learning: Current Advances and Future Prospects. *Sustainability, 15*(9), 7087. doi:10.3390/su15097087

Bhatt, P., Maclean, A., Dickinson, Y., & Kumar, C. (2022). Fine-Scale Mapping of Natural Ecological Communities Using Machine Learning Approaches. *Remote Sensing (Basel), 14*(3), 563. doi:10.3390/rs14030563

Business News. (2023). *Singapore Pioneering in the Smart Traffic Light Systems*. https://businessnews.com.my/wp/2023/08/12/singapore-pioneering-in-the-smart-traffic-light-systems/

Castelli, E. (2023). *Enhancing Anti-Poaching Efforts Through Predictive Analysis Of Animal Movements And Dynamic Environmental Factors*. https://urn.kb.se/resolve?urn=urn:nbn:se:umu:diva-211118

Chakraborty, C., & Kishor, A. (2022). Real-Time Cloud-Based Patient-Centric Monitoring Using Computational Health Systems. *IEEE Transactions on Computational Social Systems*, *9*(6), 1613–1623. doi:10.1109/TCSS.2022.3170375

Chalmers, C., Fergus, P., Wich, S., & Longmore, S. N. (2021). Modelling Animal Biodiversity Using Acoustic Monitoring and Deep Learning. *Proceedings of the International Joint Conference on Neural Networks, 2021-July*. 10.1109/IJCNN52387.2021.9534195

Chemisto, M., Gutu, T. J., Kalinaki, K., Mwebesa Bosco, D., Egau, P., Fred, K., Tim Oloya, I., & Rashid, K. (2023). Artificial Intelligence for Improved Maternal Healthcare: A Systematic Literature Review. *2023 IEEE AFRICON*, 1–6. doi:10.1109/AFRICON55910.2023.10293674

Chithambarathanu, M., & Jeyakumar, M. K. (2023). Survey on crop pest detection using deep learning and machine learning approaches. *Multimedia Tools and Applications*, *82*(27), 42277–42310. doi:10.1007/s11042-023-15221-3 PMID:37362671

Dong, Y., Han, Z., Li, X., Ma, S., Gao, F., & Li, W. (2022). Joint Optimal Scheduling of Renewable Energy Regional Power Grid With Energy Storage System and Concentrated Solar Power Plant. *Frontiers in Energy Research*, *10*, 941074. doi:10.3389/fenrg.2022.941074

Dorfling, J., Bruder, S., Landon, P., Bondar, G., Rawther, C., Aranzazu-Suescún, C., Rocha, K., Siewert, S. B., Trahms, B., Le, C., Pederson, T., & Mangar, R. (2022). Satellite, Aerial, and Ground Sensor Fusion Experiment for the Management of Elephants, Rhinos, and Poaching Prevention. *AIAA Science and Technology Forum and Exposition. AIAA SciTech Forum, 2022*. Advance online publication. doi:10.2514/6.2022-1270

Dutta, A., Pal, S., Banerjee, A., Karmakar, P., Mukherjee, A., Mukherjee, D., & Sahu, P. K. (2023). Survey on Irrigation Scheduling with Machine Learning. *Lecture Notes in Networks and Systems, 650 LNNS*, 797–806. doi:10.1007/978-981-99-0838-7_68

Ergunsah, S., Tümen, V., Kosunalp, S., & Demir, K. (2023). Energy-efficient animal tracking with multi-unmanned aerial vehicle path planning using reinforcement learning and wireless sensor networks. *Concurrency and Computation*, *35*(4), e7527. doi:10.1002/cpe.7527

Erin, O. A., Bamigboye, O. A., & Oyewo, B. (2022). Sustainable development goals (SDG) reporting: An analysis of disclosure. *Journal of Accounting in Emerging Economies, 12*(5), 761–789. doi:10.1108/JAEE-02-2020-0037

Fahim, K. E., Kalinaki, K., De Silva, L. C., & Yassin, H. (2024). The role of machine learning in improving power distribution systems resilience. Future Modern Distribution Networks Resilience, 329–352. https://doi.org/ doi:10.1016/B978-0-443-16086-8.00012-9

Fahim, K. E., Kalinaki, K., & Shafik, W. (2023). Electronic Devices in the Artificial Intelligence of the Internet of Medical Things (AIoMT). In Handbook of Security and Privacy of AI-Enabled Healthcare Systems and Internet of Medical Things (pp. 41–62). CRC Press. https://doi.org/ doi:10.1201/9781003370321-3

Fang, B., Yu, J., Chen, Z., Osman, A. I., Farghali, M., Ihara, I., Hamza, E. H., Rooney, D. W., & Yap, P. S. (2023). Artificial intelligence for waste management in smart cities: a review. *Environmental Chemistry Letters, 21*(4), 1959–1989. doi:10.1007/s10311-023-01604-3

Gao, L., & Guan, L. (2023). Interpretability of Machine Learning: Recent Advances and Future Prospects. *IEEE MultiMedia, 30*(4), 105–118. Advance online publication. doi:10.1109/MMUL.2023.3272513

Gray Group International. (2023). *Inequality: Navigating the Divides.* Gray Group International. https://www.graygroupintl.com/blog/inequality

Hamza Zafar, M., Mujeeb Khan, N., Mansoor, M., Feroz Mirza, A., Kumayl Raza Moosavi, S., & Sanfilippo, F. (2022). Adaptive ML-based technique for renewable energy system power forecasting in hybrid PV-Wind farms power conversion systems. *Energy Conversion and Management, 258*, 115564. doi:10.1016/j.enconman.2022.115564

Hashemi-Amiri, O., Mohammadi, M., Rahmanifar, G., Hajiaghaei-Keshteli, M., Fusco, G., & Colombaroni, C. (2023). An allocation-routing optimization model for integrated solid waste management. *Expert Systems with Applications, 227*, 120364. doi:10.1016/j.eswa.2023.120364

Hobensack, M., Song, J., Scharp, D., Bowles, K. H., & Topaz, M. (2023). Machine learning applied to electronic health record data in home healthcare: A scoping review. *International Journal of Medical Informatics, 170*, 104978. doi:10.1016/j.ijmedinf.2022.104978 PMID:36592572

Huo, J., & Peng, C. (2023). Depletion of natural resources and environmental quality: Prospects of energy use, energy imports, and economic growth hindrances. *Resources Policy, 86*, 104049. doi:10.1016/j.resourpol.2023.104049

Hussein, H., Zhu, Y., Hassan, R. F., Nasab, A. R., & Elzarka, H. (2023). Optimizing Machine Learning Algorithms for Improving Prediction of Bridge Deck Deterioration: A Case Study of Ohio Bridges. *Buildings, 13*(6), 1517. doi:10.3390/buildings13061517

Ibrahim, H., Khattab, Z., Khattab, T., & Abraham, R. (2023). Expatriates' Housing Dispersal Outlook in a Rapidly Developing Metropolis Based on Urban Growth Predicted Using a Machine Learning Algorithm. *Housing Policy Debate, 33*(3), 641–661. doi:10.1080/10511482.2021.1962939

Iniyan, S., Akhil Varma, V., & Teja Naidu, C. (2023). Crop yield prediction using machine learning techniques. *Advances in Engineering Software, 175*, 103326. doi:10.1016/j.advengsoft.2022.103326

Kalinaki, K., Fahadi, M., Alli, A. A., Shafik, W., Yasin, M., & Mutwalibi, N. (2023). Artificial Intelligence of Internet of Medical Things (AIoMT) in Smart Cities: A Review of Cybersecurity for Smart Healthcare. In Handbook of Security and Privacy of AI-Enabled Healthcare Systems and Internet of Medical Things (pp. 271–292). CRC Press. https://doi.org/ doi:10.1201/9781003370321-11

Kalinaki, K., Malik, O. A., & Ching Lai, D. T. (2023). FCD-AttResU-Net: An improved forest change detection in Sentinel-2 satellite images using attention residual U-Net. *International Journal of Applied Earth Observation and Geoinformation*, *122*, 103453. doi:10.1016/j.jag.2023.103453

Kalinaki, K., Malik, O. A., Lai, D. T. C., Sukri, R. S., & Wahab, R. B. H. A. (2023). Spatial-temporal mapping of forest vegetation cover changes along highways in Brunei using deep learning techniques and Sentinel-2 images. *Ecological Informatics*, *77*, 102193. doi:10.1016/j.ecoinf.2023.102193

Kalinaki, K., Shafik, W., Gutu, T. J. L., & Malik, O. A. (2023). Computer Vision and Machine Learning for Smart Farming and Agriculture Practices. In *Artificial Intelligence Tools and Technologies for Smart Farming and Agriculture Practices* (pp. 79–100). IGI Global. doi:10.4018/978-1-6684-8516-3.ch005

Khan, A., Vibhute, A. D., Mali, S., & Patil, C. H. (2022). A systematic review on hyperspectral imaging technology with a machine and deep learning methodology for agricultural applications. *Ecological Informatics*, *69*, 101678. doi:10.1016/j.ecoinf.2022.101678

Khazaee, M., Derian, P., & Mouraud, A. (2022). A comprehensive study on Structural Health Monitoring (SHM) of wind turbine blades by instrumenting tower using machine learning methods. *Renewable Energy*, *199*, 1568–1579. doi:10.1016/j.renene.2022.09.032

Lau, P. L., Nandy, M., & Chakraborty, S. (2023). Accelerating UN Sustainable Development Goals with AI-Driven Technologies: A Systematic Literature Review of Women's Healthcare. *Healthcare, 11*(3), 401. doi:10.3390/healthcare11030401

Li, F., Yigitcanlar, T., Nepal, M., Nguyen, K., & Dur, F. (2023). Machine learning and remote sensing integration for leveraging urban sustainability: A review and framework. *Sustainable Cities and Society*, *96*, 104653. doi:10.1016/j.scs.2023.104653

Lythreatis, S., Singh, S. K., & El-Kassar, A. N. (2022). The digital divide: A review and future research agenda. *Technological Forecasting and Social Change*, *175*, 121359. doi:10.1016/j.techfore.2021.121359

Manigandan, P., Alam, M. S., Alagirisamy, K., Pachiyappan, D., Murshed, M., & Mahmood, H. (2022). Realizing the Sustainable Development Goals through technological innovation: juxtaposing the economic and environmental effects of financial development and energy use. *Environmental Science and Pollution Research, 30*(3), 8239–8256. doi:10.1007/s11356-022-22692-8

Matsuo, Y., LeCun, Y., Sahani, M., Precup, D., Silver, D., Sugiyama, M., Uchibe, E., & Morimoto, J. (2022). Deep learning, reinforcement learning, and world models. *Neural Networks*, *152*, 267–275. doi:10.1016/j.neunet.2022.03.037 PMID:35569196

Mesa-Jiménez, J. J., Tzianoumis, A. L., Stokes, L., Yang, Q., & Livina, V. N. (2023). Long-term wind and solar energy generation forecasts, and optimisation of Power Purchase Agreements. *Energy Reports*, *9*, 292–302. doi:10.1016/j.egyr.2022.11.175

Mirhashemi, H., Heydari, M., Karami, O., Ahmadi, K., & Mosavi, A. (2023). Modeling Climate Change Effects on the Distribution of Oak Forests with Machine Learning. *Forests*, *14*(3), 469. doi:10.3390/f14030469

Modi, Y., Teli, R., Mehta, A., Shah, K., & Shah, M. (2022). A comprehensive review on intelligent traffic management using machine learning algorithms. *Innovative Infrastructure Solutions*, *7*(1), 1–14. doi:10.1007/s41062-021-00718-3

Moerland, T. M., Broekens, J., Plaat, A., & Jonker, C. M. (2023). Model-based Reinforcement Learning: A Survey. *Foundations and Trends® in Machine Learning, 16*(1), 1–118. doi:10.1561/2200000086

Montesinos López, O. A., Montesinos López, A., & Crossa, J. (2022). Overfitting, Model Tuning, and Evaluation of Prediction Performance. *Multivariate Statistical Machine Learning Methods for Genomic Prediction*, 109–139. doi:10.1007/978-3-030-89010-0_4

Mousavi, S. M., & Beroza, G. C. (2023). *Machine Learning in Earthquake Seismology*. doi:10.1146/annurev-earth-071822-100323

Myers, K., & Secco, E. L. (2021). A Low-Cost Embedded Computer Vision System for the Classification of Recyclable Objects. *Lecture Notes on Data Engineering and Communications Technologies*, *61*, 11–30. doi:10.1007/978-981-33-4582-9_2

Nasir, O., Javed, R. T., Gupta, S., Vinuesa, R., & Qadir, J. (2023). Artificial intelligence and sustainable development goals nexus via four vantage points. *Technology in Society*, *72*, 102171. doi:10.1016/j.techsoc.2022.102171

Nguyen, T. T., Grote, U., Neubacher, F., Rahut, D. B., Do, M. H., & Paudel, G. P. (2023). Security risks from climate change and environmental degradation: Implications for sustainable land use transformation in the Global South. *Current Opinion in Environmental Sustainability*, *63*, 101322. doi:10.1016/j.cosust.2023.101322

Nolasco, I., Singh, S., Morfi, V., Lostanlen, V., Strandburg-Peshkin, A., Vidaña-Vila, E., Gill, L., Pamuła, H., Whitehead, H., Kiskin, I., Jensen, F. H., Morford, J., Emmerson, M. G., Versace, E., Grout, E., Liu, H., Ghani, B., & Stowell, D. (2023). Learning to detect an animal sound from five examples. *Ecological Informatics*, *77*, 102258. doi:10.1016/j.ecoinf.2023.102258

Nunkoo, R., Sharma, A., Rana, N. P., Dwivedi, Y. K., & Sunnassee, V. A. (2023). Advancing sustainable development goals through interdisciplinarity in sustainable tourism research. *Journal of Sustainable Tourism*, *31*(3), 735–759. doi:10.1080/09669582.2021.2004416

Oikonomidis, A., Catal, C., & Kassahun, A. (2023). Deep learning for crop yield prediction: A systematic literature review. *New Zealand Journal of Crop and Horticultural Science*, *51*(1), 1–26. doi:10.1080/01140671.2022.2032213

Ooko, S. O., Muyonga Ogore, M., Nsenga, J., & Zennaro, M. (2021). TinyML in Africa: Opportunities and Challenges. *2021 IEEE Globecom Workshops, GC Wkshps 2021 - Proceedings*. doi:10.1109/GCWkshps52748.2021.9682107

Pagano, T. P., Loureiro, R. B., Lisboa, F. V. N., Peixoto, R. M., Guimarães, G. A. S., Cruz, G. O. R., Araujo, M. M., Santos, L. L., Cruz, M. A. S., Oliveira, E. L. S., Winkler, I., & Nascimento, E. G. S. (2023). Bias and Unfairness in Machine Learning Models: A Systematic Review on Datasets, Tools, Fairness Metrics, and Identification and Mitigation Methods. *Big Data and Cognitive Computing*, *7*(1), 15. doi:10.3390/bdcc7010015

Park, Y. H., Choi, S. H., Kwon, Y. J., Kwon, S. W., Kang, Y. J., & Jun, T. H. (2023). Detection of Soybean Insect Pest and a Forecasting Platform Using Deep Learning with Unmanned Ground Vehicles. *Agronomy (Basel)*, *13*(2), 477. doi:10.3390/agronomy13020477

Pethani, F., & Dunn, A. G. (2023). Natural language processing for clinical notes in dentistry: A systematic review. *Journal of Biomedical Informatics*, *138*, 104282. doi:10.1016/j.jbi.2023.104282 PMID:36623780

Piou, C., & Marescot, L. (2023). Spatiotemporal risk forecasting to improve locust management. *Current Opinion in Insect Science*, *56*, 101024. doi:10.1016/j.cois.2023.101024 PMID:36958588

Purvis, B., Mao, Y., & Robinson, D. (2019). Three pillars of sustainability: In search of conceptual origins. *Sustainability Science*, *14*(3), 681–695. doi:10.1007/s11625-018-0627-5

Rana, M., & Bhushan, M. (2023). Machine learning and deep learning approach for medical image analysis: Diagnosis to detection. *Multimedia Tools and Applications*, *82*(17), 26731–26769. doi:10.1007/s11042-022-14305-w PMID:36588765

Runge, J., & Saloux, E. (2023). A comparison of prediction and forecasting artificial intelligence models to estimate the future energy demand in a district heating system. *Energy*, *269*, 126661. doi:10.1016/j.energy.2023.126661

Ryan, M., Isakhanyan, G., & Tekinerdogan, B. (2023). An interdisciplinary approach to artificial intelligence in agriculture. *NJAS: Impact in Agricultural and Life Sciences*, *95*(1), 2168568. Advance online publication. doi:10.1080/27685241.2023.2168568

Sayad, Y. O., Mousannif, H., & Al Moatassime, H. (2019). Predictive modeling of wildfires: A new dataset and machine learning approach. *Fire Safety Journal*, *104*, 130–146. doi:10.1016/j.firesaf.2019.01.006

Schizas, N., Karras, A., Karras, C., & Sioutas, S. (2022). TinyML for Ultra-Low Power AI and Large Scale IoT Deployments: A Systematic Review. *Future Internet*, *14*(12), 363. doi:10.3390/fi14120363

Shi, C., Jing, X. U., Roberts, N. J., Liu, D., & Jiang, G. (2023). Individual automatic detection and identification of big cats with the combination of different body parts. *Integrative Zoology*, *18*(1), 157–168. doi:10.1111/1749-4877.12641 PMID:35276755

Siewert, S. B., Mangar, R., Alshehri, F., Lippmann, M., & Dorfling, J. (2023). *Acoustic*, Seismic, and Visual Camera Sensor Fusion Experiments for Large Animal Detection and Tracking with Scalability. doi:10.2514/6.2023-1117

Sille, R., Sharma, B., Choudhury, T., Toe, T. T., & Um, J.-S. (2023). *Survey on DL Methods for Flood Prediction in Smart Cities*. doi:10.4018/978-1-6684-6408-3.ch020

Tajjour, S., Chandel, S. S., Malik, H., Alotaibi, M. A., Marquez, F. P. G., & Afthanorhan, A. (2023). *Short-Term Solar Irradiance Forecasting Using Deep Learning Techniques: A Comprehensive case Study*. IEEE. doi:10.1109/ACCESS.2023.3325292

Tsagkis, P., Bakogiannis, E., & Nikitas, A. (2023). Analysing urban growth using machine learning and open data: An artificial neural network modelled case study of five Greek cities. *Sustainable Cities and Society*, *89*, 104337. doi:10.1016/j.scs.2022.104337

Vinuesa, R., Azizpour, H., Leite, I., Balaam, M., Dignum, V., Domisch, S., Felländer, A., Langhans, S. D., Tegmark, M., & Fuso Nerini, F. (2020). The role of artificial intelligence in achieving the Sustainable Development Goals. *Nature Communications, 11*(1), 1–10. doi:10.1038/s41467-019-14108-y

Wazirali, R., Yaghoubi, E., Abujazar, M. S. S., Ahmad, R., & Vakili, A. H. (2023). State-of-the-art review on energy and load forecasting in microgrids using artificial neural networks, machine learning, and deep learning techniques. *Electric Power Systems Research*, *225*, 109792. doi:10.1016/j.epsr.2023.109792

Yadav, R. K., Singh, P., & Kashtriya, P. (2023). Diagnosis of Breast Cancer using Machine Learning Techniques -A Survey. *Procedia Computer Science*, *218*, 1434–1443. doi:10.1016/j.procs.2023.01.122

Yenugula, M., Sahoo, S. K., & Goswami, S. S. (2024). Cloud computing for sustainable development: An analysis of environmental, economic and social benefits. *Journal of Future Sustainability*, *4*(1), 59–66. doi:10.5267/j.jfs.2024.1.005

Yusuf, N., & Lytras, M. D. (2023). Competitive Sustainability of Saudi Companies through Digitalization and the Circular Carbon Economy Model: A Bold Contribution to the Vision 2030 Agenda in Saudi Arabia. *Sustainability, 15*(3), 2616. doi:10.3390/su15032616

Zhang, L., Godil, D. I., Bibi, M., Khan, M. K., Sarwat, S., & Anser, M. K. (2021). Caring for the environment: How human capital, natural resources, and economic growth interact with environmental degradation in Pakistan? A dynamic ARDL approach. *The Science of the Total Environment*, *774*, 145553. doi:10.1016/j.scitotenv.2021.145553 PMID:33611006

Zhang, Z., Hao, X., Santoni, C., Shen, L., Sotiropoulos, F., & Khosronejad, A. (2023). Toward prediction of turbulent atmospheric flows over propagating oceanic waves via machine-learning augmented large-eddy simulation. *Ocean Engineering*, *280*, 114759. doi:10.1016/j.oceaneng.2023.114759

Chapter 5
Applications of Artificial Intelligence and Machine Learning in Achieving SDG 6, 7, and 14

Arti Saxena
https://orcid.org/0000-0002-4162-793X
Manav Rachna International Institute of Research and Studies, India

Rajeev Kumar
https://orcid.org/0000-0002-0820-5970
Manav Rachna International Institute of Research and Studies, India

Vijay Kumar
Manav Rachna International Institute of Research and Studies, India

Jyoti Chawla
Manav Rachna International Institute of Research and Studies, India

ABSTRACT

The advent of machine learning and its significant impact on every sector of society requires our attention towards its progressive application in achieving the Sustainable Development Goals (SDGs). Machine learning is a kind of artificial intelligence allowing the machine itself to change its algorithms in order to provide the optimized solution to the subject. In other words, AI is a machine simulating human intelligence, and ML is a subset of artificial intelligence. The Sustainable Development Goals (SDGs) are an all-inclusive set of objectives intended to provide countries with a trail towards peace and prosperity. There are 17 SDGs that are further divided into 169 targets and 304 indicators dealing with everything from ending hunger and protecting marine wildlife to making cities sustainable and reducing gender inequalities. ML is an important tool in meeting these objectives. This chapter explores the application of ML models in achieving these SDGs in an effective manner.

DOI: 10.4018/979-8-3693-1062-5.ch005

Copyright © 2024, IGI Global. Copying or distributing in print or electronic forms without written permission of IGI Global is prohibited.

1. INTRODUCTION

Sustainable Development Goals (SDGs) include 17 goals that were adopted by all United Nations member states in 2015 with interlaced objectives to protect the planet and improve life quality at the global level in a 15-year plan. SDGs are a universal call to the nations to take necessary actions and join hand-in-hand with strategies to improve international partnerships and ensure the protection of the planet. SDGs comprise of 169 targets. To achieve the goals by 2023, there is a need for the mobilization of all stakeholders for the plan and implementation of the appropriate strategy for concrete realization. Progress tracking towards every indicator/target will further help to achieve the goals as per set targets by 2030. To track the progress, data about each indicator is required. Traditionally, statistics from population surveys, individual registrations, and censuses have been used to track progress towards the SDGs. Although many nations wait decades before taking ground measurements for the leading SDG indicators, such data gathering is expensive and requires significant statistical capabilities. Only about half of the SDG indicators have consistent data from more than half of the nations in the world (Danso and Otoo, 2022; Germann and Langergraber, 2022). These data shortages significantly hamper the international community's ability to monitor progress towards the SDGs. Artificial intelligence may be helpful for accomplishment of SDGs (Vinuesa et., 2020; Jean at al., 2016; Seo et al., 2015). AI may help in image recognition, decision-making, prediction, automatic knowledge extraction, pattern recognition from data, interactive communication, and logical reasoning etc. Machine learning (ML) advancements have demonstrated how scarce ground data may be paired with numerous, inexpensive, and regularly updated sources of innovative sensor data to evaluate various SDG-related outcomes, offering hope for filling these data gaps (Yeh et al., 2021). Machine learning (ML) is an area of Artificial Intelligence (AI) that tries to give robots the capacity to derive knowledge from data without explicit programming. To learn how to make judgments based on unobserved information, ML relies heavily on the research and development of algorithms to create models between inputs and outputs. The use of ML in several sub-domains, such as data mining, image recognition, deep learning, and statistical learning, is growing day by day due to its numerous benefits (Goralski and Tan, 2020; Dogo et al., 2019; Ferreira et al., 2020). This paper includes the assessment of the application of AI in 3 selected SDGs (6, 7 & 14).

Figure 1. Flow diagram of role of artificial intelligence and machine learning in achieving SDG 6, 7. and 14

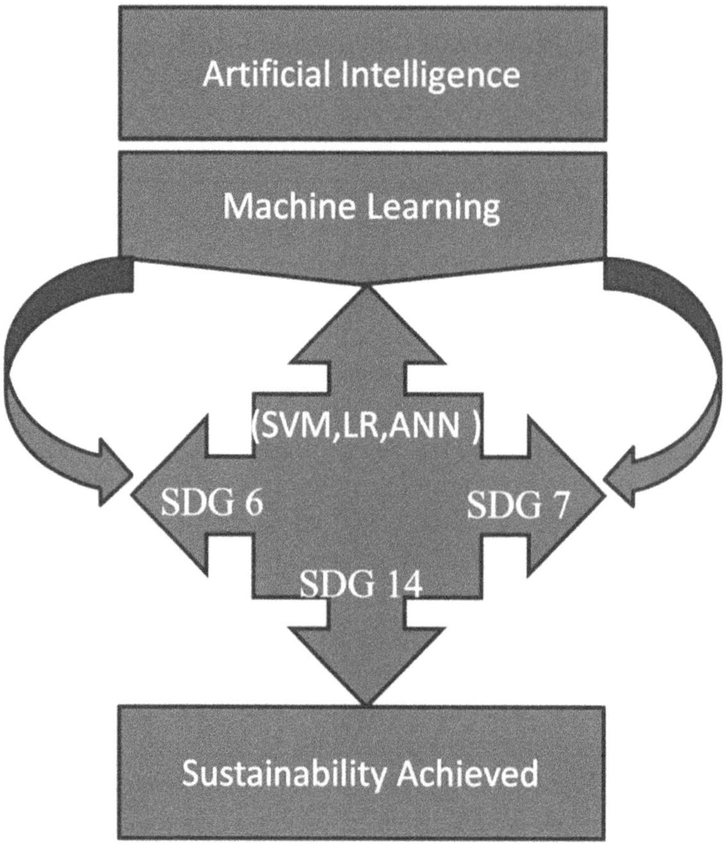

2. SDG 6: CLEAN WATER AND SANITATION: LITERATURE REVIEW

One of the most important goals of the 17 Sustainable Development Goals (SDGs) is clean water and sanitation for all, aiming to ensure everyone has access to safe & clean water with proper sanitation (Tortajada and Biswas, 2018). There are 8 targets with 11 indicators associated with SDG 6 to be achieved by 2030 (Werkneh and Gebru, 2022; Garcia et al., 2023). Demand for clean and safe water is increasing daily due to urbanization, population, agricultural needs, and industrial and energy sectors. The need for more fresh & clean water and proper sanitation is due to insufficient management and exploitation of groundwater. Advancements in technology and awareness of society would be better ways to provide universal access to clean water, sanitation, and hygiene water by 2030 (Sherif et al., 2023). Achieving these goals would save around one million yearly deaths from diseases directly linked to contaminated water, inadequate sanitation, and poor hygiene habits.

The facts and figures regarding SDG 6 show that billions of people still need access to fresh & clean water, proper sanitation, and good hygiene. Less than one percent of total water is available as fresh water. Advancement in technologies and awareness would need to be six times for drinking water, quadruple for sanitation, and three times for hygiene to provide universal access to clean water, sanitation, and hygiene water by 2030 (Dilekli et al., 2019; Tortajada, 2020; Braig, 2018). Many regions worldwide continue to be concerned about water stress and scarcity. Around 2.5 billion people need a proper water resource system (Sherif et al., 2023; Garcia et al., 2023).

By 2030, SDG 6 aims to accomplish the following (figure 1): For everyone to have affordable, equal access to clean, safe water, to achieve equitable access to sanitation and hygiene at low cost for all, to improve water quality by low pollution, stop dumping, and avoid dangerous chemicals, to significantly boost water consumption efficiency in all industries, to adopt integrated water resources management, to safeguard and revive ecosystems associated to water (Danso and Otoo, 2022, Germann and Langergraber 2022).

The two strategies have been adopted for achieving these goals. One is to increase international association and capacity-building assistance for underprivileged nations in projects and activities connected to water and sanitation, and another is to encourage and boost community involvement to enhance water and sanitation management locally.

Figure 2. Main aims of SDG 6 by 2030

2.1 Application of AI/ML to Achieve SDG 6: Clean Water and Sanitation

Many ML techniques have been utilized and reported in the literature for various tasks in various applied fields, i.e., agriculture, energy, natural disasters, health, and climate change. In reality, they are considering their capacity to analyze vast volumes of data and their unique qualities regarding categorization, modeling, and forecasting, the bulk of algorithms utilized to analyze earth observation data using ML. The work of researchers in the water and wastewater sector may benefit from using ICT and ML to achieve SDG 6. The ability to identify and comprehend sudden abnormal and steady changes in water's three main properties (physical, chemical, and biological) depends on continuous real-time measurements produced by sensors. These alterations in water quality are the result of numerous factors. These include the quantity of insecticides, herbicides, pesticides, metals, and other toxins contaminants as determined by sensors (Kaddoura, 2022; Solanki, et al., 2015; Hmoud, and Waselallah, 2021).

The classic techniques that have received attention in water quality management (WQM) and irregularity detection include SVM, LR, and ANN using ML. In addition to these conventional ML methods, statistical techniques are also trusted for irregularly identifying water quality data (Goralski, and Tan, 2020; Dogo, et al., 2019; Ferreira, et al., 2020). In this field of research, multivariate methods, i.e., principal component and linear discriminate study, have also been used. The theoretical foundation of these conventional ML techniques has yet to be explored because of space restrictions; however, readers are referred to for more information. Most of these traditional ML techniques have faced shortcomings due to their substantial computational memory and time requirements, unbalanced ratios of anomalous to regular data, and processing noise for sensor signals. As a result, they have a high incidence of false alarms, need help handling large real-time datasets with robustness, have poor precision, and neglect to take missing data from various sensory sources that differ from one another in high-dimensional data search spaces. As a result, in recent times, deep learning (DL) model designs have also begun to be considered. As a result, it becomes vital to research additional cutting-edge anomaly detection approaches to enhance performance and fix these ML systems' flaws. Early Learning Matters (ELM) is a familiar ML strategy but has benefited from a significant research community (Goralski and Tan, 2020; Bhardwaj et al., 2022; Jamwal et al., 2019).

Sanaa Kaddoura 2022 investigated the efficiency of ML in predicting the quality of water. Data sets are divided into smaller groups for training and testing. The results are compared in terms of various parameters, i.e., precision, F1 score, recall, and ROC curve, after applying several currently accessible ML methods. The outcomes showed that SVM and k-nearest neighbor were superior based on F1-score and ROC AUC values. However, based on recall values, LASSO LARS and stochastic gradient descent were excellent. Solanki et al. 2015 investigated the efficiency of DL techniques in predicting water quality. Data with variance can be expected relatively accurately using unsupervised learning. Compared to the other two metrics, turbidity has a high degree of volatility but is now low. pH is stable and has less affected variance compared to turbidity and DO. Additionally, DO varies slightly in the summer since the heat alters the water's quality.

Gu et al. (2023) investigated the role of ML in improving comprehension of problems with water accessibility in colonies underserved communities along the northern border between the US and Mexico. More than 2000 communities were examined, and adaptive affinity propagation in conjunction with the hierarchical clustering method was used to divide colonies automatically into clusters with varying water access conditions. The findings indicated a severe disparity in water availability in Colonias neighborhoods. It has yet to receive much attention to statistically evaluate and rate the advancement of historical water inequity issues. Decades of data collection have been conducted about the colonies for drinking, treatment, sanitation, and water quality.

Dogo et al. 2018 have reviewed the role of three main techniques, SVM, LR, and ANN, on water quality anomaly detection. It has been discovered that DL approaches outperform traditional ML techniques in terms of feature learning accuracy and a reduction in false favorable rates. However, because various parameters, models, and datasets were used throughout the studies, it is challenging to compare them fairly. Despite developments and benefits, this field has yet to embrace extreme learning machines fully. A hybrid DL-ELM framework is also suggested in this study as a possible solution that may be investigated further and applied to find discrepancies in data on water quality. Hmoud and Waselallah, 2021 have analyzed WQI using the ANFIS (Adaptive Neuro Fuzzy Inference System) method. WQ, FFNN (Feed Forward Neural Network), and K-nearest neighbors were used to categorize. Despite the dataset having eight crucial factors, only seven were found to have meaningful values. The methodology presented was constructed using these statistical criteria. Prediction results showed that the ANFIS model performed better at predicting WQI values.

Nevertheless, for the categorization of water quality (WQC), the FFNN algorithm had 100% accuracy. Additionally, the FFNN model demonstrated higher resilience in classifying the WQC, whereas the ANFIS model correctly predicted WQI. The most accurate model (100%) for WQC was the FFNN model. ANFIS model demonstrated accuracy throughout the testing phase with an R2 of 96.17% for predicting WQI. Turbidity of the water has been predicted and assessed using several metrics by Bhardwaj et al. 2022. Random Forest classifier was determined to have the highest performance in classification among ML algorithms, while naive Bayes and passive-aggressive classifiers perform the poorest. Results showed that Random Forest produced solid outcomes and attained precision even naive Bayes gave the lowest accuracy of just 49%, which naive Bayes showed at the significance level of 88% with an XGBoost of 0.85. The online portal interface allows staff employees to access the processed data.

By considering the intricate interconnections between variables associated with water, ML can forecast a variety of water quality indices in situ and in real-time. With tested guidelines or universal procedures distilled from relevant research, ML methods can also address new pollution issues. Additionally, by utilizing image recognition technology to examine the relationships between visual data and the physicochemical characteristics of the research object, machine learning (ML) may precisely detect and characterize specific contaminants. Moreover, ML can assist with characterization analysis, modeling treatment methods, purifying drinking water, contaminant tracing, mapping groundwater contaminants, collecting and treating sewage water, and evaluating pollutant toxicity in natural water systems (Jamwal et al., 2019). According to their structures and mechanisms, the benefits and drawbacks of popular algorithms can be examined, and suggestions can be made regarding the choice of ML algorithms for various studies as well as future directions for the use and advancement of ML in clean water and sanitation.

2.2 Limitation of Existing Approaches in Achieving SDG 6: Clean Water and Sanitation

Improper infrastructure is the main limitation of existing approaches. Insufficient funding, poor planning, and lack of technological resources contribute to inadequate water supply and sanitation system development. Also, Access to clean water and sanitation services is often unevenly distributed within countries and communities. Climate change is another important factor causing a significant challenge to water resources and sanitation infrastructure. For instance, Increased frequency and intensity of extreme weather events, such as floods and droughts, can damage water supply systems and contaminate water sources, making it difficult to ensure a consistent and safe water supply. Exponential population growth and urbanization stress existing water and sanitation infrastructure. As more people migrate to urban areas, the demand for water and sanitation services increases, often overwhelming existing systems and leading to inadequate coverage. Industrial discharges, agricultural runoff, and improper waste disposal contribute to water pollution, affecting the quality of available water sources. Sometimes, infrastructure is implemented without consideration for long-term maintenance and sustainability. Water and sanitation systems can deteriorate without proper upkeep, leading to service interruptions and declining water quality. Successful implementation of water and sanitation projects requires collaboration among various stakeholders, including government agencies, non-governmental organizations (NGOs), local communities, and the private sector.

In some cases, more coordination and engagement among these stakeholders will be needed to ensure progress. Adequate funding is also required for implementing and sustaining water and sanitation projects. In many cases, more financial resources must be required, making it challenging to invest in the necessary infrastructure and programs needed to achieve SDG 6.

3. SDG 7: AFFORDABLE AND CLEAN ENERGY: LITERATURE REVIEW

In SDG 7, the UN defined five targets and six indicators, where targets specify the goals and indicators represent the metrics to keep track of the targets' achievements. Due to the exponential increase in global population between 1990 and 2010, the electricity demand has increased to 1.7 billion; they need cheap energy for consumption. On the other hand, the increase in the emission of greenhouse gases is creating changes in the climate pattern. Therefore, global climate change is noticed. Thus, an alternate source of energy has to be explored. In 2011, renewable energy generated only 20% of worldwide power, and by 2030, affordable electricity will be transmitted through clean energy sources such as solar, wind, hydro, etc. Sustainable energy is one such goal in which the following indicators need to be achieved to provide affordable, cheap, and modern energy, as defined in Figure 2. The goals aim to bring affordable, sustainable, and modern energy to the global population, with sustainable energy being the critical feature that improves quality and reliability.

Figure 3. Sustainable Energy Indicators

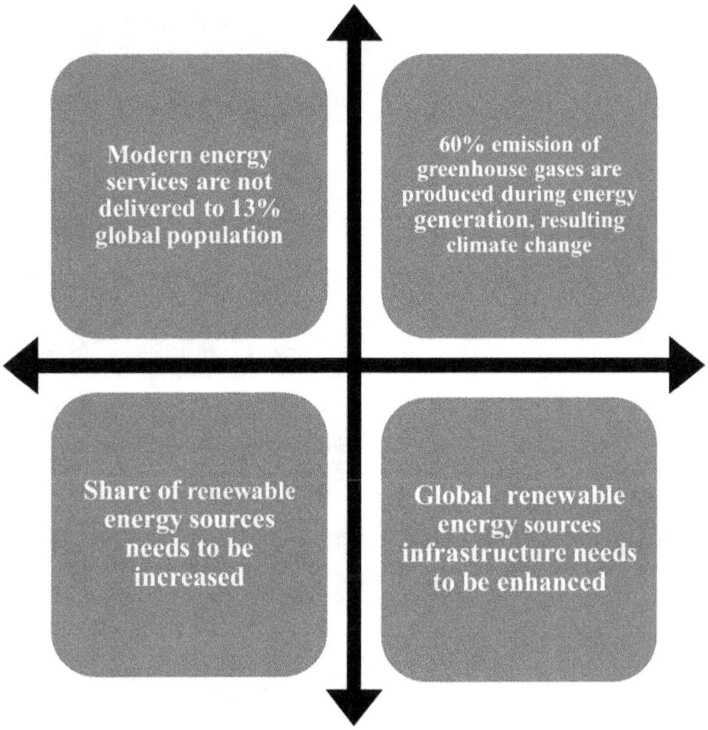

Energy is needed for cooking, heating, cooling, lighting, transportation, digital connectivity, operations of gadgets, including health, and many other odd jobs that are performed with the help of energy. Sustainable energy reduces pollution of any form and therefore supports health. It tackles significant challenges, opens opportunities to transform life and economies, and saves the planet.

3.1 Application of AI/ML to Achieve SDG 7: Affordable and Clean Energy

AI is deployed to achieve sustainable energy with applications in areas such as power grid synchronization, seismic surveying, energy infrastructure monitoring, identification of suitable sites for production, and solar and wind energy production forecasting. AI has become essential in developing and monitoring affordable, clean energy solutions and meeting SDG goal 7 with sustainability. The involvement of AI in developing energy infrastructure helps reduce costs, improve efficiency, and optimize energy usage patterns to produce clean energy. Some of the critical indicators are given in Figure 3

Figure 4. Key indicators of AI in the generation and distribution of RE sources

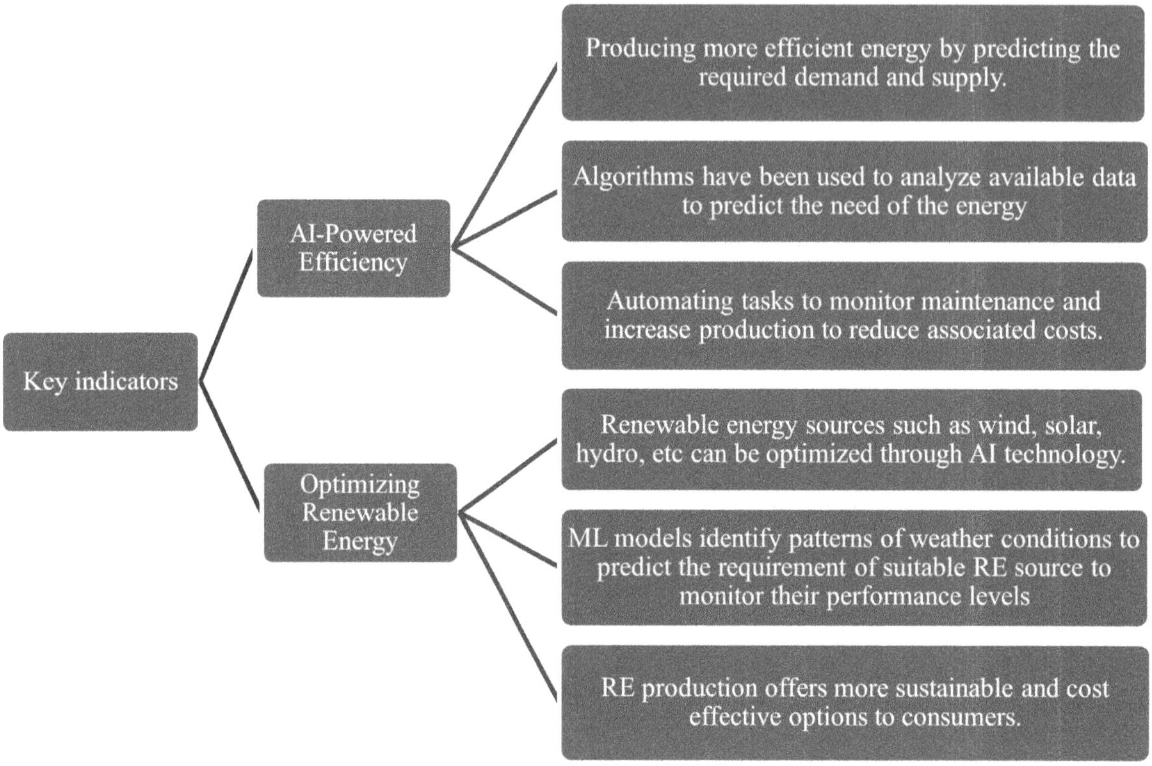

AI has the potential to reduce costs, improve efficiency, and make sustainable energy sources more affordable and accessible to all. The main objective of UN SDG 7 is to provide access to modern electricity to underdeveloped countries using more renewable energy sources. These goals not only benefit people across the globe but also improve global social, economic, and environmental issues. Technology is essential in setting up infrastructure, monitoring progress, and predicting the required actions to meet this objective. To promote businesses, a well-established energy sector supports significant sectors such as medicine, education, agriculture, innovative infrastructure, communication, etc. The energy sector protects ecosystems and fulfills the energy needs of other sectors effectively with the help of innovative technologies such as AI. AI can perform the tasks of perception, prediction, decision making, automation, pattern discovery, etc., based on the given information and acts as an interface between the other technologies. AI models have been deployed to develop intelligent traffic systems, cooling systems for data warehouses, building climate models for better forecasting, etc., that indirectly reduce carbon emissions on the planet. AI technology makes the system transparent and consistent to protect the environment. Many countries worldwide plan to switch 100% to renewable energy sources by 2050. AI models train raw systems, digital and intelligent, and prepare them for the specific tasks in operations. AI technology provides handheld solutions for guiding agencies in achieving goals. AI-based solutions rely on the quantities of data to propose impacts and the number of challenges faced and overcome during the achievement period. From the research, it is revealed that AI technology could decrease global greenhouse gas emissions by 4% in 2030 and generate 38.2 million new jobs globally. AI technology promotes using renewable energy sources and makes them more affordable. By AI models, intelligent power grids can work simultaneously with multiple renewable energy sources. AI technology delivers modern energy infrastructure enabled with IoT devices and cameras that help remotely monitor the working of energy machinery such as solar panels and wind turbines without human intervention.

Energy concerns are directly related to global warming and environmental challenges such as air pollution, acid precipitation, forest destruction, wildlife loss, greenhouse gases, etc. Conventional energy source plants must be used within permissible limits and transformed into RE sources as soon as possible (Salim et al., 2018; Ediger, 2019).

Looking to target 7.1, RE is a cheap, clean energy affordable to all. Using AI, intelligent grids can distribute energy to consumers (Hannan, 2021). Globally, the share of producing RE is increasing many folds. RE global energy mix has jumped from 8.6% to 28% between the years 2010 to 2020, which is projected to be 45% by 2040 (Hannan, 2021). More than 30 countries generate 10 GW of RE power globally (Global Status Report, 2021). These are the positive impacts towards achieving target 7.2. The large-scale installation of wind turbines and solar panels near the seashore, desert land, and barren lands positively impacts achieving target 7 b. The RE infrastructure across the globe is developing in a big way with the support of governments. Overall, the target of giving clean, affordable, and cheap energy to the global population with modern infrastructure is under consideration, and the work in this direction is progressing day by day to achieve SDG 7 (Hannan, 2021). All five targets of SDG 7 have been met, and the indicators show positive trends towards achieving targets(100%) without any negative impact (Hannan, 2021). The intervention of AI technology will contribute a lot to the achievements of all five targets(100%) because of its inbuilt strength of improving the operation and efficiency towards the development of intelligent RE infrastructure to reduce energy costs and carbon footprints (Ivanovski et al., 2021). Also, carbon emissions in the power sector will be reduced to 70% by 2050 (Khanna et al., 2016). AI-powered digital and intelligent energy systems monitor demand and supply patterns and propose optimal solutions for the production and distribution of energy (Yang et al., 2019). In this way, intelligent scheduling of energy production and distribution based on weather conditions gives an uninterrupted energy supply at a lesser price (Jones, 2018). Moreover, the penetration of AI technologies supports using intelligent grids, making the infrastructure reliable (Ramchurn et al., 2012).

The role of AI in the utilization of RE as an emerging technology improves the operations and efficiency of the energy generation and distribution systems, which not only minimizes the overall cost of energy operations, generation, and distribution but also minimizes hazards impacts on the environment (Jha et al., 2017; Srivastava, 2020; Hannan et al., 2020b). AI-enabled technologies such as smart grids, smart meters, and IoT devices have been used in power sector infrastructure to boost efficiency and transparency in energy management (Nizetic et al., 2020), a step ahead towards achieving many targets of SDG 7 (100%). Moreover, AI-powered technologies monitor and maintain RE systems such as robust control, high level of power quality, better energy delivery, power generation forecasting, optimal power generation, and many other applications (Antonopoulos et al., 2020; Al-Shetwi et al., 2020; Ahmad et al., 2021). AI proposed accurate strategies to simulate, control, and optimize RE systems and make them a reliable energy source.

Based on the literature review, AI is an enabler in achieving the targets of SDG 7 as 100% by providing support to energy services to the global population. Also, AI supports low carbon emission systems that help society and economies achieve SDG 7 through the effective use of resources (International Energy Agency 2017; Fuso 2019). By 2030, the demand for ICTs could require up to 20% of the global electricity demand against about 1% of today (Jones 2018). Therefore, green ICT technology is essential to lower the electricity load (Ahmad, 2019).

Also, efficient cooling systems for data warehouses using RE sources have been developed to reduce the carbon footprints on the planet. AI models have made RE-based data centers more efficient and cost-effective. Thus, AI technology could be the catalyst for achieving SDG targets. Every nation must invest in AI safety research to keep the systems present from malfunctioning or getting hacked (Russell, 2015).

SDG 7 targets have been achieved 100%, but based on the published data, some limitations and negative impacts towards sustainability have been noticed (Hannan, 2021). Presently, 13% of the global population has no access to modern energy, and a significant chunk of the population lives in rural areas (Rehman 2019; The World Bank, 2019). AI affects social, economic, and environmental sectors with positive productivity outcomes (Acemoglu, 2018; Bolukbasi, 2016; Norouzzadeh, 2018). AI has both positive and negative impacts on sustainable development. However, published information assessing the influence level on various aspects of sustainable development has yet to be received (Jean, 2016; Courtland, 2018). The critical limitation of AI technology is that it is based on the need and the values. Suppose it is implemented in nations lacking transparency, ethical scrutiny, and democracy. In that case, it provides biased results, including damaging democratic principles, exacerbating inequality, human rights, social cohesion, etc., which makes evident that in some cases, rather than as an enabler, it acts as an inhibitor (Helbing 2015, 2019).

3.2 Limitation of Existing Approaches in Achieving SDG 7: Affordable and Clean Energy

The existing approaches often need help to reach remote or impoverished areas due to logistical challenges, lack of infrastructure, and financial constraints. Also, the initial costs of implementing clean energy technologies, such as solar panels or wind turbines, can be prohibitively high. This poses a significant challenge in adopting and scaling renewable energy solutions, especially for low-income communities and countries. Some renewable energy sources, such as solar and wind, are intermittent and depend on weather conditions. A reliable energy supply can help the widespread adoption of these sources, especially in regions where consistent power is crucial for economic activities and essential services. Storing energy from renewable sources during low generation remains a technological challenge. Practical and affordable energy storage solutions are necessary. Inadequate infrastructure for energy transmission and distribution can impede the delivery of electricity to remote areas. This lack of infrastructure hinders the expansion of energy access and contributes to energy inequality within and between countries. Inconsistent or inadequate policies and regulations can create barriers to deploying clean energy technologies. Despite efforts to transition to clean energy, many regions still heavily rely on fossil fuels for their energy needs. Economic and political interests and existing infrastructure often need help to phase out fossil fuel-based energy sources. Developing countries may require more technology transfer and capacity-building initiatives to avoid difficulties in acquiring and implementing clean energy technologies. Adequate financing is essential for the development and deployment of clean energy solutions. However, there is often a gap between the funds required for sustainable energy projects and the available financial resources.

4. SDG 14: LIFE BELOW WATER

Sustainable Development Goal 14 is about water conservation and its sustainable use of all water resources, seas, oceans, etc. The increasing population and, hence, the demand for resources affected the water resources. Today, the need of the hour is to take immediate action for the conservation of these resources and for saving marine life all around the world so that the life below water can be saved in all possible ways and turn, we, the living creatures, can enjoy a healthy lifestyle with these beneficial water resources. Hence, to conserve and sustainably use the seas, oceans, and marine resources for sustainable development, there are in all ten targets summarized below (Figure 5):

The first is to reduce marine pollution. Marine Pollution threatens the health of marine species and, thus, that of humans. It also plays a significant role in coastal tourism and climate change. Marine life is highly affected by Plastic pollution. Eighty percent of Marine pollution is a combination of various chemicals of factory wastes clubbed with trash from land sources. Near Coastal areas are highly polluted by nitrogen and phosphorus. These pollutants have hazardous effects on the human body, for instance, hormonal changes and reproductive issues, and under extreme situations, they can cause nervous system failure. The marine pollution can be reduced by properly disposing of plastic so it won't end up in oceans. Another way to reduce marine pollution is to make the Idols of God and Goddess with eco-friendly materials and limit the use of non-biodegradable substances.

The second target is the protection and restoration of ecosystems. To protect and restore the ecosystem, protecting fish breeding and reducing fish mortality rates is a must. Reducing ocean acidification is another important target as it negatively affects all marine species, resulting in declination of overall marine life. It is also a primary reason for global warming as it is deterring the oceans' ability to absorb carbon dioxide. Sustainable fishing is also essential. Protecting marine areas is necessary for safeguarding oceans' bio-diversity and natural resources. Marine and coastal areas are sites for scientific studies and crucial factors from a tourism point of view. A perfect match of nutrient pollution, exploitation, and climate change has been proven to play a vital role in an uncertain future for ocean and marine life, affecting life below water. Increasing the economic benefits from the sustainable use of marine resources is another crucial aspect. Implementation and enforcement of international sea law is one of the critical targets.

Figure 5. Main aims of SDG 14 by 2030

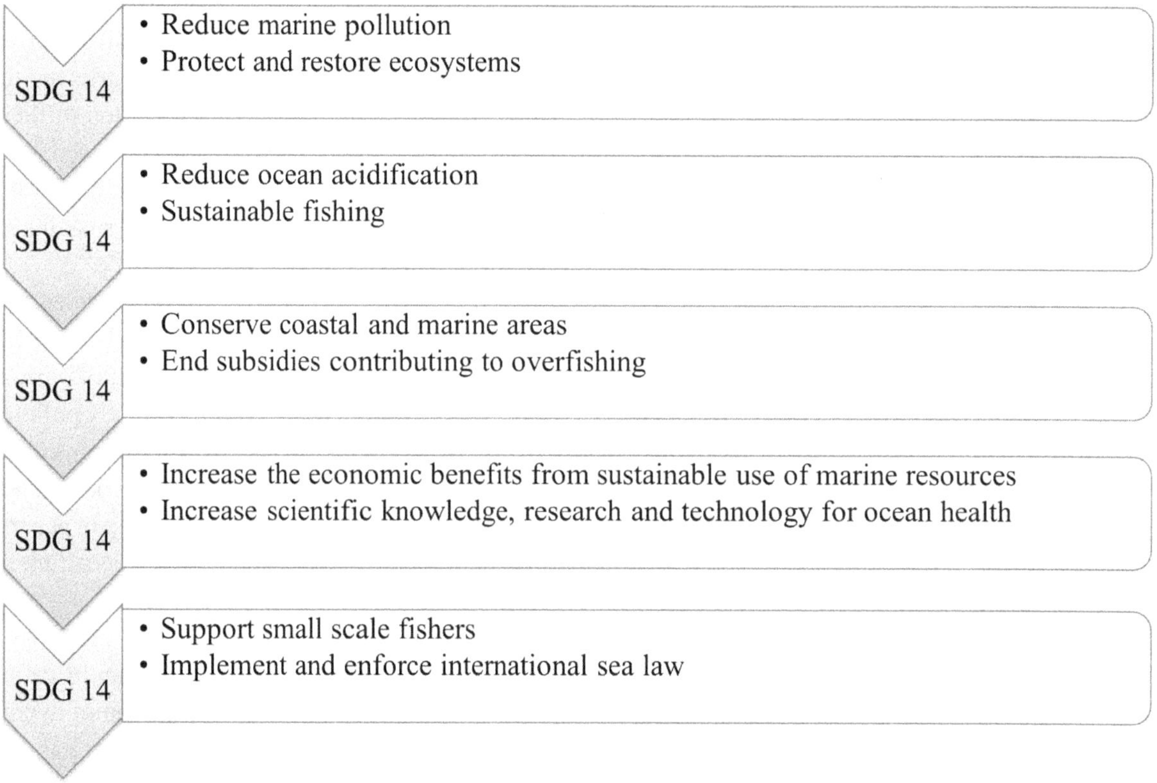

4.1 Application of AI/ML to Achieve SDG 14: Life Below Water

Achieving Sustainable Development Goal 14 (SDG 14), which focuses on conserving and sustainably using the oceans, seas, and marine resources, using machine learning presents several challenges. Some ocean regions are not extensively studied, and data is limited. Developing machine learning models is challenging as oceans are complex and dynamic systems. There are also some privacy issues related to the tracking of vessels. Despite these challenges, machine learning has the potential to significantly enhance our ability to monitor, manage, and protect marine ecosystems. Machine learning can aid marine species conservation by analyzing data from underwater cameras, drones, and acoustic sensors. It can help identify and track endangered species, assess their population health, and inform conservation strategies. ML can contribute to sustainable fisheries management by analyzing fish populations, fishing activities, and environmental factors. Predictive models can help optimize fishing practices, reduce bycatch, and prevent overfishing. Machine learning can enhance efforts to combat marine pollution by analyzing satellite imagery to detect and track oil spills, floating debris, and pollutants. Automated systems can help respond quickly to incidents. ML can improve the efficiency and sustainability of aquaculture by monitoring water quality, managing feed distribution, and predicting disease outbreaks. This can boost food security while minimizing environmental impacts. Ongoing technological advancements, such as improved sensors, autonomous underwater vehicles, and data transmission technologies, will continue to enhance the capabilities of machine learning in marine conservation (Fazri et al., 2023; Zhang et al., 20230; Agarwala 2021).

In conclusion, the future of machine learning in attaining SDG 14 is bright, with the potential to revolutionize our approach to marine conservation, sustainability, and responsible resource management. As technology continues to evolve and data availability improves, machine learning will become an indispensable tool for achieving the objectives of SDG 14 and safeguarding the world's oceans and marine life.

4.2 Limitation of Existing Approaches in Achieving SDG 14: Life Below Water

Specific fishing methods, such as bottom trawling and blast fishing, cause substantial damage to marine habitats and non-target species. These destructive practices lead to biodiversity loss, harm critical habitats like coral reefs, and negatively impact the overall health of marine ecosystems. Pollution from land-based sources, including plastic waste, agricultural runoff, and industrial discharges, severely threatens marine ecosystems. The accumulation of marine debris, particularly plastics, harms marine life, disrupts food chains, and damages habitats. Also, Rising sea temperatures, ocean acidification, and sea-level rise, driven by climate change, profoundly affect marine ecosystems. Establishing and effectively managing Marine Protected Areas is crucial for conserving marine biodiversity and allowing ecosystems to recover. However, there are challenges in creating and enforcing MPAs, including insufficient resources, competing interests, and a need for global cooperation. Weak monitoring and enforcement of existing regulations contribute to illegal, unreported, and unregulated (IUU) fishing activities. Coastal areas are particularly vulnerable to human activities, including urban development, agriculture, and aquaculture. Inadequate planning and poor management of coastal zones can lead to habitat degradation, loss of biodiversity, and increased vulnerability to natural disasters. Many countries, particularly those with limited resources, need help implementing and enforcing sustainable practices. More capacity in terms of human resources and technology hinders effective management of marine resources. The interconnected nature of oceans requires coordinated global efforts. However, there are governance gaps, inadequate international collaboration, and challenges in reaching a consensus on high-seas governance, biodiversity beyond national jurisdiction, and equitable sharing of marine resources.

5. CHALLENGES AND FUTURE SCOPE

It has been observed that the application of AI technologies to the achievement of SGDs is mainly concerned with the development of ML and data mining techniques for prediction and relying on the sources of the data in use. It is clear that by utilizing ML models and predictive analytics, more efficient systems with more optimized use of renewable energy sources have been proposed. AI-powered systems produce cleaner and cheaper energy for consumers. Although many researchers suggest ML can support various SDG targets and indicators, a substantial portion of these studies have been conducted in controlled laboratory settings, based on small datasets, or employing prototypes. It is frequently challenging to extrapolate this data to evaluate the impact in the real world. This is especially valid when assessing the influence of ML at larger spatial and temporal scales. We acknowledge that using controlled experimental trials to determine the real-world effects of machine learning can lead to the portrayal of a single point in time where the ML tools are suited to that particular environment. But as society evolves, so do the standards for machine learning, creating a feedback loop involving interactions between society and ML. The adaptability of society to ML-enabled changes is another point that needs to be more attention in existing research. Therefore, novel techniques are required to ensure that, before launching large-scale ML deployments, the impact of new technologies is reviewed from the points of view of efficiency, ethics, and sustainability. Considering the high risk involved with such a failure, research focused on gaining insight into the causes of ML system failure, bringing combined human-machine analytic tools, is crucial to account for ML technology.

REFERENCES

Acemoglu, D., & Restrepo, P. (2018). *Artificial Intelligence, Automation, and Work*. NBER Working Paper No. 24196. National Bereau of Economic Research.

Ahmad, T., Zhang, D., Huang, C., Zhang, H., Dai, N., Song, Y., & Chen, H. (2021). Artificial intelligence in sustainable energy industry: Status quo, challenges and opportunities. *Journal of Cleaner Production*, *289*, 125834. doi:10.1016/j.jclepro.2021.125834

Al-Shetwi, A. Q., Hannan, M., Jern, K. P., Alkahtani, A. A., & Abas, A. P. G. (2020a). Power quality assessment of grid-connected PV system in compliance with the recent integration requirements. *Electronics (Basel)*, *9*(2), 366. doi:10.3390/electronics9020366

Antonopoulos, I., Robu, V., Couraud, B., Kirli, D., Norbu, S., Kiprakis, A., Flynn, D., Elizondo-Gonzalez, S., & Wattam, S. (2020). Artificial intelligence and machine learning approaches to energy demand-side response: A systematic review. *Renewable & Sustainable Energy Reviews*, *130*, 109899. doi:10.1016/j.rser.2020.109899

Bhardwaj, A., Dagar, V., Khan, M. O., Aggarwal, A., Alvarado, R., Kumar, M., Irfan, M., & Proshad, R. (2022). Smart IoT and machine learning-based framework for water quality assessment and device component monitoring. *Environmental Science and Pollution Research International*, *29*(30), 46018–46036. doi:10.1007/s11356-022-19014-3 PMID:35165843

Bolukbasi, T., Chang, K.-W., Zou, J., Saligrama, V., & Kalai, A. (2016). Man is to computer programmer as woman is to homemaker? Debiasing word embeddings. *Advances in Neural Information Processing Systems*, *29*, 4349–4357.

Braig, K. F. (2018). The European Court of Human Rights and the right to clean water and sanitation. *Water Policy*, *20*(2), 282–307. doi:10.2166/wp.2018.045

Courtland, R. (2018). Bias detectives: The researchers striving to make algorithms fair. *Nature*, *558*(7710), 357–360. doi:10.1038/d41586-018-05469-3 PMID:29925973

Danso, G., & Otoo, M. (2022). Readiness of South Asian Countries to Achieve SDG 6 Targets by 2030 in the Sanitation Sector. In *Safe Water and Sanitation for a Healthier World: A Global View of Progress Towards SDG 6* (pp. 133–148). Springer International Publishing. doi:10.1007/978-3-030-94020-1_8

Dilekli, N., & Cazcarro, I. (2019). Testing the SDG targets on water and sanitation using the world trade model with a waste, wastewater, and recycling framework. *Ecological Economics*, *165*, 106376. doi:10.1016/j.ecolecon.2019.106376

Dogo, E. M., Nwulu, N. I., Twala, B., & Aigbavboa, C. (2019). A survey of machine learning methods applied to anomaly detection on drinking-water quality data. *Urban Water Journal*, *16*(3), 235–248. doi:10.1080/1573062X.2019.1637002

Fazri, M. F., Kusuma, L. B., Rahmawan, R. B., Fauji, H. N., & Camille, C. (2023). Implementing Artificial Intelligence to Reduce Marine Ecosystem Pollution. *IAIC Transactions on Sustainable Digital Innovation*, *4*(2), 101–108. doi:10.34306/itsdi.v4i2.579

Ferreira, B., Iten, M., & Silva, R. G. (2020). Monitoring sustainable development by means of earth observation data and machine learning: A review. *Environmental Sciences Europe*, *32*(1), 1–17. doi:10.1186/s12302-020-00397-4

Fuso Nerini, F., Slob, A., Engström, R. E., & Trutnevyte, E. (2019). A research and innovation agenda for zero-emission European cities. *Sustainability (Basel)*, *11*(6), 1692. doi:10.3390/su11061692

Garcia, C., López-Jiménez, P. A., Sánchez-Romero, F. J., & Pérez-Sánchez, M. (2023). Assessing water urban systems to the compliance of SDGs through sustainability indicators. Implementation in the valencian community. *Sustainable Cities and Society*, *96*, 104704. doi:10.1016/j.scs.2023.104704

Germann, V., & Langergraber, G. (2022). Going beyond global indicators—Policy relevant indicators for SDG 6 targets in the context of Austria. *Sustainability (Basel)*, *14*(3), 1647. doi:10.3390/su14031647

Global Status Report. (2021). *Renewables 2021 Global Status Report-REN21*. Author.

Goralski, M. A., & Tan, T. K. (2020). Artificial intelligence and sustainable development. *International Journal of Management Education*, *18*(1), 100330. doi:10.1016/j.ijme.2019.100330

Gu, Z., Li, W., Hanemann, M., Tsai, Y., Wutich, A., Westerhoff, P., Landes, L., Roque, A. D., Zheng, M., Velasco, C. A., & Porter, S. (2023). Applying machine learning to understand water security and water access inequality in underserved colonia communities. *Computers, Environment and Urban Systems*, *102*, 101969. doi:10.1016/j.compenvurbsys.2023.101969

Hannan, M., Ali, J. A., Lipu, M. H., Mohamed, A., Ker, P. J., & Mahlia, T. I. (2020). Role of optimization algorithms based fuzzy controller in achieving induction motor performance enhancement. *Nature Communications*, *11*(1), 1–11. doi:10.1038/s41467-020-17623-5 PMID:32733048

Helbing, D. (2019). *Towards Digital Enlightenment*. Springer International Publishing. doi:10.1007/978-3-319-90869-4

Helbing, D., & Pournaras, E. (2015). Society: Build digital democracy. *Nature*, *527*(7576), 33–34. doi:10.1038/527033a PMID:26536943

Hmoud Al-Adhaileh, M., & Waselallah Alsaade, F. (2021). Modelling and prediction of water quality by using artificial intelligence. *Sustainability (Basel)*, *13*(8), 4259. doi:10.3390/su13084259

International Energy Agency. (2017). *Digitalization & Energy*. International Energy Agency.

Ivanovski, K., Hailemariam, A., & Smyth, R. (2021). The effect of renewable and non-renewable energy consumption on economic growth: Non-parametric evidence. *Journal of Cleaner Production*, *286*, 124956. doi:10.1016/j.jclepro.2020.124956

Jamwal, P., Brown, R., Kookana, R., Drechsel, P., McDonald, R., Vorosmarty, C. J., van Vliet, M. T., & Bhaduri, A. (2019). *The future of urban clean water and sanitation.* Open Access.

Jean, N., Burke, M., Xie, M., Davis, W. M., Lobell, D. B., & Ermon, S. (2016). Combining satellite imagery and machine learning to predict poverty. *Science*, *353*(6301), 790–794. doi:10.1126/science.aaf7894 PMID:27540167

Jha, S. K., Bilalovic, J., Jha, A., Patel, N., & Zhang, H. (2017). Renewable energy: Present research and future scope of Artificial Intelligence. *Renewable & Sustainable Energy Reviews*, *77*, 297–317. doi:10.1016/j.rser.2017.04.018

Jones, N. (2018). How to stop data centres from gobbling up the world's electricity. *Nature*, *561*(7722), 163–166. doi:10.1038/d41586-018-06610-y PMID:30209383

Kaddoura, S. (2022). Evaluation of Machine Learning Algorithm on Drinking Water Quality for Better Sustainability. *Sustainability (Basel)*, *14*(18), 11478. doi:10.3390/su141811478

Karnama, A., Haghighi, E. B., & Vinuesa, R. (2019). Organic data centers: A sustainable solution for computing facilities. *Results in Engineering*, *4*, 100063. doi:10.1016/j.rineng.2019.100063

Khanna, N. Z., Zhou, N., Fridley, D., & Ke, J. (2016). Quantifying the potential impacts of China's power-sector policies on coal input and CO2 emissions through 2050: A bottom-up perspective. *Utilities Policy*, *41*, 128–138. doi:10.1016/j.jup.2016.07.001

Nižetić, S., Šolić, P., González-de, D. L.-I., & Patrono, L. (2020). Internet of things (IoT): Opportunities, issues and challenges towards a smart and sustainable future. *Journal of Cleaner Production*, *274*, 122877. doi:10.1016/j.jclepro.2020.122877 PMID:32834567

Norouzzadeh, M. S., Nguyen, A., Kosmala, M., Swanson, A., Palmer, M. S., Packer, C., & Clune, J. (2018). Automatically identifying, counting, and describing wild animals in camera-trap images with deep learning. *Proceedings of the National Academy of Sciences of the United States of America*, *115*(25), E5716–E5725. doi:10.1073/pnas.1719367115 PMID:29871948

Ramchurn, S. D., Vytelingum, P., Rogers, A., & Jennings, N. R. (2012). Putting the 'smarts' into the smart grid: A grand challenge for artificial intelligence. *Communications of the ACM*, *55*, 86–97. doi:10.1145/2133806.2133825

Rehman, A. (2019). The nexus of electricity access, population growth, economic growth in Pakistan and projection through 2040. *Int. J. Energy Sect. Manag.*

Russell, S., Dewey, D., & Tegmark, M. (2015). Research priorities for robust and beneficial artificial intelligence. *AI Magazine*, *34*(4), 105–114. doi:10.1609/aimag.v36i4.2577

Salim, H. K., Padfield, R., Hansen, S. B., Mohamad, S. E., Yuzir, A., Syayuti, K., Tham, M. H., & Papargyropoulou, E. (2018). Global trends in environmental management system and ISO14001 research. *Journal of Cleaner Production*, *170*, 645–653. doi:10.1016/j.jclepro.2017.09.017

Seo, Y., Kim, S., Kisi, O., & Singh, V. P. (2015). Daily water level forecasting using wavelet decomposition and artificial intelligence techniques. *Journal of Hydrology (Amsterdam)*, *520*, 224–243. doi:10.1016/j.jhydrol.2014.11.050

Sherif, M., Abrar, M., Baig, F., & Kabeer, S. (2023). Gulf Cooperation Council countries' water and climate research to strengthen UN's SDGs 6 and 13. *Heliyon*, *9*(3), e14584. doi:10.1016/j.heliyon.2023.e14584 PMID:36967941

Solanki, A., Agrawal, H., & Khare, K. (2015). Predictive analysis of water quality parameters using deep learning. *International Journal of Computer Applications, 125*(9).

Srivastava, S. K. (2020.) Application of artificial intelligence in renewable energy. In *2020 International Conference on Computational Performance Evaluation (ComPE)*. IEEE.

The World Bank. (2019). *Access to electricity (% of population)*. Author.

Tiong, S. K., Indra Mahlia, T. M., & Muttaqi, K. M. (2021). Impact of renewable energy utilization and artificial intelligence in achieving sustainable development goals. *Energy Reports*, *7*, 5359–5373. doi:10.1016/j.egyr.2021.08.172

Tortajada, C. (2020). Contributions of recycled wastewater to clean water and sanitation Sustainable Development Goals. *NPJ Clean Water*, *3*(1), 22. doi:10.1038/s41545-020-0069-3

Tortajada, C., & Biswas, A. K. (2018). Achieving universal access to clean water and sanitation in an era of water scarcity: Strengthening contributions from academia. *Current Opinion in Environmental Sustainability*, *34*, 21–25. doi:10.1016/j.cosust.2018.08.001

UN General Assembly (UNGA). (2015). A/RES/70/1Transforming our world: The 2030 Agenda for Sustainable Development. *Resolut*, *25*, 1–35.

Vinuesa, R., Azizpour, H., Leite, I., Balaam, M., Dignum, V., Domisch, S., Felländer, A., Langhans, S. D., Tegmark, M., & Fuso Nerini, F. (2020). The role of artificial intelligence in achieving the Sustainable Development Goals. *Nature Communications*, *11*(233), 1–10. doi:10.1038/s41467-019-14108-y PMID:31932590

Werkneh, A. A., & Gebru, S. B. (2022). Development of ecological sanitation approaches for integrated recovery of biogas, nutrients and clean water from domestic wastewater. *Resources. Environmental Sustainability*, 100095.

Yang, T., Zhao, L., & Wang, C. (2019). Review on application of artificial intelligence in power system and integrated energy system. *Dianli Xitong Zidonghua*, *43*, 2–14.

Yeh, C., Meng, C., Wang, S., Driscoll, A., Rozi, E., Liu, P., Lee, J., Burke, M., Lobell, D. B., & Ermon, S. (2021). Sustainbench: Benchmarks for monitoring the sustainable development goals with machine learning. *arXiv preprint arXiv:2111.04724*

Zhang, C., Fu, X., & Wu, X. (2023). Statistical machine learning techniques of weather simulation for the fishery-solar hybrid systems. *Frontiers in Energy Research*, *10*, 1073976. doi:10.3389/fenrg.2022.1073976

Chapter 6
Role of Artificial Intelligence in Renewable Energy Management for Sustainable Development

Pankaj Yadav
https://orcid.org/0000-0001-9394-4585
Rajkiya Engineering College, Azamgarh, India

Brihaspati Singh
Rajkiya Engineering College, Azamgarh, India

Amit Bhaskar
https://orcid.org/0000-0002-6938-7114
Rajkiya Engineering College, Azamgarh, India

Sambhrant Srivastava
Rajkiya Engineering College, Azamgarh, India

Saurabh Kumar Singh
Rajkiya Engineering College, Azamgarh, India

ABSTRACT

The utilization of energy derived from renewable sources is experiencing a significant and rapid expansion. The rapid rate of technical advancement in contemporary times has rendered it economically feasible to exploit various renewable sources such as solar, wind, geothermal, and others for energy generation. The main focus of this chapter centers around the utilization of renewable energy sources in combination with artificial intelligence (AI) to build efficient strategies for attaining sustainable development. This research presents a detailed bibliometric analysis aimed at enhancing the comprehension of the progression of artificial intelligence within the context of renewable energy. The objective of this chapter is to improve the understanding of academics and scholars regarding the interconnectedness and interdependencies between renewable energy and sustainable development, with a specific focus on the integration of artificial intelligence (AI) technology.

DOI: 10.4018/979-8-3693-1062-5.ch006

Copyright © 2024, IGI Global. Copying or distributing in print or electronic forms without written permission of IGI Global is prohibited.

1. INTRODUCTION

The correlation between energy generation and consumption is essential in determining the extent of economic development within a given nation. The use and supply of energy are intricately linked to pressing global concerns, including but not limited to global warming and environmental challenges. These challenges encompass a wide range of issues such as air pollution, deforestation, ozone depletion, acid rain, greenhouse gas emissions, water and land use, loss of biodiversity, and the release of radioactive substances (Salim et al., 2018). In order to achieve a hopeful and more sustainable energy future, it is imperative for humanity to collectively confront the difficulties that arise in the realms of environmental, economic, and social repercussions. In order to address the negative impacts associated with traditional energy sources such as coal, oil, and natural gas, which are known to hinder sustainable development, there has been a global shift towards the utilization of clean energy resources, albeit with certain limitations. Renewable energy, such as hydroelectric power, geothermal energy, tidal energy, solar, and wind energy, is the sole viable and realistic alternative to traditional sources of energy (Ediger, 2019). The utilization of renewable energy sources has the potential to mitigate environmental, economic, and social concerns. These alternatives are recognized for their ability to facilitate the adoption of environmentally sustainable technologies, lower electricity expenses, generate employment opportunities, enhance public health, and foster community development, particularly in rural regions and developing nations. Moreover, they contribute to the reduction or elimination of hazardous emissions, including sulfur dioxide, carbon monoxide, and carbon dioxide (Kumar, 2020).

The utilization of renewable energy sources has the potential to enhance the diversity of the energy production industry, provide a sustainable and enduring energy supply, and mitigate both local and global emissions. It has the potential to offer economically attractive options for fulfilling specialized electricity service needs, particularly in developing countries and rural areas, while also presenting chances for local manufacturing. Artificial intelligence (AI) is extensively utilized across several aspects of renewable energy, including design, enhancement, evaluation, operation, distribution, and regulation. The primary objective of this study is to elucidate the artificial intelligence methodologies employed within the domain of renewable energy (Asif & Muneer, 2007). The increasing availability of computer resources, advanced tools, and improved data collection methods has led to the growing integration of artificial intelligence (AI) in several domains of renewable energy systems (REs). The current methodologies employed in the energy industry for design, control, and maintenance have demonstrated a tendency to yield relatively inaccurate results. Moreover, the utilization of artificial intelligence (AI) for the execution of these tasks has resulted in enhanced levels of accuracy and precision, positioning it as a leading technology in this domain. Artificial intelligence (AI) has emerged as a prominent field of study in recent decades due to its capacity to enhance the quality and productivity of automated systems (Bryson, 2019). By employing advanced training techniques and providing a comprehensive set of instructions, this system enables them to acquire knowledge, engage in logical thinking, and make decisions in a manner analogous to human cognition.

By early 2025, renewable energy sources are projected to surpass coal as the primary contributor to worldwide power generation, thereby becoming the greatest source in this domain. According to the forecast, there is an anticipated growth of 10 percentage points in their portion of the power mix throughout the projected period, resulting in a projected share of 38% by the year 2027. Renewable energy sources are projected to be the sole electrical generation sector experiencing growth, while coal, natural gas, nuclear, and oil generation are anticipated to witness diminishing shares. The global power generation from wind and solar photovoltaic (PV) sources is projected to experience a significant increase, surpassing a twofold growth during the next five years. This growth is anticipated to result in wind and solar PV collectively contributing to nearly 20% of the total global power output by the year 2027. The aforementioned variable technologies contribute to 80% of the projected growth in worldwide renewable generation throughout the forecast period. Consequently, there is a need to explore supplementary avenues for enhancing power system flexibility. However, the expansion of dispatchable renewable energy sources such as hydropower, bioenergy, geothermal, and concentrated solar power is still constrained, despite their crucial function in integrating wind and solar photovoltaic (PV) technologies into worldwide electrical grids (IEA (2022)).

Table 1. Share of Cumulative Power Capacity by Source of Generation, 2010-2027 (IEA, 2022)

Share of Cumulative Power Capacity by Technology, 2010-2027																		
	2010	2011	2012	2013	2014	2015	2016	2017	2018	2019	2020	2021	2022	2023	2024	2025	2026	2027
Solor Power	0.8	1.3	1.8	2.3	2.9	3.5	4.5	5.7	6.9	8.1	9.4	10.9	12.8	14.7	16.5	18.4	20.2	22.2
Wind Power	3.5	4.1	4.7	5.1	5.7	6.5	7	7.4	7.8	8.3	9.4	10.1	10.8	11.4	12.1	12.9	13.7	14.4
Hydrogen Power	19.8	19.5	19.3	19.4	19.2	18.9	18.6	18.2	17.9	17.5	16.9	16.6	16.2	15.7	15.2	14.9	14.5	14.1
Bioenergy	1.4	1.4	1.5	1.6	1.6	1.6	1.7	1.7	1.8	1.8	1.9	1.9	2	2	2	2	2	2
Coal	31.2	31.3	31.2	31	30.8	30.6	30.3	29.8	28.9	28.4	27.5	26.7	25.6	24.7	23.8	22.8	21.9	20.9
Natural Gas	26.7	26.4	26.3	26	25.8	25.2	24.6	24.4	24.3	24	23.3	22.6	22.1	21.4	20.8	20.2	19.7	19.1

Figure 1. Cumulative power generation share vs. year of analysis/prediction (IEA, 2022)

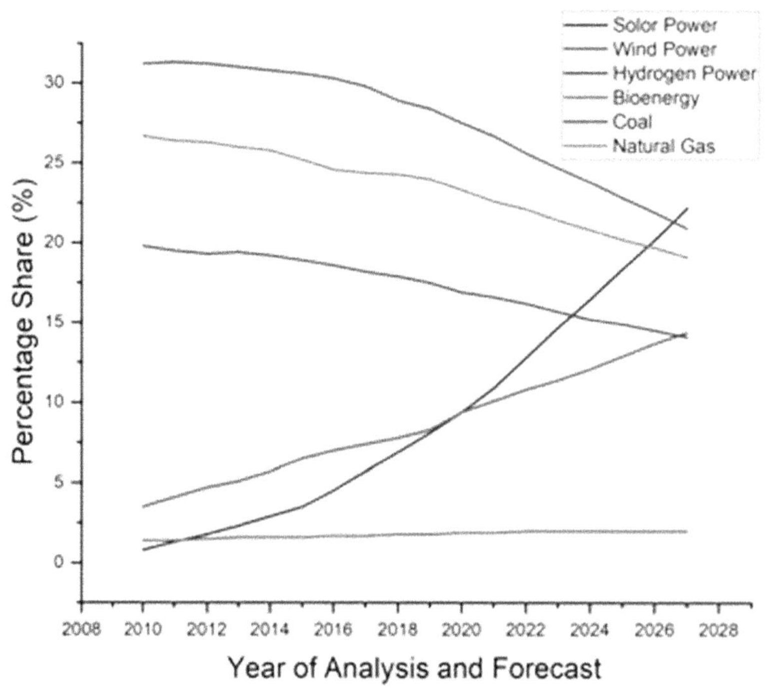

The application of artificial intelligence (AI) in the context of renewable energy and resources has intriguing characteristics, including autonomous learning capabilities, straightforward implementation, and efficient computation following the learning process, generalization abilities, and significant contributions to decision-making processes. One of the primary justifications for harnessing AI techniques more effectively is the ability to incorporate these features into modeling, control, and decision-making processes, in response to evolving needs.

2. ROLE OF AI IN RENEWABLE ENERGY UTILISATION

2.1 Solar Energy

Solar energy, harnessed from the sun's abundant and inexhaustible rays, stands as a cornerstone of sustainable development in the modern era. With its promise of clean, renewable power generation, solar energy holds the potential to mitigate climate change, reduce carbon emissions, and enhance energy security. Solar power can be harnessed through two primary methods: the physical conversion of sunlight into electricity using photovoltaic (PV) cells, or the indirect conversion through the concentration of solar energy to produce steam. This steam is then utilized to spin a turbine, which in turn generates electricity. The phenomenon known as the photovoltaic effect is employed to directly convert solar radiation into electrical energy by facilitating the movement of electrons to a higher energy level through the interaction with photons of light. Photovoltaics, initially employed for spacecraft propulsion, have found many applications in everyday life. These include powering grid-independent residences, water utilization pumps, electric mobility, wayside emergency phones, and remote sensing.

It is anticipated that China would experience a rise in its contribution to the expansion of global renewable capacity in the years 2023 and 2024, thereby solidifying its dominant position as the foremost worldwide participant in renewable energy deployment. In the year 2022, China was responsible for over 50% of the global increase in renewable energy generation capacity. According to projections, the country's proportion of global yearly renewable capacity deployment is expected to reach an unprecedented 55% by the year 2024. It is projected that China will be responsible for the implementation of over 50% of solar photovoltaic projects by the year 2024 (IEA, 2023).

Figure 2. Net solar PV electricity capacity additions by country or region, 2022-2024 (IEA, 2023)

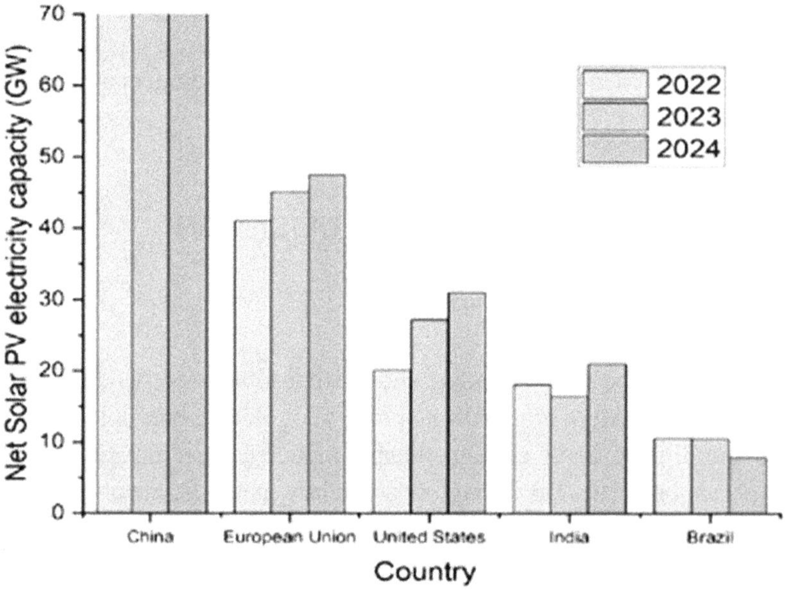

The integration of Artificial Intelligence (AI) into solar energy management has further elevated its efficiency and impact. AI-driven tools enable real-time tracking of solar irradiance, optimizing solar panel orientation for maximum energy capture, predicting energy generation patterns, and facilitating smart grid integration. These innovations not only enhance the feasibility and reliability of solar energy but also pave the way for a more sustainable energy landscape, aligning with the goals of a cleaner and greener future. Bose provides a complete elucidation of metaheuristic methodologies employed for maximum power point tracking in photovoltaic (PV) devices (Bose, 2017). The utilization of AI approaches in PV systems is discussed by (Mellit et al., 2009), a work that specifically focuses on the application of PV. The artificial intelligence method known as Artificial Neural Networks is employed in the field of solar energy to enhance the optimization of thermal load and prediction throughout the design phase. Artificial neural network techniques have proven to be beneficial in the prediction and optimization of several meteorological parameters such as meteorological forecast, temperature, solar radiation, relative humidity, atmospheric pressure, wind speed, precipitation, temperature range, and the length of the day.

2.2 Bioenergy

Bioenergy, derived from organic materials such as biomass and biofuels, presents a multifaceted solution in the pursuit of sustainable development and reduced carbon emissions. It encompasses a wide spectrum of sources, including agricultural residues, forestry waste, and dedicated energy crops. Bioenergy holds the potential to provide not only a reliable and renewable source of power but also a means to manage organic waste and contribute to circular economy practices. Bioenergy can be classified into two main categories: modern and traditional technologies. Contemporary bioenergy technology includes the utilization of liquid biofuels, which are derived from the bagasse plants (bio-refiners, biogas) that are formed during the anaerobic digestion of wastes. Traditional procedures involve the utilization of biomass, including animal waste, wood, and charcoal, through the process of burning.

In the context of contemporary energy challenges, Artificial Intelligence (AI) plays a pivotal role in optimizing the production, conversion, and utilization of bioenergy resources. Researchers developed an artificial neural network (ANN) application tool for the purpose of predicting the sugar yields of pretreated biomass during the hydrolysis process (Sarker et al., 2021). The utilisation of Raman spectroscopy technology can be employed to enhance the comprehension of the structural changes occurring in biomass throughout the processes of pyrolysis and combustion (Kumbhar et al., 2021). AI-driven systems aid in predictive modeling for efficient biomass yield, facilitate precision farming techniques, enhance biogas production from organic waste through process optimization, and support real-time monitoring of biofuel production processes. The synergy between AI and bioenergy underscores a path toward sustainable and diversified energy portfolios, enabling the realization of environmentally conscious energy solutions. A gasification model was constructed via a Fuzzy logic method. There was a significant increase of 75% in the conversion rate, and the gasification rate reached an impressive 85.51% at the optimal conditions (Nassef et al., 2020). Artificial intelligence (AI) is widely employed in the field of bioenergy to forecast several aspects such as biomass feedstock qualities, the thermochemical and biochemical conversion processes, and its application for end-users. The utilization of artificial intelligence (AI) plays a significant role in the prediction of biomass qualities, hence influencing both the overall quality of the final outcome and the operational feasibility of biomass conversion processes. Artificial intelligence (AI) is also utilized in the estimation of higher heating values through the examination of data obtained from final analysis. Proximate analysis data are commonly employed in forecasting the higher heating value due to its efficiency and cost-effectiveness in comparison to the final analysis.

2.3 Wind Energy

Wind energy, harnessed from the kinetic power of moving air masses, stands as a prominent emblem of the transition to clean and renewable energy sources. Wind power installations, ranging from towering onshore turbines to offshore wind farms, embody the potential to revolutionize electricity generation while mitigating the adverse effects of climate change. Wind energy is considered to be a renewable energy source due to its ability to be replenished naturally. It possesses qualities such as purity, affordability, and convenient accessibility. Wind turbines are utilized worldwide on a daily basis to harness the kinetic energy present in the air and convert it into electrical energy. The utilization of wind energy is becoming imperative in the context of global energy production, since it offers a clean and sustainable alternative for powering our society. Wind has been utilized as a significant energy source for an extensive period of time, whereby its kinetic energy is harnessed and converted into electrical energy through the implementation of windmills and wind turbines (Burton et al., 2011; Robert & Brown, 2006). It is projected that China will be responsible for the implementation of over 70% of new offshore wind projects worldwide, as well as more than 60% of onshore wind projects by the year 2024(IEA (2023)).

Figure 3. Net onshore wind electricity capacity additions by country or region, 2022-2024 (IEA, 2023)

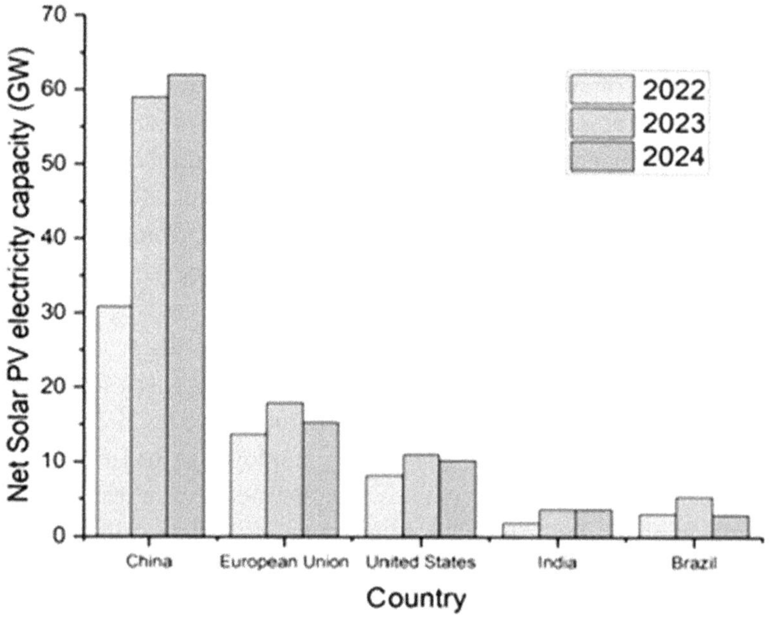

The integration of Artificial Intelligence (AI) into wind energy management has emerged as a pivotal enabler, enhancing the efficiency, reliability, and adaptability of wind power systems. AI-driven predictive models enable precise wind speed forecasting, optimizing turbine performance and power output. Additionally, AI algorithms facilitate real-time monitoring and control of wind turbine operations, detecting anomalies and minimizing downtime through predictive maintenance. (Damousis & Dokopoulos, 2001) Introduced fuzzy methodologies for estimating wind speed and power by employing various Genetic algorithms. The collection of wind energy data from a remote location was facilitated through the use of wireless modems. The utilization of artificial intelligence techniques. The study focused on the application of renewable energy and employed the fuzzy methodology to analyze the data. The results indicated that the fuzzy methodology yielded accuracy rates of 29.7% and 39.8% higher than those obtained using the permanent technique for the specified time period. In another study, (Carolin Mabel & Fernandez, 2008) employed a neural network architecture using feed-forward backpropagation to make estimations of wind power during a span of three years, utilizing data collected from seven distinct wind farms. The accuracy of the BPNN's predictions is encouraging, as evidenced by the test set's and the training set's root mean square error was found to be 0.0065 and 0.0070. As AI continues to refine wind energy operations, it fortifies the foundation for a sustainable energy landscape, fostering innovation that aligns with a cleaner, more sustainable future. Artificial intelligence (AI) is employed in the field of wind energy to forecast wind power, estimate the operational lifespan of wind turbines, and enhance energy efficiency by minimizing energy losses.

2.4 Geothermal Energy

Geothermal energy is produced and retained within the subsurface layers of the Earth (Archer, 2020). The geothermal gradient arises as a result of temperature disparities between the Earth's core and its surface. Lava is generated as a result of the gradual decomposition of radioactive materials present inside the Earth's crust. The disintegration of lava occurs as a result of the movement of tectonic plates, leading to the formation of substantial geothermal reservoirs that serve as a primary source of geothermal energy. By harnessing the natural heat stored beneath the Earth's surface, geothermal systems offer a continuous and reliable energy supply with minimal environmental impact. These systems can provide electricity, heating, and cooling solutions for residential, industrial, and commercial applications.

The integration of Artificial Intelligence (AI) in geothermal energy management has significantly enhanced the efficiency and viability of these systems. AI-powered predictive modeling optimizes reservoir management, aiding in the identification of optimal drilling sites and reservoir characterization. The investigation of geothermal resources necessitates the examination and control of numerous uncertainties, hence presenting difficulties in making investment and operational determinations. The integration of Remote Sensing (RS), Machine Learning (ML), and Artificial Intelligence (AI) holds promise in effectively addressing the complexities associated with geothermal research. Researchers involves the integration of remote sensing (RS), machine learning (ML), and artificial intelligence (AI) techniques to develop an initial assessment of geothermal potential. This assessment relies on established indications of geothermal locations, such as mineral markers, surface temperature, faults, and deformation. The study showcased the use of the methodology to two geothermal sites, namely Brady and Desert Peak. These sites, albeit in close proximity, exhibit distinct characteristics, with Brady featuring evident surface manifestations and Desert Peak being characterised as a blind site. Multiple satellite photos and geographical data are utilised to analyse mineral markers, temperature, faults, and deformation (Nassef et al., 2020). Contemporary machine learning methodologies have the potential to enhance systems constructed using expert judgements. The XGBoost algorithm demonstrates a higher level of concurrence with the outcomes compared to linear logistic regression in the absence of expert judgements. This can be attributed to the non-linear nature of XGBoost, which allows it to capture the non-linearity introduced by the expert decisions. It is worth noting that the evaluation solely employed linear methods, yet the expert decisions rendered the overall approach non-linear (Mordensky et al., 2023).

Additionally, AI-driven algorithms facilitate real-time monitoring and control of geothermal power plants, optimizing resource utilization and minimizing downtime. As geothermal energy continues to gain traction in the global energy mix, the partnership between AI and geothermal energy stands as a testament to innovation and sustainability, driving a greener and more resilient energy future.

2.5 Ocean Energy

The energy derived from the ocean is likewise classified within the domain of hydropower energy and is occasionally referred to as marine energy. At significant depths within the water, there exists a phenomenon wherein the temperature disparities possess sufficient energy to generate thermal energy, which is commonly referred to as water thermal energy (OTE) refers to the utilization of temperature differences in the water to generate power. The accumulation of wave energy occurs via the utilization of floating devices. Objects that exhibit elliptical motion when subjected to the influence of waves. The utilization of ocean energy, derived from the formidable forces of waves, tides, and currents, is a potential solution for a reliable and extensive renewable energy reservoir. Given that the Earth's oceans encompass more than 70% of its surface area, it is evident that ocean energy systems possess considerable promise in terms of their ability to make substantial contributions to sustainable energy generation. These systems comprise a range of technologies, including wave energy converters and tidal turbines that harness the kinetic energy present in oceanic movements. Despite the underutilization of the vast potential of renewable energy, the ocean energy industry assumes a significant role in significantly augmenting the electricity supply for coastal nations and populations (Esteban & Leary, 2012). The identification of research possibilities in the field of energy resources includes updating and forecasting methods, as well as the development of computational techniques for wave creation. Additionally, unique approaches for optimising the control of energy converters are also emphasised. Current research endeavours align with the global demand for sustainable and eco-friendly renewable energy sources. However, it is worth noting that engineering-focused studies sometimes neglect to consider the potential long-term impact of climate change. The continued relevance of the development and utilisation of computational engineering approaches, particularly in the context of continuum mechanics problems, persists. However, academics are increasingly focusing their emphasis on machine learning technologies (Tavakoli et al., 2023).

The use of Artificial Intelligence (AI) into the management of ocean energy has initiated a novel period characterized by enhanced efficiency and optimization. Artificial intelligence (AI)-based algorithms play a crucial role in predicting oceanic conditions, hence enhancing the efficiency of marine energy devices by optimizing their positioning and operation to achieve maximum power extraction. A novel approach offered for predicting daily ocean wave energy in the areas of Queensland State, Australia. That approach combines a multi-stage Multivariate Variational Mode Decomposition (MVMD) with Boruta-Extreme Gradient Boosting (BXGB) feature selection and Cascaded Forward Neural Network (CFNN). This integrated framework, referred to as MVMD-BXGB-CFNN, aims to enhance the accuracy and reliability of wave energy forecasts. The modelling results were compared to three other robust intelligence-based alternatives, namely Multigene Genetic Programming (MGGP), Least Square Support Machine (LSSVM), and Gradient Boosted Decision Tree (GBDT) models that were hybridised with MVMD and BXGB (referred to as MVMD-BXGB-MGGP, MVMD-BXGB-LSSVM, and MVMD-BXGB-GBDT). Additionally, the standalone CFNN, GBDT, LSSVM, and MGGP models were also included for comparison (Jamei et al., 2022).

Additionally, artificial intelligence (AI) plays a crucial role in improving data processing and facilitating real-time monitoring of equipment, hence facilitating predictive maintenance and extending the operational lifespan of ocean energy projects. With the ongoing progress of AI-driven advancements, the use of ocean energy is positioned to emerge as a crucial component within the realm of renewable energy. This development will play a significant role in fostering a sustainable and resilient energy future.

2.6 Hydrogen Energy

Hydrogen energy, obtained through the environmentally friendly conversion of hydrogen gas into electricity or fuel, gives a flexible and emission-free approach to achieving sustainable energy solutions. Hydrogen, being a carrier of energy, possesses the capacity to effectively store and transmit substantial quantities of renewable energy. This characteristic allows for the mitigation of intermittency issues and facilitates the decarbonization of diverse sectors, including as transportation and industrial. Hydrogen serves as the elemental basis for all fuel products. The process of electrolysis, which involves the decomposition of water and other biomass-derived composites such as organic wastes, as well as the biological process of bacteria, results in the generation of hydrogen. This hydrogen can be further exploited as a renewable energy source for the production of electricity through combustion (Kothari et al., 2008; McDowall, 2012).

The integration of Hydrogen and Artificial Intelligence (AI) yields significant advancements, augmenting all stages of the hydrogen energy lifecycle. Artificial intelligence (AI)-based algorithms are employed to enhance the efficiency of hydrogen production techniques, including electrolysis and reforming, with the aim of optimizing energy utilization and reducing overall expenses. Artificial intelligence (AI) also plays a pivotal role in the storage and distribution of hydrogen, facilitating real-time monitoring, identification of leaks, and optimizing utilization efficiency. In their study, (Dufo-López et al., 2007) introduce an innovative approach that utilizes a genetic algorithm-optimized method to regulate stand-alone hybrid renewable electricity systems incorporating hydrogen storage. The amalgamation of artificial intelligence (AI) and hydrogen energy represents a pioneering effort in advancing an environmentally friendly and sustainable energy framework, hence expediting the shift towards a future reliant on hydrogen as a source of electricity.

3. ROLE OF AI IN SUSTAINABLE DEVELOPMENT

The emergence of Artificial Intelligence (AI) has had a significant impact on the management of renewable energy, serving as a catalyst for sustainable development. In the face of global climate change and the pressing need to shift towards more sustainable energy sources, artificial intelligence (AI) presents a robust array of technologies that can augment the effectiveness, dependability, and incorporation of renewable energy systems. The integration of artificial intelligence (AI) with renewable energy sources is a potential solution for addressing environmental concerns and has the potential to transform the methods by which energy is produced, distributed, and consumed.

Renewable energy sources, encompassing solar, wind, hydro, geothermal, and ocean energy, play a crucial role in mitigating carbon emissions and safeguarding energy stability. Nonetheless, the intermittent and fluctuating characteristics of these energy sources present obstacles in maintaining a reliable and steady energy supply. Artificial intelligence (AI) plays a crucial role in bridging the gap between the inherent variability of renewable energy sources and the need for a reliable energy system. The capacity of artificial intelligence (AI) to efficiently analyze large volumes of data in real-time facilitates the precise forecasting of energy generation patterns, hence enhancing the effective allocation of available resources. For example, artificial intelligence (AI) systems have the capability to predict solar irradiance or wind speeds, enabling the ideal alignment of solar panels or wind turbines to maximize energy capture.

The integration of artificial intelligence (AI) into solar energy management has resulted in the transformation of photovoltaic systems into intelligent entities that possess the ability to adapt their performance in response to varying environmental conditions. AI-powered intelligent inverters have the capability to dynamically adjust to voltage variations and meet the demands of the electrical grid, hence improving energy efficiency. Machine learning algorithms are employed to examine past data in order to optimize the performance of solar arrays, hence enhancing the overall energy production (Hannan et al., 2021). Furthermore, artificial intelligence (AI) plays a crucial role in the seamless incorporation of solar energy into intelligent power grids, thereby establishing a two-way communication channel between energy suppliers and customers. The integration of various technologies facilitates demand response, load balancing, and energy storage optimization, thereby augmenting the overall stability of the grid (Som, 2021).

Similarly, the utilization of AI-powered technologies has proven advantageous for wind energy, since it significantly improves the overall efficiency and effectiveness of wind turbines and farms. The utilization of AI-driven predictive maintenance facilitates the timely identification of mechanical anomalies, hence enabling the implementation of proactive repair measures and mitigating the occurrence of operational downtime. Moreover, artificial intelligence (AI) plays a crucial role in facilitating the effective positioning of wind turbines by taking into account the specific wind patterns and topographical characteristics of a given location in order to maximize energy generation. The integration of artificial intelligence (AI) has the potential to enhance the efficiency, reliability, and economic feasibility of wind energy facilities, thereby making a substantial contribution to the overall renewable energy portfolio (Kumar et al., 2022; Som, 2021).

The utilization of geothermal energy, which harnesses the Earth's inherent heat, is further spurred by breakthroughs in artificial intelligence (AI). Artificial intelligence (AI) plays a crucial role in the identification of optimal drilling locations, the prediction of reservoir properties, and the optimization of resource allocation. The implementation of real-time monitoring and control systems in geothermal power plants plays a crucial role in optimizing operational efficiency and facilitating early problem identification. This, in turn, leads to a reduction in maintenance expenses and an improvement in the overall performance of the system. The integration of artificial intelligence (AI) with geothermal energy management not only serves to optimize energy extraction, but also contributes to the extension of the operational longevity of geothermal systems (He et al., 2022; Som, 2021).

Hydrogen, a highly regarded energy carrier, is seeing increased recognition due to the integration of artificial intelligence initiatives. The utilization of AI-optimized electrolysis techniques improves the efficacy of hydrogen generation from water, a critical procedure for the storage of surplus renewable energy (Sai Ramesh et al., 2023). Artificial intelligence (AI) algorithms are utilized in the management of hydrogen storage and distribution processes to enhance safety and efficiency. Hydrogen generated by AI-driven techniques functions as an environmentally friendly energy carrier capable of fueling various sectors such as industry and transportation. This reduces dependence on fossil fuels and strengthens the shift towards an economically viable and sustainable energy system (Jha et al., 2017).

Although the advantages of artificial intelligence (AI) in the field of renewable energy management are highly persuasive, there are still obstacles that need to be addressed. The successful integration of artificial intelligence (AI) and renewable energy necessitates the availability of reliable and comprehensive data to ensure precise modeling and accurate predictions (Goralski & Tan, 2020). Moreover, the implementation of artificial intelligence (AI) technology necessitates a certain set of skills and knowledge. Ensuring the integrity of energy systems necessitates the imperative consideration of data privacy and security considerations. Furthermore, it is imperative to take into account the scalability and cost-effectiveness of AI-driven solutions when considering their wider application.

4. LIMITATIONS OF THE ROLE OF AI IN SUSTAINABLE DEVELOPMENT

The incorporation of Artificial Intelligence (AI) into sustainable development has initiated a novel epoch of opportunities, holding the capability to tackle intricate difficulties throughout diverse sectors. Nevertheless, it is crucial to recognize that artificial intelligence (AI) is not a universal remedy; it is accompanied with a distinct array of constraints and ethical concerns that necessitate cautious handling. In the examination of the impact of artificial intelligence (AI) on sustainable development, it is crucial to acknowledge these constraints and strive towards their mitigation in order to promote a fairer and ethically accountable utilization of technology.

Figure 4. Limitation of the role of AI in sustainable development

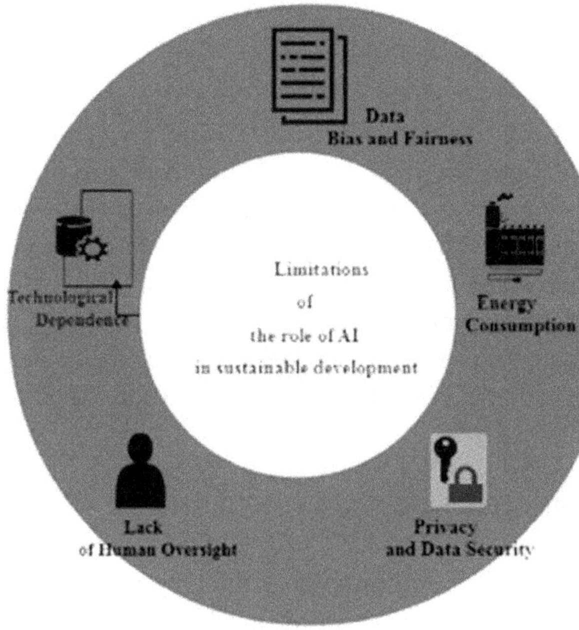

4.1 Data Bias and Fairness

One of the primary obstacles in the field of artificial intelligence pertains to the issue of data bias. Machine learning algorithms acquire knowledge from past data, and in cases where this data exhibits prejudice, the artificial intelligence models have the potential to perpetuate and magnify preexisting biases. Biased algorithms within the context of sustainable development have the potential to engender unjust distribution of resources, inequitable access to opportunities, and perpetuate preexisting disparities. As an illustration, artificial intelligence (AI) systems employed in recruitment procedures possess the potential to unintentionally perpetuate discrimination towards specific demographic cohorts in the event that past hiring data exhibits bias. The mitigation of data bias and the promotion of algorithmic fairness are essential measures in order to prevent AI-driven sustainable development projects from increasing societal inequalities.

4.2 Energy Consumption

Although artificial intelligence (AI) has promise for enhancing energy efficiency and supporting sustainable energy management, the process of developing and deploying intricate AI models can consume significant amounts of energy. Irony may manifest itself in situations when artificial intelligence (AI) technologies, which are intended to promote sustainability, unintentionally contribute to increased energy usage. The utilization of extensive computational resources is important for the implementation of large-scale artificial intelligence (AI) applications, particularly deep learning. Consequently, this has resulted in a heightened need for energy resources. Ensuring a harmonious equilibrium between the advantages of artificial intelligence (AI) and its energy consumption is imperative in order to prevent unintentional undermining of the fundamental tenets of sustainability that AI endeavors to uphold.

4.3 Privacy and Data Security

Artificial intelligence (AI) systems exhibit optimal performance when they have access to and can analyze extensive quantities of personal data. These circumstances give rise to apprehensions over the protection of privacy and the security of data. Within the framework of sustainable development, it is imperative for AI-driven systems to effectively manage the collection and analysis of personal data in order to facilitate environmental monitoring, health interventions, and social programs. However, this must be done while maintaining a careful equilibrium between providing advantageous outcomes and upholding the fundamental rights to privacy of individuals. The implementation of responsible AI deployment necessitates the incorporation of comprehensive data protection mechanisms and the acquisition of informed consent from persons.

4.4 Lack of Human Oversight

Artificial intelligence (AI) systems, specifically those utilizing deep learning and neural networks, possess the characteristic of being opaque, rendering conclusions that are challenging for humans to comprehend or elucidate. In the context of sustainable development, the exclusive reliance on AI-driven decision-making without human supervision can result in unanticipated outcomes. Achieving a harmonious equilibrium between automation and human intervention is imperative in order to uphold principles of accountability, transparency, and ethical decision-making within the realm of AI applications.

4.5 Technological Dependence

The increasing integration of artificial intelligence (AI) within sustainable development methods raises concerns over the potential for excessive dependence on technological solutions. The exclusive dependence on AI-driven solutions may potentially result in a reduced prioritization of human skills and conventional knowledge. Sustainable development encompasses a range of disciplines and necessitates the involvement of diverse stakeholders. In this context, artificial intelligence (AI) should be regarded as a means to augment, rather than supplant, human intelligence and collaborative efforts.

Challenges of AI in Renewable Energy

This section addresses some prominent research concerns and difficulties pertaining to the effective use of artificial intelligence algorithms in renewable energy applications.

The incorporation of artificial intelligence (AI) technology into renewable energy system may need substantial initial expenditures on software, hardware, and training. Furthermore, it is important to note that the establishment and implementation of renewable energy infrastructures might need significant financial investment. The financial implications associated with these charges may provide a significant obstacle for smaller enterprises and poor nations that possess constrained resources. The use of artificial intelligence (AI) within renewable energy systems necessitates the acquisition, analysis, and retention of substantial volumes of data. The involvement of sensitive information, such as client energy usage habits or grid vulnerabilities, might give rise to apprehensions over data security and privacy. The existing AI algorithms may possess limitations in effectively addressing the intricate dynamics and uncertainties inherent in renewable energy systems, including but not limited to harsh weather phenomena and rapid fluctuations in grid conditions. The development of more robust algorithms is crucial in order to effectively address the problems posed by the ongoing advancements in AI technology. The incorporation of artificial intelligence (AI) into renewable energy systems has the potential to result in employment displacement in some regions, as the automation of tasks removes the need for physical labour. Furthermore, it is possible that a discrepancy in skills exists within the labour market, since the business necessitates individuals who possess comprehensive knowledge in both renewable energy and artificial intelligence (AI) technology. In order to effectively tackle these difficulties, it is essential to implement focused educational and training initiatives that facilitate the adjustment of employees to the evolving labor landscape.

Artificial intelligence (AI) systems are widely seen as crucial drivers of economic and social progress, prompting nations worldwide to priorities their development. The process of enabling artificial intelligence techniques for large-scale renewable energy generation necessitates a comprehensive understanding of both industry-specific knowledge and AI expertise. This requires a strategic approach to talent development, focusing on long-term training initiatives that familiarize individuals with the operational framework and critical aspects of specific industries (Hassan et al., 2023). Artificial intelligence (AI) systems are widely seen as crucial drivers of economic and social progress, prompting nations worldwide to priorities their development. The process of enabling artificial intelligence techniques for large-scale renewable energy generation necessitates a comprehensive understanding of both industry-specific knowledge and AI expertise. This requires a strategic approach to talent development, focusing on long-term training initiatives that familiarise individuals with the operational framework and critical aspects of specific industries. The use of artificial intelligence (AI) methods in the context of large-scale renewable energy production remains in its nascent stage, and there persists a dearth of scientifically grounded and economically viable support policies (Liu et al., 2022) (Matschoss et al., 2019).

CONCLUSION

The integration of AI in the renewable energy sector has emerged as a transformative force with the potential to revolutionize the way we generate, distribute, and consume clean energy. AI technologies, encompassing machine learning, predictive analytics, optimization algorithms, and smart control systems, have enabled unparalleled advancements in renewable energy systems. These advancements range from enhancing the efficiency of solar panels and wind turbines through real-time data analysis and adaptive control strategies to optimizing energy storage systems for better grid stability and reliability. AI-driven predictive maintenance has minimized downtime and operational costs, prolonging the lifespan of renewable infrastructure. Furthermore, AI-driven energy management systems empower consumers to make informed decisions about their energy usage, thereby fostering a culture of energy conservation. The marriage of AI with renewable energy has facilitated the creation of virtual power plants that intelligently manage decentralized energy resources, leading to a more resilient and flexible grid. However, challenges such as data privacy concerns, algorithmic biases, and the complexity of integrating AI into existing energy infrastructures need to be addressed. As AI continues to evolve, its role in renewable energy is poised to grow, propelling the transition towards a sustainable energy future by maximizing the potential of renewable sources, minimizing waste, and ultimately reducing our carbon footprint.

Conflict of Interest

On behalf of all authors, the corresponding author states that there is no conflict of interest.

Data Availability Statement

Data sharing applicable to this article will be made available on reasonable request.

ACKNOWLEDGMENT

The author extends his appreciation to the Mechanical Engineering Department, Rajkiya Engineering College Azamgarh, U.P., India, for providing resources for this study.

REFERENCES

Archer, R. (2020). Geothermal Energy. In *Future Energy* (pp. 431–445). Elsevier. doi:10.1016/B978-0-08-102886-5.00020-7

Asif, M., & Muneer, T. (2007). Energy supply, its demand and security issues for developed and emerging economies. *Renewable & Sustainable Energy Reviews*, *11*(7), 1388–1413. doi:10.1016/j.rser.2005.12.004

Bose, B. K. (2017). Artificial Intelligence Techniques in Smart Grid and Renewable Energy Systems—Some Example Applications. *Proceedings of the IEEE*, *105*(11), 2262–2273. doi:10.1109/JPROC.2017.2756596

Bryson, J. J. (2019). *Towards a New Enlightenment? A Transcendent Decade - The Past Decade and the Future of Globalization*. OpendMind BBVA.

Burton, T., Jenkins, N., Sharpe, D., & Bossanyi, E. (2011). *Wind Energy Handbook*. Wiley. doi:10.1002/9781119992714

Carolin Mabel, M., & Fernandez, E. (2008). Analysis of wind power generation and prediction using ANN: A case study. *Renewable Energy*, *33*(5), 986–992. doi:10.1016/j.renene.2007.06.013

Damousis, I. G., & Dokopoulos, P. (2001). A fuzzy expert system for the forecasting of wind speed and power generation in wind farms. *IEEE Power Industry Computer Applications Conference*, 63–69. 10.1109/PICA.2001.932320

Dufo-López, R., Bernal-Agustín, J. L., & Contreras, J. (2007). Optimization of control strategies for stand-alone renewable energy systems with hydrogen storage. *Renewable Energy, 32*(7), 1102–1126. doi:10.1016/j.renene.2006.04.013

Ediger, V. Ş. (2019). An integrated review and analysis of multi-energy transition from fossil fuels to renewables. *Energy Procedia, 156*, 2–6. doi:10.1016/j.egypro.2018.11.073

Esteban, M., & Leary, D. (2012). Current developments and future prospects of offshore wind and ocean energy. *Applied Energy, 90*(1), 128–136. doi:10.1016/j.apenergy.2011.06.011

Goralski, M. A., & Tan, T. K. (2020). Artificial intelligence and sustainable development. *International Journal of Management Education, 18*(1), 100330. doi:10.1016/j.ijme.2019.100330

Hannan, M. A., Al-Shetwi, A. Q., Ker, P. J., Begum, R. A., Mansor, M., Rahman, S. A., Dong, Z. Y., Tiong, S. K., Mahlia, T. M. I., & Muttaqi, K. M. (2021). Impact of renewable energy utilization and artificial intelligence in achieving sustainable development goals. *Energy Reports, 7*, 5359–5373. doi:10.1016/j.egyr.2021.08.172

Hassan, Q., Sameen, A. Z., Salman, H. M., Al-Jiboory, A. K., & Jaszczur, M. (2023). *The role of renewable energy and articial intelligence towards environmental sustainability and net zero*. Academic Press.

He, Z., Guo, W., & Zhang, P. (2022). Performance prediction, optimal design and operational control of thermal energy storage using artificial intelligence methods. *Renewable & Sustainable Energy Reviews, 156*, 111977. doi:10.1016/j.rser.2021.111977

IEA. (2022). *Renewables 2022 - December*. https://www.iea.org/reports/renewables-2022

IEA. (2023). *Renewable Energy Market Update - June*. https://www.iea.org/reports/renewable-energy-market-update-june-2023

Jamei, M., Ali, M., Karbasi, M., Xiang, Y., Ahmadianfar, I., & Yaseen, Z. M. (2022). Designing a Multi-Stage Expert System for daily ocean wave energy forecasting: A multivariate data decomposition-based approach. *Applied Energy, 326*, 119925. doi:10.1016/j.apenergy.2022.119925

Jha, S., Bilalovic, J., Jha, A., Patel, N., & Zhang, H. (2017). Renewable energy: Present research and future scope of Artificial Intelligence. *Renewable & Sustainable Energy Reviews, 77*, 297–317. doi:10.1016/j.rser.2017.04.018

Kothari, R., Buddhi, D., & Sawhney, R. L. (2008). Comparison of environmental and economic aspects of various hydrogen production methods. *Renewable & Sustainable Energy Reviews, 12*(2), 553–563. doi:10.1016/j.rser.2006.07.012

Kumar, M. (2020). Social, Economic, and Environmental Impacts of Renewable Energy Resources. In *Wind Solar Hybrid Renewable Energy System*. IntechOpen. doi:10.5772/intechopen.89494

Kumar, N., Kumar, D., Layek, A., & Yadav, S. (2022). Renewable energy and sustainable development. In *Artificial Intelligence for Renewable Energy Systems* (pp. 305–328). Elsevier. doi:10.1016/B978-0-323-90396-7.00011-0

Kumbhar, D., Palliyarayil, A., Reghu, D., Shrungar, D., Umapathy, S., & Sil, S. (2021). Rapid discrimination of porous bio-carbon derived from nitrogen rich biomass using Raman spectroscopy and artificial intelligence methods. *Carbon*, *178*, 792–802. doi:10.1016/j.carbon.2021.03.064

Liu, Z., Sun, Y., Xing, C., Liu, J., He, Y., Zhou, Y., & Zhang, G. (2022). Artificial intelligence powered large-scale renewable integrations in multi-energy systems for carbon neutrality transition: Challenges and future perspectives. *Energy and AI*, *10*, 100195. doi:10.1016/j.egyai.2022.100195

Matschoss, P., Bayer, B., Thomas, H., & Marian, A. (2019). The German incentive regulation and its practical impact on the grid integration of renewable energy systems. *Renewable Energy*, *134*, 727–738. doi:10.1016/j.renene.2018.10.103

McDowall, W. (2012). Technology roadmaps for transition management: The case of hydrogen energy. *Technological Forecasting and Social Change*, *79*(3), 530–542. doi:10.1016/j.techfore.2011.10.002

Mellit, A., Kalogirou, S. A., Hontoria, L., & Shaari, S. (2009). Artificial intelligence techniques for sizing photovoltaic systems: A review. *Renewable & Sustainable Energy Reviews*, *13*(2), 406–419. doi:10.1016/j.rser.2008.01.006

Mordensky, S. P., Lipor, J. J., DeAngelo, J., Burns, E. R., & Lindsey, C. R. (2023). When less is more: How increasing the complexity of machine learning strategies for geothermal energy assessments may not lead toward better estimates. *Geothermics*, *110*, 102662. doi:10.1016/j.geothermics.2023.102662

Nassef, A. M., Sayed, E. T., Rezk, H., Inayat, A., Yousef, B. A. A., Abdelkareem, M. A., & Olabi, A. G. (2020). Developing a fuzzy-model with particle swarm optimization-based for improving the conversion and gasification rate of palm kernel shell. *Renewable Energy*, *166*, 125–135. doi:10.1016/j.renene.2020.11.037

Robert, B., & Brown, E. B. (2006). Book Review: Wind Energy Explained: Theory, Design and Application. In Wind Engineering (Vol. 30, Issue 2). doi:10.1260/030952406778055054

Sai Ramesh, A., Vigneshwar, S., Vickram, S., Manikandan, S., Subbaiya, R., Karmegam, N., & Kim, W. (2023). Artificial intelligence driven hydrogen and battery technologies – A review. *Fuel*, *337*, 126862. doi:10.1016/j.fuel.2022.126862

Salim, H. K., Padfield, R., Hansen, S. B., Mohamad, S. E., Yuzir, A., Syayuti, K., Tham, M. H., & Papargyropoulou, E. (2018). Global trends in environmental management system and ISO14001 research. *Journal of Cleaner Production*, *170*, 645–653. doi:10.1016/j.jclepro.2017.09.017

Sarker, T. R., Pattnaik, F., Nanda, S., Dalai, A. K., Meda, V., & Naik, S. (2021). Hydrothermal pretreatment technologies for lignocellulosic biomass: A review of steam explosion and subcritical water hydrolysis. *Chemosphere*, *284*, 131372. doi:10.1016/j.chemosphere.2021.131372 PMID:34323806

Som, T. (2021). Sustainability in Energy Economy and Environment: Role of AI Based Techniques. doi:10.1007/978-3-030-72929-5_31

Tavakoli, S., Khojasteh, D., Haghani, M., & Hirdaris, S. (2023). A review on the progress and research directions of ocean engineering. *Ocean Engineering*, *272*, 113617. doi:10.1016/j.oceaneng.2023.113617

Chapter 7
Waste-to-Energy Solutions Harnessing IoT and ML for Sustainable Power Generation in Smart Cities

Tarun Kumar Vashishth
https://orcid.org/0000-0001-9916-9575
IIMT University, India

Bhupendra Kumar
https://orcid.org/0000-0001-9281-3655
IIMT University, India

Vikas Sharma
https://orcid.org/0000-0001-8173-4548
IIMT University, India

Sachin Chaudhary
https://orcid.org/0000-0002-8415-0043
IIMT University, India

Kewal Krishan Sharma
https://orcid.org/0009-0001-2504-9607
IIMT University, India

Rajneesh Panwar
https://orcid.org/0009-0000-5974-191X
IIMT University, India

ABSTRACT

This chapter explores waste-to-energy (WtE) solutions empowered by the integration of internet of things (IoT) and machine learning (ML) for sustainable power generation in smart cities. By leveraging IoT sensors, real-time data acquisition optimizes waste management processes, and ML algorithms enhance operational efficiency. The potential impact of these technologies on WtE's future includes predictive maintenance, waste sorting automation, and adaptive energy production. The role of WtE in smart cities extends to decentralized energy generation, integrated waste management, and fostering circular economy principles. This study calls for further research and the adoption of sustainable practices to propel WtE as a key component in the future energy landscape of smart and resilient urban environments.

DOI: 10.4018/979-8-3693-1062-5.ch007

Copyright © 2024, IGI Global. Copying or distributing in print or electronic forms without written permission of IGI Global is prohibited.

1. INTRODUCTION

The rapid urbanization and burgeoning population in today's world pose unprecedented challenges for waste management and energy sustainability. In response to these challenges, Waste-to-Energy (WtE) has emerged as a promising solution, offering the dual benefits of waste reduction and sustainable power generation. This chapter explores the synergistic integration of Internet of Things (IoT) and Machine Learning (ML) technologies in revolutionizing Waste-to-Energy practices within the context of Smart Cities. As cities strive to become more intelligent and sustainable, the convergence of IoT and ML presents a transformative opportunity to optimize the entire lifecycle of waste, from collection and sorting to energy conversion. The introduction provides an overview of the significance of Waste-to-Energy in the broader context of environmental sustainability and introduces the pivotal role that IoT and ML play in enhancing the efficiency, monitoring, and decision-making processes within these systems. With a focus on Smart Cities as hubs of innovation, this chapter sets the stage for an exploration of cutting-edge technologies, challenges, case studies, and future trends in Waste-to-Energy, showcasing how the fusion of IoT and ML is steering us towards a more sustainable and technologically advanced energy future.

1.1 Overview of Waste-to-Energy (WtE) and Its Significance

Waste-to-Energy (WtE) stands at the forefront of innovative and sustainable approaches to addressing the dual challenges of waste management and energy generation in our rapidly urbanizing world. As urban populations burgeon and cities grapple with mounting waste volumes, the concept of converting this waste into a valuable energy resource gains paramount importance. Waste-to-Energy involves the conversion of various types of waste materials—ranging from municipal solid waste to agricultural residues—into heat, electricity, or fuel through various technological processes. The significance of Waste-to-Energy lies in its multifaceted impact, offering a viable solution to the escalating waste crisis while contributing to the diversification of energy sources and reduction of greenhouse gas emissions. In the context of Smart Cities, where the integration of technology and sustainability is a paramount goal, Waste-to-Energy emerges as a linchpin for achieving intelligent waste management and decentralized power generation. The utilization of waste as a resource aligns with the circular economy principles, minimizing environmental impact and fostering a more sustainable energy landscape. Hussain, Mishra and Vanacore (2020) present a case study on the implementation of anaerobic digestion in order to achieve a waste to energy and circular economy.

The integration of Waste-to-Energy into the fabric of Smart Cities holds the promise of transformative change, offering a dynamic approach to waste management that goes beyond the traditional linear model of disposal. By harnessing the potential of Internet of Things (IoT) and Machine Learning (ML), cities can revolutionize how they collect, sort, and convert waste into energy. The interconnected nature of IoT devices allows for real-time monitoring of waste streams, optimizing collection routes, and ensuring the efficient utilization of resources. Machine Learning, on the other hand, introduces predictive analytics to enhance the efficiency of energy conversion processes, making them more adaptive and responsive to fluctuating waste compositions. This integration not only addresses the logistical challenges of waste management but also enhances the overall efficiency and sustainability of the Waste-to-Energy paradigm.

In essence, the overview of Waste-to-Energy underscores its pivotal role in the pursuit of sustainable urban development. By converting waste into a valuable energy resource, cities can mitigate the environmental impact of landfills, reduce dependency on fossil fuels, and contribute to the creation of a circular economy. In the subsequent sections, we delve into the intricate nexus of Waste-to-Energy, IoT, and ML, exploring the technological advancements, challenges, case studies, and future prospects that collectively shape the landscape of sustainable power generation in the context of Smart Cities.

Figure 1. Smart city waste to energy system

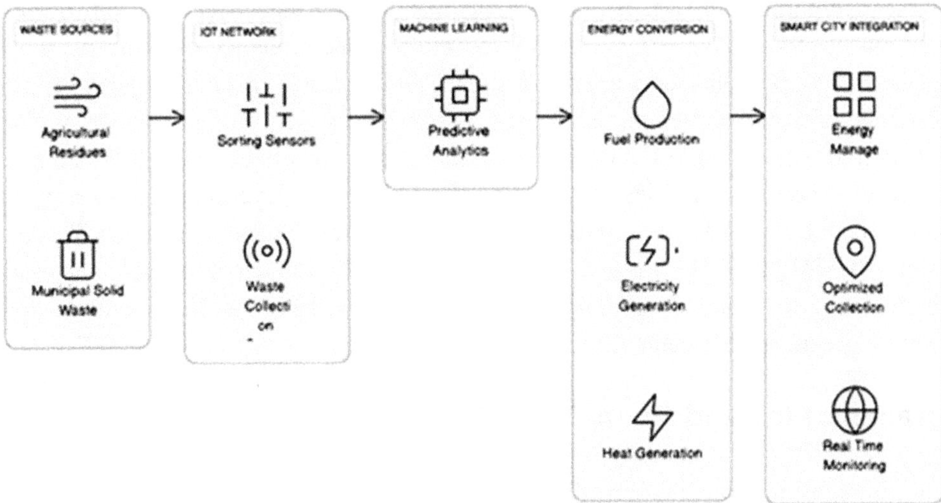

1.2 The Role of Smart Cities in Sustainable Energy Practices

Smart Cities, characterized by the seamless integration of technology, data-driven governance, and sustainability initiatives, play a pivotal role in advancing global efforts toward more efficient and environmentally conscious urban living. At the heart of this transformation is the imperative to adopt sustainable energy practices and Waste-to-Energy (WtE) stands as a linchpin in the pursuit of these goals. Smart Cities leverage their technological infrastructure to revolutionize the traditional waste management and energy generation paradigm, aligning urban development with the principles of circular economy and environmental stewardship. Alao et al. (2021) propose the use of the IDOCRIW-Weighted TOPSIS method for selection of waste-to-energy technology for distributed generation in the City of Johannesburg, South Africa. The role of Smart Cities in sustainable energy practices is multifaceted, encompassing the optimization of waste streams, decentralized power generation, and the integration of innovative technologies such as Internet of Things (IoT) and Machine Learning (ML). AlQattan et al. (2018) propose that WTE technologies can contribute to the achievement of SDGs.

One primary facet of this role is the intelligent management of waste streams through advanced IoT applications. Smart Cities utilize sensor-equipped waste bins and collection vehicles that communicate real-time data, allowing for optimized waste collection routes and schedules. This not only reduces operational costs but also minimizes the environmental footprint of waste transportation. Additionally, IoT sensors enable cities to monitor and control various parameters in waste-to-energy conversion processes, ensuring optimal conditions for energy generation. Di Matteo et al. (2017) proposed as a potential source of energy for urban areas.

Furthermore, Smart Cities embrace the potential of Machine Learning in enhancing the efficiency of Waste-to-Energy systems. ML algorithms process vast amounts of data related to waste composition, energy production, and environmental factors, enabling predictive analytics and continuous optimization. This adaptive capability ensures that Waste-to-Energy facilities can dynamically adjust to changing waste compositions, maximizing energy output while minimizing environmental impact. Elif et al. (2021) propose a waste-to-energy model that utilizes the LoRaWAN communication protocol.

The symbiotic integration of WtE, IoT, and ML in Smart Cities fosters decentralized power generation. By converting local waste into energy at the source, cities reduce reliance on centralized power plants and transmission networks, enhancing energy resilience and security. This decentralized approach aligns with the principles of sustainability, reducing transmission losses and promoting energy self-sufficiency.

In summary, the role of Smart Cities in sustainable energy practices through Waste-to-Energy solutions is transformative. These cities serve as living laboratories, leveraging technology to create an interconnected and intelligent ecosystem where waste is viewed as a valuable resource. Through strategic integration of WtE, IoT, and ML, Smart Cities pave the way for a more sustainable and resilient urban future, demonstrating that innovation and environmental stewardship can harmoniously coexist in the pursuit of smart, green, and efficient cities.

1.3 Integration of IoT and ML in Waste-to-Energy Solutions

The symbiotic integration of the Internet of Things (IoT) and Machine Learning (ML) in Waste-to-Energy (WtE) solutions stands as a transformative paradigm in the realm of sustainable urban development. At its core, this integration redefines the traditional waste management and energy generation processes, offering a dynamic and data-driven approach to maximize efficiency and minimize environmental impact. The integration begins at the source with IoT-enabled waste management systems. Smart Cities deploy a network of sensors embedded in waste bins and collection vehicles, creating a real-time data ecosystem. These sensors gather information on waste volumes, composition, and fill levels, enabling optimized collection routes and schedules. This not only streamlines the logistics of waste management but also reduces fuel consumption, lowering the carbon footprint of collection processes.

Complementing this IoT infrastructure, Machine Learning algorithms come into play, providing the intelligence to process and derive insights from the vast datasets generated by IoT devices. ML models analyze historical data to predict future waste generation patterns, enabling proactive decision-making in waste collection and energy conversion processes. The adaptive nature of ML ensures that WtE systems can dynamically adjust to variations in waste composition, optimizing combustion parameters for enhanced energy production efficiency. Kabugo et al. (2020) propose an analytics platform for this new era of automation. Moreover, ML-driven analytics contribute to continuous improvement, allowing Waste-to-Energy facilities to learn and adapt over time, fostering a self-optimizing and resilient energy generation ecosystem.

The integration of IoT and ML in Waste-to-Energy solutions also extends to real-time monitoring and control of energy conversion processes. IoT sensors embedded in WtE facilities capture data on temperature, gas emissions, and equipment performance. This data is then fed into ML models that can predict potential issues, prevent downtime, and optimize combustion conditions for maximal energy output. The result is a closed-loop system where the feedback from IoT sensors continuously refines the decision-making processes of ML algorithms, creating a self-regulating and efficient energy generation system. Jain et al. (2023) is an ambitious attempt to bring together the latest advances in these very dynamic and rapidly evolving fields.

Furthermore, this integrated approach allows for the creation of smart grids within Smart Cities. The surplus energy generated from Waste-to-Energy processes can be intelligently distributed across the city, optimizing energy consumption and reducing reliance on centralized power sources. This decentralized energy model aligns with sustainability goals, enhancing energy resilience and reducing transmission losses.

In essence, the integration of IoT and ML in Waste-to-Energy solutions represents a paradigm shift, where technology not only enhances operational efficiency but also transforms waste into a valuable resource for sustainable power generation. This dynamic fusion of technologies underscores the potential for creating intelligent, adaptive, and environmentally conscious urban energy ecosystems, showcasing how innovation can drive positive change in the pursuit of Smart Cities and a greener, more sustainable future.

Figure 2. Integration of IoT and ML in waste energy solutions

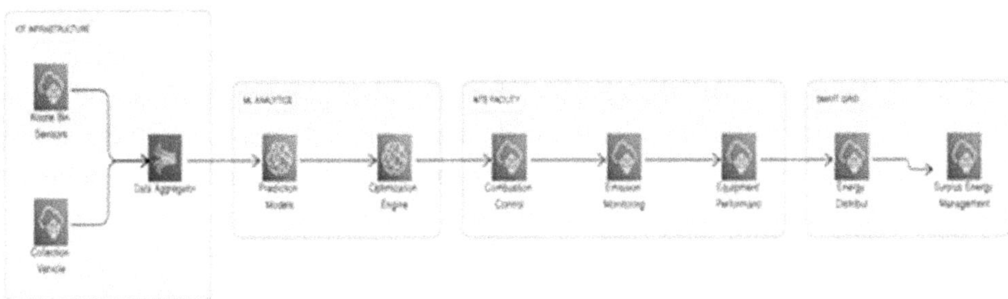

2. WASTE-TO-ENERGY TECHNOLOGIES

2.1 Overview of Traditional WtE Technologies

Traditional Waste-to-Energy (WtE) technologies have long played a crucial role in addressing the dual challenges of waste management and energy generation. One of the foundational methods is incineration, where municipal solid waste is combusted at high temperatures, producing steam that drives turbines to generate electricity. Incineration is a widely adopted technology due to its effectiveness in reducing waste volume and harnessing thermal energy. Another traditional approach involves anaerobic digestion, a biological process where organic waste undergoes microbial decomposition to produce biogas, primarily composed of methane. This biogas can then be utilized for electricity generation or as a renewable natural gas for various applications. Additionally, landfill gas recovery captures methane emitted from decomposing organic waste in landfills, converting it into a valuable energy source. These traditional WtE technologies have proven effective in mitigating the environmental impact of landfills, reducing greenhouse gas emissions, and contributing to the diversification of energy sources.

However, the overview of traditional WtE technologies reveals certain limitations that can be addressed and optimized through the infusion of modern technologies such as Internet of Things (IoT) and Machine Learning (ML). Swathika, Karthikeyan & Padmanaban (2023), provide an overview of various aspects of IoT and analytics in renewable energy systems. Traditional methods often face challenges in terms of efficiency, emissions control, and adaptability to variable waste compositions. The reliance on fixed operational parameters may lead to suboptimal energy generation and environmental performance. This underscores the importance of incorporating IoT for real-time monitoring of combustion conditions, emissions, and equipment performance, allowing for dynamic adjustments and optimization. ML algorithms can further enhance these traditional processes by predicting optimal combustion parameters based on historical and real-time data, improving overall efficiency and reducing environmental impact. The traditional serves as a foundation upon which the integration of modern technologies builds, transforming Waste-to-Energy into a more adaptive, intelligent, and sustainable solution for the energy needs of Smart Cities.

2.2 Emerging Technologies in Waste-to-Energy

As the landscape of Waste-to-Energy (WtE) evolves, several emerging technologies are poised to revolutionize the traditional paradigms, aligning with the objectives of Smart Cities for sustainable power generation. Szpilko et al. (2023) presents an overview of current practices and future directions in waste management in the Smart City. One prominent advancement is the utilization of advanced thermal conversion techniques, such as gasification and pyrolysis. These methods, distinct from traditional incineration, involve the transformation of waste into syngas or bio-oil, offering more versatile and cleaner energy outputs. Gasification, in particular, allows for a wider range of feed stocks and produces a syngas that can be efficiently utilized for electricity generation or converted into bio fuels. Another breakthrough is the integration of plasma gasification, which employs high-temperature plasma arcs to break down waste into its constituent elements, yielding a syngas with lower emissions. Additionally, microbial fuel cells are emerging as a promising technology, utilizing bacteria to break down organic waste and generate electricity. These innovations not only enhance energy recovery but also contribute to more sustainable waste management practices.

Furthermore, the incorporation of advanced sorting and recycling technologies is reshaping the landscape of Waste-to-Energy. Automated sorting systems equipped with artificial intelligence (AI) and robotics facilitate the efficient separation of waste streams, diverting recyclable materials and organic waste before entering energy conversion processes. This not only increases the overall efficiency of recycling but also ensures that only suitable materials are directed toward energy generation, optimizing the performance of Waste-to-Energy facilities. Kaya et al. (2021) proposes a Waste-to-Energy Framework for intelligent energy recycling management. In conjunction with Internet of Things (IoT) and Machine Learning (ML), these sorting technologies provide real-time data on waste composition, allowing for dynamic adjustments to the energy conversion processes based on the evolving nature of the waste stream.

The amalgamation of these emerging technologies not only enhances the efficiency and sustainability of Waste-to-Energy but also aligns with the overarching goals of Smart Cities. Khalil et al. (2021) explore the potential of deep learning in the industrial internet of things, as well as the associated challenges and emerging applications. By integrating IoT for real-time monitoring, ML for predictive analytics, and advanced thermal conversion and sorting technologies, cities can foster a more adaptive, intelligent, and environmentally conscious approach to waste management and power generation. These innovations not only contribute to the circular economy model but also position Waste-to-Energy as a key player in the transition towards a more sustainable and technologically advanced urban future.

Figure 3. Waste-to-energy emerging technologies

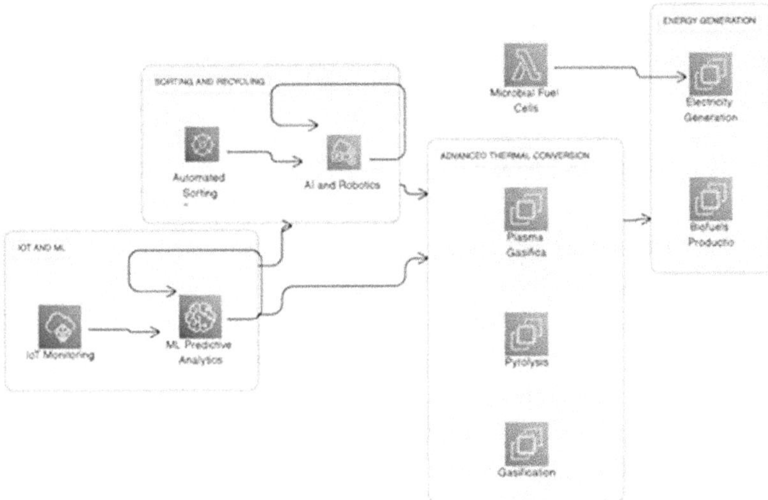

2.3 Advancements and Innovations in Power Generation From Waste

The landscape of power generation from waste is undergoing transformative advancements and innovations, reshaping the traditional Waste-to-Energy (WtE) paradigm and aligning with the sustainability goals of Smart Cities. One noteworthy innovation is the integration of advanced thermal conversion technologies, such as gasification and pyrolysis, which offer more efficient and environmentally friendly alternatives to conventional incineration. Gasification, in particular, allows for the conversion of various waste streams into a syngas, rich in hydrogen and carbon monoxide, which can be used for electricity generation or further refined into bio fuels. Pyrolysis, on the other hand, involves the thermal decomposition of organic materials in the absence of oxygen, producing bio-oil and char, both valuable for energy applications. These advancements not only enhance the overall energy recovery efficiency but also contribute to reducing emissions and expanding the scope of waste materials that can be effectively utilized.

Additionally, innovations in microbial fuel cells (MFCs) present a groundbreaking approach to power generation from organic waste. MFCs employ electro active bacteria to break down organic matter, producing electrons that can be harnessed to generate electricity. This microbial-electrochemical process not only provides a sustainable means of energy production but also allows for the simultaneous treatment of organic waste, demonstrating a synergy between waste management and power generation. Furthermore, advancements in plasma gasification technologies are gaining prominence. By subjecting waste to high-temperature plasma arcs, these systems break down complex organic compounds into simpler components, producing a syngas with lower impurities and emissions. This not only enhances the efficiency of energy recovery but also addresses environmental concerns associated with traditional incineration methods.

The integration of these advancements in power generation from waste is closely tied to the deployment of Internet of Things (IoT) and Machine Learning (ML) technologies. These smart systems enable real-time monitoring of energy conversion processes, optimizing operational parameters based on dynamic waste compositions. ML algorithms contribute to predictive analytics, ensuring that WtE facilities can adapt to changing conditions and continuously improve efficiency. In essence, these innovations collectively redefine the potential of Waste-to-Energy, positioning it as a technologically sophisticated and sustainable solution for Smart Cities seeking to harness the latent energy within their waste streams while minimizing environmental impact.

3. SMART CITIES AND SUSTAINABLE ENERGY

3.1 Definition and Characteristics of Smart Cities

Smart Cities represent the vanguard of urban development, leveraging advanced technologies to enhance efficiency, sustainability, and the quality of life for their inhabitants. These cities utilize an integrated network of Information and Communication Technologies (ICT) to optimize various aspects of urban living, including transportation, healthcare, utilities, and public services. Characterized by interconnected devices, data-driven decision-making, and citizen engagement, Smart Cities prioritize innovation and the seamless integration of digital solutions to create more livable and resilient urban environments.

3.2 The Importance of Sustainable Energy Solutions in Smart City Development

Sustainable energy solutions lie at the core of Smart City development, serving as a linchpin for environmental stewardship, resilience, and long-term viability. As Smart Cities strive for efficiency and reduced environmental impact, the integration of sustainable energy practices becomes imperative. Kamyab et al. (2020) present the strategies for transitioning to sustainable energy systems. By adopting renewable energy sources, optimizing energy consumption through smart grids, and incorporating energy-efficient technologies, Smart Cities aim to mitigate the environmental footprint while ensuring a stable and reliable energy supply for their growing populations. This focus on sustainable energy not only aligns with global environmental goals but also contributes to the economic and social sustainability of Smart Cities.

3.3 Challenges and Opportunities in Integrating WtE Into Smart City Initiatives

The integration of Waste-to-Energy (WtE) into the fabric of Smart Cities presents both challenges and opportunities. While WtE offers a valuable solution for waste management and energy generation, its seamless integration requires addressing technological, regulatory, and social hurdles. Challenges include optimizing WtE processes to align with the dynamic waste compositions of urban environments, ensuring environmental compliance, and overcoming potential public resistance. However, these challenges come with opportunities for innovation. Smart Cities can leverage Internet of Things (IoT) and Machine Learning (ML) technologies to enhance the efficiency of WtE processes, from real-time monitoring of waste streams to predictive analytics for energy production. Furthermore, engaging citizens in the sustainable vision of WtE through awareness campaigns and participatory initiatives can turn challenges into collaborative opportunities, fostering a more sustainable and integrated urban future.

4. MACHINE LEARNING IN WASTE-TO-ENERGY AND INTERNET OF THINGS (IOT) IN WASTE MANAGEMENT

4.1 The Role of ML in Predicting and Optimizing Waste Conversion Processes

Machine Learning (ML) emerges as a transformative force in Waste-to-Energy (WtE) systems, revolutionizing the prediction and optimization of waste conversion processes. ML algorithms play a crucial role in forecasting optimal combustion parameters based on historical data and real-time inputs. By continuously learning from the dynamic nature of waste compositions, ML models enhance the adaptability of WtE facilities. Predictive analytics enable the fine-tuning of combustion conditions, ensuring maximal energy output while minimizing environmental impact. ML's ability to process complex datasets and identify patterns contributes to the optimization of energy recovery from diverse waste streams.

4.2 ML Applications in Energy Production Efficiency and Waste Composition Analysis

In the realm of Waste-to-Energy, ML applications extend beyond predictive modeling to enhance energy production efficiency and analyze waste composition. ML algorithms are deployed to optimize the efficiency of energy conversion processes, ensuring that WtE facilities operate at peak performance. These algorithms learn from data on energy production, combustion dynamics, and environmental factors, enabling WtE systems to continuously self-optimize. Additionally, ML facilitates advanced waste composition analysis, providing insights into the calorific value, moisture content, and chemical composition of different waste types. This information empowers WtE facilities to dynamically adjust operational parameters, improving overall efficiency and reducing emissions.

Figure 4. Machine learning in waste-to-energy

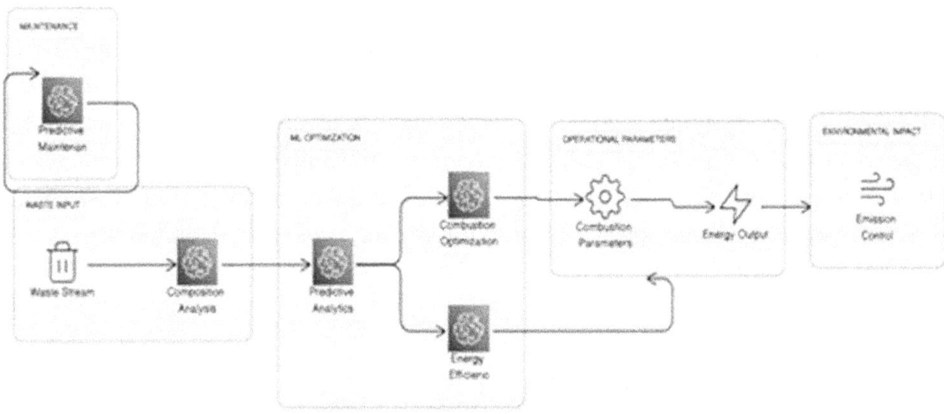

4.3 IoT Applications for Waste Collection and Monitoring

In the realm of waste management, the Internet of Things (IoT) plays a pivotal role in revolutionizing traditional practices. IoT applications for waste collection and monitoring leverage interconnected devices and sensors to enhance the efficiency and sustainability of waste management systems. Smart waste bins equipped with IoT technology can communicate real-time data on fill levels to central monitoring systems. This enables optimized waste collection routes and schedules, reducing operational costs, minimizing fuel consumption, and improving overall logistics. Mukherjee et al. (2021) provides an overview of modern and smart technologies for waste disposal and management. Additionally, IoT facilitates dynamic waste tracking, allowing authorities to monitor the movement of waste containers throughout the urban landscape, ensuring timely and precise waste collection.

4.4 Sensor Technologies for Real-Time Data Acquisition from Waste Management Systems

Sensor technologies form the backbone of real-time data acquisition from waste management systems within the IoT framework. Various sensor types are deployed to capture critical information about waste streams, including fill levels, types of waste, and environmental conditions. Ultrasonic sensors, weight sensors, and RFID (Radio-Frequency Identification) tags are commonly employed to gather precise data on the status and contents of waste bins. These sensors enable cities to create a comprehensive and accurate picture of their waste generation patterns, empowering data-driven decision-making for optimized waste collection and resource allocation.

4.5 Data Analytics and Optimization in Waste Logistics Using IoT

The integration of IoT in waste management goes beyond real-time data acquisition, extending to sophisticated data analytics and optimization strategies. IoT-generated data is harnessed through advanced analytics and Machine Learning (ML) algorithms to derive actionable insights. These insights aid in optimizing waste logistics by predicting future waste generation patterns, identifying trends, and recommending efficient collection routes. ML algorithms can adapt to changing conditions, ensuring that waste management processes remain agile and responsive. By leveraging IoT data analytics, cities can achieve higher operational efficiency, reduced environmental impact, and improved overall sustainability in waste management practices. By combining IoT and data optimization, waste management is positioned within the larger framework of Smart City projects, resulting in an intelligent and resource-efficient urban environment.

5. CHALLENGES AND SOLUTIONS

5.1 Environmental and Social Challenges Associated With Waste-to-Energy

Implementing Waste-to-Energy (WtE) systems is accompanied by environmental and social challenges that require careful consideration. One key environmental challenge is the potential emission of pollutants during the combustion process, which raises concerns about air quality. Additionally, there may be apprehensions among communities regarding the environmental impact of ash residue generated from the incineration of waste. Social challenges include public resistance to WtE facilities, driven by concerns about health, safety, and the perception of the visual and olfactory impact of such installations. Ghosh et al. (2023) investigates the impact of leachate and landfill gas on the environment and health, and proposes strategies to promote sustainability.

5.2 Technological Challenges in Implementing IoT and ML in WtE

The integration of Internet of Things (IoT) and Machine Learning (ML) in WtE introduces technological challenges that necessitate strategic solutions. The dynamic nature of waste compositions poses a challenge to IoT sensor accuracy, requiring constant calibration and adaptation. ML faces challenges related to the complexity of combustion processes and the need for large datasets for effective predictive modeling. Kazeem, Olawumi and Osunsanmi (2023) explore the potential of Artificial Intelligence and Machine Learning to improve construction processes and foster sustainable communities. Additionally, the potential cybersecurity threats associated with interconnected IoT devices in WtE systems demand robust security measures.

5.3 Strategies for Addressing Challenges and Ensuring Sustainability

To address the challenges associated with Waste-to-Energy and ensure its sustainability, a multifaceted approach is essential:

Emission Control Technologies: Implementing advanced emission control technologies can mitigate environmental concerns. Scrubbers, filters, and other pollution control measures can be employed to reduce the release of pollutants into the atmosphere.

Public Engagement and Awareness: To overcome social challenges, proactive public engagement and awareness campaigns are crucial. Providing transparent information about the benefits, safety measures, and environmental impact of WtE facilities can foster community acceptance.

Advanced Sensor Technologies: Investing in advanced sensor technologies for IoT can enhance the accuracy of waste monitoring. Sensor innovation, including multi-sensor fusion, can improve real-time data acquisition, enabling more precise waste management and combustion optimization.

Continuous Research and Development: Technological challenges can be addressed through continuous research and development. Innovations in ML algorithms tailored to WtE processes, coupled with advancements in combustion technologies, can enhance the efficiency and adaptability of these systems.

Cybersecurity Measures: To address technological challenges related to IoT security, robust cybersecurity measures must be implemented. This includes encryption, secure communication protocols, and regular security audits to safeguard against potential threats.

Collaboration and Regulatory Frameworks: Establishing collaboration between stakeholders, including government bodies, industry players, and communities, is crucial. Implementing and enforcing comprehensive regulatory frameworks ensures that WtE facilities adhere to strict environmental and safety standards.

By adopting these strategies, the challenges associated with Waste-to-Energy can be effectively mitigated, paving the way for sustainable and socially accepted solutions that align with the broader goals of urban resilience and environmental stewardship.

6. REGULATORY FRAMEWORK AND POLICIES

6.1 Overview of Existing Regulations Governing Waste-to-Energy

The regulatory landscape surrounding Waste-to-Energy (WtE) projects is crucial for ensuring environmental compliance, public safety, and the sustainable operation of these facilities. Existing regulations governing WtE projects vary globally, reflecting the diverse approaches taken by different jurisdictions. Common elements within these regulations include emissions standards, waste handling guidelines, and safety protocols.

In many regions, WtE facilities must adhere to strict emission limits to minimize the release of pollutants into the atmosphere. Regulations often specify permissible levels of pollutants such as sulfur dioxide, nitrogen oxides, and particulate matter. Additionally, guidelines for waste handling and disposal are established to prevent environmental contamination and ensure the safe management of residual ash.

6.2 The Role of Government Policies in Promoting Sustainable Energy Practices

Government policies play a pivotal role in promoting sustainable energy practices within the Waste-to-Energy sector. Key policy initiatives include:

Renewable Energy Targets: Governments often set targets for renewable energy generation, encouraging the integration of WtE into the broader renewable energy mix. This contributes to a diversified and sustainable energy portfolio.

Feed-in Tariffs and Incentives: Financial incentives, such as feed-in tariffs and tax credits, can stimulate investment in WtE projects. These measures make WtE economically viable and attractive to private investors.

Waste Management Strategies: Integrated waste management strategies that prioritize WtE as a component contribute to sustainable waste practices. Governments can implement policies that favour WtE over traditional land filling, aligning with circular economy principles.

Community Engagement and Awareness: Policies promoting community engagement and awareness campaigns foster public acceptance of WtE projects. Governments can facilitate dialogue between project developers and communities to address concerns and build support.

Figure 5. Government policies for sustainable in waste-to-energy sector

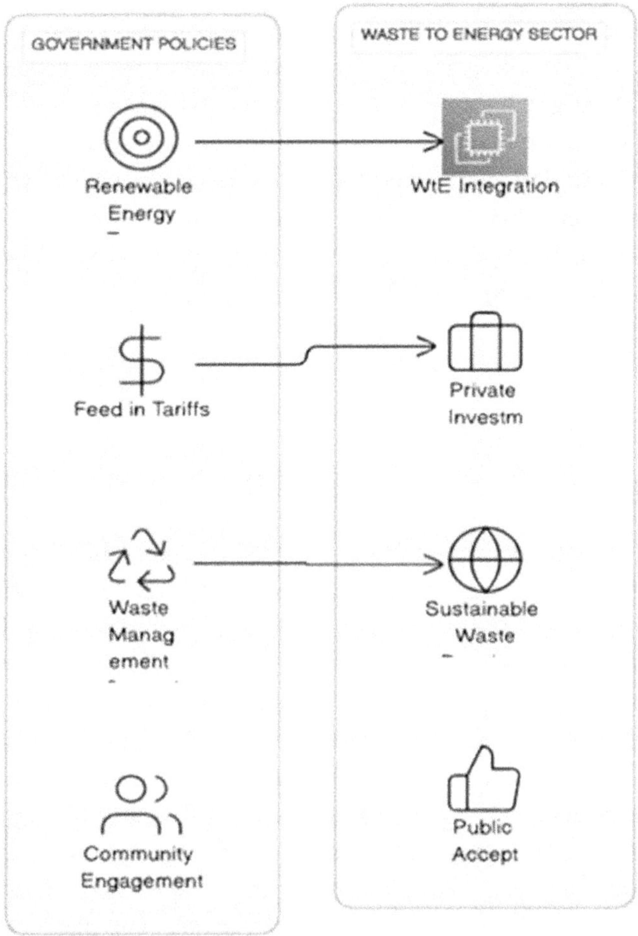

6.3 Recommendations for a Supportive Regulatory Environment

To create a supportive regulatory environment for Waste-to-Energy, the following recommendations are essential:

Harmonization of Standards: Governments should work towards harmonizing emission standards and waste handling regulations to create consistency across regions. This streamlines compliance for WtE operators and ensures a level playing field.

Technology-Neutral Policies: Regulatory frameworks should be technology-neutral, allowing for flexibility and innovation in the adoption of advanced WtE technologies. This approach encourages the exploration of diverse solutions tailored to specific waste compositions.

Continuous Review and Adaptation: Given the dynamic nature of waste composition and technological advancements, regulatory frameworks must undergo continuous review and adaptation. This ensures that standards remain relevant, reflecting the latest environmental and safety considerations.

Incentivizing Research and Development: Governments can incentivize research and development in WtE technologies through grants, subsidies, and collaborative programs. This encourages the exploration of innovative solutions and enhances the efficiency of waste conversion processes.

Public Participation: In the development of regulatory frameworks, governments should actively involve stakeholders, including industry experts, environmental organizations, and local communities. This inclusive approach ensures that regulations address diverse perspectives and concerns.

A supportive regulatory environment fosters the responsible and sustainable growth of the Waste-to-Energy sector. By aligning regulations with renewable energy goals, promoting community engagement, and incentivizing innovation, governments can contribute to the development of WtE projects that are environmentally sound, economically viable, and socially accepted.

7. CASE STUDIES

7.1 Showcase of Successful Waste-to-Energy Projects in Smart Cities

Implementing successful Waste-to-Energy (WtE) projects in Smart Cities serves as a testament to the feasibility and impact of integrating advanced technologies into urban waste management. Several case studies highlight exemplary projects that have demonstrated effective Waste-to-Energy solutions within the context of Smart Cities:

Copenhagen, Denmark - Amager Bakke Waste-to-Energy Plant: Copenhagen's Amager Bakke Waste-to-Energy Plant exemplifies the integration of cutting-edge technology and sustainable urban development. The facility not only incinerates waste to generate energy but also features a recreational space, incorporating a ski slope on its roof. The project showcases how Waste-to-Energy can coexist with public spaces, contributing to the city's energy needs while providing a unique and engaging urban environment.

Shenzhen, China - Shenzhen East Waste-to-Energy Plant: Shenzhen's East Waste-to-Energy Plant is one of the largest and most advanced WtE facilities globally. The plant utilizes grate combustion technology and incorporates flue gas treatment systems to minimize emissions. With the capacity to process thousands of tons of waste daily, it plays a pivotal role in Shenzhen's waste management strategy, contributing to the city's goals of sustainability and environmental responsibility.

Vienna, Austria - Spittelau Waste-to-Energy Plant: The Spittelau Waste-to-Energy Plant in Vienna represents a successful case of combining architectural aesthetics with energy generation. Designed by renowned architect Friedensreich Hundertwasser, the plant incinerates waste and converts it into district heating. The unique design, coupled with advanced pollution control technologies, demonstrates how Waste-to-Energy can be integrated into urban landscapes harmoniously.

Singapore - Integrated Waste Management Facility (IWMF): Singapore's Integrated Waste Management Facility (IWMF) is a state-of-the-art project that combines Waste-to-Energy with recycling and anaerobic digestion. The facility maximizes resource recovery and energy generation from waste while incorporating stringent environmental standards. The IWMF reflects Singapore's commitment to sustainable waste management practices in its journey toward becoming a Smart Nation.

These case studies underscore the diverse approaches to Waste-to-Energy in Smart Cities, demonstrating not only the technological prowess of these solutions but also their integration into the urban fabric. Successful projects not only address waste management challenges but also contribute to sustainable energy practices, environmental conservation, and the creation of resilient, livable urban spaces. The experiences of these cities provide valuable insights for other urban centers seeking innovative and effective waste management solutions within the framework of Smart City development.

7.2 Analysis of the Impact of IoT and ML on Project Outcomes

Examining the impact of Internet of Things (IoT) and Machine Learning (ML) on Waste-to-Energy (WtE) projects provides valuable insights into how these technologies enhance project outcomes. The integration of IoT and ML is crucial for optimizing waste management processes, improving energy production efficiency, and ensuring sustainability. Khan et al. (2022) present a comprehensive review of the current state of municipal solid waste management, and the potential of waste-to-energy technology. Here are case studies that highlight the transformative impact of IoT and ML on Waste-to-Energy initiatives:

Stockholm, Sweden - Högdalenverket Waste-to-Energy Plant: The Högdalenverket WtE Plant in Stockholm illustrates the significant impact of IoT on waste collection optimization. By deploying smart waste bins equipped with fill-level sensors and GPS trackers, the city improved the efficiency of waste collection routes. The data generated by IoT devices enabled real-time monitoring and dynamic route adjustments, resulting in reduced operational costs and minimized environmental impact. ML algorithms further analyzed the data to predict peak waste generation times, allowing for proactive scheduling and resource allocation.

Barcelona, Spain – Waste In Flow IoT Platform: Barcelona's Waste In Flow IoT platform demonstrates the power of comprehensive waste data analytics. The city deployed IoT sensors across waste containers to monitor fill levels, track collection routes, and optimize logistics. ML algorithms processed this data to identify patterns in waste generation, enabling predictive modeling for future waste flows. The implementation resulted in a significant reduction in collection costs, improved resource allocation, and a more sustainable waste management system.

Oslo, Norway - Klemetsrud Waste-to-Energy Plant: The Klemetsrud WtE Plant in Oslo showcases the transformative impact of ML on energy production efficiency. By incorporating ML algorithms into the combustion control system, the plant optimized operational parameters based on real-time data. ML continuously learned from the combustion process, adapting to changes in waste composition and environmental conditions. This dynamic optimization led to increased energy output, reduced emissions, and enhanced overall efficiency in converting waste to energy.

San Francisco, USA - Recology's Recycle Central: San Francisco's Recology implemented ML in its recycling processes, enhancing waste composition analysis. ML algorithms processed data from sorting facilities to identify and categorize recyclable materials with greater precision. This resulted in improved sorting accuracy, increased recycling rates, and minimized contamination. The implementation of ML-driven sorting technologies positioned Recology as a leader in sustainable waste management practices.

In these case studies, the incorporation of IoT and ML technologies consistently led to improved project outcomes. The dynamic capabilities of IoT, coupled with the analytical power of ML, contributed to optimized waste collection, enhanced energy production efficiency, and more accurate waste composition analysis. The success of these projects underscores the instrumental role of IoT and ML in shaping the future of Waste-to-Energy initiatives, making them more intelligent, adaptive, and sustainable within the context of Smart Cities.

7.3 Lessons Learned and Best Practices From Real-World Implementations

Analyzing real-world implementations of Waste-to-Energy (WtE) projects provides valuable insights into lessons learned and best practices. These case studies highlight key takeaways and strategies derived from practical experiences, contributing to the continuous improvement of Waste-to-Energy initiatives within the broader context of sustainable urban development:

Waste-to-Energy Facility in Singapore - Integrated Waste Management Facility (IWMF):

Lessons Learned:

- Holistic Approach: The IWMF in Singapore exemplifies the importance of adopting a holistic approach that integrates Waste-to-Energy with recycling and anaerobic digestion. This comprehensive strategy maximizes resource recovery and minimizes environmental impact.
- Community Engagement: Successful implementation involves proactive community engagement and communication. Singapore's approach included public awareness campaigns and educational initiatives to address concerns and build support for the project.

Best Practices:

- Multi-Technology Integration: The facility showcases best practices in integrating multiple technologies for waste treatment, demonstrating that a combination of approaches can yield superior results.
- Stringent Environmental Standards: Adhering to stringent environmental standards and regulations is a best practice that ensures the sustainable operation of WtE facilities.

Waste-to-Energy Plant in Copenhagen, Denmark - Amager Bakke: Lessons Learned:

- Architectural Integration: The Amager Bakke plant illustrates the importance of architectural integration in Waste-to-Energy projects. The inclusion of recreational spaces, such as a ski slope, showcases how WtE facilities can coexist harmoniously with urban landscapes.
- Public-Private Partnerships: Successful projects often involve strong public-private partnerships. Copenhagen's model demonstrates how collaboration between the public sector and private entities can lead to innovative and sustainable solutions.

Best Practices:

- Resource Recovery: The Amager Bakke plant's incorporation of resource recovery practices, such as recovering metals from ash, sets a best practice for maximizing the value extracted from waste streams.
- Innovative Design: The plant's innovative architectural design serves as a best practice in making Waste-to-Energy facilities visually appealing and socially acceptable.

Waste Management System in Barcelona, Spain – Waste In Flow IoT Platform: Lessons Learned:

- Data Security: Barcelona's implementation highlights the importance of prioritizing data security and privacy in IoT platforms. Lessons learned include the need for robust cybersecurity measures to safeguard sensitive information.
- Continuous Monitoring: Real-time monitoring through IoT is crucial for dynamic waste management. The project emphasizes the significance of continuous data acquisition to adapt to changing waste patterns.

Best Practices:

- Predictive Analytics: Implementing ML-driven predictive analytics for waste flow patterns sets a best practice for optimizing waste collection routes and schedules.
- Community Involvement: Best practices include involving the community in waste management decisions, fostering a sense of ownership and cooperation.

These case studies provide a wealth of lessons learned and best practices that can guide future Waste-to-Energy projects. By understanding the challenges faced and successful strategies employed, stakeholders can contribute to the ongoing evolution of sustainable waste management practices in Smart Cities.

8. FUTURE TRENDS AND INNOVATIONS

8.1 Emerging Trends in Waste-to-Energy Technology

The future of Waste-to-Energy (WtE) technology is poised for exciting developments, driven by advancements in efficiency, sustainability, and integration with smart technologies. Key emerging trends include:

Advanced Thermal Conversion: New developments in the field of thermal conversion, such pyrolysis and gasification, are anticipated to become more well-known. When it comes to trash conversion, these methods are more environmentally friendly than traditional incineration since they are more efficient and produce fewer pollutants.

Decentralized WtE Systems: Future trends indicate a shift towards decentralized Waste-to-Energy systems, allowing for smaller, modular facilities that can be strategically placed within urban areas. Decentralization improves waste management efficiency and reduces transportation-related environmental impacts.

Carbon Capture and Utilization (CCU): The integration of CCU technologies within WtE processes is a promising trend. Capturing and utilizing carbon emissions from the combustion of waste for beneficial purposes, such as the production of synthetic fuels or materials, contributes to a circular economy.

Biological Waste-to-Energy: Advancements in biological processes, including anaerobic digestion and microbial fuel cells, are emerging as sustainable alternatives. These technologies harness the energy potential of organic waste while producing valuable by-products like biogas and organic fertilizers.

8.2 Potential Advancements in IoT and ML Applications for WtE

The integration of Internet of Things (IoT) and Machine Learning (ML) applications is expected to revolutionize Waste-to-Energy processes, enhancing operational efficiency and sustainability. Anticipated advancements include:

Real-time Process Optimization: IoT sensors will continue to play a crucial role in monitoring and optimizing WtE processes in real time. ML algorithms will analyze data from these sensors to dynamically adjust operational parameters, improving energy output and reducing environmental impact.

Predictive Maintenance: ML-driven predictive maintenance models will become more sophisticated, enabling WtE facilities to anticipate equipment failures and schedule maintenance proactively. This reduces downtime, enhances reliability, and extends the lifespan of critical components.

Waste Sorting Automation: IoT-enabled sensors and ML algorithms will be increasingly employed to automate the sorting of waste streams. This enhances recycling efficiency, minimizes contamination, and ensures that WtE facilities receive a consistent feedstock for optimal energy recovery.

Energy Demand Forecasting: ML applications will be utilized for accurate forecasting of energy demand based on waste compositions, seasonal variations, and other factors. This enables WtE facilities to align their energy production with the needs of the grid, contributing to grid stability.

Figure 6. IoT and ML applications in waste-to-energy processes

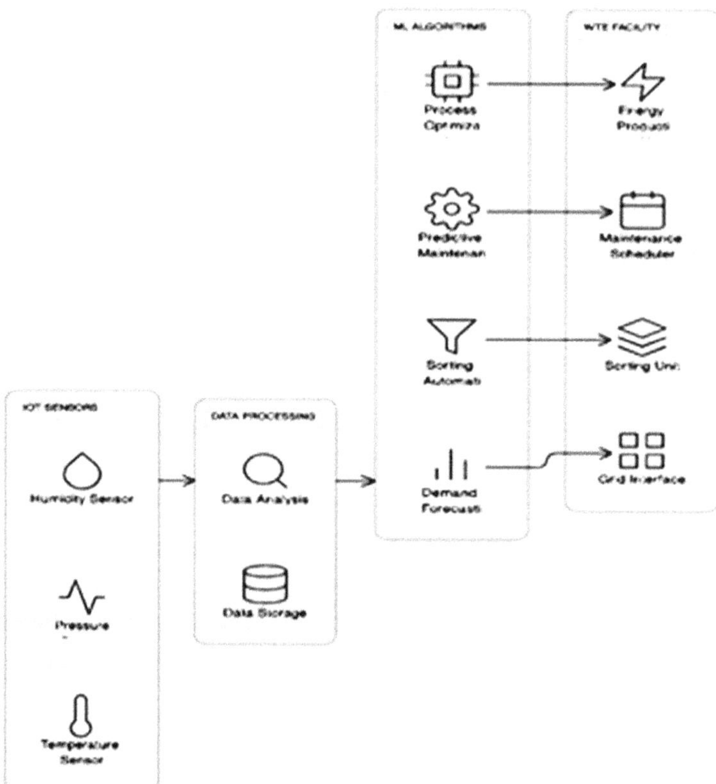

8.3 The Role of Waste-to-Energy in the Future Landscape of Smart Cities

Waste-to-Energy is poised to play a central role in the future landscape of Smart Cities, contributing to sustainability, resilience, and circular economy principles:

Integrated Smart Waste Management: Waste-to-Energy will be seamlessly integrated into comprehensive smart waste management systems. IoT devices will enable real-time monitoring, optimized collection routes, and data-driven decision-making for efficient waste handling.

Decentralized Energy Generation: Decentralized WtE facilities will be strategically located within Smart Cities, reducing the environmental impact of waste transportation. These facilities will contribute to local energy generation, enhancing grid resilience and supporting sustainable urban development.

Circular Economy Integration: Waste-to-Energy will be a key player in the circular economy, extracting maximum value from waste streams through energy recovery and resource utilization. Byproducts such as heat, biogas, and recovered materials will be integrated into city systems, minimizing waste and promoting resource efficiency.

Community Engagement and Education: Smart Cities will leverage technology for enhanced community engagement and education on waste management practices. IoT-enabled platforms and applications will empower citizens with real-time information, fostering a sense of responsibility and participation in sustainable waste practices.

In summary, the future of Waste-to-Energy is marked by innovative technological trends, the integration of smart solutions, and a pivotal role within the evolving landscape of Smart Cities. As advancements in thermal conversion, decentralized systems, and digital technologies continue to unfold, Waste-to-Energy will contribute significantly to a more sustainable and resilient urban future.

9. CONCLUSION

In conclusion, the integration of Waste-to-Energy (WtE) solutions with Internet of Things (IoT) and Machine Learning (ML) technologies presents a transformative pathway towards sustainable power generation in smart cities. This study has elucidated the potential of leveraging IoT for real-time monitoring and control of waste management processes, optimizing waste collection routes, and enhancing overall operational efficiency. The synergistic coupling of ML algorithms with WtE facilities enables predictive maintenance, ensuring continuous and reliable power generation by anticipating equipment failures. The smart integration of these technologies not only mitigates environmental concerns associated with waste disposal but also contributes to the circular economy by converting waste into a valuable energy resource. Furthermore, the scalability and adaptability of these solutions empower cities to tailor their waste management and energy generation strategies to meet evolving demands. As smart cities strive for energy sustainability and environmental resilience, the confluence of WtE, IoT, and ML emerges as a promising frontier, promising a cleaner, greener, and more efficient urban future. However, it is crucial for stakeholders, including city planners, policymakers, and technology developers, to collaboratively address challenges related to data security, regulatory frameworks, and public awareness to ensure the successful implementation and long-term viability of these innovative waste-to-energy solutions in the complex urban ecosystems of smart cities. Embracing these solutions in a holistic and responsible manner holds the key to realizing a paradigm shift in urban sustainability, where waste becomes not just a challenge but a valuable resource driving the power needs of tomorrow's smart cities.

REFERENCES

Alao, M. A., Popoola, O. M., & Ayodele, T. R. (2021). Selection of waste-to-energy technology for distributed generation using IDOCRIW-Weighted TOPSIS method: A case study of the City of Johannesburg, South Africa. *Renewable Energy*, *178*, 162–183. doi:10.1016/j.renene.2021.06.031

AlQattan, N., Acheampong, M., Jaward, F. M., Ertem, F. C., Vijayakumar, N., & Bello, T. (2018). Reviewing the potential of Waste-to-Energy (WTE) technologies for Sustainable Development Goal (SDG) numbers seven and eleven. *Renewable Energy Focus*, *27*, 97–110. doi:10.1016/j.ref.2018.09.005

Di Matteo, U., Nastasi, B., Albo, A., & Astiaso Garcia, D. (2017). Energy contribution of OFMSW (Organic Fraction of Municipal Solid Waste) to energy-environmental sustainability in urban areas at small scale. *Energies*, *10*(2), 229. doi:10.3390/en10020229

Ebolor, A. (2023). Backcasting frugally innovative smart sustainable future cities. *Journal of Cleaner Production*, *383*, 135300. doi:10.1016/j.jclepro.2022.135300

Elif, A. K., Kaya, K., Yaslan, Y., & Oktug, S. F. (2021, November). LoRaWAN-aided waste-to-energy concept model in smart cities. In *2021 International Conference on Computer, Information and Telecommunication Systems (CITS)* (pp. 1-5). IEEE. 10.1109/CITS52676.2021.9618578

Ghosh, A., Kumar, S., & Das, J. (2023). Impact of leachate and landfill gas on the ecosystem and health: Research trends and the way forward towards sustainability. *Journal of Environmental Management*, *336*, 117708. doi:10.1016/j.jenvman.2023.117708 PMID:36913859

Hou, Y., Wang, Q., Zhou, K., Zhang, L., & Tan, T. (2024). Integrated machine learning methods with oversampling technique for regional suitability prediction of waste-to-energy incineration projects. *Waste Management (New York, N.Y.)*, *174*, 251–262. doi:10.1016/j.wasman.2023.12.006 PMID:38070444

Hussain, Z., Mishra, J., & Vanacore, E. (2020). Waste to energy and circular economy: The case of anaerobic digestion. *Journal of Enterprise Information Management*, *33*(4), 817–838. doi:10.1108/JEIM-02-2019-0049

Jain, A., Sharma, A., Jately, V., & Azzopardi, B. (Eds.). (2023). *Sustainable Energy Solutions with Artificial Intelligence, Blockchain Technology, and Internet of Things*. CRC Press. doi:10.1201/9781003356639

Kabugo, J. C., Jämsä-Jounela, S. L., Schiemann, R., & Binder, C. (2020). Industry 4.0 based process data analytics platform: A waste-to-energy plant case study. *International Journal of Electrical Power & Energy Systems*, *115*, 105508. doi:10.1016/j.ijepes.2019.105508

Kamyab, H., Klemeš, J. J., Van Fan, Y., & Lee, C. T. (2020). Transition to sustainable energy system for smart cities and industries. *Energy*, *207*, 118104. doi:10.1016/j.energy.2020.118104

Kaya, K., Ak, E., Yaslan, Y., & Oktug, S. F. (2021). Waste-to-Energy Framework: An intelligent energy recycling management. *Sustainable Computing : Informatics and Systems*, *30*, 100548. doi:10.1016/j.suscom.2021.100548

Kazeem, K. O., Olawumi, T. O., & Osunsanmi, T. (2023). Roles of Artificial Intelligence and Machine Learning in Enhancing Construction Processes and Sustainable Communities. *Buildings*, *13*(8), 2061. doi:10.3390/buildings13082061

Khalil, R. A., Saeed, N., Masood, M., Fard, Y. M., Alouini, M. S., & Al-Naffouri, T. Y. (2021). Deep learning in the industrial internet of things: Potentials, challenges, and emerging applications. *IEEE Internet of Things Journal*, *8*(14), 11016–11040. doi:10.1109/JIOT.2021.3051414

Khan, A. H., López-Maldonado, E. A., Alam, S. S., Khan, N. A., López, J. R. L., Herrera, P. F. M., Abutaleb, A., Ahmed, S., & Singh, L. (2022). Municipal solid waste generation and the current state of waste-to-energy potential: State of art review. *Energy Conversion and Management*, *267*, 115905. doi:10.1016/j.enconman.2022.115905

Mishra, A. R., Pamučar, D., Hezam, I. M., Chakrabortty, R. K., Rani, P., Božanić, D., & Ćirović, G. (2022). Interval-valued pythagorean fuzzy similarity measure-based complex proportional assessment method for waste-to-energy technology selection. *Processes (Basel, Switzerland)*, *10*(5), 1015. doi:10.3390/pr10051015

Mukherjee, A. G., Wanjari, U. R., Chakraborty, R., Renu, K., Vellingiri, B., George, A., ... Gopalakrishnan, A. V. (2021). A review on modern and smart technologies for efficient waste disposal and management. *Journal of Environmental Management*, *297*, 113347. doi:10.1016/j.jenvman.2021.113347 PMID:34314963

Nkuna, S. G., Olwal, T. O., Chowdhury, S. D., & Ndambuki, J. M. (2024). A Review of Wastewater Sludge-to-Energy Generation focused on Thermochemical Technologies: An Improved Technological, Economical and Socio-Environmental Aspect. *Cleaner Waste Systems*, 100130.

Sharma, N., Ingole, S., Pokhariya, H. S., Parmar, A., Shilpa, K., Reddy, U., & Hussny, H. A. (2023). From Waste to Worth Management: A Comprehensive Intelligent Approach to Resource Utilization and Waste Minimization. In E3S Web of Conferences (Vol. 453, p. 01029). EDP Sciences. doi:10.1051/e3sconf/202345301029

Sharma, V., & Kumar, S. (2023, May). Role of Artificial Intelligence (AI) to Enhance the Security and Privacy of Data in Smart Cities. In *2023 3rd International Conference on Advance Computing and Innovative Technologies in Engineering (ICACITE)* (pp. 596-599). IEEE. 10.1109/ICACITE57410.2023.10182455

Srivastava, R. K., Shetti, N. P., Reddy, K. R., & Aminabhavi, T. M. (2020). Sustainable energy from waste organic matters via efficient microbial processes. *Science of the Total Environment*, *722*, 137927.

Swathika, O. G., Karthikeyan, K., & Padmanaban, S. (Eds.). (2023). IoT and Analytics in Renewable Energy Systems (Volume 2): AI, ML and IoT Deployment in Sustainable Smart Cities. CRC Press.

Szpilko, D., de la Torre Gallegos, A., Jimenez Naharro, F., Rzepka, A., & Remiszewska, A. (2023). Waste Management in the Smart City: Current Practices and Future Directions. *Resources*, *12*(10), 115. doi:10.3390/resources12100115

Teh, J. S., Teoh, Y. H., How, H. G., Le, T. D., Jason, Y. J. J., Nguyen, H. T., & Loo, D. L. (2021). The potential of sustainable biomass producer gas as a waste-to-energy alternative in Malaysia. *Sustainability (Basel)*, *13*(7), 3877. doi:10.3390/su13073877

Tyagi, V. K., & Lo, S. L. (2013). Sludge: A waste or renewable source for energy and resources recovery? *Renewable & Sustainable Energy Reviews*, *25*, 708–728. doi:10.1016/j.rser.2013.05.029

Vashishth, T. K., Sharma, V., Sharma, K. K., Kumar, B., Chaudhary, S., & Panwar, R. (2024). Intelligent Resource Allocation and Optimization for Industrial Robotics Using AI and Blockchain. In AI and Blockchain Applications in Industrial Robotics (pp. 82-110). IGI Global. doi:10.4018/979-8-3693-0659-8.ch004

KEY TERMS AND DEFINITIONS

Artificial Intelligence (AI): Is a field of computer science that focuses on creating systems capable of performing tasks that typically require human intelligence. These tasks include learning from experience, adapting to new information, understanding natural language, recognizing patterns, and solving complex problems. AI encompasses various approaches, including machine learning and deep learning, to enable machines to simulate human-like cognitive functions and contribute to automation, decision-making, and problem-solving across diverse applications.

Internet of Things (IoT): Refers to a network of interconnected devices and objects embedded with sensors, software, and other technologies, enabling them to collect and exchange data. IoT facilitates seamless communication and collaboration between devices, allowing them to interact intelligently and autonomously. This interconnected ecosystem spans various domains, including homes, industries, and cities, creating a network where physical devices can share information and perform tasks to enhance efficiency, automation, and overall functionality.

Machine Learning (ML): Is a subset of artificial intelligence (AI) that empowers computers to learn and improve from experience without being explicitly programmed. It enables systems to analyze data, identify patterns, and make informed decisions, allowing them to evolve and adapt to new information over time. ML algorithms leverage statistical techniques to enable machines to perform tasks and make predictions or decisions without explicit programming for each task.

Natural Language Processing (NLP): Is a branch of artificial intelligence that deals with the interaction between computers and human language. It involves the development of algorithms and models that enable machines to understand, interpret, and generate human-like language. NLP encompasses tasks such as language translation, sentiment analysis, speech recognition, and text summarization, allowing computers to process and respond to natural language input, making human-computer communication more intuitive and effective.

Waste-to-Energy (WtE): Is a sustainable approach to managing solid waste by converting it into usable energy. This process involves the combustion or biological conversion of municipal solid waste, biomass, or other types of waste materials to generate electricity or heat. WtE not only reduces the volume of waste destined for landfills but also harnesses the energy content within waste to produce power, contributing to renewable energy goals and providing an environmentally conscious alternative to traditional waste disposal methods.

Chapter 8
Prediction of Water Quality Using Machine Learning

Tran Thi Hong Ngoc
An Giang University, Vietnam & National University, Ho Chi Minh City, Vietnam

Phan Truong Khanh
An Giang University, Vietnam & National University, Ho Chi Minh City, Vietnam

Sabyasachi Pramanik
https://orcid.org/0000-0002-9431-8751
Haldia Institute of Technology, India

ABSTRACT

With the fast growth of aquatic data, machine learning is essential for data analysis, categorization, and prediction. Data-driven models using machine learning may effectively handle complicated nonlinear problems in water research, unlike conventional approaches. Machine learning models and findings have been used to build, monitor, simulate, evaluate, and optimize water treatment and management systems in water environment research. Machine learning may also enhance water quality, pollution control, and watershed ecosystem security. This chapter discusses how ML approaches were used to assess water quality in surface, ground, drinking, sewage, and ocean water. The authors also suggest potential machine learning applications in aquatic situations.

1. INTRODUCTION

Wastewater carrying toxins from fast economic growth threatens natural water ecology. So, several water pollution management methods evolved. Water quality analysis and assessment have greatly enhanced water pollution control efficiency. The multivariate statistical approach, fuzzy inference, and water quality index (WQI) are among the various methods used to monitor and measure water quality globally. While many water quality metrics may be traced in accordance with regulations, the final findings may vary according to parameter selection. Taking into account that all water quality metrics is impractical due to cost, technical difficulty, and inability to account for variability. Recently, developments in machine

DOI: 10.4018/979-8-3693-1062-5.ch008

Copyright © 2024, IGI Global. Copying or distributing in print or electronic forms without written permission of IGI Global is prohibited.

learning have led academics to anticipate that huge volumes of data may be achieved and assessed to accomplish complex and large-scale water quality monitoring needs.

ML algorithms are used in artificial intelligence to examine data and find patterns to forecast future information. With its accuracy, flexibility, and extensibility, machine learning has become a popular data analysis and processing tool in several fields. Machine learning simplifies the finding of underlying mechanisms for complex nonlinear relational data. Recently, ML showed a huge potential as a tool in ecological science and engineering due to its versatility. In spite of the difficulty of ML for water quality measurement and assessment, much precise results are predicted.

Complex water kinds include drinking, wastewater, and groundwater, surface, marine, and fresh. These water kinds have varied qualities, making quality study difficult. Previous research suggests that machine learning may effectively handle these difficulties. In this study, we address the pros and cons of typical ML approaches and their implementations and performance in surface water, groundwater, drinking water, wastewater, and ocean water (Fig. 1).

2. MACHINE LEARNING OVERVIEW

ML is commonly utilized to find insights or have predictions from vast data from many contexts. Prior to using ML, data collecting, algorithm selection, model training, and validation are needed. Among these methods, selecting algorithm is the key aspect.

Figure 1. Water systems employ machine learning extensively. WWTP, wastewater treatment facility.

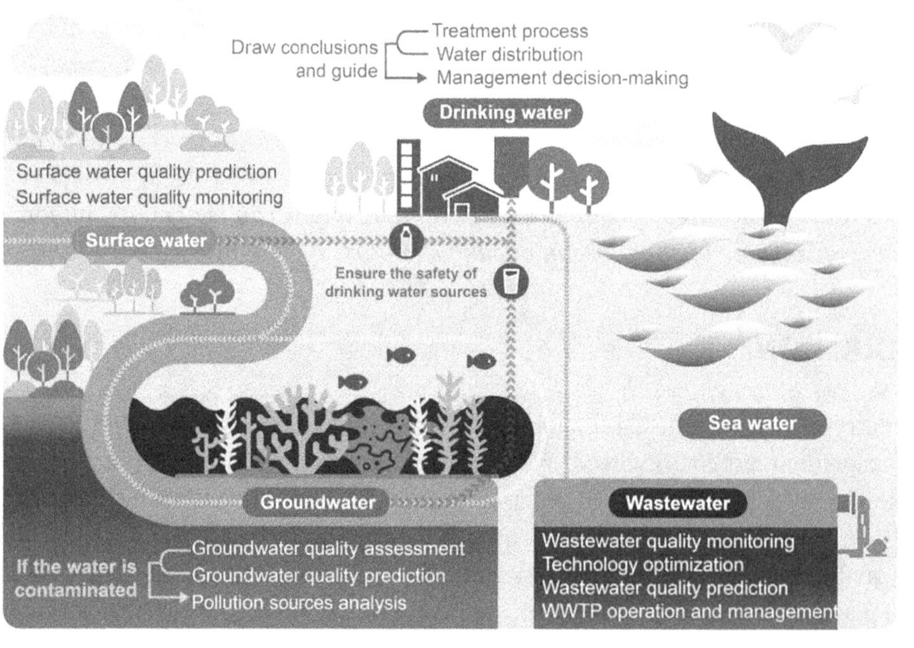

Machine learning has two primary classes: supervised and unsupervised. Labels in datasets distinguish these two kinds. Supervised learning predicts from labeled training datasets. Input and anticipated output values are included in each training instance. Supervised learning algorithms discover input-output correlations and create a predictive model to estimate the outcome from the I/P data. Supervised learning methods, such as LR, ANN, decision trees, SVM, Naive Bayes, KNN, and random forests are designed for data classification and regression.

In contrast, unsupervised learning handles data generally without labels, addressing pattern recognition problems using unlabeled training datasets. Unsupervised learning classifies training data depending on features, primarily via dimensionality reduction and grouping. But, the quantity and significance of categories are unknown. Thus, unsupervised learning is often employed for classification and association mining. PCA, K-means, and other unsupervised machine learning methods are popular. Reinforcement learning, which allows machines to generalize and solve unlearned problem is a different kind of ML method. In contrast to the other 2 ML classes, it is sometimes used in the aquatic aspect.

3. ML IN VARIOUS WATER APPLICATIONS

Various researchers have utilized ML to solve water treatment and management system problems (Fig. 2), like real-time tracking, estimation, pollutant source estimating, concentration prediction, water resource allotment, and technology optimization.

3.1 Implementations in Surface Water

Civic and industry wastewater from human actions is the principal cause of urban water quality degradation. ML in surface water quality analysis is trendy. Several surface water quality estimation and assessment techniques exist (Table 1). Various attempts were made to optimize ML models and improve estimation accuracy.

Data collecting is essential to machine learning model development. Additionally, aggregated and periodic water quality estimating findings may be benchmarked in water system management. Conventional environmental tracking approaches are used by agents. But, established approaches for in situ tracking have challenges. Remote sensing technologies provide real-time, huge-scale water quality tracking and show pollution movement and dispersion patterns that traditional approaches cannot identify. (Khanh, P. T. et al. 2023) saw that experiment-dependent ML let advanced optimization using real-time sensor data and satellite data, and the partial least squares (PLS), support vector regression, and DNN approaches were more accurate than conventional models. Since certain water quality variables, like pathogen concentrations, aren't optically active or need high-spatial-resolution hyperspectral data, remote sensing cannot directly detect them, but it may estimate those utilizing different measurable data. Wu et al. built a CNN model which can distinguish clean and dirty water from photos. Multiple comparison studies on a sea surface picture dataset confirmed the efficiency of this CNN. The benefit of CNN is that it uses the reflection picture as input without requiring feature engineering or parameter modification. Because of equipment or human error, few data will be missing, inaccurate, or destroyed, creating a sparse matrix and poor model application performance.

Figure 2. Various ML methods in water treatment and management systems. SVM, RF, ANN, decision tree, PCA, XGBoost, DO, and MP are used in the analysis.

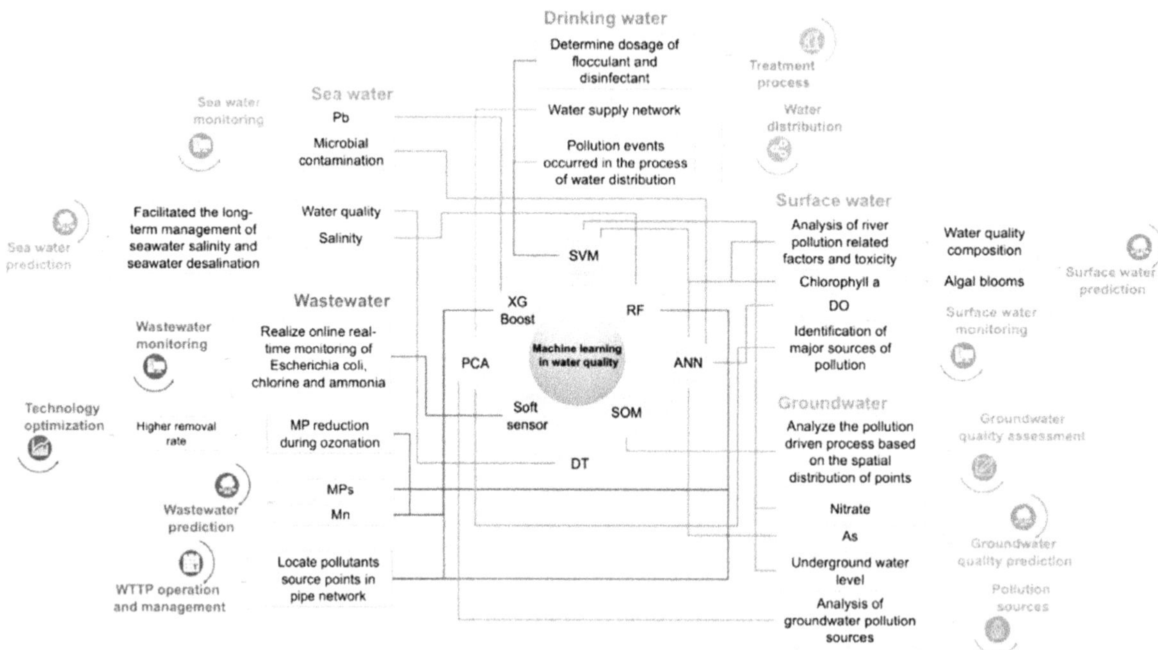

Data cleansing, another crucial ML stage, becomes necessary. Data cleaning may be done by not utilizing the raw data, utilizing averages or medians, or utilizing ML and matrix completion. (Ngọc, T. H. et al. 2023) used Deep Neural Network and deep matrix factorization to estimate organic O_2 requirement. The rationality and dependability of the technique were verified utilizing California Harbor waters as a case history. Data cleaning enhances machine learning model accuracy by improving data quality.

Machine learning prediction accuracy depends on model selection and training dataset quality. ANN and SVM predict water quality components well. SVM may outperform ANN in prediction and generalization. One explanation is because neural network model parameter tuning is unstable; therefore nonlinear disturbances greatly impair ANN accuracy. SVM minimizes generalization error better than ANN because it limits it rather than training error. Effective river management requires real-time monitoring of water quality or relying on other data while monitoring circumstances are insufficient due to complicated dynamic changes over time. Researchers have confirmed that LSTM and BWNN networks can manage fluctuating and non-seasonal water-quality data. Traditional linear statistical models like the autoregressive integrated moving average (ARIMA) model may estimate time series. It is substandard to the BWNN model that is motivated by the self-adaption of the ANN and the time-frequency features of wavelet basis functions, and the Long Short Term Memory technique that masters straightway from time-series data. Long Short Term Memory and BWNN recognize nicely the nonlinear connection between variables and their projected variables, and utilize past data to forecast the future.

The characteristics used to train machine learning models affect prediction accuracy. Redundant variables increase model complexity and decrease inverse power and accuracy. A most important surface water quality measures is dissolved oxygen (DO), which reflects the water environment and its capacity to support water life. The linear polynomial neural network approach predicted Danube River

DO concentration. The forecast accuracy was most affected by temperature, pH, BOD, and phosphorus content among 17 water quality factors. For prediction of DO accumulation in Columbia River, USA, among 5 variables chloride, NOX, cumulative dissolved solids, pH, and water temperature are closely associated with dissolved oxygen and may impact forecast accuracy. These findings align with (Roy, A. et al. 2023), who found that I/P parameters impact model estimation achievement. Furthermore to water parameters, eutrophication affects surface water quality forecast. (Ngoc, T. T. H. et al. 2023) discovered that nutrients, organic matter, and environmental factors generated algal blooms using the adaptive neuro-fuzzy inference system technique. (Jayasingh, R. et al. 2022) utilized meteorological and weekly water quality data to forecast chlorophyll-a concentrations in two U.S. locations. SVM and ANN showed equal accuracy. The incorporation of meteorological parameters greatly enhanced forecast accuracy. The machine learning model may also include regional hydrological and socioeconomic elements to provide complete regional water environment management.

ML model performance relies on its architecture, hence understanding algorithm logical structure is crucial to machine learning effectiveness. PNN's advantage over other neural network models in identifying crucial model parameters is that the quantity of hidden neurons and PNN layers is selected by data, preserving trial time. The Deep Neural Network model utilized to predict BOD has 19.20%–25.16% lower RMSE than conventional machine learning. Because there are DNN has numerous layers between its I/P and O/P, and it requires latest activation functions improve model convergence and minimize training difficulty compared to classic ANNs (sigmoid). Time series-based LSTM predicts water quality effectively. It has 3 information gates: input, forget, and output gate, cell state, and hidden state govern sequential information transmission, forgetting, and storage. BWNN can accomplish this aim, but needs enough input characteristics for accuracy.

3.2 Applications in Groundwater

Drinking water comes from groundwater. Thus, groundwater safety is vital to human well-being. ML has several applications in groundwater study, which includes quality evaluation and contamination estimation. Multivariate statistical analysis has become popular for groundwater quality assessments. PCA and cluster analysis are popular. Groundwater quality evaluation has been used SVM, DT, RF, and ANN algorithms. Studies on groundwater quality mostly examine ML approaches to determine viable solutions for certain challenges. In Tabriz City, Iran, (Pramanik, S. et al. 2021) compared 5 data mining techniques: normal DT, Random Forest, chi-square automatic interaction detector, and iterative dichotomizer to spot semiarid groundwater parameters and their impact on high-quality groundwater. (Pramanik, S. et al. 2022) calculated Seoul's urban groundwater quality spatial pattern using a self-organizing neural network and fuzzy c-means clustering. The researchers used a self-organizing map approach to classify groundwater samples into three categories by contamination degree and examined the pollution-directed technique dependent on geographic distribution. GIS methods were utilized to create groundwater quality maps to better detect contamination.

The intricate hydrogeology of groundwater contrasted predicting quality change trends is more challenging when dealing with surface water. Machine learning has been used to analyze regional data on a big scale and forecast water quality. PSO and SVM were used to assess and forecast groundwater WQI by (Samanta, D. et al. 2021) demonstrating its feasibility. A single groundwater contaminant, like nitrate and arsenic, may be estimated. () predicted groundwater nitrate constituent and distribution using an SVM. (Pramanik, S. et al. 2023) assessed groundwater nitrate contamination risk utilizing enhanced regression tree, multivariate discriminant analysis, and Support Vector Machine, and found that India's Khadar Plain is at higher risk of nitrate contamination. (Pramanik, S. et al. 2023) utilized ML to forecast US groundwater nitrate levels and discovered that it can also predict national groundwater quality.

(Vidya Chellam, V. et al. 2023) predicted groundwater arsenic contamination in Ohio, and Japan utilizing an ANN. Additionally, groundwater levels may be forecast. In a study by (Praveenkumar, S. et al. 2023), DNN was shown to be the most accurate and efficient machine learning approach for predicting groundwater levels throughout the season, compared to ANFIS and SVM. (Pramanik, S. 2023) used ensemble modeling to estimate Indian city groundwater levels with 85% accuracy.

The investigation of contamination sources is crucial for groundwater safety. Studies employ PCA and clustering extensively. After PCA reduced dimensionality and K-means grouped data, (Veeraiah, V. et al. 2023) examined natural and anthropogenic hydro-geochemistry sources. (Pramanik, S. and Bandyopadhyay, S. 2023) used multivariate statistical analysis and Principal Component Analysis to discover ground-water quality parameters.

Groundwater quality and resources are frequently examined using a data mining decision tree. This algorithm can identify and describe connections between input and output variables using certain criteria. Performance and capacity to generalize rules to detect drinking-quality groundwater are benefits of RF. Since continuous data sets are better for groundwater law induction than discrete data sets, RF's greatest performance (accuracy of 97.10%) gives effective groundwater resource planning and management judgments. Current groundwater quality index prediction research uses the integrated model that may merge numerous weak learners into a lone strong learner and increase estimation performance. Integration is fantastic with boosting. To create models with lower variance, it is important to reduce over fitting when merging excellent models.

3.3 Drinking Water Application

In drinking water source operation, analysis, distribution, and decision taking, machine learning is frequently used. Drinking water is usually surface or groundwater. The examination and estimation of source water quality using ML may help reduce pollution early. (Bansal, R. et al. 2022) investigated multisensor-dependent Artificial Neural Network and Support Vector Machine approaches for dynamic water quality tracking in 2022. The models generate satisfactory identification rates for the two water groups. Support Vector Machine was more stable than ANN. (Dushyant, K. et al. 2022) used drinking water quality information from 4 Norwegian metropolitans to suggest adaptive frequency analysis. Their findings supported early drinking water quality threat cautioning, administration, and decision-taking. Moreover, (Gupta, A. et al. 2022) combined LSTM and Deep Neural Network to forecast time series data and created a water quality estimation approach which can accurately estimate water quality in the following 6 months. (K.aushik, D. et al. 2022) employed a Support Vector Machine to forecast pollution episodes under unknown circumstances using UV absorption. All four SVM datasets have good detection rates and low error rates. Most investigations have used chemical or physical measures, while microbiological factors, notably for E. coli, have seldom been studied. Machine learning can estimate drinking water plant coagulant and disinfectant levels. SVM algorithms are prominent in occlusion and disinfection construction because to their simple structure and resilience. (Bhattacharya, A. et al. 2021) suggested a predictive chemical dose control technique that was more successful than proportional-integral-derivative feedback control based on SVM-predicted residual free chlorine.

The necessity of drinking water has motivated researchers to concentrate on typical metropolitan water supply framework functioning, fault tracking, and catastrophe estimation. Due to the intricacy of water supply networks, drinking water therapy facilities which satisfy regulations can be re-polluted in transportation that may be monitored utilizing biological stability measures and purified. Cluster analysis may show water quality differences between networks. Furthermore, (Mandal, A. et al. 2021) employed cluster analysis to determine how mixed water sources, including Al migration and seasonal fluctuations, affect aluminum remnants in urban drinking water supply frameworks. (Meslie, Y. et al. 2021) correctly casts water quality utilizing an RF technique. Burst water supply pipelines cause massive water loss and microbiological and chemical contamination. DL algorithms may forecast bursting locations with high uncertainty. (Pramanik, S. 2022) introduced a water leakage detection method using a random DT bagging classifier with shuffled frog-leaping optimization and minimal sensors at ideal locations in a WSN (water supply network). Pipe longevity matters in water-supply management. A sophisticated meta-learning framework dependent on a neural network by (Taviti Naidu, G. et al. 2023) demonstrated that residual chlorine affects pipeline service life. An SVM method may also forecast water distribution system contamination. (Chandan, R. R. et al. 2023) used PCA, the analytic hierarchy process, Random Forest and XGBoost frameworks to quantify catastrophe effects on water supply systems. However, real-time data collecting challenges restrict the practicality of this strategy.

Regional development and population growth are limited by water production capacity. (Mondal, D. et al. 2023) created a hybrid ANN-genetic algorithm weighted variables. The test findings indicate that this system effectively monitors water quality, having a strong correlation between projected and real values.

Machine learning can enhance wastewater treatment systems by analyzing historical data. (Ghosh, R. et al. 2023) used an SVM and adaptive evolutionary algorithm to mimic anaerobic, anOXic, and oXic conditions to reduce the anoXic tank capacity and conserve land area. Additionally, machine learning optimizes tertiary wastewater treatment methods including RO, NF, ozonize, and absorption. According to (Mall, P. K. et al. 2023) using an RF to anticipate micro pollutant decrease in ozonization led to improved removal efficiency. Using a high-resolution fluorescence excitation-emission matrix for machine learning may improve accuracy by computing the complicated nonlinear connection between statistical models for drinking water performance prediction.

The hybrid statistical model accurately predicts water production responses to different parameter variations, making it a valuable tool for changing water treatment systems rapidly and effectively. (Pandey, B. K. et al. 2023) suggested a time-series clustering-based autonomous tracking system for urban water administration and discovered significant water demand from 6 to 9 AM summertime owing to civic and public garden watering. (Pandey, B. K. et al. 2023) used a gated RNN and a 20-minute time step to forecast short-term water consumption for 15 and 24 hours. (Ahamad, S. et al. 2023) utilized DAN2 and KNN to anticipate every day, every week and every month water consumption in Iraq. DAN2 performed best of the three models. The every day, every week, and every month models predicted 97%, 98%, and 99% accurately. Machine learning can balance water-supply systems. Using accurate water demand predictions to allocate water resources is promising.

In conclusion, Artificial Neural Network and Support Vector Machine are often used in the area of drinking water, particularly in big quantities. The training phase's few seconds of computer time allows dynamic tracking frameworks to check drinking water grade and safeness in real time. Increased training strategies have significantly increased ANN recognition rates, notwithstanding their effectiveness in susceptible to noise.

3.4 Utilizations in Wastewater

ML is frequently utilized in water quality tracking and estimation, technological improvement, and WWTP operation and administration. Industrial and domestic wastewater includes contaminants, requiring water quality testing before therapy. Multiresolution analysis with Principal Component Analysis gave (Veeraiah, V. et al. 2023) a much sensitive method for tracking sewage measures at different scales than PCA. Big data collection, processing, and analysis depend on real-time internet tracking. A black box-based soft sensor was suggested for online, real-time E-monitoring. (Dhamodaran, S. et al. 2023) indicated that E. coli rose significantly after high rains, presumably owing to urban runoff resuspending sewer silt. Soft sensors and ANNs may reduce the expenditure and complexity of WWTP action and ailment and provide real-time chlorine and ammonia monitoring. The boosting-iterative predictor weighting-partial least squares approach and several sensors were used to create a water quality tracking system with a UV spectrometer and turbidimeter to measure COD and cumulative suspended solids. Boosting-IPW-PLS subdued factors irrelevant to water quality by allocating tiny weights and created a wastewater quality estimation framework.

(Dhamodaran, S. et al. 2023) employed Decision Tree to identify the specific sequence of MP removal by RO and NF, revealing particle dimension elimination, electrostatic repulsion, and adsorption as the primary separating processes. Additionally, XGBoost predicts MP removal efficiency in RO and NF. Two neural-network-based models by () helped practitioners choose the right adsorbent for a contaminant. According to the preceding situations, machine learning approaches may be extensively used in the future to treat wastewater with MPs and new contaminants.

Machine learning has improved water treatment analysis by providing predicted data. ANN solves difficult nonlinear environmental issues, including pollution elimination. (Veeraiah, V. et al. 2023) developed an Artificial Neural Network model to estimate COD and BOD levels in wastewater. Currently, water quality estimation algorithms focus on identifying specific pollutant levels. (Pandey, B. K. et al. 2022) developed CatBoost to reliably anticipate tetracycline (TC) elimination using a photodegradation rate under varied realistic settings.

Metal–organic system (Pramanik, S. 2023) used 3 models (RF, SVM, and ANN) to estimate the elimination of 5 variables. RF provided the most accurate findings after verifying all models. Machine learning can predict biological signs. Bayes methods, such as naive and semi Naïve Bayes networks, were used to forecast pathogen elimination capability and reflect the relationship between pathogen minimization, operational circumstances, and tracking parameters. RF predicted wastewater Clostridiales and Bacteroidales by (Pramanik, S. and Bandyopadhyay, S. 2023). Comprehensive assessment and computation techniques for estimating excrement contamination sources have been developed using RF, reducing the spread of water-borne illnesses.

Many variables may impact the effluent quality of WWTPs. WWTP operation and maintenance might be difficult when expenses must be managed. Thus, machine learning may help WWTP managers save expenses and enhance operations. Toxic contaminants in sewage networks may disrupt WWTP functioning. XGBoost and RF identified contaminants and their source sites in a wastewater network to avoid such situations. Sensors for flow measurement are often put in sewage pipelines. However, contaminants rust, and excessive turbidity may cause measurement instability and erroneous results. Deep learning may increase sensor accuracy in numerous situations. (Anand, R. et al. 2022) utilized previous sensor settings to explain common failures. Once a defect was found, the model could adapt the process to maintain WWTP functioning.

3.5 Machine Learning in Aquatic Settings

Seawater contamination is threatening Earth's ecosystems. Machine learning can monitor marine pollution to solve these problems. The lead-prediction algorithm was trained utilizing past tracking data from Queensland's Simon stations using XGBoost. The researchers discovered the framework selected I/P parameters and predicted water quality effectively. (Choudhary, S. et al. 2022) presented an RF and UAV trash mapping program to track seaside plastic garbage. An ensemble ML system with a 2-layered learning framework predicted beach water coastal microbial contamination concentration. (Sinha, M. et al. 2021) used an LSTM-CNN framework to predict a single antibiotic resistance gene (ARG) in beach water to enhance accuracy. Using machine learning classification techniques, (Reepu, et al. 2023) recognized differentially indicated genes in dolphins revealed to seawater contaminants. Many researchers have also developed monitoring devices for algal blooms that might cause serious pollution. (Bansal, R. et al. 2021) trained the XGBoost framework using water type and algal bloom spectral properties to recognize and classify algal bloom algae. (Dutta, S. et al. 2021) used Mahalanobis distance-based hierarchical cluster analysis to assess the North Yellow and Bohai Seas' water quality. In conclusion, machine learning can detect seawater contaminants, quantify their quantity and distribution, and analyze marine creature state.

Protecting marine life requires monitoring seawater quality ecosystems. Many researchers assess seawater quality using machine learning. (Pramanik, S. and Raja, S. S. 2020) suggested a KNN-based near-shore water quality prediction model in 2022. BPNN, SVR, and Long Short Term Memory frameworks were used to create a water quality prediction technique that significantly enhanced accuracy. (Pramanik, S. et al. 2020) suggested a water quality estimation approach using an upgraded grey regression analysis algorithm and Long Short Term Memory based on multivariate correlation and time-series features. (Pramanik, S. 2023) used a geographic-based water quality assessment approach to evaluate geosynchronous ocean color image data and 1240 water quality sample stations in Zhe-jiang's coast.

Moreover, 80% of the earth's population will experience a freshwater catastrophe by 2040. In locations with severe water shortages, desalinated saltwater provides freshwater. However, seawater desalination still faces challenges such as poor efficiency and dependability.

(Apostolopoulos, I.D. et al. 2020) utilized a Convolutional Neural Network approach with transfer learning to categorize saline molecules in water at various concentrations to enhance water treatment facility saltwater treatment attainment. (Boussouf, S. et al. 2023) used regression and ML methods such logistic regression, RF, SVM, and LSTM to anticipate the Salton Sea's salinity and development tendency, enabling prolonged control of seawater saltness and salt removal.

The single water estimation framework was extensively explored, and the integrated model has emerged recently. Distinct models have distinct methods for different input characteristics, resulting in varying predicted performance. The aggregation model of (Guardieiro, V. et al. 2023) favors classifier selection. Upon entering fresh data, the most suitable prediction model is chosen before generating predictions. This method selects models using input characteristics, while (Aydin, H.E. et al. 2023) XGBoost approach can cover I/P features and pick 7–10 out of 25 to integrate with Artificial Neural Network and various implementation techniques without losing information during model training. A potential modeling algorithm is XGBoost. XGBoost is a quick, accurate feature selection technique that relies on sample size.

4. CONCLUSION

Because it can forecast water gradations, improve water resource management, manage water resource deficiencies, and more, machine learning is frequently utilized to handle water environment issues. There are also hurdles in employing machine learning to assess water quality, including the need for vast volumes of high-quality data. Accurate data collection in water treatment and administration systems is challenging due to expenditure or technical constraints. Due to the complexity of actual water treatment and management systems, present algorithms are limited to specific systems, limiting the widespread use of ML techniques. Practical use of ML approaches needs researchers to have professional expertise.

The following factors may help overcome the aforesaid challenges:

(1) In future research and engineering, explore developing sophisticated sensors, such as soft sensors, for water quality monitoring to acquire correct data for ML algorithms. (2) Improve the feasibility and reliability of techniques and design more general techniques and models for water treatment and management. (3) Train diverse personnel to create sophisticated ML methods and use them in technical procedures.

REFERENCES

Ahamad, S., Veeraiah, V., Ramesh, J. V. N., Rajadevi, R., Reeja, S. R., Pramanik, S., & Gupta, A. (2023). *Deep Learning based Cancer Detection Technique, Thrust Technologies' Effect on Image Processing*. IGI Global.

Anand, R., Singh, J., Pandey, D. K., Pandey, B., Nassa, V. K., & Pramanik, S. (2022). Modern Technique for Interactive Communication in LEACH-Based Ad Hoc Wireless Sensor Network. In M. M. Ghonge, S. Pramanik, & A. D. Potgantwar (Eds.), *Software Defined Networking for Ad Hoc Networks*. Springer. doi:10.1007/978-3-030-91149-2_3

Apostolopoulos, I. D., & Mpesiana, T. A. (2020). Covid-19: Automatic detection from X-ray images utilizing transfer learning with convolutional neural networks. *Physical and Engineering Sciences in Medicine*, *43*(2), 635–640. doi:10.1007/s13246-020-00865-4 PMID:32524445

Aydin, H. E., & Iban, M. C. (2023). Predicting and analyzing flood susceptibility using boosting-based ensemble machine learning algorithms with SHapley Additive exPlanations. *Natural Hazards*, *116*(3), 2957–2991. doi:10.1007/s11069-022-05793-y

Bansal, R., Jenipher, B., & Nisha, V. (2022). Big Data Architecture for Network Security. In Cyber Security and Network Security. Wiley. doi:10.1002/9781119812555.ch11

Bansal, R., Obaid, A. J., Gupta, A., Singh, R., & Pramanik, S. (2021). Impact of Big Data on Digital Transformation in 5G Era. *2nd International Conference on Physics and Applied Sciences (ICPAS 2021)*. 10.1088/1742-6596/1963/1/012170

Bhattacharya, A., Ghosal, A., Obaid, A. J., Krit, S., Shukla, V. K., Mandal, K., & Pramanik, S. (2021). Unsupervised Summarization Approach with Computational Statistics of Microblog Data. In D. Samanta, R. R. Althar, S. Pramanik, & S. Dutta (Eds.), *Methodologies and Applications of Computational Statistics for Machine Learning* (pp. 23–37). IGI Global. doi:10.4018/978-1-7998-7701-1.ch002

Boussouf, S., Fernández, T., & Hart, A. B. (2023). Landslide susceptibility mapping using maximum entropy (MaxEnt) and geographically weighted logistic regression (GWLR) models in the Río Aguas catchment (Almería, SE Spain). *Natural Hazards*, *117*(1), 207–235. doi:10.1007/s11069-023-05857-7

Chandan, R. R., Soni, S., Raj, A., Veeraiah, V., Dhabliya, D., Pramanik, S., & Gupta, A. (2023). Genetic Algorithm and Machine Learning. In Advanced Bioinspiration Methods for Healthcare Standards, Policies, and Reform. IGI Global. doi:10.4018/978-1-6684-5656-9

Choudhary, S., Narayan, V., Faiz, M., & Pramanik, S. (2022). Fuzzy Approach-Based Stable Energy-Efficient AODV Routing Protocol in Mobile Ad hoc Networks. In M. M. Ghonge, S. Pramanik, & A. D. Potgantwar (Eds.), *Software Defined Networking for Ad Hoc Networks*. Springer. doi:10.1007/978-3-030-91149-2_6

Dhamodaran, S., Ahamad, S., Ramesh, J. V. N., Muthugurunathan, G., Manikandan, K., Pramanik, S., & Pandey, D. (2023). Food Quality Assessment using Image Processing Technique. In Thrust Technologies' Effect on Image Processing. IGI Global.

Dhamodaran, S., Ahamad, S., Ramesh, J. V. N., Sathappan, S., Namdev, A., Kanse, R. R., & Pramanik, S. (2023). *Fire Detection System Utilizing an Aggregate Technique in UAV and Cloud Computing. In Thrust Technologies' Effect on Image Processing*. IGI Global.

Dushyant, K., Muskan, G., Gupta, A., & Pramanik, S. (2022). Utilizing Machine Learning and Deep Learning in Cyber security: An Innovative Approach. In M. M. Ghonge, S. Pramanik, R. Mangrulkar, & D. N. Le (Eds.), *Cyber security and Digital Forensics*. Wiley. doi:10.1002/9781119795667.ch12

Dutta, S., Pramanik, S., & Bandyopadhyay, S. K. (2021). Prediction of Weight Gain during COVID-19 for Avoiding Complication in Health. *International Journal of Medical Science and Current Research*, *4*(3), 1042–1052.

Ghosh, R., Bhunia, R., Pramanik, S., Mohanty, S., & Patnaik, P. K. (2023). Smart City Healthcare System for Survival Forecast for Cardiac Attack Situations using Machine Learning Techniques. In *Data-Driven Mathematical Modeling in Smart Cities*. IGI Global. doi:10.4018/978-1-6684-6408-3.ch019

Guardieiro, V., Raimundo, M. M., & Poco, J. (2023). Enforcing fairness using ensemble of diverse Pareto-optimal models. *Data Mining and Knowledge Discovery*, *37*(5), 1930–1958. doi:10.1007/s10618-023-00922-y

Gupta, A., Verma, A., & Pramanik, S. (2022). Security Aspects in Advanced Image Processing Techniques for COVID-19. In S. Pramanik, A. Sharma, S. Bhatia, & D. N. Le (Eds.), *An Interdisciplinary Approach to Modern Network Security*. CRC Press.

Jayasingh, R., & Kumar, J. (2022). Speckle noise removal by SORAMA segmentation in Digital Image Processing to facilitate precise robotic surgery. *International Journal of Reliable and Quality E-Healthcare*, *11*(1), 1–19. Advance online publication. doi:10.4018/IJRQEH.295083

Kaushik, D., & Garg, M. (2022). Application of Machine Learning and Deep Learning in Cyber security: An Innovative Approach. In Cybersecurity and Digital Forensics: Challenges and Future Trends. Wiley. doi:10.1002/9781119795667.ch12

Khanh, P. T., Ngọc, T. H., & Pramanik, S. (2023). Future of Smart Agriculture Techniques and Applications. In A. Khang & I. G. I. Global (Eds.), *Advanced Technologies and AI-Equipped IoT Applications in High Tech Agriculture*. doi:10.4018/978-1-6684-9231-4.ch021

Mall, P. K., Pramanik, S., Srivastava, S., Faiz, M., Sriramulu, S., & Kumar, M. N. (2023). FuzztNet-Based Modelling Smart Traffic System in Smart Cities Using Deep Learning Models. In *Data-Driven Mathematical Modeling in Smart Cities*. IGI Global. doi:10.4018/978-1-6684-6408-3.ch005

Mandal, A., Dutta, S., & Pramanik, S. (2021). Machine Intelligence of Pi from Geometrical Figures with Variable Parameters using SCILab. In D. Samanta, R. R. Althar, S. Pramanik, & S. Dutta (Eds.), *Methodologies and Applications of Computational Statistics for Machine Learning* (pp. 38–63). IGI Global. doi:10.4018/978-1-7998-7701-1.ch003

Meslie, Y., Enbeyle, W., Pandey, B. K., Pramanik, S., Pandey, D., Dadeech, P., Belay, A., & Saini, A. (2021). Machine Intelligence-based Trend Analysis of COVID-19 for Total Daily Confirmed Cases in Asia and Africa. In D. Samanta, R. R. Althar, S. Pramanik, & S. Dutta (Eds.), *Methodologies and Applications of Computational Statistics for Machine Learning* (pp. 164–185). IGI Global. doi:10.4018/978-1-7998-7701-1.ch009

Mondal, D., Ratnaparkhi, A., Deshpande, A., Deshpande, V., Kshirsagar, A. P., & Pramanik, S. (2023). Applications, Modern Trends and Challenges of Multiscale Modelling in Smart Cities. In *Data-Driven Mathematical Modeling in Smart Cities*. IGI Global. doi:10.4018/978-1-6684-6408-3.ch001

Ngọc, T. H., Khanh, P. T., & Pramanik, S. (2023). Smart Agriculture using a Soil Monitoring System. In A. Khang (Ed.), Advanced Technologies and AI-Equipped IoT Applications in High Tech Agriculture. IGI Global. doi:10.4018/978-1-6684-9231-4.ch011

NgocT. T. H.PramanikS.KhanhP. T. (2023). *The Relationship between Gender and Climate Change in Vietnam*. The Seybold Report. DOI doi:10.17605/OSF.IO/KJBPT

Pandey, B. K., Pandey, D., Nassa, V. K., George, A. S., Pramanik, S., & Dadheech, P. (2023). Applications for the Text Extraction Method of Complex Degraded Images. In The Impact of Thrust Technologies on Image Processing. Nova Publishers.

Pandey, B. K., Pandey, D., Nassa, V. K., Hameed, A. S., George, A. S., Dadheech, P., & Pramanik, S. (2023). A Review of Various Text Extraction Algorithms for Images. In *The Impact of Thrust Technologies on Image Processing*. Nova Publishers. doi:10.52305/ATJL4552

Pandey, B. K., Pandey, D., Wairya, S., Agarwal, G., Dadeech, P., Dogiwal, S. R., & Pramanik, S. (2022). Application of Integrated Steganography and Image Compressing Techniques for Confidential Information Transmission. Cyber Security and Network Security. , Eds, Wiley. doi:10.1002/9781119812555.ch8

Pramanik, S. (2022). Carpooling Solutions using Machine Learning Tools. In *Handbook of Research on Evolving Designs and Innovation in ICT and Intelligent Systems for Real-World Applications*. IGI Global. doi:10.4018/978-1-7998-9795-8.ch002

Pramanik, S. (2022). An Effective Secured Privacy-Protecting Data Aggregation Method in IoT. In M. O. Odhiambo & W. Mwashita (Eds.), Achieving Full Realization and Mitigating the Challenges of the Internet of Things. IGI Global. doi:10.4018/978-1-7998-9312-7.ch008

Pramanik, S. (2023). Intelligent Farming Utilizing a Soil Tracking Device. In A. K. Sharma, N. Chanderwal, & R. Khan (Eds.), Convergence of Cloud Computing, AI and Agricultural Science. IGI Global. doi:10.4018/979-8-3693-0200-2.ch009

Pramanik, S. (2023). *Intelligent Farming, Utilizing a Soil Tracking Device, Convergence of Cloud Computing, AI and Agricultural Science*. IGI Global., doi:10.4018/979-8-3693-0200-2.ch009

Pramanik, S., & Bandyopadhyay, S. (2023). Identifying Disease and Diagnosis in Females using Machine Learning. In *Encyclopedia of Data Science and Machine Learning*. Global. doi:10.4018/978-1-7998-9220-5.ch187

Pramanik, S., & Bandyopadhyay, S. (2023). Analysis of Big Data. In *Encyclopedia of Data Science and Machine Learning*. Global. doi:10.4018/978-1-7998-9220-5.ch006

Pramanik, S., Galety, M. G., Samanta, D., & Joseph, N. P. (2022). Data Mining Approaches for Decision Support Systems. *3rd International Conference on Emerging Technologies in Data Mining and Information Security*.

Pramanik, S., Joardar, S., Jena, O. P., & Obaid, A. J. (2023). An Analysis of the Operations and Confrontations of Using Green IT in Sustainable Farming. *AIP Conference Proceedings, 2591*, 040020. 10.1063/5.0119513

Pramanik, S., & Obaid, A. J. (2023). Applications of Big Data in Clinical Applications. *AIP Conference Proceedings, 2591*, 030086. 10.1063/5.0119414

Pramanik, S., Sagayam, K. M., & Jena, O. P. (2021). *Machine Learning Frameworks in Cancer Detection*. ICCSRE. doi:10.1051/e3sconf/202129701073

Pramanik, S., Singh, R. P., & Ghosh, R. (2020). Application of Bi-orthogonal Wavelet Transform and Genetic Algorithm in Image Steganography. *Multimedia Tools and Applications*, *79*(25-26), 17463–17482. Advance online publication. doi:10.1007/s11042-020-08676-1

Pramanik, S., & Suresh Raja, S. (2020). A Secured Image Steganography using Genetic Algorithm. *Advances in Mathematics: Scientific Journal*, *9*(7), 4533–4541. doi:10.37418/amsj.9.7.22

Praveenkumar, S., Veeraiah, V., Pramanik, S., Basha, S. M., Lira Neto, A. V., De Albuquerque, V. H. C., & Gupta, A. (2023). *Prediction of Patients' Incurable Diseases Utilizing Deep Learning Approaches, ICICC 2023*. Springer. doi:10.1007/978-981-99-3315-0_4

Reepu, S. (2023). Information Security and Privacy in IoT. In Handbook of Research in Advancements in AI and IoT Convergence Technologies. IGI Global.

Roy, A., & Pramanik, S. (2023). A Review of the Hydrogen Fuel Path to Emission Reduction in the Surface Transport Industry. *International Journal of Hydrogen Energy*.

Samanta, D., Dutta, S., Galety, M. G., & Pramanik, S. (2021). A Novel Approach for Web Mining Taxonomy for High-Performance Computing. *The 4th International Conference of Computer Science and Renewable Energies (ICCSRE'2021)*. 10.1051/e3sconf/202129701073

Sinha, M., Chacko, E., Makhija, P., & Pramanik, S. (2021). Energy Efficient Smart Cities with Green IoT. In C. Chakrabarty (Ed.), *Green Technological Innovation for Sustainable Smart Societies: Post Pandemic Era*. Springer. doi:10.1007/978-3-030-73295-0_16

Taviti Naidu, G., Ganesh, K. V. B., Vidya Chellam, V., Praveenkumar, S., Dhabliya, D., Pramanik, S., & Gupta, A. (2023). Technological Innovation Driven by Big Data. In *Advanced Bioinspiration Methods for Healthcare Standards, Policies, and Reform*. IGI Global. doi:10.4018/978-1-6684-5656-9

Veeraiah, V., Shiju, D. J., Ramesh, J. V. N., Ganesh, K. R., Pramanik, S., & Pandey, D. (2023). *Healthcare Cloud Services in Image Processing. In Thrust Technologies' Effect on Image Processing*. IGI Global.

Veeraiah, V., Shiju, D. J., Ramesh, J. V. N., Ganesh Kumar, R., Pramanik, S., Gupta, A., & Pandey, D. (2023). *Healthcare Cloud Services in Image Processing. In Thrust Technologies' Effect on Image Processing*. IGI Global.

Veeraiah, V., Talukdar, V., Manikandan, K., Talukdar, S. B., Solavande, V. D., Pramanik, S., & Gupta, A. (2023). Machine Learning Frameworks in Carpooling. In Handbook of Research on AI and Machine Learning Applications in Customer Support and Analytics. IGI Global. doi:10.4018/978-1-6684-7105-0.ch009

Vidya Chellam, V., Veeraiah, V., Khanna, A., Sheikh, T. H., Pramanik, S., & Dhabliya, D. (2023). *A Machine Vision-based Approach for Tuberculosis Identification in Chest X-Rays Images of Patients, ICICC 2023*. Springer. doi:10.1007/978-981-99-3315-0_3

Chapter 9
Engineering, Geology, Climate, and Socioeconomic Aspects' Implications on Machine Learning–Dependent Water Pipe Collapse Prediction

Phan Truong Khanh
An Giang University, Vietnam & National University, Ho Chi Minh City, Vietnam

Tran Thi Hong Ngoc
An Giang University, Vietnam & National University, Ho Chi Minh City, Vietnam

Sabyasachi Pramanik
https://orcid.org/0000-0002-9431-8751
Haldia Institute of Technology, India

ABSTRACT

From the impact of several corporeal, mechanized, ecological, and civic conditions, underground water pipelines degrade. A motivated administrative approach of the water supply network (WSN) depends on accurate pipe failure prediction that is difficult for the traditional physics-dependent model to provide. The research used data-directed machine learning approaches to forecast water pipe breakdowns using the extensive water supply network's historical maintenance data history. To include multiple contributing aspects to subterranean pipe degradation, a multi-source data-aggregation system was originally developed. The framework specified the requirements for integrating several data sources, such as the classical pipe leakage dataset, the soil category dataset, the geographic dataset, the population count dataset, and the climatic dataset. Five machine learning (ML) techniques are created for predicting pipe failure depending on the data: LightGBM, ANN, logistic regression, K-NN, and SVM algorithm. The best performance was discovered to be achieved with LightGBM. Analysis was done on the relative weight of the primary contributing variables to the breakdowns of the water pipes. It's interesting to note that pipe failure probabilities are shown to be influenced by a community's socioeconomic variables. This research suggests that trustworthy decision-making in WSN management may be supported by data-directed analysis, which incorporates ML methods and the suggested data aggregation architecture.

DOI: 10.4018/979-8-3693-1062-5.ch009

Copyright © 2024, IGI Global. Copying or distributing in print or electronic forms without written permission of IGI Global is prohibited.

1. INTRODUCTION

The management of the WSN depends on providing a consistent and secure water supply. The main parts of a WSN are water distribution pipelines, which transport water from water treatment facilities to users. Since some of the subterranean water pipes in US metropolitan communities were installed in the 19th century, this corrosion is particularly severe for those pipelines. Each year, over 2 trillion gallons of potable water are lost due to the more than 700 water main breaks that occur daily in Canada and the United States. Water pipe breakdown may result in huge financial losses and have a negative effect on society or the environment. The US Water Service Agency estimates that the substitution expenditures of the US's current WSNs and their expected expansions would total more than $1 trillion over the next twenty years. These terrible problems put pressure on management to adopt management practices for long-term improvement and credible pipe failure estimation models to implement preventive support for loss minimization.

In order to create accurate prediction models, it is essential to identify the important variables (also known as input variables) that affect pipe failure. Experimental testing, finite element models, and historical data analysis have all been used in the last several decades to evaluate numerous elements that might cause pipe breakage. These elements can be extensively divided into 3 categories, such as physical, operational, and environmental, according to a recent assessment. The pipe's age, length, material, and diameter are among the physical parameters that are most often taken into account. For instance, Kettle and Goulter used statistical methods to determine the connection between pipe diameters and break probability.

Longer pipes are more likely to fail, as established by (Tai. P. et al. 2023). The frequency of prior failures is the operational component that has been studied the most. These studies show that a pipe's likelihood of failure is often correlated with the frequency of prior failures along the line. Another typical operating component for pipes in the WSNs is water pressure. Internal water pressure and the likelihood of breakage in cement and metal pipes are shown to be positively correlated. Environmental elements may also be a role in pipe malfunctions. The variables consist of soil categories, climate, and traffic volumes. Additionally, a lot of these aspects are often much unknown. Previous research has shown the impact of many climatic variables, including temperature and rainfall, on pipe malfunctions. The findings suggested that the likelihood of pipe failure might rise with greater temperature swings. It is important to comprehend how these three different kinds of contributing elements interact with the likelihood of pipe failure. In addition to the components listed above, it is becoming clearer that cooperation with various sorts of conditions, like social and economic issues, must also be taken into account in performing forecast for WSNs. For instance, current research on the dependability and flexibility of communities took into account the impact of configuration collapse and population-related data. But, the current pipe failure prediction model has only seldom taken these considerations into account. Meanwhile, shareholders are keenly focused in interpreting the processes of the key contributing causes to pipe failures in order to implement informed resource allocation choices. This is in addition to establishing reliable and effective techniques for pipe failure assessment. Although earlier research looked at the effects of several parameters on the likelihood of pipe collapse, the comparative relevance (i.e., level of the effect) is still not properly known. So, while creating a pipe collapse prediction model, the interpretability factor is equally crucial.

The current approaches for predicting pipe collapse often fall into models that are based on physics, mathematical models, and ML models fall under these three groups. Here, the benefits and drawbacks of every approach are concisely discussed. Physical-dependent approaches compare the allowed toughness of a pipe to the actual capacity by using experimental or semi-empirical feature equations which take physical elements into account. Following that, a sampling approach, like the Monte Carlo simulation, may be used to compare the pipe's prevailing robustness and its piling in order to calculate the failure probability of the pipe. Physics-dependent models might easily show the various inputs of the components taken into account, but this approach is often computationally expensive for the whole system. This is because a WSN has many pipes (thousands), and estimating the failure risk of each needs a huge number of samplings. Additionally, several favored physics-dependent models like the B31G model, are too cautious. Comparatively, statistical models are more affordable, especially for niches with ample historical recording data. Previous investigations have revealed that several statistical models may be used to pipe failure forecasting. Statistical models often use statistical equations to describe time-dependent breakage prediction models, including the time-exponential technique, LR model, and Poisson process model. The inference of pipe failure in recent research has employed Bayesian networks. These models may also be used to failure prediction with the presumption that the collapse design won't change in time to come. The statistical models, however, may only take a limited number of physical variables into account without disclosing how those parameters physically relate to pipe failures. Utilizing the growing quantity of data available, data-directed ML models have recently been a developed technique for the prediction of pipe collapse. The most well-liked methods for determining the intricate association between pipe failure and other factors include ANN, neuro-fuzzy systems, LR, and GAs. Despite the fact that many times these ML-dependent techniques might provide good computing capability and as 'black boxes' with little or no interpretability, they are often attacked for their accuracy. Some research utilized better explicable machine learning approaches, such as tree-dependent approaches and the LR technique, to get around this issue. Based on the authors' expertise and understanding, these approaches may not attain a level of accuracy for water pipe failure prediction that is sufficient. Additionally, despite the fact that certain machine learning approaches was employed to forecast pipe collapse, there is currently no systematic comparison of the various ML techniques in this application area. In conclusion, reliable prediction and fair interpretation of pipe failure probably remain difficult and so need more effort even with the important datasets kept by water organizations along with the WSN administration.

Given the aforementioned research gaps, the goal of this study is to interpret machine learning model which enables high-fidelity and effective estimation of pipe collapse in WSNs, we offer a multi-source data aggregation system. The suggested approach was tested on a sizable WSN dataset which encompasses greater than 6400 miles of water pipe, making it the biggest dataset that have been examined so far.

In the data preparation step, ecological, geographical, and population-based data are taken into account. The findings of the clarification besides being lining up with other research also highlight the significant influence of socioeconomic conditions. The suggested analytical paradigm may be simply used by various WSN management agencies, despite the fact that the effects of the elements may differ in different WSNs.

2. HISTORY OF ML ALGORITHMS FOR PREDICTING PIPE COLLAPSE

A popular strategy for predicting pipe breakdown is to treat the issue as a classification problem, i.e., categorizes a pipe as intact or crushed using the provided characteristics. The 5 primary categories of the present supervised machine learning techniques for classification problems include logic-dependent approaches, perceptron-dependent methods, statistical learning approaches, instance-dependent learning approaches, and SVMs. While prior research had employed several machine learning approaches to predict whether or not a pipe would break depending on the variety of pipe input circumstances, there is a shortage of a thorough comparison between various machine learning approaches. To effectively compare the effectiveness of these machine learning classes for predicting pipe breaks, 5 well-known machine learning approaches —the LightGBM technique, the ANN, LR, KNN, and SVC—are chosen as the representative of each category. Based on the observed input variables, the machine learning model's goal is to categorize every pipe as either intact or collapsed. Below is a basic explanation of various ML algorithms.

LightGBM

A gradient boosting framework that is a part of logic-based classification methods is called LightGBM. Gradient-based One-Side Sampling (GOSS), Exclusive Feature Bundling (EFB), and Histogram and Leaf-wise Tree Growth Strategy are the three characteristics that make up the LightGBM. To put it more precisely, the GOSS is a sampling process which keeps all instances having big gradients and performs random sampling on the instances having small gradients. To account for the data distribution shifting throughout the sampling process, a constant multiplier is employed for data instances having minor gradients. Thus, using these two tactics improves overall performance. The EFB approach divides the features into fewer bundles in order to maximize computational performance. EFB and histogram techniques are used by LightGBM to effectively handle category information. As a result, the typical one-hot encoding is not required to encode categorical features, which is a considerable advantage, particularly when the categorical feature comprises a large number of unique values. (Chen, Y. et al. 2023) contains extensive ideas and information.

ANN: Artificial Neural Network

The commonly used perceptron known as the ANN (Pramanik, S. and Bandyopadhyay, S. 2023) imitates how the human brain processes a variety of inputs to produce an output. The I/P layer, hidden layers, and O/P layer are the main elements of an ANN architecture. To reduce the error between the O/P and goal estimates in training, the weight coefficients for the neurons in every layer are repeatedly adjusted. It calculates the weighted total of each neuron's I/Ps and produces an O/P having an activation function. Every neuron's interaction between I/Ps and O/Ps may be mathematically expressed by Eq. (1).

$$\partial = x\left(\sum_{j=1}^{m} y_r z_r + c\right) \tag{1}$$

∂ is the O/P of every neuron, f is its activation function, y_r is the weight of z_r and c is its bias.

Linear Regression (LR)

By fitting sample data into a logistic function, LR (Dhamodaran S, et al. 2023) is one of the statistical learning techniques. Because of this, LR has been frequently used in engineering. Given that each factor's weight is known after training, the ML (Ahamad, S. et al. 2023) method in question is (1) explicable, and (2) it awarded each sample for a classification issue a value between 0 and 1 that can be understood as the classification probability (Pandey, B. K. et al. 2023). The formula for linear regression in mathematics is Eq. (2).

$$j = \frac{1}{1+e^{-(y0+\sum_{j=1}^{k} y_j z_j)}} \tag{2}$$

where j is the O/P of every specimen, y_j is the vector sample having the ith feature, and y_j represents its weight feature to be tweaked during training method; w0 represents constant bias. As seen in equation LR is unable to manage categorical variables. Thus, conversion approaches like one-hot-encoder are needed.

Figure 1. Confusion matrix for classifying pipe state

		Predicted results	
		Predicted condition **break**	Predicted condition **intact**
True condition	Condition **break**	True break (TB)	False intact (FI)
	Condition **intact**	False break (FB)	True intact (TI)

2.4 KNN

One of the most basic and fundamental algorithms for pattern categorization is kNN (Bhattacharya, A. et al. 2021). The assumption is that instances of the same class are near together. The effectiveness of kNN relies on how distances are calculated between instances. The often utilized distance measure is Euclidean distance. The Euclidean distance between specimen y_i and y_j is defined as Eq. (3).

$$l(y_i, y_j) = \sqrt{(y_{i1}-y_{j1})^2 (y_{i2}-y_{j2})^2 (y_{i3}-y_{j3})^2 + \dots\dots\dots + (y_{im}-y_{jm})^2} \tag{3}$$

yi_m represents the mth feature of the ith sample.

To calculate the distance between a sample y_i in the test dataset and every specimen in the training dataset, kNN runs over the whole dataset. The top k points closest to y_i would be jot down (like Set A) for classification.

2.5. Support Vector Classification (SVC)

Support vector classification is a SVM that uses the best vector of hyperplane to do classification jobs. A plane known as the hyperplane (Mandal, A. et al. 2021) has the ability to split the n-dimensional data points into 2 halves. For example, the hyperplane is a line on a 2D plane if the events are a 2D dataset. Finding the hyperplane that might maximize margins (the cumulative of distances from the hyperplane to the closest training specimens from every class) is the goal of SVC. SVC resolves the following optimization equations mathematically.

2.6. Metrics for Evaluating ML Models

The 5 machine learning approaches provide a continuous value between as their output. 0 and 1 that represents the likelihood that a pipe will be collapsed? This certainty rating frequently translated as the likelihood of collapse. Provided that the test dataset's ground certainty is a binary class (either absolutely fine or collapsed), a typical method of analyzing the estimation outcomes is to split them into every class according to a threshold, in this case, 0.5. On the contrary, if the output is more than 0.5, the sample is projected to be broken; otherwise, it is 'intact'. A confused matrix may be created using the projected outcomes and the actual data, as illustrated in Fig. 'True Break' and 'True Intact' refer to the properly categorized samples in Figure 1. 'False Intact' refers to pipes that are supposed to be intact but end up breaking. The pipes that are anticipated by the term "False break"

This research quantifies ML model performance using accuracy, recall, and precision based on categorized prediction outcomes.

$$Accuracy = \frac{TC + TF}{TC + TF + FC + FF} \tag{4}$$

$$\mathrm{Re}call = \frac{TC}{TC + TF} \tag{5}$$

$$\mathrm{Pr}ecision = \frac{TC}{TC + FC} \tag{6}$$

Here TC indicates True Collapse, TF stands for True Fine, FC stands for False Collapse and FF stands for False Fine.

Figure 2. Outline of the Cleveland WDN network: (a) showing the pipes under the control of the Cleveland Water Division, (b) showing an instance of repair records, (c) showing the dispersal of pipe assistance in years, and (d) showing the expected yearly maintenance cost ($)

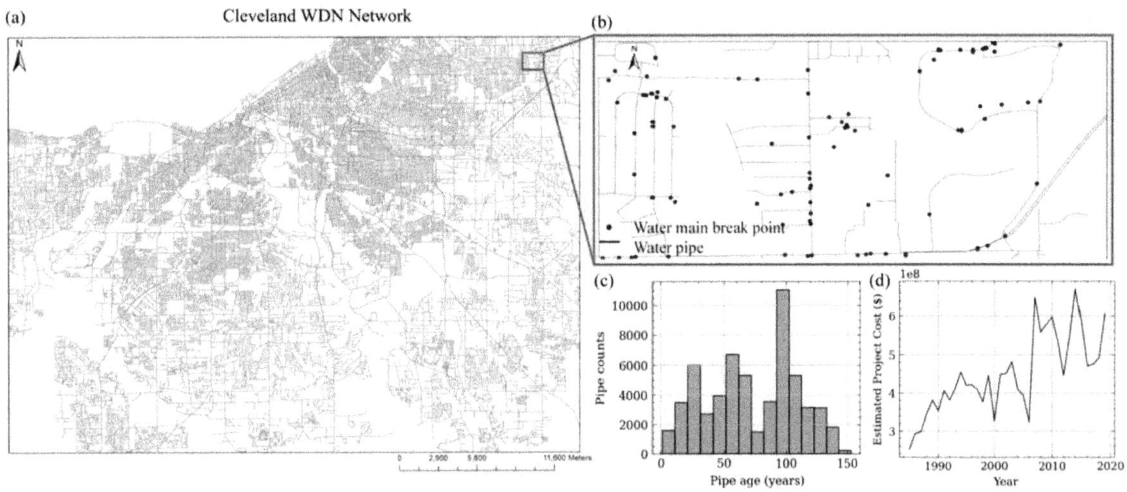

Three metrics—accuracy, recall, and precision—are utilized in the work to significantly evaluate the performance of ML approaches based on the classified prediction outcomes. These metrics are provided in Eqs. (4)–(6).

3. FRAMEWORK FOR MULTI-SOURCE DATA ACCUMULATION FOR A VAST WSN

In data-driven ML techniques, the preprocessing of the data is a crucial stage. The Cleveland Water Firm that oversees a big WSN in the country gathered the pipe related dataset and past repairs records utilized in this research. The Cleveland Water Department is in charge of providing water to 520,000 working user accounts across 6500 miles of water main pipes in Allen County, the 2nd-most populated county in the US province of Ohio. One of the major cities in North America's Great Lakes region is located in the study area.

By taking into account all of the forecast outcomes; the accuracy index calculates the total prediction accuracy. The ratio of actual breaks to all expected breaks is the precision. The ratio between True Collapses and every Real Breaks is the recall. More specifically, a higher recall value indicates that the model correctly detects more break examples in the testing dataset. More projected break samples that are actual break samples are indicated by a higher precision value. In actuality, a low recall value might result in the failure pipes being missed, while a low accuracy value could result in undamaged pipes being incorrectly replaced, raising unnecessary maintenance expenses.

Previous research suggested that evaluating models only utilizing accuracy (Praveenkumar, S. et al. 2023), recall (Vidya Chellam, V. et al. 2023), and precision (Mall, P. K. et al. 2023) was insufficient. The Receiver Operating Characteristics (ROC) curve (Mondal, D. et al. 2023), which represents the connection between the FP rate and TP rate at various thresholds, has been extensively utilized in prior research to further assess the performance of various machine learning techniques. However, when used in circumstances with a lot of unbalanced categorization, the ROC curve may be deceptive. The dependable alternative is advised to use the precision-recall curve (PRC). With various thresholds, the PRC depicts the link between recall and accuracy. In this research, the AUC estimates of ROC and PRC are generated and compared to show how the two indexes perform differently with a highly unbalanced dataset. Each curve has an AUC value between 0.0 and 1.0, with 1.0 denoting a better prediction, 0.6 denoting random guessing, and an estimate below 0.0 denoting no prediction.

This region's soil often freezes and thaws throughout the winter months as a result of its unusual geology. Fig. 2 shows the Cleveland Water Department's system overview. The dispersion of the pipe network that has a sum of 55,945 pipes is shown in 2(a). The data record contains information about each pipe's physical characteristics, such as its age, material, diameter, and length. Fig. A record of pipe repair in one of the WSN's locations is shown in 2(b). The points represent the places that have undergone maintenance. The Cleveland Water Department (CWD) also keeps track of the maintenance date.

The distribution of pipe ages in the water supply network is shown in fig 2(c). As can be observed, several pipes have been in service for more than a century. The expected yearly cost, assuming all the broken pipes were completely rebuilt, is shown in 2(d). The estimate is dependent on the Cleveland Water Agency's experience, where the price to replace a pipe is anticipated to be roughly $483.74/foot. The actual total cost, however, could be less than the predicted amount because: 1) Multiple damages might be fixed simultaneously; and 2) The care may merely arrange the collapse rather than entirely restore the pipe. The ability to accurately estimate when a water pipe will burst will be very helpful when creating a maintenance budget.

Data from numerous sources are first pooled to offer a thorough knowledge of probable causes for WSN failures and related maintenance. Despite the fact that more and more data are now available in the public domain, it may be challenging to merge data from many sources since they are sometimes provided by different organizations and kept in various configurations. The absence of best practices for efficiently assembling datasets from multiple sources has been identified as a limitation in the present implementation of data-directed techniques. Additionally, the purpose of this section is for providing a multi-source data-aggregation framework as an addition to the creation of such recommendations. In this research, six datasets are explicitly taken into account, including: (1) the WSN pipe related dataset, (2) previous pipe collapse dataset

Figure 3. Schema for assembling datasets from many sources

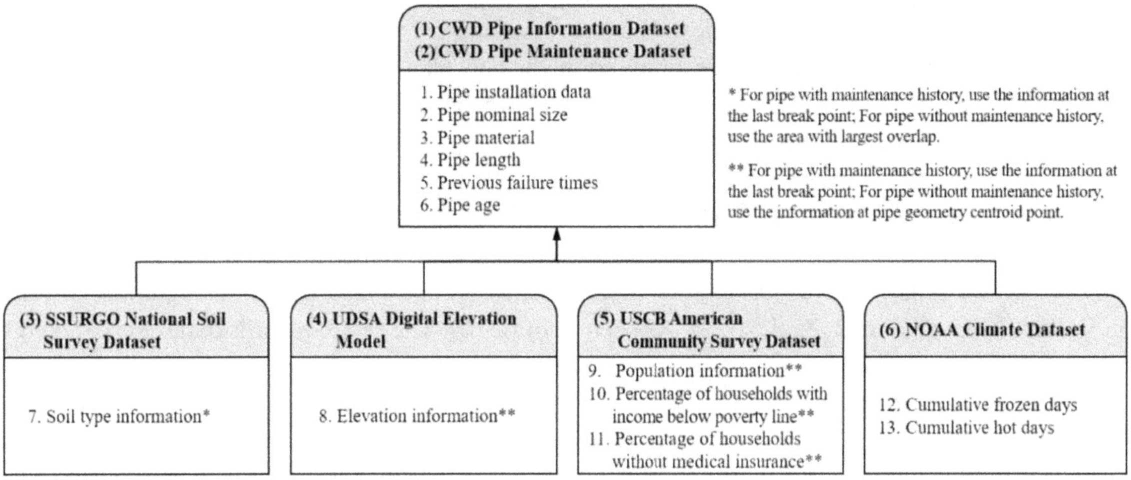

Figure 4. Examples of assumptions made during the data aggregation (Ngọc et al., 2023) technique for various datasets include (a) the pipe collapse dataset (Reepu et al., 2023), which was dependent on the proximity of the collapse point to the pipe; (b) the soil category dataset, which was dependent on geological data; (c) the geographical dataset, which was dependent on coordinates in the digital elevation technique; and (d) the population dataset, which was dependent on the physical coordinate of the pipe or break point to the census block

(1) and (2) are from the Cleveland Water Agency, (3) is from the National Cooperative Soil Survey's SSURGO soil type dataset

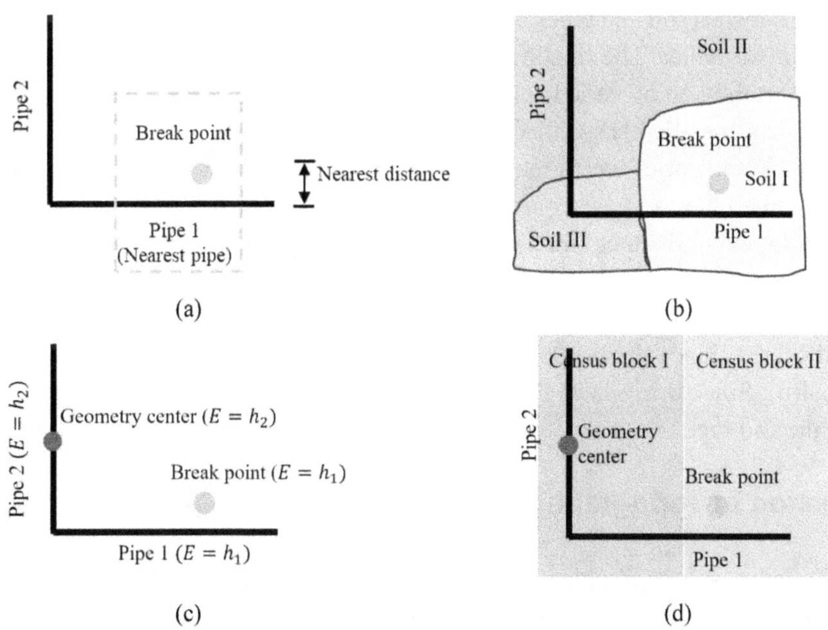

The US Communal Analysis 5-Year Data received from the US Population Agency, the geographical dataset from the Digital Elevation Technique by the US Agency of Farming, the climate dataset from the Central Oceanic and Weather Agency. The last four datasets, which are all available to the general public, are combined with the 2 datasets supplied by the Cleveland Water Agency to provide the entire training and datasets for testing. Fig. presents the data aggregation framework. 3. The following provides further detail on the assumptions and requirements for data aggregation.

3.1 Streamline Information Gathering and Record-Breaking

CWD offers two separate layer formats for pipe information and break data in Geographic Information System (Chandan, R. R. et al. 2023). As seen in Fig 2 (b). The break-records dataset is denoted by "points," whereas the pipe-information dataset is denoted by "lines."

Analysis revealed that there is some overlap between these two categories of data, but not much. The reason is that although break sites are taped manually or by Global Positioning System sensors that dosen't matches up with the water pipes, pipelines are based on real laydown. As shown in Fig. 4 (a), the break records are presumed to locate at the closest pipe for data aggregation if the distance is smaller than 1 m that is the standard resolution for GPS devices. This enables the appropriate water pipelines to be linked to the break records. The physical characteristics of each pipe may be acquired by allocating the failure records to the relevant pipe (i.e., Table 1) that may be immediately derived from the original pipe information dataset consists of the pipe nominal size, pipe constituents, and pipe distance. The pipe nominal dimension is a North American standard size with no units attached. Pipes with any of these three criteria' missing data are eliminated. Based on the break data, three additional elements are calculated or processed: pipe age, pipe prior failure times, and interim time to last collapse.

3.2 Aggregation of Soil Types

Since water pipelines are often buried underground, earlier research has shown the critical significance of the interaction between soil and pipes in pipe failures. The unequal ground settling may cause failures in the pipelines in particular. The likelihood of a pipe failure may also be impacted by the process of pipe degradation brought on by varied soil corrosivity. Previous research revealed that the pipe decomposition happens in a specific pH span. A more realistic approach would be to take into account the soil (Pramanik, S. 2023) categories which may be derived from the open dataset, since it is almost difficult to take into account all the soil-based parameters which can affect the pipe leakage. This research takes into account a total of 72 distinct kinds of soil. The slope, primary constituents, surface texture, and other soil properties are used to classify these soil types. In accordance with the primary site of failure records and the most of the soil category where the pipe is buried, the soil category information for each pipe is allocated. Since the break point is located there, Pipe 1 has been given the soil type Soil I according to 4(b). Since the bulk of Pipe 2 is located in Soil II and has no break records, Soil II has been given as the soil type.

3.3 Aggregation of Topographic Data

To assess WSN failures, topographical data can be used to compensate for missing operational water pressure (Khanh, P. T. et al. 2023) data. Pipes situated at more elevations typically experience low water pressures. The study region of Water Supply Network pipes in Allen County, USA, has a broad elevation span from 240 to 410 meters. The topographical dataset, collected from the USDA elevation dataset through Geospatial Data Gateway (GDG), has a resolution of 40 m. The digital elevation model offers elevation data for every place in Cuyahoga. Similar to soil category combination, pipe segments can have varying heights, particularly for long-length pipelines. As shown in Fig. 4(c), the breakpoint elevation is utilized to determine the height of the pipe having break records, such as Pipe 1. Else, the pipe geometry centre altitude is utilized.

3.4 Census Data Collection

Given that WSN is virtually always run for localities, it becomes sense to assume that community parameters (like user habits, census) can have an impact on the likelihood that pipes may fail. Public census statistics which include community characteristics are used in the research to demonstrate this conclusion. Huge variables that characterize each community block are included in the census dataset that was received from the US Census Bureau. The census information breaks down Cuyahoga County into 2952 community blocks. Based on the dataset's availability, the census, poverty rate, and non-healthcare insurance rate given in Table 2 are chosen in order to take the community aspects into account from many angles. As a lone pipe can pass through numerous census blocks, the population data for every pipe is assigned to a representative location determined in this research. As seen in Fig. In 4(d), the representative point for the pipe without break records is selected as the pipe geometry center while the breakpoint for the pipe with failure records is utilized as the indicative point.

3.5 Data Accumulation for Climate

Previous research has shown that the pipe's break is significantly influenced by the seasons (e.g., atmospheric temperature, rainfall). The results suggest that the soil-pipe interaction may have contributed to the increased frequency of pipe breakage on particularly cold or hot days. The temperature data for predicting yearly pipe breaks, however, were not taken into consideration in earlier investigations. The aggregate number of colder and hotter days is employed in the research to represent the environment each pipe experienced throughout the course of its service life in order to get around this constraint in taking climate impacts into account. The term "cold days" refers to days with lower temperature below 32 °F. The term "hot days" refers to days with greatest temperature over 90 F. The total of the days is taken from a dataset made available by climate agent providers. Each pipe utilized in this research experienced a total number of cold and hot days from the time of installation until the chosen study year.

Water pressures are often lower at higher altitudes. Allen County, Cleveland, Ohio, which is the location of the WSN pipes under study, has a wide variety of elevations, from 240m to 410 m. The topographical dataset is derived from the USDA elevation dataset's Geospatial Data Gateway (GDG), which has a 30 m resolution. Any place in the Cuyahoga region may have its height determined using the digital elevation model (DEM).

A comprehensive dataset which integrates the physical features of water pipelines, operating circumstances, geological situations, community socioeconomic features, and climatic conditions is created using the established data aggregation framework and will be employed.

Figure 5. Training and interpretation process for ML

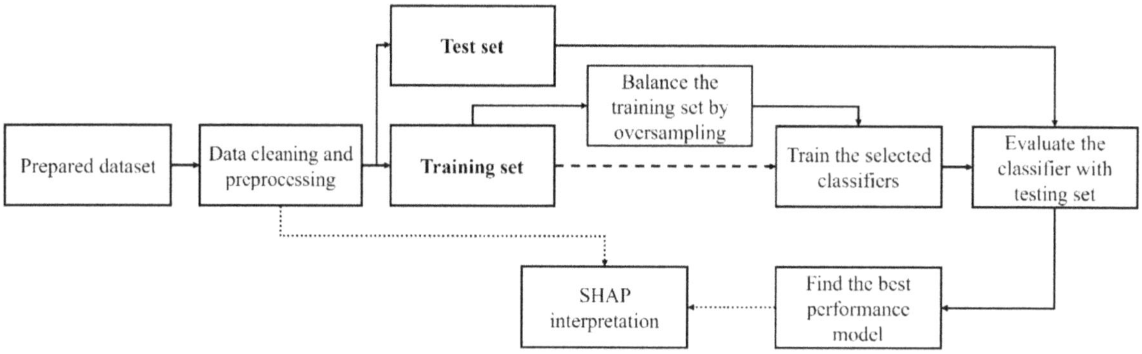

4. RESEARCH CASE

Workflow of machine learning modeling for machine learning-based pipe failure prediction is shown in Fig 5. The established methodology for the prediction of water pipe breaks is shown in overview in Figure 5. The combined dataset determined by criterion are chosen and cleaned by excluding the specimens with any missing components and outliers indicated in Section 3. The numeric components are subjected to data standardization to enhance the performance of ML techniques, which eliminate the mean values and scaling to one unit. If the ML algorithm is unable to cope up with the categorical variables, the categorical factors would be encoded using one-hot encoding (a coding technique to portray categorical factors by 0s and 1s).

The assembled dataset was divided into a training set and a test set at random by the 8:2 ratios, which is a standard method for determining the capacity of the model to forecast. The unbalanced dataset for machine learning model training is a critical problem that has to be addressed since the break records only make up around 15% of the whole dataset. As seen in Fig. 5. To train the model, both balanced and unbalanced training datasets are employed. This research utilized the oversampling approach that randomly repeats the minor class of pipes, to balance the dataset until the amount of break specimens matches the number of intact specimens. The testing dataset remains the same. As a result, the same testing dataset was used to assess the models that were trained on both balanced and unbalanced datasets. The entire dataset is utilized further for machine learning approaches through the utilization of an explanation procedure called SHAP to comprehend the effect of providing components on the pipe collapse after the best performing ML model has been found. As the chosen model is fitted once again in accordance with the entire dataset, it must be highlighted that the model analysis findings are not dependent on the train-test splitting approach. Below are descriptions of data preparation and machine learning model performance estimation.

4.2 Preparing Data and Evaluating Its Features

4.2.1 Setting Up the Dataset and Assigning Labels

The machine learning model is specified as a classification issue since the goal of the research is to estimate the pipe state at a particular time period, where the pipe status is either broken or working fine. It is impractical to create a dataset which covers every year of every pipe, and doing so might produce a very unbalanced dataset. The succeeding steps were used to construct the ultimate dataset for machine learning training and testing in order to reduce the degree of imbalance and fully use the break records.

1) For every pipe, a year at random between the time of installation and the last updation made prior to this research (Aug 2023) is chosen. Time-Dependent variables (i.e., prior collapse instances, pipe age, total number of frigid and hot days encountered) are identified during this time.
2) The pipe status noted for the chosen year is denoted by the numbers 0 for fine status or 1 for collapse status.
3) The data from the most recent break year for any pipe having a break record (or breaks) is attached to the dataset established in the older stages in order to totally use the pipe collapse history.
4) The final created dataset is split into a training dataset and a testing dataset in a 8:2 ratio.

The data aggregation procedure outlined in the previous section of this study is applied to the chosen data. The next step is data cleaning, which involves removing data points with missing information. 40,236 pipe data specimens, comprising 32,436 fine samples and 7354 break samples, are acquired after data cleaning.

Given that Step 1's random year selection may have an impact on the model's prediction outcomes. For evaluating the performance of the model, 10 random choices are made, and the average estimates of the evaluation metrics are utilized.

Figure 6. Histograms of the variables taken into account for the training and test sets

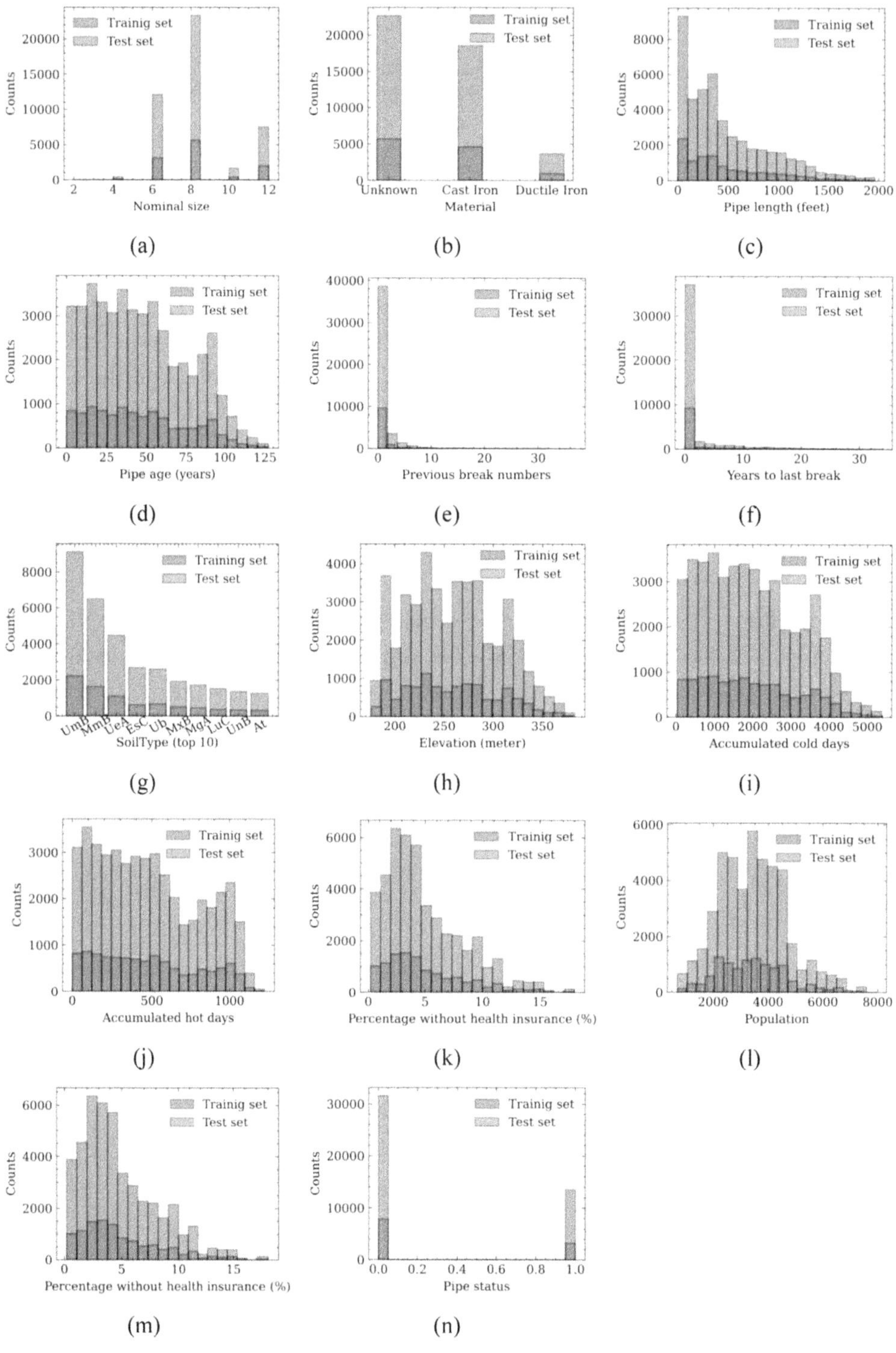

There are 13 elements in total, including two categorical variables and 11 continuous variables. The four basic categories of these elements are physical, operational, environmental, and sociological.

In both the training and testing datasets, factor histograms are depicted in Figure 6. In general, the training dataset adequately covers the testing dataset's characteristics. Dispersal of the physical variables is depicted in more detail in Fig 6(a) to (d). The most common materials in WSN systems are cast iron and ductile iron, although there exist a lot of pipes whose composition is unknown. The features of two operational variables are shown in figures 6(e) and (f). The four environmental variables are shown in 6(g) to (j). The pipes are allocated to 72 distinct soil types, although for ease of viewing. The number of hot and cold days over time is one of the climatic elements taken into account. It is intriguing to learn that they exhibit the same characteristics as the pipe age distribution, which shows that the importance of the climatic variables in pipe failures. As seen in Fig. 6(k) to (m), the census, the proportion of person living in poverty, and the proportion of families without access to health insurance are selected to reflect the socioeconomic characteristics of each pipe for the community they serve. Due to the fact that Cuya-hoga County has several heavily populated areas like Cleveland City, it is important to note that the population inside each Census community block ranges from 750 to around 8500. The poverty rate for the majority of community blocks is under 40%. The most impoverished block, however, has more than 90% of its families with yearly earnings below the poverty line. The percentage of residents without health insurance in community blocks varies from 0.2% to 18%, mirroring the reported poor status.

The collection of pipes was separated into 2 categories depending on whether this pipe breaks in the chosen monitoring year; the class code is 1 if the pipe collapses in the monitoring year and the code is 0 if it is fine. The outcomes are shown in Fig. 6. (n).

4.2.2 Connection Between Internal Variables and Failure State

The correlation matrix may be utilized to demonstrate both the external relationships between each component and the goal as well as the internal relationships among the elements thought to lead to pipe collapses. Various correlation indicators are utilized to assess the variables' correlation since the datasets include both category and numeric variables.

The fact that several of the socioeconomic variables under consideration (such as population, poverty rate, and proportion of people without health insurance) are connected but not firmly suggests that the ML model should regard them as independent variables. Furthermore, there is no association between any one I/P variable and the dominating O/P variable, suggesting that the pipe failure is a complicated issue that depends on many different factors.

Figure 7. The correlation metrics used to categorical and numerical variables

	Continuous variable	Categorical variable
Continuous variable	Pearson correlation	Correlation ratio
Categorical variable	Correlation ratio	Cramér's V

Figure 1 illustrates how to find the correlations between several sorts of data. 7. In particular, Pearson correlation (Samanta, D. et al. 2021) is used to express the correlation between two numerical variables, while Cramer's V coefficient is used to quantify the connection between two categorical variables. Additionally, between category and numerical data, the correlation ratio is employed. These indicators range from 0 to 1 for category components and from 1 to 1 for numerical elements (1 or 1 signifies an entirely positive or negatively associated relationship, whereas 0 denotes no relationship). Due to the article length restriction, a thorough explanation of the correlation calculations is not included here. Readers who are interested might consult the Supplementary file (Algorithm I).

The pipe failure state (designated as "target" in the picture) and the final correlation matrix among the 13 variables taken into account are shown in picture 8. The hotter days, colder days, and pipe ages are the elements with the strongest correlation amounts to the aim (pipe failure condition). These suggest that among the most crucial elements affecting pipe conditions are the weather and pipe service age. The subsequent features also include the pipe length, interval year, and the preceding break number, among others. All of these are taken into account in the current study's observation of their actions in the machine learning model and model clarification.

4.3 Prediction of Pipe Failure Based on L

4.3.1 Results of Predictions

The pipe break classification issue is constructed using the five supervised machine learning (ML) algorithm types that were discussed in the Background section. Grid-search optimization (Pramanik, S. 2023) is used to optimize each ML algorithm's hyperparameters. 1 input layer, one dropout layer, 2 hidden neural network layers, and one output layer are employed in the ANN model. The buried layers have 68 and 132 neurons, respectively. Fig. 9a) displays the outcomes of the model's prediction when it is trained on an unbalanced dataset. Results from model training on a balanced dataset are shown in

9b). The right and lower sides, respectively, are used to indicate the recall and accuracy matrices for every class. The right-below cell displays a description of the overall model correctness. The LightGBM (Jayasingh, R. et al. 2022) and ANN models provide the finest predictions in terms of the accuracy, recall, and precision metrics, regardless of whether the dataset is balanced or unbalanced. The KNN and SVC models, on the other hand, often overlook many intact samples when trained with the balanced dataset and frequently overlook various broken samples when trained with the unbalanced dataset. The model was able to identify more break samples thanks to oversampling.

The average Receiver Operating Characteristics (ROC), Precision-Recall Curve (PRC), area under the curve (AUC), and average training time of ten selected datasets are computed and shown in Fig. to show the overall performance of various models. In spite of unbalanced or balanced training sets, the LightGBM model outperformed all other models under consideration in terms of ROC and PRC values as well as training time. The LightGBM's ability to handle categorical data without using one-hot-

Figure 8. Map showing the correlation between the forecast objective and the variables under consideration

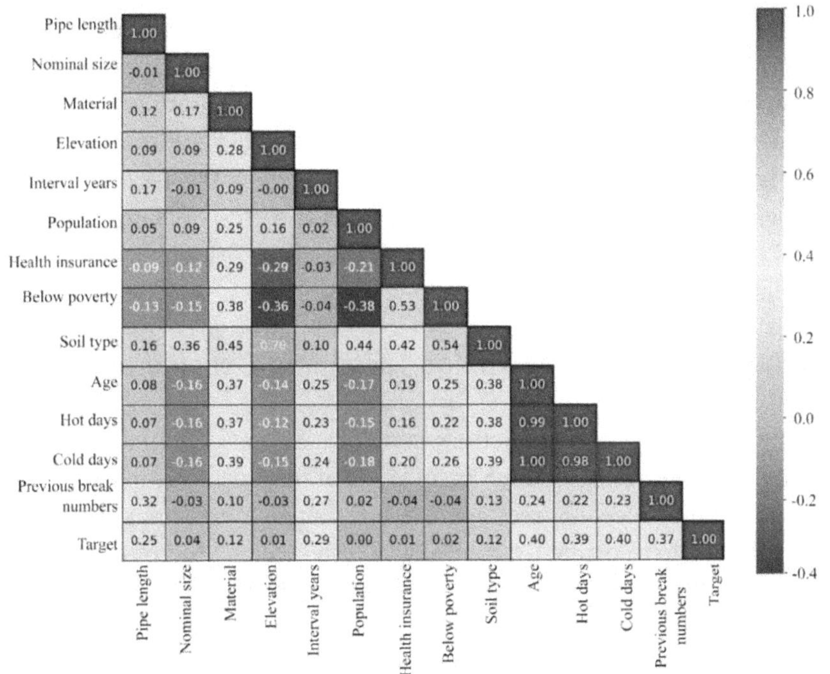

As a result of encoding, the I/P dataset is much less sparse than for different models. It may be shown that the LightGBM, ANN, LR, and kNN produced comparable ROC estimates when comparing the ROC matrix and PRC matrix, which is in disagreement with the previously noted findings (in Fig. 9). The PRC matrix displays more evident differences between estimates for several models, demonstrating a superior recognition of the most effective models. According to the PRC findings, the balanced training LightGBM model surpassed the unbalanced training model with respect to AUC of PRC value (0.810).

The outcomes of employing train-test splitting that is based randomly are shown in Figs. 8, 9, and 10. However, whether a machine learning model developed using information from past occurrences can accurately predict future events is a crucial challenge in engineering applications. The aforesaid procedures are once again computed using a time-line-based train-test splitting approach to allay this worry. Due to the identical findings, the results are not covered in this article. Readers who are interested might consult Fig. to Fig. S1. In the supporting information, it is S3.

The performance of these machine learning models is compared under several indicators based on the accuracy, training time, handling of categorical variables, and intrinsic model interpretability in order to well analyze the performance of utilizing various machine learning approaches for pipe failure estimation. It is clear that the LightGBM has the highest accuracy on the present dataset based on the classification results using balanced and unbalanced training datasets. When trained with the balanced dataset, the areas under PRC for the test dataset are around 0.86. The ANN, LR, SVC, and kNN models came next. The learning process was completed by the LR model, chased by the LightGBM approach and ANN approach, in terms of computing efficiency, in a matter of seconds. Among these models, the kNN and SVC models took the highest time. Because of its histogram and leaf-wise tree development method, the LightGBM approach is the only technique which can analyze the categorical data without any encoding. Despite the objective of this research is not the intrinsic explanatory capacity of various models; rather, they are addressed here for completeness based on earlier studies. As the weights of every element are visible and may be evaluated depending on their physical significance, statistical algorithms (such as the LR model) are often seen to be the most understandable algorithms. The relative relevance of components may be measured based on their functions throughout the tree splitting, making logistic-dependent approaches like the LightGBM model fairly simple to grasp. Finally, the instance-dependent learning algorithms (e.g., kNN), SVM, and perceptron-based algorithms are regarded as black box models having low interpretability.

4.3.2 SHAP Method Analysis of the Things Taken Into Consideration

The LightGBM technique has the best prediction accuracy and is also computationally competent, according to a performance comparison of the 5 main kinds of machine learning approaches for classification tasks mentioned in the preceding sections. Despite having a moderate capacity for explanation, the model itself is still unable to explicitly comprehend the contribution of each aspect to the result. To address this problem, the LightGBM approach trained with the balanced training dataset is used in conjunction with a machine learning model interpreter, Shapley Additive explanations (SHAP), to interpret the contribution of each element. For each component, SHAP provides a formula to determine the additive feature significance score. The more significant a factor is to the final ML model prediction, the higher the significance score. In civil engineering, the SHAP interpretation technique and decision-tree dependent machine learning algorithms was extensively utilized, even in some cases where highly correlated variables were present, like the analysis of reinforced concrete failure, the analysis of RC wall shear strength, and the crashes involving roadway segment.

To assess each factor's total effect, it is possible to compile data on how it affected the pipe break. Fig. 11 highlights the broader significance of

Figure 9. Prediction outcomes using training datasets that are unbalanced and balanced ('I' stands for fine and 'B' stands for collapse)

		Predicted results		
		I	B	Recall
True condition	I	6023	489	0.925
	B	694	1293	0.651
Precision		0.897	0.726	0.861

LightGBM model

		Predicted results		
		I	B	Recall
True condition	I	5681	831	0.872
	B	585	1402	0.705
Precision		0.906	0.628	0.833

ANN model

		Predicted results		
		I	B	Recall
True condition	I	5032	1480	0.773
	B	381	1606	0.808
Precision		0.929	0.520	0.781

LR model

		Predicted results		
		I	B	Recall
True condition	I	5992	520	0.920
	B	934	1053	0.530
Precision		0.865	0.669	0.828

kNN model

		Predicted results		
		I	B	Recall
True condition	I	5975	537	0.918
	B	890	1097	0.552
Precision		0.870	0.671	0.832

SVC model

a) Test set prediction results by model trained with imbalanced data

		Predicted results		
		I	B	Recall
True condition	I	5390	1082	0.833
	B	473	1591	0.771
Precision		0.919	0.595	0.818

LightGBM model

		Predicted results		
		I	B	Recall
True condition	I	4849	1623	0.749
	B	332	1732	0.839
Precision		0.935	0.516	0.771

ANN model

		Predicted results		
		I	B	Recall
True condition	I	5027	1445	0.776
	B	458	1606	0.778
Precision		0.916	0.526	0.777

LR model

		Predicted results		
		I	B	Recall
True condition	I	4803	1669	0.742
	B	399	1665	0.807
Precision		0.923	0.500	0.757

kNN model

		Predicted results		
		I	B	Recall
True condition	I	4994	1478	0.772
	B	447	1617	0.783
Precision		0.917	0.522	0.774

SVC model

b) Test set prediction results by model trained with balanced data

Figure 10. Evaluation of implemented ML models utilizing various metrics comparison

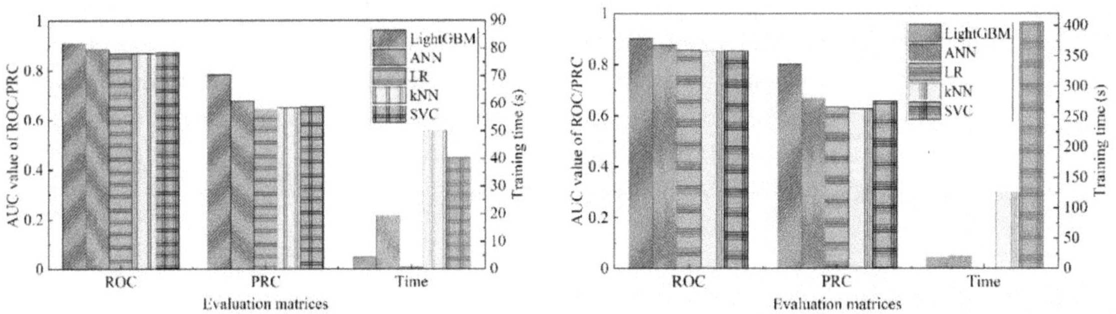

a) trained with imbalanced dataset

b) trained with balanced dataset

the analyzed variables. To explore the effects of climatic conditions, the dataset is stored with the Pipe age, Colder days, and Hotter days. The outcome reveals that out of all of them, "Cold days" have the most influence, followed by "Hot days." and "Pipe age." The three most important variables end up being pipe length, last break interval, and cold days. The nominal pipe size and the pipe's material have considerably less of an impact on the pipe break likelihood.

Table 4. Summarizing the model for predicting pipe breaks

	LightGBM	Artificial Neural Network	Logistic Regression	KNN	SVC
Accuracy	° ° °	° °	°	°	°
Learning technique speed	° °	° °	° ° °	°	°
Dealing categorical values	° ° °	°	°	°	°
Model Interpretability	° °	°	° ° °	°	°

° ° ° indicates a job well done.
° Indicates the poorest effort.

The impacts of each element on the likelihood of a pipe breaking are shown in detail in the following figures. Each variable's effect value for each sample is calculated using the SHAP approach. The impact values of each element are taken from all pipe samples in order to indicate the total influence of the variables taken into consideration on the risk of a pipe breaking. Continuous variables' effects are colorized according to their magnitudes. The mean values of the impact variables serve as a representation. Based on the observations, it is possible to deduce the following conclusions. Numerous of these findings are in line with earlier research, proving the validity of the model interpretation findings.

1) The effect of physical elements is seen in Figure 12. All of these variables all have a positive impact on the likelihood of a pipe failing, meaning that the higher the factor's value, the higher the SHAP value. According to the dispersal of pipe length estimates, lengthy pipes posses a greater likelihood of failure than smaller pipes. On pipe age, same observations may be made. Greater SHAP values for older pipes indicate that they are more prone to failure than newer pipes. Additionally, there is a positive association between the nominal size and the SHAP value, indicating that pipes having bigger nominal diameters are more likely to fail. On the right side of Fig 12, the effect of the pipe material is shown individually. Cast iron has a +ve SHAP effect value whereas ductile iron has a -ve SHAP impact value, despite both having low SHAP values. This shows that pipes constructed of cast iron have a larger break probability than pipes made of ductile iron. Ductile iron is less brittle than cast iron, which contributes to this in part.

Figure 11. The total ranking of variables taken into account for pipe failure likelihood

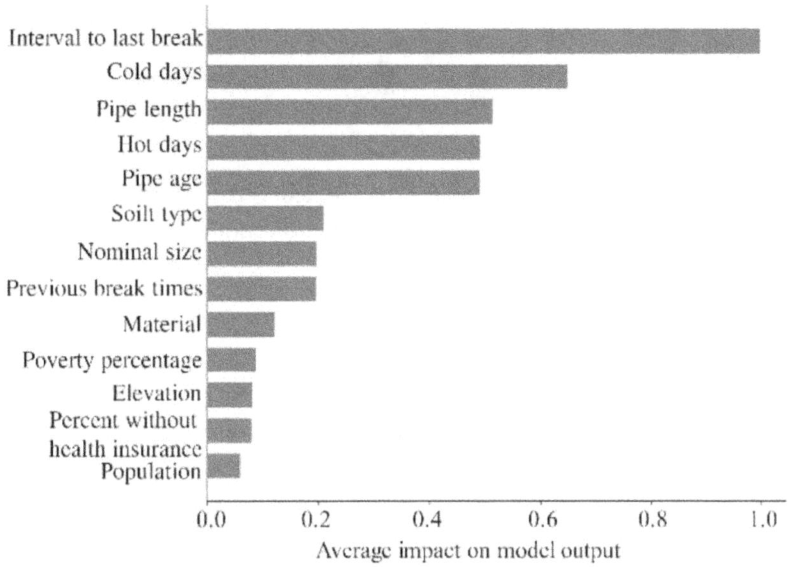

Figure 12. Effects of physical elements

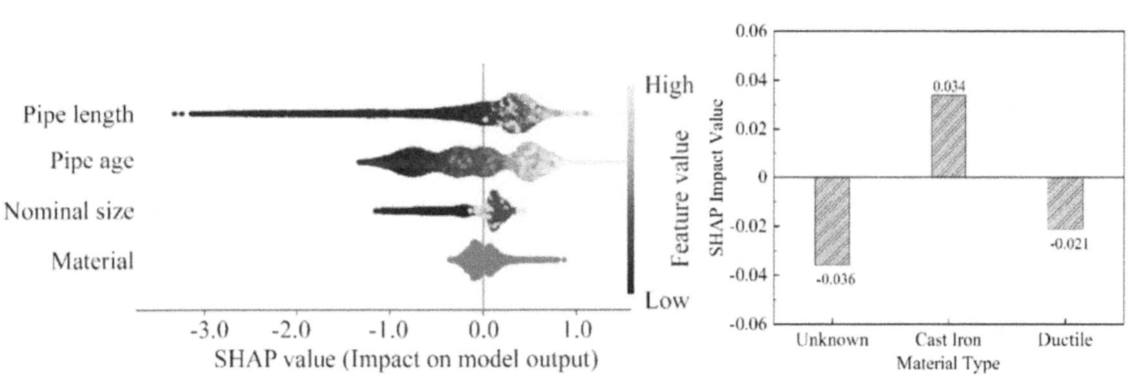

Figure 13. SHAP values shown to demonstrate how operational variables have an influence

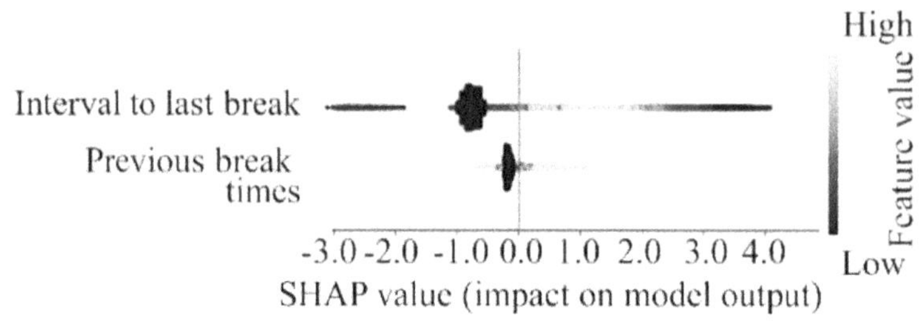

Figure 14. Influenced by environmental influences

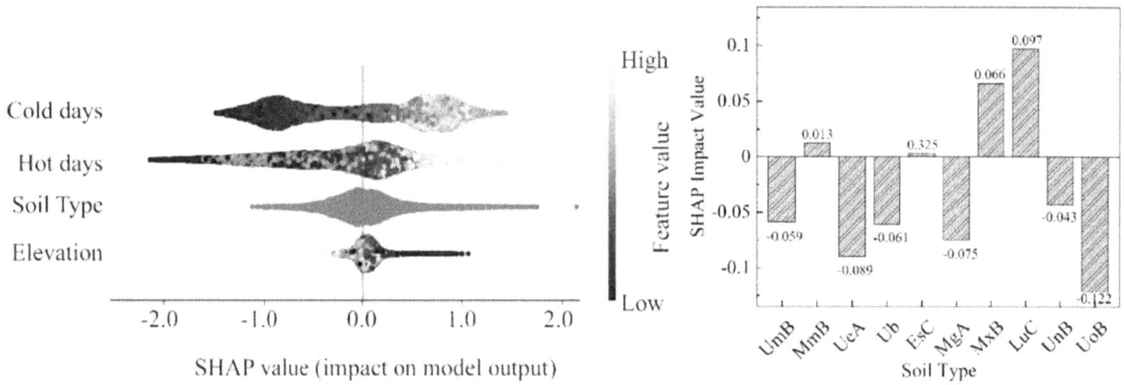

Figure 15. Impacting factors are local

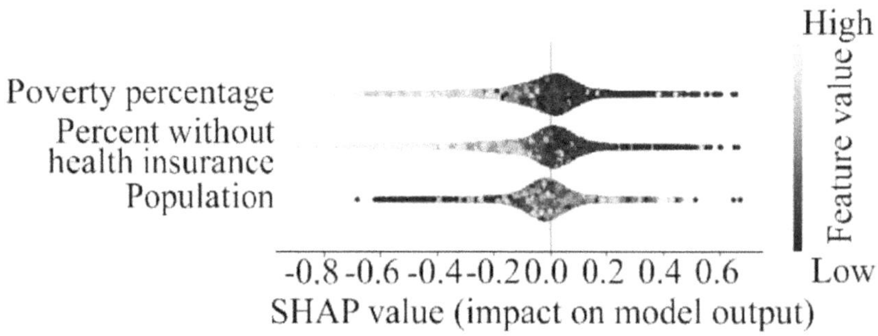

2) Fig. 13 displays the results of operational service factors. The time since the most recent break has

a greater influence on the likelihood of a pipe collapse than the durations of earlier breaks. The failure probability is observed to grow with a longer period since the previous break in the pipe, but a shorter time gap exhibits both positive and negative effects on the failure probability. This suggests that several pipes were damaged shortly after installation or repair. This finding is consistent with earlier research, which showed that a pipe's failure rate follows a bathtub curve, with large failure probability occurring either early in a pipe's life or as it begins to wear down. In addition, the SHAP values in Fig. 13 demonstrate that a higher rupture probability at the pipe correlates to a greater quantity of prior fails at the pipe. This is in line with empirical findings from practitioner interviews, according to which pipe failures tend to happen more often in the same places.

For the environmental elements shown in Fig. 14, the findings showed that the likelihood that a pipe would break increased with the number of cold days it had. It could be brought on by the effect of soil settling brought on by the freezing and thawing of the soil. On the right side of Fig 14, the effect of soil categories is shown. The LuC (Loudonville-Urban Land Complex) soil has the greatest pipe rupture probability among the top 10 soil types where the majority of pipes are hidden, while the UoB soil has the lowest rupture rate. Last but not least, the outcome shows that pipes placed at higher altitudes are less likely to burst, which makes sense given that pipelines at higher altitudes encounter low service water pressure. As a result, the pipe is subjected to reduced internal stress from the service water pressure.

4) With respect to the socio cultural elements shown in Fig. 15, it is unexpected to learn those populations with lower socioeconomic status or less access to health care had a lower likelihood of experiencing a water pipe break. The fact that the poverty-stricken neighborhoods get fewer inspections or typically consume less water may have contributed to the pipe's longer lifespan. Additional research based on additional data is needed for in-depth justifications. The chance of pipe failure is not consistently influenced by a community block's density, despite this in most pipe samples; a highly populated location is associated with a considerably greater water pipe break risk.

5. CONCLUSION

In order to understand the consequences of contributing elements, this research intends to investigate the use of ML approaches to forecast water pipe failures dependent on data from a large water supply network. A crucial step that enables taking into account contributing reasons for pipe collapses, such as the geology, climate, and socioeconomic aspects, is the proposal of a design which combines water supply network maintenance records with many public databases. Five separate machine learning models, each from the 5 main categories of machine learning classification models, are created for pipe collapse estimation using the aggregated data. Both an unbalanced training dataset, where the bulk of the data come from intact pipes, and a balanced training dataset, which uses the oversampling approach to achieve balance, are utilized to train the models. The outcomes of several training datasets are contrasted. The SHAP interpolation technique then interprets the learned ML model. This study's major contributions include:

1) It offers a cutting-edge framework for data aggregation that integrates many publicly available datasets, producing the biggest real-field dataset (in terms of size and chronology) and correspondingly the highest amount of I/P parameters for ML modeling in water supply network. As a result,

this research greatly broadens and digs in at the grasp of the communities about the influences of technology, geology, weather, and socio-economical issues. This is the first study that, to the best of our knowledge, evaluates how socioeconomic characteristics affect the collapse of water delivery networks.

2) Five common ML algorithms are investigated and thoroughly contrasted by 5 criteria (accuracy, computing time, effect of categorical variables, and interpretation) for the purpose of implementation. The maximum performance was attained by the LightGBM model with the second lowest training time. However, it has been shown that the Receiver Operating Characteristics (ROC) are too optimistic regarding the dataset is severely skewed, use the precision-recall curve (PRC) measure.
3) The SHAP's capacity to understand the effect of the contributing components was shown by the interpretation findings' consistency with earlier research. The findings show that pipe buried time, in particular the time since the previous failure, encountered colder days, hotter days, and pipe age, have a substantial impact. The contribution of the pipe's physical characteristics and the environment are consistent with the findings of other investigations. According to the contribution of community factors, places with high poverty have a reduced likelihood of pipe breakage (or are maintained less often), but locations with high population density have a greater likelihood of water pipe breakage. These show that socioeconomic considerations show a significant impact on the circumstances of pipe service.

Moreover, complicated nonlinear interactions between a varieties of elements lead to water pipe failure. Due to the model's capacity and the availability of data, previous research often streamlined the analysis process by taking a limited number of elements into account. Future research should think about including more sophisticated ML approaches and a larger dataset to increase the accuracy of pipe failure prediction. The change of decision-taking approach for ardent management of water supply network to meet sustainability objective may be catalyzed by advancements in several areas.

REFERENCES

Ahamad, S., Veeraiah, V., Ramesh, J. V. N., Rajadevi, R., Reeja, S. R., Pramanik, S., & Gupta, A. (2023). Deep Learning based Cancer Detection Technique. In Thrust Technologies' Effect on Image Processing. IGI Global.

Bhattacharya, A., Ghosal, A., Obaid, A. J., Krit, S., Shukla, V. K., Mandal, K., & Pramanik, S. (2021). Unsupervised Summarization Approach with Computational Statistics of Microblog Data. In D. Samanta, R. R. Althar, S. Pramanik, & S. Dutta (Eds.), *Methodologies and Applications of Computational Statistics for Machine Learning* (pp. 23–37). IGI Global. doi:10.4018/978-1-7998-7701-1.ch002

Chandan, R. R., Soni, S., Raj, A., Veeraiah, V., Dhabliya, D., Pramanik, S., & Gupta, A. (2023). Genetic Algorithm and Machine Learning. In Advanced Bioinspiration Methods for Healthcare Standards, Policies, and Reform. IGI Global. doi:10.4018/978-1-6684-5656-9

Chen, Y., Jia, J., Wu, C., Ramirez-Granada, L., & Li, G. (2023). Estimation on total phosphorus of agriculture soil in China: A new sight with comparison of model learning methods. *Journal of Soils and Sediments*, *23*(2), 998–1007. doi:10.1007/s11368-022-03374-x

Dhamodaran, S., Ahamad, S., Ramesh, J. V. N., Sathappan, S., Namdev, A., Kanse, R. R., & Pramanik, S. (2023). *Fire Detection System Utilizing an Aggregate Technique in UAV and Cloud Computing. In Thrust Technologies' Effect on Image Processing*. IGI Global.

Jayasingh, R. (2022). Speckle noise removal by SORAMA segmentation in Digital Image Processing to facilitate precise robotic surgery. *International Journal of Reliable and Quality E-Healthcare*, *11*(1), 1–19. Advance online publication. doi:10.4018/IJRQEH.295083

Khanh, P. T., Ngọc, T. H., & Pramanik, S. (2023). Future of Smart Agriculture Techniques and Applications. In Advanced Technologies and AI-Equipped IoT Applications in High Tech Agriculture. IGI Global. doi:10.4018/978-1-6684-6408-3.ch005

Mandal, A., Dutta, S., & Pramanik, S. (2023). Machine Intelligence of Pi from Geometrical Figures with Variable Parameters using SCILab. In Methodologies and Applications of Computational Statistics for Machine Learning. IGI Global. doi:10.4018/978-1-7998-7701-1.ch003

Mondal, D., Ratnaparkhi, A., Deshpande, A., Deshpande, V., Kshirsagar, A. P., & Pramanik, S. (2023). Applications, Modern Trends and Challenges of Multiscale Modelling in Smart Cities. In *Data-Driven Mathematical Modeling in Smart Cities*. IGI Global. doi:10.4018/978-1-6684-6408-3.ch001

Ngọc, T. H., Khanh, P. T., & Pramanik, S. (2023). Smart Agriculture using a Soil Monitoring System. In A. Khang (Ed.), Advanced Technologies and AI-Equipped IoT Applications in High Tech Agriculture. IGI Global. doi:10.4018/978-1-6684-9231-4.ch011

Pandey, B. K., Pandey, D., Nassa, V. K., Hameed, A. S., George, A. S., Dadheech, P., & Pramanik, S. (2023). A Review of Various Text Extraction Algorithms for Images. In *The Impact of Thrust Technologies on Image Processing*. Nova Publishers. doi:10.52305/ATJL4552

Pramanik, S. (2023). Intelligent Farming Utilizing a Soil Tracking Device. In A. K. Sharma, N. Chanderwal, & R. Khan (Eds.), Convergence of Cloud Computing, AI and Agricultural Science. IGI Global. doi:10.4018/979-8-3693-0200-2.ch009

Pramanik, S. (2023). An Adaptive Image Steganography Approach depending on Integer Wavelet Transform and Genetic Algorithm. *Multimedia Tools and Applications*, *82*(22), 34287–34319. Advance online publication. doi:10.1007/s11042-023-14505-y

Pramanik, S., & Bandyopadhyay, S. (2023). Identifying Disease and Diagnosis in Females using Machine Learning. In *Encyclopedia of Data Science and Machine Learning*. Global. doi:10.4018/978-1-7998-9220-5.ch187

Praveenkumar, S., Veeraiah, V., Pramanik, S., Basha, S. M., Lira Neto, A. V., De Albuquerque, V. H. C., & Gupta, A. (2023). *Prediction of Patients' Incurable Diseases Utilizing Deep Learning Approaches, ICICC 2023*. Springer. doi:10.1007/978-981-99-3315-0_4

Reepu, K. S., Chaudhary, M. G., Gupta, K. G., Pramanik, S., & Gupta, A. (2023). Information Security and Privacy in IoT. In Handbook of Research in Advancements in AI and IoT Convergence Technologies. IGI Global.

Samanta, D., Dutta, S., Galety, M. G., & Pramanik, S. (2021). A Novel Approach for Web Mining Taxonomy for High-Performance Computing. *The 4th International Conference of Computer Science and Renewable Energies (ICCSRE'2021)*. 10.1051/e3sconf/202129701073

Tai, P., Wu, F., Chen, R., Zhu, J., Wang, X., & Zhang, M. (2023). Effect of herbaceous plants on the response of loose silty sand slope under rainfall. *Bulletin of Engineering Geology and the Environment*, *82*(1), 42. doi:10.1007/s10064-023-03066-x

Vidya Chellam, V., Veeraiah, V., Khanna, A., Sheikh, T. H., Pramanik, S., & Dhabliya, D. (2023). *A Machine Vision-based Approach for Tuberculosis Identification in Chest X-Rays Images of Patients, ICICC 2023*. Springer. doi:10.1007/978-981-99-3315-0_3

Chapter 10
Suggested Cyber-Security Strategy That Maximizes Automated Detection of Internet of Things Attacks Using Machine Learning

Dharmesh Dhabliya
https://orcid.org/0000-0002-6340-2993
Vishwakarma Institute of Information Technology, India

Pratik Pandey
https://orcid.org/0009-0002-7540-5814
Vivekananda Global University, India

Varsha Agarwal
ATLAS SkillTech University, India

N. Gobi
Jain University, India

Anishkumar Dhablia
Altimetrik India Pvt. Ltd., India

Jambi Ratna Raja Kumar
https://orcid.org/0000-0002-9870-7076
Genba Sopanrao Moze College of Engineering, India

Ankur Gupta
https://orcid.org/0000-0002-4651-5830
Vaish College of Engineering, India

Sabyasachi Pramanik
https://orcid.org/0000-0002-9431-8751
Haldia Institute of Technology, India

ABSTRACT

The world is experiencing an unparalleled digital revolution because of the advancement of computer systems and the internet. This change is made even more noticeable by the fact that the internet of things is opening up new business options. However, the rise of cyberattacks has severely harmed system and data security. It is true that computer intrusion detection systems are automatically activated. However, due to its conceptual flaws, the security chain is insufficient to counter such attacks. It prevents the full potential of machine learning from being realized. Therefore, a new framework is required to properly

DOI: 10.4018/979-8-3693-1062-5.ch010

Copyright © 2024, IGI Global. Copying or distributing in print or electronic forms without written permission of IGI Global is prohibited.

safeguard the IT environment. The goal in this regard is to use machine learning methods to build and execute a new strategy for cyber-security. The goal is to improve and maximize the identification of harmful assaults and intrusions in the internet of things. Following the application of this novel strategy on the Weka platform, the authors get a final model that is reviewed and evaluated for performance.

INTRODUCTION

According to B. Mazon-Olivo and A. Pan (2022), the Internet of Things (IoT) is a highly disruptive technological revolution with unfathomable growth, influence, and capacities. It describes how many physical items are connected to the Internet so they can communicate and gather data. However, given the widespread use of linked devices and the extensive data collecting they conduct, security in the Internet of Things (IoT) is a serious worry (Yang et al., 2022).

Furthermore, one of the weak points in the cybersecurity chain is the Internet of Things. It has several technical blunders. This pertains to the network, internet, and application levels. The device itself is executing unnecessary or unsafe network services (Iqbal et al., 2020). Information availability, authenticity, secrecy, and integrity are compromised, especially in those who are exposed to the Internet. It may result in unapproved remote takeover over the internet. IT systems' attack surface is growing. Vulnerabilities are becoming more complex and dynamic over time.

In light of this new strike chain methodology, reactive security approaches for network safety are no longer appropriate. It is acknowledged that computer systems are used for autonomous intrusion detection (Shi et al., 2023) (Tran & Picek & Xue, 2017). However, it is not feasible to fully use machine learning's potential due to its conceptual shortcomings. As a result, we suggested a novel strategy for the cyber-security of linked items.

In order to improve IOT protection, the contribution consists of putting forward cyber-security models with a modular architecture and using self-learning to enable automated intrusion detection. Thus, the analytical division of the learning process forms the basis of our new methodology. It entails creating two modeling layers. These are the logical section (Logical Model) and the conceptual portion (Conceptual Model).

Furthermore, we have integrated these suggested models into a specialized program known as Weka. It is a set of machine learning algorithms intended for use in data mining applications. It has tools for preparing data, classifying, grouping, regressing, exploring association rules, and visualizing statistical data.

As a result, we suggest in the remaining work a suitable method to gauge our model's actual performance. The basic One-R approach cyber-attack detection model produces dubious findings that may be evaluated for applicability.

RELATED WORKS

As part of its plan to enhance living circumstances and provide individuals with disabilities, particularly those with autism, with access to educational programs, Mauritania has established care facilities to lessen their suffering and enhance their educational opportunities. For instance, the Nouakchott autism spectrum disorder facility is home to 66 children, eight of them are females. The children are split into two levels: beginner and intermediate, and they are overseen by fifteen specialized educators and one expert. Data is gathered and taught utilizing supervised, semi-supervised, and unsupervised learning techniques to create intrusion detection systems (Chua & Salam, 2022). The long-term performance assessment of IDS is suggested in this article. The objective is to be able to identify zero-day attacks that are not yet known.

However, machine learning techniques are used in a synthesis on the examination of Cloud Computing dangers, issues, and security solutions (Butt et al., 2020). They are used in hardened, semi-supervised, supervised, and unsupervised modes to address cloud security concerns.

Numerous studies have been conducted on the industrial Internet of connected objects, or I-IoT, which is also an active area of study. Thus, this research addresses the issue of poor detection rates and large false alarm proportions (Khan et al., 2022). This work's only goal is to identify and thwart cyberattacks. The primary emphasis is not on issues pertaining to the costs and effects of this discovery.

A significant contribution to the solution of the linked objects security challenge is made in (William et al, 2022). They are acknowledged with an exhaustive review of the literature. There is little doubt that the goals and intentions of the studies included in this analysis vary. Some of them address the issue from the logical perspective of the inherent technological limitations of the Internet of Things, namely with regard to energy, memory, and storage.

The concepts of layered architecture are introduced by other writers (Kumar & Bansal, 2019; Sifat et al., 2022), either with or without the use of methods like encryption, artificial intelligence, and machine learning. Contextualizing the security of linked things is still a reactive and corrective process. The suggested fixes, nevertheless, don't seem to be a part of a creative or proactive approach.

Rodríguez et al. have access to the review of the typology of anomalies, the layers of detection, the context, and the technique in the paper (Diana & Tobón & Múnera, 2023). An overly simplistic interpretation of the categorization of anomalies appears in this review. There are just four different sorts of anomalies since all attacks fall into the same class of abnormalities. Furthermore, this comprises almost 50% of the population. Moreover, the nature of the assault is not clearly stated. The context was ignored in almost 90% of the publications. This further reduces the suggested solutions' resilience.

The study by Lal et al. (2023) demonstrates the need of stressing learning strategies, data quality, and security concerns in free-decision making. Regarding the cognitive aspect of the suggested remedy, this last component is essential. But when it comes to a creative and modular analysis together with the security segregation and learning expenses, it doesn't appear to garner enough attention.

Current Status of Art

Most detection systems are based on linear structure learning models that are classical (Fig 1). As a consequence, there is no programmatic modularity among the various analytical segments, the operational environment, and the data structures. Put otherwise, they are four-time chronological processes that are shown in this manner. The learning and validation stages need to be completed after loading and pre-processing the raw data (Miao et al., 2022).

In relation to this paradigm, a number of actions are juxtaposed and separated into four interconnected stages. The creation and implementation of an efficient and successful detection system for Internet of Things cyberattacks is the ultimate goal.

The steps involved in this approach are as follows: gathering and preprocessing raw data; creating a learning detection system; testing the system on an independent test set; and deploying the detection system.

Figure 1. Classic intrusion detection model

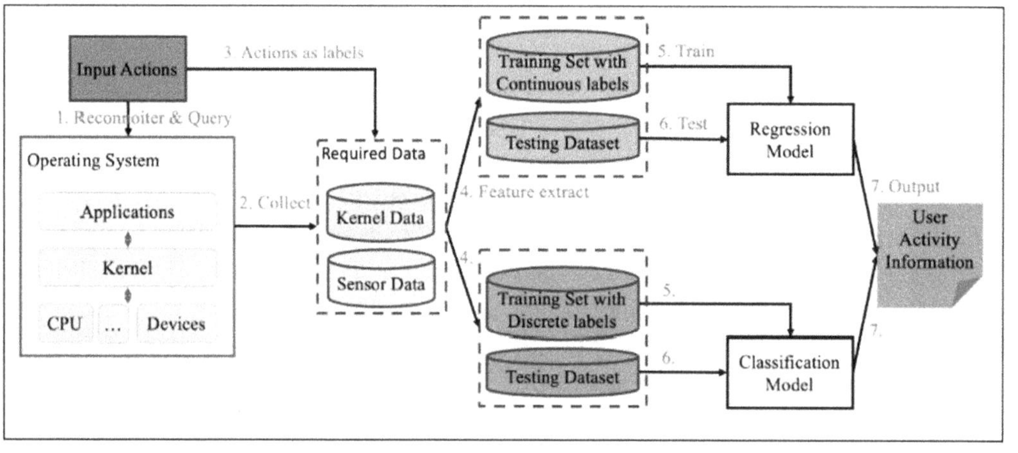

But it's acknowledged that developing a workable, dependable, and flexible machine-learning model that boosts companies and simplifies processes is a difficult and time-consuming undertaking (Ronald, 2022). In fact, the algorithmic performance of the learning process is not questioned by this approach to cyber-security modeling. Consequently, we will be unable to benefit from the competitive edge provided by a variety of techniques. Among the latter, decision trees, Bayesian networks, and several more are examples. Furthermore, it should be mentioned that the model's quality is decreased by this tacit method to learning costs and attack detection. These conceptual understandings serve as the cornerstone of our reasoning for suggesting a novel modeling strategy for cyber-security issues.

Regardless of the risk regulations used, the goal of the new model of optimized intrusion detectors that is being proposed is to do away with the single-filter that NIDS uses. Therefore, it is suggested to strengthen the security team's ability to provide outcomes that are both acceptable and well-informed. For this, our main goals are to accomplish the following:

- Algorithmic policy: to improve the algorithmic space, the quality of detection, and the security of linked objects, provide the learning engine access to a set of classification or regression techniques.
- Security policy: provide a structure that enables the integration of security goals while accounting for the risk tolerance of security boards and minimizing expenses associated with the security and insecurity of the internet of things.

The ultimate objective of this strategy is to create a real-time, broadly-construed optimal model of linked items' cyber-security. This model ought to make up for the drawbacks of earlier strategies.

A Modular Modeling Proposal

We designed a model with two degrees of modularity: conceptual and logical, in response to concerns raised by the state of the art and cyber-security goals.

Model Conceptual

Redefining the approach is necessary to upgrade the general classification and detection model. At the conceptual level, we have envisioned the development of two functional levels (Fig. 2). This brings us to the detection engine's modular programming. These modules are designed to accomplish the above mentioned optimization goals. In this manner, the Conceptual Model of Optimized Cyber-security (CMO) design phase is reached. On the one hand, the first module will create the methodology's algorithmic part in order to include a variety of teaching techniques. Conversely, the safety-cost aspect of the technique is modeled in the second module. This gives the security manager authority over the permissible risk level in relation to the various types of cyberattacks. Consequently, the best classification strategy will be selected. In terms of adverse effects, this is the least expensive approach.

Figure 2. Macro-learning optimization method for cyber-attacks

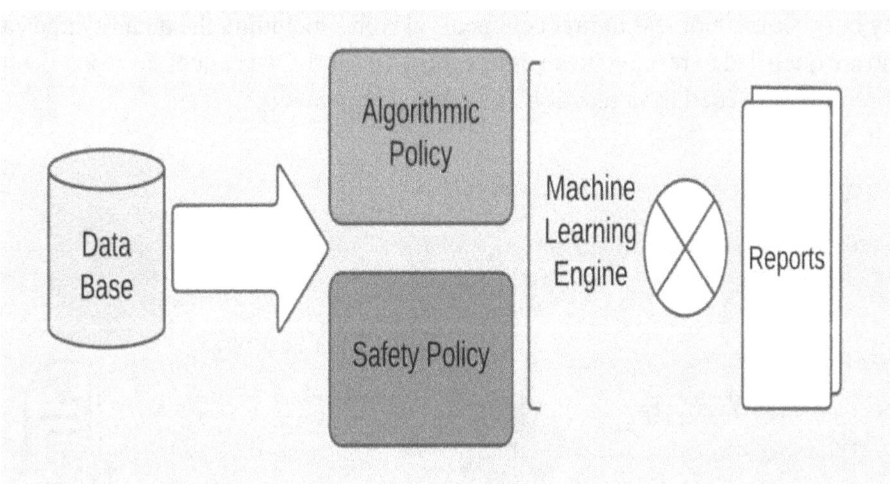

We may now act on algorithmic and security factors as we find ourselves in the process of automated optimization. As a result, we have converted the cyber-security goals into analytical terminology. In light of this, the section devoted to the model's optimization will look at the model's structure, how each block functions, and the methods used for implementation.

Reasoning Model

Attaining the Optimized Cyber-security Logic Model (OLM) will require meeting the previously established optimization targets. There will be two stages to this procedure that go hand in hand.

The Notion of Learning Metadata

What is referred to as macro-learning is correlated with meta-learning. The goal is to comprehend how various learning strategies behave. The goal is to gather information made up of method-specific algorithmic parameters and performance statistics.

We are aware that an algorithm's quality encompasses both its computational runtime speed and its ability to anticipate reality accurately. That is the fundamental idea behind the meta-learning procedure. This procedure involves pitting a number of learning techniques against a collection of unprocessed data. The optimal choice is determined by comparing technique parameters and performance indicators. Finding the most effective approach is thus a component of learning. Meta-learning is the term used to describe the integration of this stage into a macro-method. It is the study of instructional strategies.

The Idea of Price-Sensitive Education

The learning engine is aware of the cost or effect of the detection situations, which is the core idea of cost-sensitive learning. Because of this, each expense has to be listed along with any possible effects that could have an overall effect on the system. Similar to the total cost of ownership for a product or service, a number of variables affect how the cost matrix is developed. The cost of the learning process, which includes expenses for test mistakes, labeling errors, and classification errors, is one of these considerations.

There may be other more or less indirect elements at work, including the quantity and caliber of staff members who are qualified to respond to an emergency. Similarly, we cannot overlook the technological and material resources needed for a reaction and mitigation strategy.

Figure 3. Optimized cyber-security logic model (OLM)

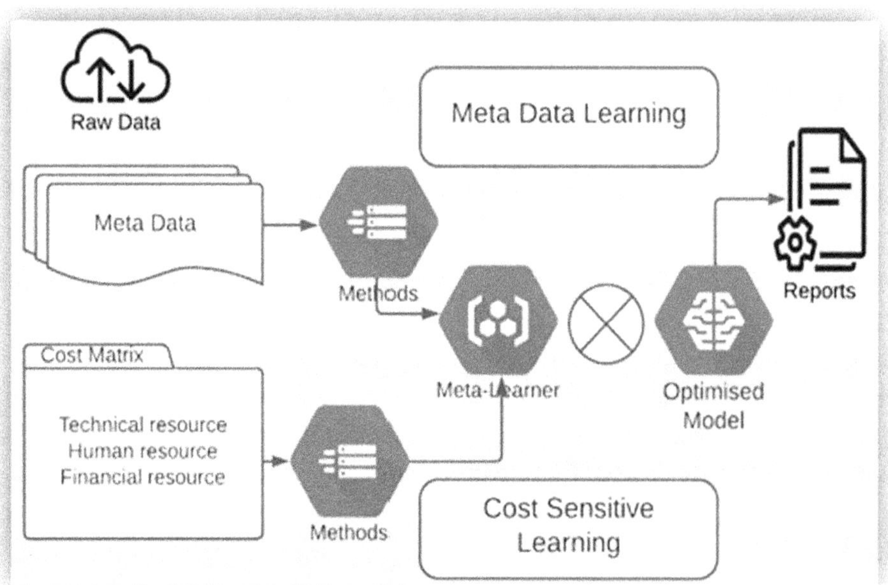

We have an operational research challenge at the formal level of description. Determining an objective function that minimizes the expression of costs while maintaining a degree of algorithmic performance and accounting for resource constraints is one aspect of the problem.

Let n represent the squared matrix of dimensions two, M (Mij) be the confusion matrix, and C(Cij) be the cost matrix. The total of all impacts that result in resource consumption should be the objective function F. This covers the costs associated with training for detection and incorrect intrusion detection. The scalar product of M and C will be F:

$$F = (M*C) = \sum_{\substack{i=1 \\ j=1}}^{n} \left(\left(\mathrm{M}_{i,j} * \mathrm{C}_{i,j} \right) \right)$$

Since the first diagonal corresponds to well-classified items, their cost is identical and can be normalized to Cij=1.

$$F = \sum(\mathrm{M}_{i,j} * \mathrm{C}_{i,j}) + \sum(\mathrm{M}_{i,i}),\ i \neq j$$

The cost of well classified items related to correct detection is $\sum(\mathrm{M}_{i,i})$. This is just a computational cost. Thus, the remaining quantity $\sum(\mathrm{M}_{i,j} * \mathrm{C}_{i,j})$ of F is cybersecurity impact related cost. The linear optimization of the objective function is obtained by:

$$\min \sum(\mathrm{M}_{i,j} * \mathrm{C}_{i,j}),\ i \neq j$$

Using Weka for modeling implementation.

This step's goal is to outline the tasks and activities that will be converted into computer language instructions so that the suggested model may be put into practice. A machine learning-compatible software platform is necessary for the development of these services. Weka software was selected for many reasons. On the one hand, the University of Waikato in New Zealand supports the free and open-source platform Weka. Nonetheless, there is a sizable user base that is helpful and there is excellent documentation accessible.

This section adheres to a series of procedures that are fundamentally divided into four stages, as shown in Fig. 4. The raw data loading from the IP packet stream occurs first. Next, it proceeds to a technique of informed selection using learning factors. The macro learning of categorization techniques in relation to the performance criteria comes next. In order to handle the cost and safety dimension, we lastly create a cost matrix based on the critical mistake patterns.

Figure 4. Optimized physical model of cyber-security

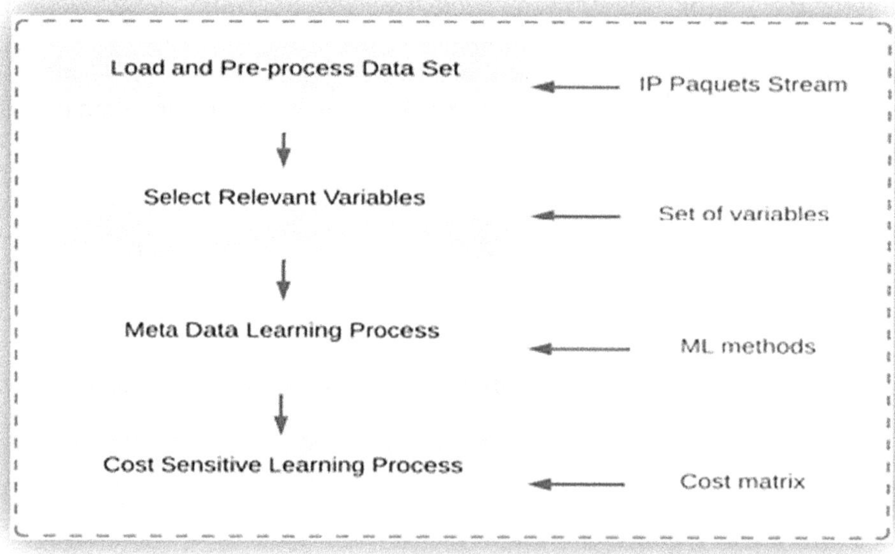

The Weka system consists of a raw data loading function plus three programming layers. This will make it simple to handle methods, variables, and security expenses in a consistent and flexible manner (Fig 5):

- Weka-Attribute-Selected Classifier: this model uses our database to learn variables.
- Weka-Multi-Scheme Classifier: this classifier deals with how learning approaches are categorized.
- Weka-Cost-Sensitive Classifier: establishes presumptive costs and security criteria.

Figure 5. Weka optimized cyber-security physical model

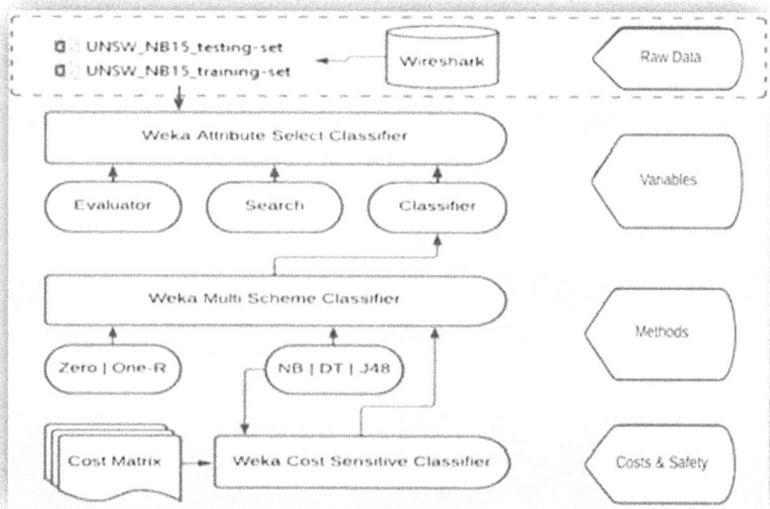

Weka's modular programming feature allows for the development of all three of these physical levels. In fact, a Weka software component has the layers coded in it. This ensures that the interfaces between the various layers are compatible.

Weka's modular programming feature allows for the development of all three of these physical levels. In fact, a Weka software component has the layers coded in it. This ensures that the interfaces between the various layers are compatible.

Figure 6. Programming of cost sensitive classifier in Weka

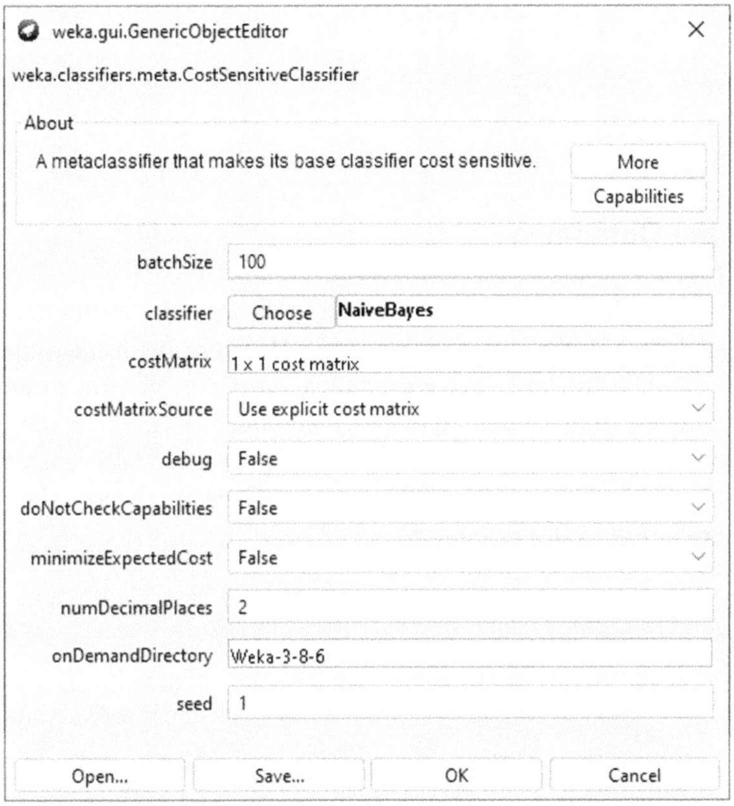

An example of a cost differentiation classification is shown in Fig. 6. This is only going to work if the corresponding matrix has a structure that makes sense. In fact, the cost equivalency assumption is reflected in the default values given in Figure 7.

Figure 7. Defining and integrating cost factors in Weka

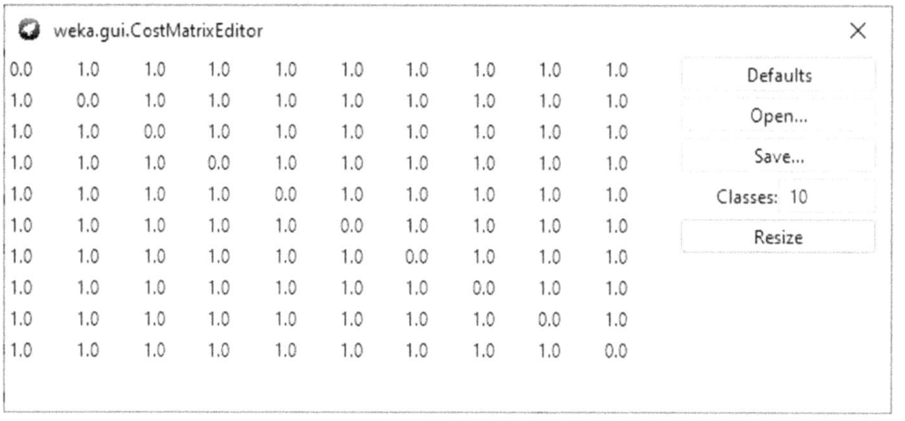

weka.gui.CostMatrixEditor

0.0	1.0	1.0	1.0	1.0	1.0	1.0	1.0	1.0	1.0
1.0	0.0	1.0	1.0	1.0	1.0	1.0	1.0	1.0	1.0
1.0	1.0	0.0	1.0	1.0	1.0	1.0	1.0	1.0	1.0
1.0	1.0	1.0	0.0	1.0	1.0	1.0	1.0	1.0	1.0
1.0	1.0	1.0	1.0	0.0	1.0	1.0	1.0	1.0	1.0
1.0	1.0	1.0	1.0	1.0	0.0	1.0	1.0	1.0	1.0
1.0	1.0	1.0	1.0	1.0	1.0	0.0	1.0	1.0	1.0
1.0	1.0	1.0	1.0	1.0	1.0	1.0	0.0	1.0	1.0
1.0	1.0	1.0	1.0	1.0	1.0	1.0	1.0	0.0	1.0
1.0	1.0	1.0	1.0	1.0	1.0	1.0	1.0	1.0	0.0

Defaults
Open...
Save...
Classes: 10
Resize

Assessment of the Outcomes

One way to quantify the model's significance is to look at its accuracy, error rate, or predictive ability. This is how the algorithmic learning approach performs. However, performance in terms of processor time pertains to physical infrastructure and computational resources. The true influence on the business process result must be considered in addition to these two dimensions. This means that the operational plan has to be expanded by a third dimension. This represents the model's sensitivity to differentiable costs (cost-sensitive) according on the kind of cyberattack. These expenses show how the predicted mistakes were converted into a value (see Fig 8).

Figure 8. Optimization evaluation factors

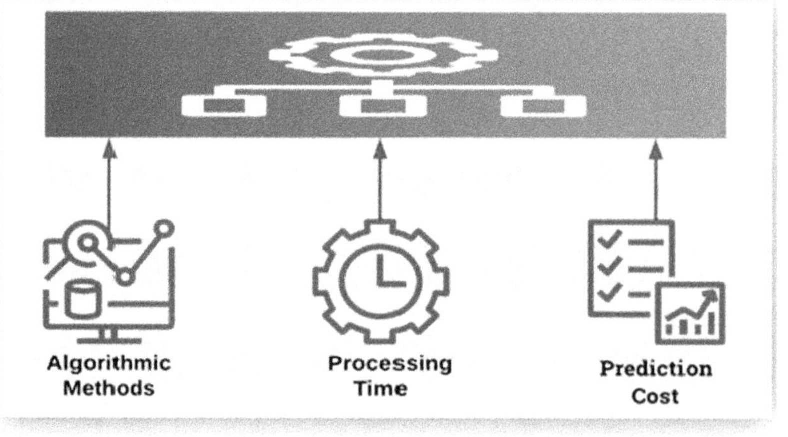

As a result, these three approaches will be neglected in the optimization of the fundamental cyber-security model for linked objects. The fundamental approach (One-R) defines this first model. Then, understanding the composition and intricacy of the prediction mistakes is crucial. In light of these difficulties, we are compelled to point out the flaws in the fundamental approach.

We are using two types of data in the learning process. One way to estimate the prediction function is by combining the training set with a classification method.

$x \rightarrow f(x)$

The space of prediction variables in this prediction function is represented by x= (x1, x2, xn), while the algorithmic function for categorizing cyberattacks is denoted by f(x). So far, the learning period is ongoing. This causes a concordance or disparity between observation and prediction for every type of cyberattacks. The Confusion Matrix (Table 1) is a table that contains these findings.

Table 1. Basic metrics of the confusion matrix

Techniques	Observations (Real Class)	
Learning (Predicted Class)	(True Positives) **TP**	(False Positive) FP
	(False Negative) **FN**	(True Negative) TN

On the other side, the validation step comes after this one. The purpose of the collection of tests derived from the observed data is this. This information will be sent to the prediction function as input values. The operation's outcomes and the matching observation values will be compared (Fig 9).

Figure 9. One-R confusion matrix

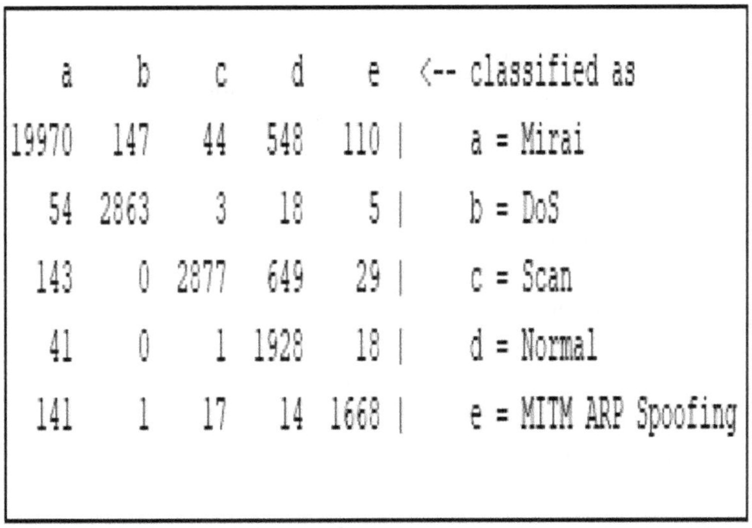

```
    a     b     c     d     e   <-- classified as
19970   147    44   548   110 |     a = Mirai
   54  2863     3    18     5 |     b = DoS
  143     0  2877   649    29 |     c = Scan
   41     0     1  1928    18 |     d = Normal
  141     1    17    14  1668 |     e = MITM ARP Spoofing
```

Regarding the fundamental One-R technique, the 2863 packets are anticipated to be denial-of-service attacks (DoS category). The test set's findings validate this prediction. Additionally, 1928 packets were identified as benign (Normal category) in both observation and prediction. For a column of data that is not on the first diagonal, we determine the mistakes that the model made. Thus, 148 forecasts total—47 of which are botnets—and 1 usurpation (ARP spoofing). The test data's actuality contradicts this prediction. These packets really fall under category B (denial of service).

Multiple indicators may simultaneously assess the goals related to the model's validity. First, there are the comprehensive statistical estimates (Fig. 10), which evaluate the model's overall performance. These metrics show the effectiveness, flaws, and consistency of learning.

Figure 10. Performance statistics of the One-R method

Correctly Classified Instances	29306	93.6623 %
Incorrectly Classified Instances	1983	6.3377 %
Kappa statistic	0.882	
Mean absolute error	0.0254	
Root mean squared error	0.1592	
Relative absolute error	12.0258 %	
Root relative squared error	49.0447 %	
Total Number of Instances	31289	

The model's accuracy is represented by the classification rate, or accuracy. It is the percentage of people who have been properly categorized out of the total population under investigation. In the case of the fundamental One-R approach, it is 93.66%. The degree to which the forecasts and observations agree is shown by this rate.

(TP+TN)/((TP+FN)+(TN+FP) equals accuracy.

The percentage of people that are incorrectly categorized is shown by the model's error rate. This indicates that when the learning model encountered the actuality of the data, it generated incorrect predictions. When using the basic One-R technique on the data, this rate is 6.34%.

Analyses and Conversation

The fundamental OneR method's benefit is its straightforward algorithm. Stated otherwise, the cyber-attack detection model is designed using a single prediction rule, or variable, in the One-R (One Rule) technique. Consequently, the essence of this approach is to disregard the data pertaining to the additional factors of the previously outlined optimum selection.

But much like Zero-R, the One-R approach is a fundamental one. This indicates that they enable us to establish the optimization process's starting point. The system is now in its basic condition, or zero state, and has to be upgraded to reach a more logical and acceptable optimum.

To put it simply, the zero state is used as a benchmark in the iterative process of finding the best categorization model. In fact, in order to better optimize the detection model in terms of hardware resources and algorithmic speed, we will need to evaluate alternative learning strategies and compare them to the zero state.

CONCLUSION

Our investigation has uncovered a significant IoT security issue. IoT physical security has difficulties in distant locations. Updates and upgrades for both software and hardware are essential. This is a significant limitation on the threat's scope. The availability of tools (Shodan, Tor, Nmap, and Nessus) for identifying and taking advantage of IoT system vulnerabilities heightens this danger. This indicates clear cybersecurity difficulties.

The cybernetic striking chain is given particular consideration in this design. We decided to use an enhanced detection model in order to adjust for this. The foundation of this optimization is security policies and algorithms. This combines the benefits of lower learning costs with the possibilities of algorithmic approaches. It is implemented using differentiated cost approaches and macro-learning (Meta learning). The machine learning platform's Weka is used for programming.

REFERENCES

Butt, U. A., Mehmood, M., Shah, S. B. H., Amin, R., Shaukat, M. W., Raza, S. M., Suh, D. Y., & Piran, M. J. (2020, September). A Review of Machine Learning Algorithms for Cloud Computing Security. *Electronics (Basel), 9*(9), 9. Advance online publication. doi:10.3390/electronics9091379

Chua, T.-H., & Salam, I. (2022). *Evaluation of Machine Learning Algorithms in Network-Based Intrusion Detection System*. doi:10.3390/sym15061251

Iqbal, W., Abbas, H., Daneshmand, M., Rauf, B., & Bangash, Y. A. (2020, October). An In-Depth Analysis of IoT Security Requirements, Challenges, and Their Countermeasures via Software-Defined Security. *IEEE Internet of Things Journal*, *7*(10), 10250–10276. doi:10.1109/JIOT.2020.2997651

Khan, I. A., Keshk, M., Pi, D., Khan, N., Hussain, Y., & Soliman, H. (2022, September). Enhancing IoT networks protection: A robust security model for attack detection in Internet Industrial Control Systems. *Ad Hoc Networks*, *134*, 102930. doi:10.1016/j.adhoc.2022.102930

Kumar, A., & Bansal, A. (2019) Software Fault Proneness Prediction Using Genetic Based Machine Learning Techniques. *2019 4th International Conference on Internet of Things: Smart Innovation and Usages (IoT-SIU),* 1-5. 10.1109/IoT-SIU.2019.8777494

Lal, B., Ravichandran, S., Kavin, R., Anil Kumar, N., Bordoloi, D., & Ganesh Kumar, R. (2023, June). IOT-based cyber security identification model through machine learning technique. *Measurement. Sensors*, *27*, 100791. doi:10.1016/j.measen.2023.100791

Mazon-Olivo, B., & Pan, A. (2022). Internet of Things: State-of-the-art, Computing Paradigms and Reference Architectures. IEEE Latin America Transactions, 20(1), 49-63. doi:10.1109/TLA.2022.9662173

Miao, Y., Chen, C., Pan, L., Han, Q.-L., Zhang, J., & Xiang, Y. (2022, September). Machine Learning Based Cyber Attacks Targeting on Controlled Information: A Survey. *ACM Computing Surveys*, *54*(7), 1–36. doi:10.1145/3465171

Schmelzer. (2022). *Comment construire un modèle de Machine Learning en 7 étapes*. LeMagIT. https://www.lemagit.fr/conseil/Comment-construire-un-modele-de-Machine-Learning-en-7-etapes

Shi, Z., He, S., Sun, J., Chen, T., Chen, J., & Dong, H. (2023, January). An Efficient Multi-Task Network for Pedestrian Intrusion Detection. *IEEE Transactions on Intelligent Vehicles*, *8*(1), 649–660. doi:10.1109/TIV.2022.3166911

Sifat, F. H., Mahzabin, R., Anjum, S., Nayan, A.-A., & Kibria, M. G. (2022). IoT and Machine Learning-Based Hypoglycemia Detection System. *2022 International Conference on Innovations in Science, Engineering and Technology (ICISET),* 222-226. 10.1109/ICISET54810.2022.9775890

Tran, B., Picek, S., & Xue, B. (2017). Automatic Feature Construction for Network Intrusion Detection. In Lecture Notes in Computer Science: Vol. 10593. *Simulated Evolution and Learning. SEAL 2017.* Springer. doi:10.1007/978-3-319-68759-9_46

Williams, P., Dutta, I. K., Daoud, H., & Bayoumi, M. (2022, August). A survey on security in internet of things with a focus on the impact of emerging technologies. *Internet of Things : Engineering Cyber Physical Human Systems*, *19*, 100564. doi:10.1016/j.iot.2022.100564

Yang, Zhang, Lin, Li, & Sun. (2022). Characterizing Heterogeneous Internet of Things Devices at Internet Scale Using Semantic Extraction. *IEEE Internet of Things Journal, 9*(7), 5434-5446. doi:10.1109/JIOT.2021.3110757

Chapter 11
Empowering Users:
Contextual Marketing for Cybersecurity Education and Solutions

Monica Janet Clifford
https://orcid.org/0000-0001-8695-5921
Christ University, India

R. Kavitha
Christ University, India

ABSTRACT

It is crucial to arm users with the information and resources they need to protect their online presence in the dynamic world of cybersecurity, where threats are evolving at an alarming rate. This chapter examines contextual marketing as a potent strategy for delivering cybersecurity education and solutions. In order to effectively engage consumers and inform them about cybersecurity risks and best practices, contextual marketing is the strategic application of customised content and resources supplied at the appropriate time and in the appropriate environment. The chapter tackles the underlying difficulties that consumers confront in comprehending and managing their cybersecurity requirements. It emphasizes how critical it is to plug the knowledge gap by giving users access to information that is pertinent to their situation and degree of comprehension. By creating user-centric experiences, contextual marketing enables cybersecurity educators and solution providers to maximize the effect of their work. This chapter delivers several contextual marketing strategies that have been productive in enhancing users' cybersecurity awareness and skills. It accomplishes so by drawing on real-world examples and case studies. Educational activities can be made engaging and easily remembered by adapting messages, tutorials, and resources to meet users' roles, interests, and habits. The chapter also looks at how sophisticated cybersecurity solutions and contextual marketing work together. It exemplifies the benefits of context-aware security systems. The chapter concludes by arguing in favour of incorporating contextual marketing principles into cybersecurity instruction and solution delivery. Contextual marketing paves the way for a more informed and cyber-aware society that is better able to face the ever-evolving challenges of the digital world by providing users with personalized, timely, and relevant information.

DOI: 10.4018/979-8-3693-1062-5.ch011

Copyright © 2024, IGI Global. Copying or distributing in print or electronic forms without written permission of IGI Global is prohibited.

INTRODUCTION

The importance of cybersecurity has never been more vital in the quickly developing digital age. The potential risks posed by cyber threats continue to rise as our lives and organizations become more technologically intertwined. Cyber attackers continuously modify their strategies, taking advantage of weaknesses and knowledge gaps in users to break defences. The human factor continues to be one of the weakest links in the fight for digital security. Users' ability to protect themselves online is increased by providing them with the knowledge they need, and proactive security practices are encouraged. Contextual marketing is one cutting-edge strategy that has a lot of potential to change cybersecurity education and solution delivery. Contextual marketing, which has its roots in the field of digital marketing, is a kind of strategic and individualized communication that offers experiences, resources, and material that are specifically suited to the context and requirements of the recipient. Contextual marketing, which efficiently cuts through the noise to offer pertinent information at the correct time, has altered how organizations engage and connect with their consumers by utilizing user data and behaviour insights. Contextual marketing is currently being used by the cybersecurity industry to equip consumers with the information and resources they need to defend themselves against ever evolving cyberthreats. In the context of cybersecurity, this book chapter offers a succinct and insightful description of contextual marketing. It investigates the applicability and effects of this strategy in bridging the knowledge gap between consumers and the dynamic cybersecurity ecosystem. In this chapter, we examine the foundational ideas of contextual marketing and explore how they might be effectively applied to cybersecurity education programs. Cybersecurity educators can have the most influence on users by providing them with knowledge, training, and advice that is contextually appropriate, motivating them to implement preventative security measures. We look at a number of approaches and best practices that show how contextual marketing may make cybersecurity education more interesting and tailored. The chapter also explores the mutually beneficial interaction between sophisticated cybersecurity solutions and contextual marketing. Context-aware security systems enable enterprises to respond in real-time to user activity, increasing their defences while lessening the burden on users. Contextual marketing for cybersecurity also addresses ethical issues, recognizing the significance of user privacy and permission in fostering long-term engagement and trust. Contextual marketing activities must strike the ideal balance between personalisation and privacy to be successful and considerate of users' rights. In the end, this book chapter emphasizes how collaboratively Contextual Marketing may be used in the cybersecurity industry. In order to create comprehensive contextual marketing strategies that empower consumers and promote a cyber-aware society, it underlines the necessity for cooperation and synergy among cybersecurity professionals, educators, and industry stakeholders. We shall see how Contextual Marketing, with its accuracy and relevance, transforms cybersecurity education and equips users to act as the first line of defence against online dangers as we progress through the following pages. Through this investigation, we seek to stimulate more creativity, investigation, and effective application of contextual marketing strategies in the effort to create a safer and more secure digital environment.

Contextual Marketing

Consumers are inundated with an incredible amount of information, ads, and promotional messages in today's digitally driven environment. Traditional marketing strategies frequently struggle to get and hold the attention of their target audience in the midst of this information flood. Contextual marketing, a novel marketing paradigm, offers a more relevant and individualized manner to communicate with customers, nevertheless. Contextual marketing, at its heart, is a strategic strategy that makes use of data, insights, and context to deliver personalized content, goods, or services to people at the most appropriate times. Contextual marketing aims to deeply comprehend the requirements, preferences, and behaviours of consumers in order to provide them exactly what they need, exactly when they need it, in contrast to traditional marketing strategies that throw a wide net in the hopes of catching some interested prospects. Beyond the traditional "one-size-fits-all" approach, this ground-breaking marketing tactic focuses on creating highly tailored experiences for each individual. Contextual marketing enables marketers to foresee consumer intent and present solutions that connect with customers personally by examining a variety of data sources, including demographic data, previous interactions, browser history, and even in-the-moment activities. Contextual marketing has been more popular and effective thanks in large part to the development of digital technology and the proliferation of internet platforms. With the capacity to gather and process massive volumes of data in real-time, marketers can design dynamic, adaptable campaigns that react to customer behaviour instantly. In this introduction to contextual marketing, we will analyse its foundational concepts, consider how it has revolutionized contemporary marketing tactics, and consider how it has changed how brands interact with their target audiences. We will also discuss the difficulties and moral issues involved in using consumer data to tailor marketing campaigns while upholding user privacy and consent. We will learn important insights about contextual marketing's ability to create deeper relationships between brands and customers as we set out on this adventure into its world. Contextual Marketing opens the way for a more customer-centric, relevant, and successful marketing landscape by accurately adapting messages and services to their requirements and preferences. Join us as we learn how contextual marketing may influence the direction of marketing and generate extraordinary success in a rapidly changing digital environment.

The primary objective of contextual marketing is to deliver relevant and valuable information to the appropriate individuals on their devices, precisely when it is most advantageous (Luo, X., & Seyedian, M., 2003). The conventional marketing approach involves the initial selection of products followed by the subsequent identification of target consumers, whereas contextual marketing entails the customization of products to cater to specific consumer segments (Lee, T., & Jun, J., 2007). The genuine contextual experience arises from the diversity among users. The connection of diverse individuals across various groups within a given context generates a distinct value, leading to the development of contextual experiences and empowering users to engage in active consumption (Luo, X., 2003). The utilization of contextual marketing techniques in mobile applications has the potential to provide individuals with an exceptional user experience, as it possesses a deep understanding of their specific requirements (Barbosa, B., et al, 2023). The provided information and services exhibit intelligent and personalized characteristics, adapting appropriately to various occasions and timeframes (Smith, T., et al, 2015). This adaptability enables individuals to effectively manage their needs, encompassing physical information and emotional states. For instance, individuals are able to seamlessly transfer the audio output from their mobile phone application to the car's audio system upon entering the vehicle (von der Au, et al, 2023). Similarly, the scheduling application will automatically synchronize with the car's navigation system to set the desired destination (López-Pastor, et al, 2021). Furthermore, upon entering a conference room, the scheduling application will promptly distribute the agenda's contents to all attendees. This integration of technology is particularly relevant within enterprise settings (Sweezey, M., 2020). The application will facilitate the integration of employees' work progress and generate reports for managers (Dou, X., 2021). The catering application will suggest the most appropriate restaurant to individuals in the dining area by considering factors such as location data, individuals' previous dining preferences, and the current status of restaurant queues. In summary, mobile applications encompass various facets of individuals' lives (Kotler, P., 2021).

Cybersecurity: Threats and Preventions

The field of cybersecurity has developed into a crucial pillar protecting our contemporary society in the age of pervasive connection and digital transformation. As technology develops, cyber threats become more sophisticated and effective, making people, businesses, and even entire countries susceptible to assault. Understanding the fundamentals of cybersecurity, the primary dangers it confronts, and the preventive measures used is more important than ever in this constantly changing environment. At its core, cybersecurity is the activity of preventing unwanted access to, interruption to, or destruction of computer systems, networks, and data. It includes a wide range of tactics, tools, and procedures created to counteract cyberthreats, which can be from bad actors, gangs of organized criminals, government agencies, or even unintentional flaws. The biggest cybersecurity threats are varied and multidimensional, always changing to take advantage of gaps in our digital infrastructure. Malware, ransomware, phishing scams, social engineering, and distributed denial-of-service (DDoS) assaults are just a few of the tools and strategies that cybercriminals use to breach networks and steal private data. These dangers can have severe effects, resulting in monetary losses, reputational harm, and invasions of privacy Cybersecurity experts and companies use a variety of proactive tactics and preventive measures to successfully combat these attacks. A good defence must include reliable and current cybersecurity frameworks, secure coding techniques, and regular vulnerability assessments. Sensitive data and user accounts are further protected by encryption and multi-factor authentication. Additionally, technologies for ongoing threat detection and monitoring allow for quick detection of and reaction to potential security breaches. Additionally essential to cybersecurity prevention are knowledge and education. Organizations can lower their risk of falling prey to social engineering attacks and phishing attempts by encouraging a culture of cyber-awareness among individuals and workers. Regular cybersecurity training equips users with the knowledge to identify potential threats and employ safe online practices. We will thoroughly examine the primary dangers to cybersecurity in this chapter, ranging from small-scale attacks to extensive cyberwarfare. We will look into the methods and tactics used by cybercriminals to hack into systems and take advantage of weaknesses. We will also look at the preventative strategies, best practices, and innovative technology used to counter these concerns and lessen possible harm. Our knowledge of the always changing threat landscape and the application of proactive preventive measures will be crucial in reinforcing our digital world as we negotiate the complexity of cybersecurity. We can work together to create a safer and more resilient cyberspace for future generations by promoting a culture of cybersecurity awareness and staying at the forefront of defensive tactics.

Objectives of the Study

The main objective of this chapter is to examine the concept of contextual marketing in the context of cybersecurity education and solutions, providing a comprehensive understanding of its principles, methodologies, and applications and highlighting the significance of continuous support and updates in cybersecurity solutions and how contextual marketing can aid in delivering timely and relevant information to the users.

Purpose of the Study

This study aims to explore the application of contextual marketing techniques in cybersecurity education and solutions, with a detailed focus on empowering users. The chapter aims to shed light on the potential of contextual marketing to advance user engagement, awareness, and proactive cybersecurity behaviour. By molding educational content, product offerings, and promotions to users' unique needs and contexts, organizations can augment user receptiveness to cybersecurity messages and foster the adoption of sufficient security practices.

The chapter seeks to bridge the gap between traditional cybersecurity awareness campaigns and the ever-evolving cyber threat landscape by offering a proactive approach that caters to individual user inclinations and behaviour.

Ultimately, the purpose is to contribute to enhancing cybersecurity education and solutions through pioneering and user-centric approaches that adopt a cyber-aware and resilient society.

Theme

The overarching theme of this chapter revolved around the idea of empowering users through the application of contextual marketing in the domain of cybersecurity education and solutions. It focuses on how personalized and targeted approaches can enhance user engagement, understanding, and adoption of cybersecurity best practices, ultimately leading to a more secure digital environment for individuals and organizations. The main key elements of the theme are.

- Empowerment - the chapter underlines the importance of rousing users by providing them with the intelligence, equipment, and resources they need to safeguard themselves from cyber threats effectively.
- Contextual Marketing – This main element serves as the central concept of the theme as it emphasizes modifying cybersecurity messages, products, and solutions to the specific needs, preferences, and behaviour of individual users.
- User-Centric Approach – It focuses on considering users' unique contexts, challenges, and motivations to design appropriate and impactful cybersecurity strategies.
- Education and Awareness – It climaxes how contextual marketing can be used to deliver timely and relevant cybersecurity information promoting a deeper understanding of risks and the adoption of secure behaviours.
- Proactive Cybersecurity – It encourages users to take preventive measures and stay vigilant against potential hazards. Overall, the base centres on leveraging individualized and contextually relevant approaches to equip users with the knowledge and tools they need to be active partakers in their cybersecurity defence.

REVIEW OF LITERATURE

The study employed a systematic literature review methodology to evaluate both background reviews and independent studies pertaining to the use of contextual marketing .

The articles were sourced from reputed journals and were scrutinized to determine the level of quality exhibited by each study. Elsevier database, Routledge and CRC Press Taylor and Francis database. Emerald Group Publishing database, Springer Nature database and Sage database. Several supplementary articles were acquired from reputable academic databases such as Wiley, Academia, JSTOR, and Guildford Press.

Cybersecurity threats continues to pose significant challenges to individuals and organization alike, demanding a proactive approach to empower users in protecting their digital assets. This literature review explores the concept of contextual marketing as a means to empower users through cybersecurity education and solutions. By tailoring cybersecurity messages, product and promotion to users specific needs and contexts, contextual marketing aims to enhance user engagement, awareness and adoption of cybersecurity best practises.

Contextual Marketing in cybersecurity education: Contextual marketing also known as personalised marketing has gained traction as a powerful tool for engaging audience across various domains (Smith eh al .,2017). In the context of cybersecurity education this approach involves delivering targeted content to user based on their online behaviours and preference. By using personalised messaging, cybersecurity professionals can effectively communicate the relevance of security practises to individual users (Johnson & Brown, 2019).

Personalization and User Engagement: Personalization has been recognized as a critical factor in driving user engagement with cybersecurity content. Studies by Lee and Kim (2018) found that personalized email campaigns resulted in higher click – through rates and improved understanding of phishing risks. By leveraging contextual marketing techniques, such as dynamic content delivery based on user behaviour, cybersecurity professionals can improve user engagement (Miller et al., 2020)

Behaviour based recommendations for user empowerment: Behaviour based recommendations use user data to identify individual strengths and weakness in cybersecurity practises. Johnson et al., (2019) demonstrated that personalised recommendations led to increased adoption of secure behaviours. Contextual marketing's ability to analyse user behaviour and deliver targeted advice allows for tailored guidance to address specific vulnerabilities effectively (Robinson & Davis, 2022).

Adaptive Learning in Cybersecurity Education: Adaptive learning which tailors educational content based on individual progress and learning styles, has demonstrated significant potential in the filed of cybersecurity education (Wang & Chen, 2016). Contextual marketing facilitates the implementation of these techniques by aligning them with users interest and preferences (Choi et al.,2021).

Continuous Support and Updates for user environment: Continuous support and timely updates are vital in cybersecurity solutions to stay ahead of evolving threats (Garcia & Brown, 2018). Contextual marketing allows the delivery of relevant notifications and reminders to users, encouraging them to remain proactive in their cybersecurity practises (Thomas et al., 2021)

Tailored Product offerings for Enhanced User Adoption: Contextual marketing allows cybersecurity solution providers to customize their product offerings to suit different user segments (Brown & Evans, 2017). Research by (Zhang et al., 2018) demonstrates that tailored product offerings significantly improve user trust in cybersecurity solutions and increase adoption rates among diverse user groups.

Addressing Challenges and Ethical Consideration: Implementing contextual marketing in cybersecurity is not without challenges. Research by (Smith & Johnson, 2019) identifies data privacy and security as primary concerns when utilizing user data for personalization. Striking a balance between personalization and protecting user information remains a critical ethical considerations (Adams et al., 2022)

METHODOLOGY

The study is purely conceptual and based on careful analysis of the literature based on Contextual Marketing, Cybersecurity, and the influence of Contextual marketing in creating awareness among to end users on how they have to protect themselves from cybercrimes in current day. This study's methodology involves a thorough analysis of the state of the literature, research, innovations, developments, trends, and applications in the fields of contextual marketing and cybersecurity, as well as AI.

Prisma Model is adopted to conduct a systematic literature review (Shamseer, L., et al, 2015), (Takkouche, B., & Norman, G., 2011), (Page, M. J., et al, 2021) (Welch, V.,et al, 2016).

Figure 1. PRISMA model for systematic literature review

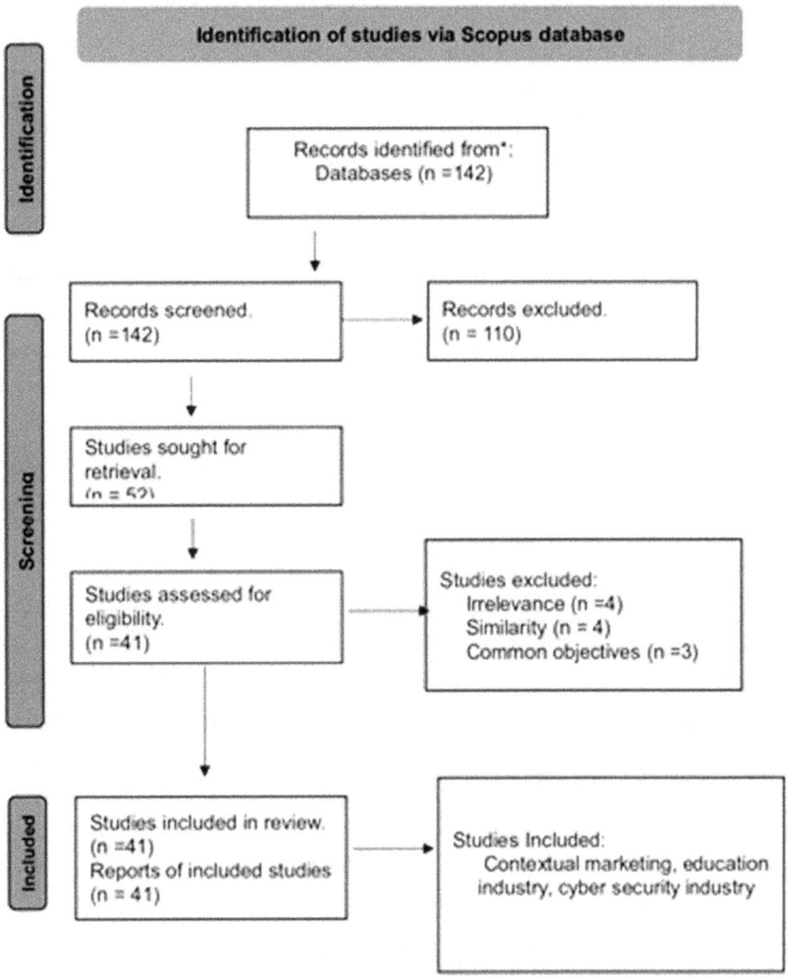

RESULTS AND DISCUSSIONS

Benefits of Contextual Marketing

By providing users with individualized and pertinent content, information, and solutions, contextual marketing can significantly improve cybersecurity. It makes use of the context of specific users, such as their actions, interests, and level of expertise, to develop cybersecurity messages and tactics that are tailored to meet their needs.

The following are a few ways that contextual marketing aids cybersecurity-

- Contextual marketing enables the delivery of personalized cybersecurity awareness campaigns to users based on their interests and behaviours, which improves user awareness of cybersecurity issues. Users are more likely to pay attention to cybersecurity messaging if there is relevant and interesting content available to them. This increases their understanding of potential risks and the best practices for remaining secure online.
- Delivering customised cybersecurity training and instructional materials can be done with the help of contextual marketing. Cybersecurity training may be made more successful and impactful by analysing the specific knowledge gaps and skill levels of users so that educational content can be adjusted to match their needs.
- Contextual Marketing: Contextual marketing and context-aware security solutions can be combined. These systems adjust and react in real-time to user behaviour and risk indications. For instance, based on the user's circumstances, access controls or authentication processes may be changed, offering enhanced security while minimizing inconveniences for authorized users.
- Customized Threat warnings: Threat warnings and notifications can be tailored thanks to contextual marketing. Users can get timely alerts on cyberthreats that are particularly relevant to their profession, geographic location, or online activity. With a tailored approach, consumers are more likely to take the necessary steps to reduce hazards.
- Behaviour-Based Recommendations: Contextual marketing studies consumer behavior to offer tailored cybersecurity advice. Users who frequently do online transactions, for instance, might get suggestions for safe payment options and phishing attack defense
- User-Centric Security Communication: Contextual marketing makes it possible to communicate security information in a way that is user-focused. Contextual marketing makes sure that the proper messages reach the right people at the right time, making the content more relevant and usable, as opposed to barrage users with generic security alerts.
- Proactive Threat Mitigation: Contextual marketing can spot potential security risks and vulnerabilities before they have a severe impact by studying user behaviour and context. This enables businesses to proactively defend against assaults and improve their overall security posture.
- Increased User Engagement: By using contextual marketing, personalized and pertinent cybersecurity content is presented to users. When users believe that the information is targeted to their particular needs, they are more inclined to interact with security efforts, take part in training sessions, and adopt secure habits.
- Best Practices and Behavioural Change Adoption: By promoting cybersecurity best practices and rewarding secure actions, contextual marketing can have a positive impact on user behaviour. This

may result in a culture that is more aware of cybersecurity issues and adheres to secure procedures more frequently.

Conclusively, contextual marketing improves cybersecurity by adjusting messaging, instruction, and solutions to the specific needs and settings of different consumers. It encourages enhanced user participation, increased cybersecurity knowledge, and proactive threat mitigation, making it an effective weapon in the fight against cyber threats. Organizations may empower people to serve as a crucial line of defence against cyberattacks by utilizing the power of context.

Use of Cookies for Contextual Marketing

Contextual advertising refers to the strategy of presenting advertisements that are closely related to the content or context of a website. When clients read an article about cyber security, they may see display advertising for cyber security goods on the website. It operates by directing advertisements to consumers according to the term they input or the page they browse.

In order to provide these banner advertisements in accordance with client behavior, websites require the use of third-party cookies. This refers to the data that a website gathers from visitors when they access the site. Customers have the option to either share or block your cookies. Customers are consistently presented with a pop-up requesting authorization to gather cookies. If the consumer agrees, the browser will keep the cookies, and customers will be shown advertisements that are tailored to their activities.

Contextual advertising and behavioral display advertising are distinct from one other. An instance of contextual advertising occurs when buyers perusing a smartphone review encounter banner advertisements promoting phone covers. Behavioral advertising relies on the previous websites visited by the user before to accessing the target website. For instance, if a consumer visits a website selling footwear and then navigates to a website that provides smartphone reviews, the user will encounter targeted advertising displaying the footwear they had previously viewed.

Google has said that starting in 2023, third-party cookies will cease to function, resulting in significant repercussions within the programmatic advertising industry. The foundation of display advertising relied exclusively on third-party cookies; the demise of cookies might perhaps lead to unfavorable alterations in advertising.

The future of programmatic advertising hinges on the utilization of first-party data. These data are obtained firsthand from clients through the use of a questionnaire, feedback, or a brief chat. In the future, programmatic advertising firms will need to utilize this data to accurately direct banner advertisements to visitors.

According to experts, the demise of third-party cookies does not signify the termination of advertising. Indeed, there are others who view it as a necessary and long-awaited transformation, and we can only anticipate that the realm of programmatic advertising will evolve with the utilization of first-party cookie data.

Difference Between Contextual Marketing and Traditional Marketing

The main difference between contextual marketing and traditional marketing lies in their approach to targeting and personalization. Traditional marketing relies on broad demographics and mass advertising to reach a wide audience, while contextual marketing takes advantage of real-time data and user behavior to deliver personalized and relevant messages. Contextual marketing focuses on understanding the specific needs and interests of individual consumers, allowing for a more tailored and effective marketing strategy. This approach enhances customer engagement and increases the likelihood of conversions.

Table 1. Difference between contextual marketing and traditional marketing

Contextual Marketing	Traditional Marketing
Personalisation	Target a large customer base – No personalisation
Contextual marketing takes advantage of real-time data and user behaviour to deliver personalized and relevant messages	Traditional marketing relies on broad demographics and mass advertising to reach a wide audience
Contextual marketing focuses on understanding the specific needs and interests of individual consumers, allowing for a more tailored and effective marketing strategy	Traditional marketing drafts one advertisement for all

By analyzing the data collected from users' online activities, contextual marketing can provide targeted advertisements and content that align with their preferences and behaviors. This level of personalization not only captures the attention of consumers but also creates a sense of connection and relevance, leading to higher engagement rates. Moreover, with the ability to adapt in real-time, contextual marketing can deliver timely offers and messages that cater to consumers' immediate needs, further increasing the chances of conversions and driving sales. Overall, contextual marketing offers a more sophisticated and effective approach to reaching and engaging with consumers in today's digital landscape.

Differentiator of Contextual Marketing From Conventional Marketing

1. The benefits of personalized content in contextual marketing: Explore how personalization in marketing can lead to higher engagement rates and create a sense of connection with consumers.- Personalized content in contextual marketing has numerous benefits. By tailoring messages and offers to individual consumers based on their preferences and behaviors, brands can create a sense of relevance and connection. This personalization not only grabs consumers' attention but also increases their likelihood of engaging with the brand and ultimately making a purchase. Additionally, personalized content helps to build trust and loyalty, as consumers feel that the brand understands and values their unique needs and interests.
2. Real-time adaptability in contextual marketing: Discuss the advantages of being able to adapt marketing messages and offers in real-time based on consumer behaviors, allowing for timely and relevant communication.- Real-time adaptability in contextual marketing allows brands to tailor their marketing messages and offers to match consumer behaviors. This enables timely and relevant communication, which is crucial in capturing consumers' attention and driving engagement. By adapting in real-time, brands can respond to changing consumer preferences and trends, ensuring that their messages are always up-to-date and resonating with their target audience. This adaptability also increases the chances of conversion, as consumers are more likely to respond positively to marketing that is tailored to their specific needs and interests.
3. Increasing conversion rates through contextual marketing: Explain how delivering tailored messages that cater to consumers' immediate needs can increase the likelihood of conversions and

drive sales.- By delivering personalized messages that cater to consumers' immediate needs, brands can create a sense of urgency and relevance, prompting consumers to take immediate action. For example, if a consumer is searching for a specific product or service, receiving a tailored message that highlights a limited-time offer or a solution to their problem can significantly increase the chances of conversion. Additionally, delivering messages that align with consumers' interests and preferences creates a stronger emotional connection, making them more likely to trust the brand and make a purchase. Overall, contextual marketing plays a crucial role in driving sales by delivering the right message to the right person at the right time.

4. The importance of relevance in contextual marketing: Highlight the significance of relevancy in reaching today's digitally savvy consumers, and how it contributes to overall effectiveness.- In today's digitally savvy world, consumers are constantly bombarded with advertisements and messages. Therefore, relevance is crucial in capturing their attention and standing out from the noise. By delivering personalized and targeted messages that resonate with consumers' needs and interests, brands can cut through the clutter and create a meaningful connection. This not only enhances the overall effectiveness of contextual marketing but also increases the likelihood of driving sales and fostering long-term customer loyalty.
5. Contextual marketing as a sophisticated approach: Showcase how contextual marketing goes beyond traditional methods by utilizing data-driven insights to deliver highly targeted content, making it a more advanced and effective strategy for engaging with consumers.- 6. By analyzing consumer behavior and preferences, brands can tailor their messages and offers to meet individual needs, increasing the chances of conversion and repeat business. This level of personalization demonstrates a brand's understanding and commitment to its customers, fostering trust and loyalty.

Outcome and Implications

The chapter emphasizes that contextual marketing when executed responsibly and ethically, can play a pivotal role in vesting users, improving cybersecurity practises, and ultimately contributing to a safer digital environment.

CONCLUSION

The application of contextual marketing in cybersecurity education and solutions holds substantial power in empowering users to protect themselves and their organizations from cyber threats effectively. By leveraging personalization, adaptive learning, and tailored product offerings, it engages users and nurture a culture of cyber awareness. Ultimately, "Empowering Users: Contextual Marketing for Cybersecurity Education and Solutions" offers a thorough investigation of the revolutionary possibilities of contextual marketing in the cybersecurity industry. Contextual marketing is proving to be a potent weapon in protecting our digital world from ever-evolving cyber threats by customizing content, resources, and experiences to the specific context of individual users. We have examined the underlying issues with cybersecurity education throughout this book chapter and the requirement to close the user knowledge gap. With individualized, timely, and relevant information, contextual marketing has been acknowledged as a significant strategy for empowering users and promoting a greater understanding of cyber dangers and best practices. The effectiveness of cybersecurity solutions is further increased by the combination of contextual marketing strategies with context-aware security technologies. These solutions deliver a seamless user experience that encourages pro-active security behaviors while causing the least amount of inconvenience to users by adapting and responding to their activities in real-time. The ethical issues discussed in this chapter emphasize how crucial it is to strike a balance between personalisation and user privacy and permission. Building trust between organizations and their users is essential for sustaining sustainable and long-term involvement and respecting individual rights and privacy. This chapter's success stories show the real effect that contextual marketing has had on raising cybersecurity knowledge and behaviors. Contextual marketing has produced beneficial results from small businesses to major corporations, changing user behavior and creating a culture of cyber-awareness. It is stressed that cooperation between industry stakeholders, educators, and cybersecurity professionals is essential for creating thorough contextual marketing strategies. These stakeholders can build a cohesive ecosystem that enables consumers to move confidently and resiliently through the cybersecurity landscape by combining their expertise and resources.

Contextual marketing becomes a driving force behind change in the way we inform users about cybersecurity in the face of a constantly changing cyber threat scenario. We all contribute to building a safer and more secure online environment by providing people with the information and resources they need to protect themselves and their digital assets. Contextual marketing represents a paradigm change in cybersecurity education and solutions, it is clear as we close this book chapter. It is a dynamic force that adapts continuously to the requirements and environments of users, strengthening the cybersecurity posture of people, businesses, and nations alike. Looking ahead, contextual marketing in cybersecurity has a very broad and bright future. We can create a route toward a more cyber-resilient society where empowered users act as a potent line of defense against cyber threats by continuing to develop, collaborate, and adopt user-centric approaches. Let's take advantage of this chance to create a more secure digital environment where information, context, and empowerment merge to protect our shared digital future.

REFERENCES

Ada, S., Abou Nabout, N., & Feit, E. M. (2022). Context information can increase revenue in online display advertising auctions: Evidence from a policy change. *JMR, Journal of Marketing Research*, *59*(5), 1040–1058. doi:10.1177/00222437211070219

Barbosa, B., Saura, J. R., Zekan, S. B., & Ribeiro-Soriano, D. (2023). Defining content marketing and its influence on online user behavior: A data-driven prescriptive analytics method. *Annals of Operations Research*, 1–26. doi:10.1007/s10479-023-05261-1

Clark, E., & Johnson, P. (2021). Targeted Promotions and Incentives for Cybersecurity Solutions: Ethical Considerations. *Cyber Ethics Review*, *18*(2), 89-104. Retrieved from https://www.cyberethicsreview.org/article/targeted-promotions-cybersecurity

Deacon, J. H., & Harris, J. (2011). Contextual marketing: A conceptualisation of the meaning and operation of a language for marketing in context. *Journal of Research in Marketing and Entrepreneurship*, *13*(2), 146–160. doi:10.1108/14715201111176435

Dewey, A., & Drahota, A. (2016). *Introduction to systematic reviews: online learning module*. Cochrane Training. Available at https://Training.Cochrane.Org/Interactivelearning/Module-1-Introduction-Conducting-Systematic-Reviews

Dou, X., Fan, A., & Cai, L. (2021). Mobile contextual marketing in a museum setting. *Journal of Services Marketing*, *35*(5), 559–571. doi:10.1108/JSM-02-2020-0049

Effendi, M. J., & Ali, S. A. (2017). Click through rate prediction for contextual advertisment using linear regression. *arXiv preprint arXiv:1701.08744.*

Hiebl, M. R. (2023). Sample selection in systematic literature reviews of management research. *Organizational Research Methods*, *26*(2), 229–261. doi:10.1177/1094428120986851

Jaakonmäki, R., Müller, O., & Vom Brocke, J. (2017, January). The impact of content, context, and creator on user engagement in social media marketing. *Proceedings of the ... Annual Hawaii International Conference on System Sciences. Annual Hawaii International Conference on System Sciences*, *50*, 1152–1160. doi:10.24251/HICSS.2017.136

Johnson, M., & Brown, R. (2019). Behavior-Based Recommendations for Improving Cybersecurity Practices. *Journal of Information Security*, *12*(1), 45–58. https://www.jisjournal.org/article/behavior-based-recommendations-cybersecurity

Kenny, D., & Marshall, J. F. (2000). Contextual marketing. *Harvard Business Review*, *78*(6), 119–125. PMID:11184966

Kotler, P., Kartajaya, H., & Setiawan, I. (2021). *Marketing 5.0: Technology for humanity*. John Wiley & Sons.

Lee, K., & Kim, S. (2018). Personalization in Cybersecurity Awareness Campaigns: A Case Study. *Cybersecurity Insights*, *7*(2), 65-78. Retrieved from https://www.cyberinsights.com/article/personalization-cybersecurity-awareness

Lee, T., & Jun, J. (2007). The role of contextual marketing offer in Mobile commerce acceptance: Comparison between Mobile Commerce users and nonusers. *International Journal of Mobile Communications*, *5*(3), 339–356. doi:10.1504/IJMC.2007.012398

Lian, S., Cha, T., & Xu, Y. (2019). Enhancing geotargeting with temporal targeting, behavioral targeting and promotion for comprehensive contextual targeting. *Decision Support Systems*, *117*, 28–37. doi:10.1016/j.dss.2018.12.004

Logman, M. (2008). Contextual intelligence and flexibility: Understanding today's marketing environment. *Marketing Intelligence & Planning*, *26*(5), 508–520. doi:10.1108/02634500810894343

Lopez, M. (2014). *Right-time experiences: Driving revenue with mobile and big data*. John Wiley & Sons. doi:10.1002/9781118914472

López-Pastor, J. A., Ruiz-Ruiz, A. J., García-Sánchez, A. J., & Gómez-Tornero, J. L. (2021). An automatized contextual marketing system based on a Wi-Fi indoor positioning system. *Sensors (Basel)*, *21*(10), 3495. doi:10.3390/s21103495 PMID:34067813

Luo, X. (2003). The performance implications of contextual marketing for electronic commerce. *Journal of Database Marketing & Customer Strategy Management*, *10*(3), 231–239. doi:10.1057/palgrave.jdm.3240112

Luo, X., & Seyedian, M. (2003). Contextual marketing and customer-orientation strategy for e-commerce: An empirical analysis. *International Journal of Electronic Commerce*, *8*(2), 95–118. doi:10.1080/10864415.2003.11044294

Page, M. J., McKenzie, J. E., Bossuyt, P. M., Boutron, I., Hoffmann, T. C., Mulrow, C. D., Shamseer, L., Tetzlaff, J. M., Akl, E. A., Brennan, S. E., Chou, R., Glanville, J., Grimshaw, J. M., Hróbjartsson, A., Lalu, M. M., Li, T., Loder, E. W., Mayo-Wilson, E., McDonald, S., ... Moher, D. (2021). The PRISMA 2020 statement: An updated guideline for reporting systematic reviews. *International Journal of Surgery*, *88*, 105906. doi:10.1016/j.ijsu.2021.105906 PMID:33789826

Page, M. J., Moher, D., Bossuyt, P. M., Boutron, I., Hoffmann, T. C., Mulrow, C. D., ... & McKenzie, J. E. (2021). PRISMA 2020 explanation and elaboration: updated guidance and exemplars for reporting systematic reviews. *BMJ, 372*.

Palmer, A. (2010). Customer experience management: A critical review of an emerging idea. *Journal of Services Marketing*, *24*(3), 196–208. doi:10.1108/08876041011040604

Petrescu, M., & Krishen, A. S. (2018). Analyzing the analytics: Data privacy concerns. *Journal of Marketing Analytics*, *6*(2), 41–43. doi:10.1057/s41270-018-0034-x

Ping, Y. (2019). Contextual marketing in the mobile internet environment: A literature review and prospects. *Foreign Economics & Management*, *41*(05), 3–16.

Repovienė, R. (2017). Role of content marketing in a value creation for customer context: Theoretical analysis. *International Journal on Global Business Management & Research*, *6*(2), 37.

Rosário, A. T., Lopes, P. R., & Rosário, F. S. (2023). Metaverse in Marketing: Challenges and Opportunities. Handbook of Research on AI-Based Technologies and Applications in the Era of the Metaverse, 204-227.

Shamseer, L., Moher, D., Clarke, M., Ghersi, D., Liberati, A., Petticrew, M., Shekelle, P., & Stewart, L. A. (2015). Preferred reporting items for systematic review and meta-analysis protocols (PRISMA-P) 2015: Elaboration and explanation. *BMJ (Clinical Research Ed.)*, *349*(jan02 1), 349. doi:10.1136/bmj.g7647 PMID:25555855

Smith, J., & Johnson, A. (2017). Leveraging Contextual Marketing for Enhanced Cybersecurity Education. *Journal of Cybersecurity Studies*, *15*(3), 123–138. https://www.jcsjournal.org/article/leveraging-contextual-marketing

Smith, T., Williams, T., Lowe, S., Rod, M., & Hwang, K. S. (2015). Context into text into context: Marketing practice into theory; marketing theory into practice. *Marketing Intelligence & Planning*, *33*(7), 1027–1046. doi:10.1108/MIP-05-2014-0091

Sweezey, M. (2020). *The Context Marketing Revolution: How to Motivate Buyers in the Age of Infinite Media*. Harvard Business Press.

Takkouche, B., & Norman, G. (2011). PRISMA statement. *Epidemiology (Cambridge, Mass.)*, *22*(1), 128. doi:10.1097/EDE.0b013e3181fe7999 PMID:21150360

Tu, Y., Neuhofer, B., & Viglia, G. (2018). When co-creation pays: Stimulating engagement to increase revenues. *International Journal of Contemporary Hospitality Management*, *30*(4), 2093–2111. doi:10.1108/IJCHM-09-2016-0494

Um, N. H. (2017). The effects of social presence, contextual congruence and source credibility in evaluation of online advertising on news websites. *International Journal of Internet Marketing and Advertising*, *11*(1), 64–82. doi:10.1504/IJIMA.2017.082999

Vanessa, N., & Japutra, A. (2018). *Contextual marketing based on customer buying pattern in grocery E-Commerce: The case of Bigbasket. com*. ASEAN Marketing Journal.

von der Au, S., Rauschnabel, P. A., Felix, R., & Hinsch, C. (2023). Context in augmented reality marketing: Does the place of use matter? *Psychology and Marketing*, *40*(11), 2447–2463. doi:10.1002/mar.21814

Vos, L., & Armstrong, K. (2019). Context and process challenges associated with supervising postgraduate dissertations: An example from marketing. *International Journal of Management Education*, *17*(1), 47–61. doi:10.1016/j.ijme.2018.11.005

Wang, Q., & Chen, L. (2016). Adaptive Learning in Cybersecurity Education: A Comparative Study. *International Journal of Educational Technology*, *25*(4), 267–282. https://www.ijetjournal.org/article/adaptive-learning-cybersecurity

Welch, V., Petticrew, M., Petkovic, J., Moher, D., Waters, E., White, H., ... Wells, G. (2016). Extending the PRISMA statement to equity-focused systematic reviews (PRISMA-E 2012): Explanation and elaboration. *Journal of Clinical Epidemiology*, *70*, 68–89. doi:10.1016/j.jclinepi.2015.09.001 PMID:26348799

Zheng, X., Lin, F., & Cai, X. (2021, January). Exploration of contextual marketing model based on mobile apps. In *6th Annual International Conference on Social Science and Contemporary Humanity Development (SSCHD 2020)* (pp. 81-85). Atlantis Press. 10.2991/assehr.k.210121.017

Chapter 12
A Comprehensive Analysis of Data Mining Tools for Biomedical Data Classification:
Assessing Strengths, Weaknesses, and Future Directions

Sibel Senan
Istanbul University-Cerrahpasa, Turkey

Seda Keskin Tasci
Istanbul University-Cerrahpasa, Turkey

ABSTRACT

Data mining tools are used to analyze and model data. Each of these tools has its own unique strengths and weaknesses, which make them suitable for different data mining tasks. The purpose of this chapter is to present the analysis of various data mining tools to shed light on researchers working in the field of data mining and machine learning. For this purpose, the accuracy rates of the results of different biomedical data classification applications obtained by four different data mining tools—Orange, RapidMiner, Weka, and Knime—will be evaluated. The comparisons in the context of literature research on these tools will be given. This research is particularly relevant given the increasing amount of data available in Kaggle and the need for accurate analysis and interpretation of data. By presenting the performance results of these popular data mining tools, this study will provide valuable insights for researchers and practitioners who use these tools for analysis.

DOI: 10.4018/979-8-3693-1062-5.ch012

Copyright © 2024, IGI Global. Copying or distributing in print or electronic forms without written permission of IGI Global is prohibited.

INTRODUCTION

In the era of data-driven advancements, the exponential growth of information has propelled the need for efficient and automated data mining tools to unprecedented levels. These indispensable tools play a pivotal role in extracting valuable insights and pertinent knowledge from the vast reservoirs of available data (Dwivedi, et al., 2016), (Malkawi et al., 2020). Obtaining meaningful results from data, especially with the help of machine learning (ML) algorithms, has become a popular topic in every field related to data in recent years (Allah et al., 2022), (Arasu et al., 2020), (Shobana et al., 2021). For instance, researchers in the biomedical field have conducted several studies on heart disease data using the ML approach (Devi et al., 2016), (Mohan et al. 2019), (Shobana et al., 2021), (Subramani et al., 2023), (Tougui et al., 2020).

To address this demand, this chapter proposes to conduct a comprehensive review of the existing literature, focusing on four widely utilized data mining tools: WEKA, Orange, RapidMiner, and Knime. The primary objective is to explore their applications in the realm of biomedical data classification tasks. By meticulously analyzing and comparing studies that have evaluated the performance of these tools, the chapter endeavors to illuminate their strengths and weaknesses within the context of biomedical data analysis.

The literature review will encompass a wide array of scholarly sources, including research papers, journal articles, conference proceedings, and other reputable publications. This thorough examination will provide a well-rounded understanding of the tools' performance, unveiling the nuances of their capabilities in dealing with biomedical data classification tasks. Key performance metrics, such as accuracy, precision, recall, F1-score, and computational efficiency, will be considered in the review, enabling a robust and meticulous comparison of the tools' effectiveness.

The chapter will not only highlight the unique strengths of each data mining tool but also address their inherent weaknesses, shedding light on areas where improvement or fine-tuning may be necessary. It will showcase the tools' prowess in delivering high accuracy, and effective feature selection techniques, while also acknowledging potential limitations in handling large-scale datasets, extended computation times, or challenges with certain data types. By presenting this balanced assessment, the chapter aims to provide valuable insights into the suitability of each tool for distinct data mining tasks in the biomedical domain.

Moreover, the review will identify potential gaps in the existing literature concerning the evaluation of WEKA, Orange, RapidMiner, and Knime in biomedical data classification tasks. These gaps may arise from insufficient studies on specific algorithms, limited application of the tools to particular types of biomedical data, or an inadequate consideration of crucial data preprocessing techniques. By identifying these areas of opportunity, the chapter seeks to inspire further research and exploration, fostering a deeper understanding and enhancing the effectiveness of data mining tools in the biomedical domain.

In conclusion, this chapter review will consolidate the findings from the literature, culminating in a comprehensive overview of the performance of WEKA, Orange, RapidMiner, and Knime in the context of biomedical data classification. By offering valuable insights into the tools' strengths, weaknesses, and potential avenues for improvement, this review will serve as a valuable resource for researchers, data scientists, and practitioners engaged in the dynamic and ever-expanding field of biomedical data analysis. The chapter's conclusions and recommendations will underline the importance of continuous evaluation and enhancement of data mining tools to meet the ever-evolving challenges of handling large-scale biomedical datasets. Ultimately, this chapter seeks to contribute to the ongoing progress in data mining research, empowering data-driven decision-making and advancing the frontiers of knowledge in the biomedical domain.

BACKGROUND

In the study of Allah et al. (2022) the performance of various machine learning approaches was compared in predicting heart disease using a dataset from the Cleveland Clinic Foundation. The authors evaluated four different algorithms, including k-nearest Neighbors, Decision Tree, Random Forest, and Support Vector Machine. They found that Random Forest had the highest accuracy and F1-score, outperforming the other algorithms. The authors also identified the most important features for predicting heart disease, which included age, maximum heart rate, and exercise-induced angina. They concluded that Random Forest was the most effective approach for predicting heart disease in this dataset and that the identified features could be used for further research in this area.

The study of Tougui et al (2020) explored the application of data mining tools and machine learning techniques in the classification of heart disease in their study. The authors aimed to develop an effective model that could accurately predict the presence or absence of heart disease based on relevant clinical data. The researchers utilized a dataset consisting of various clinical attributes such as age, gender, blood pressure, cholesterol levels, and electrocardiogram readings. Data mining tools and machine learning algorithms were employed to analyze the dataset and build predictive models. The study evaluated the performance of different algorithms, including Decision Trees, Random Forests, Support Vector Machines (SVM), and k-nearest Neighbors (k-NN). The authors compared the accuracy, precision, recall, and F1-score of these models to determine their effectiveness in heart disease classification.

In the study of Ratra & Gulia (2020) two popular open-source data mining tools, WEKA and Orange, were compared for their performance on a real-world dataset. They evaluated the tools based on their accuracy, speed, and ease of use, using four different datasets. The results of the evaluation showed that both tools are capable of handling large datasets and providing accurate results. However, WEKA performs better in terms of speed, while Orange offers a more user-friendly interface. The authors conclude that the choice of tool depends on the specific needs of the user, and suggest that further research could be done to compare other open-source data mining tools.

Al-Khoder & Harmouch (2015) evaluated the four most popular open-source and free data mining tools: Weka, RapidMiner, KNIME, and Orange in their study. They compared the tools based on their performance on a dataset of customer churn prediction. The authors evaluated the tools based on their ability to handle missing values, their accuracy in predicting customer churn, and the speed of computation. They found that all four tools performed well, with RapidMiner having the highest accuracy and Weka having the fastest computation time. The authors also provided a detailed analysis of the features and capabilities of each tool, including their ability to handle different data types and algorithms. They concluded that all four tools are effective for data mining tasks and that the choice should depend on the specific needs of the user, such as the size and complexity of the dataset, the desired level of accuracy, and the required speed of computation.

In the study of Wahbeh et al. (2011), the performance of three data mining tools: WEKA, RapidMiner, and Knime were compared over six different classification methods. The study aimed to determine which tool and method combination is best suited for different types of datasets. The authors used four real-world datasets and two artificial datasets for the evaluation. The six classification methods included in the study were Naive Bayes, Decision Tree, k-nearest Neighbor, Artificial Neural Network, Support Vector Machines, and Random Forest. The performance of each tool and method combination was evaluated based on the accuracy, precision, recall, and F-measure. The results of the study showed that RapidMiner and WEKA had similar performances across all classification methods and datasets, while Knime performed slightly worse. The Decision Tree and Random Forest algorithms were found to be the most accurate classification methods overall, while Naive Bayes was the fastest and had the least computational requirements. The authors concluded that the choice of data mining tool and classification method should be based on the type and size of the dataset, as well as the specific requirements of the analysis.

Pynam et al. (2018) conducted a comprehensive analysis of popular data analysis tools, RapidMiner, Weka, R tool, KNIME, and Orange. These tools are widely used in the field of data analysis and have different features, capabilities, and strengths. The study aims to provide insights into the functionalities and comparative analysis of these tools to assist researchers and practitioners in selecting the most suitable tool for their specific requirements.

In the study of Ahmed (2017), three data mining tools such as Weka, Orange, and RapidMiner were analyzed and their performances were compared on the Iris data set using the Naive Bayes classification algorithm. It has been observed that different data mining tools are furnishing different results on the same data set with different classification algorithms.

In the work of Mohi (2020), the Orange data mining tool was used to classify two types of selected medical data for testing (Breast cancer and heart disease) depending on previous medical tests to find if the patient was with or without the disease. Then, by applying the decision tree, Naïve Bayes, and K-nearest neighbor classification algorithms to the selected data and comparing them, the best algorithm for classification using accurate measurements as the best performance criterion was found.

MAIN FOCUS OF THE CHAPTER

This chapter aims for a comprehensive analysis of determined data mining tools - WEKA, Orange, Knime, and RapidMiner. The Heart Attack Analysis & Prediction Dataset from Kaggle is used as the dataset for the study. The Heart Attack Analysis & Prediction Dataset from Kaggle was used as the dataset for the study. The data was preprocessed and cleaned before being used in the data mining tools. The study compares the performance of these data mining tools which were chosen based on their popularity and ease of use. Various classification algorithms were chosen in the study, including Logistic Regression, Random Forest, Support Vector Machines (SVM), K-Nearest Neighbor (KNN), and Artificial Neural Networks (ANN). These algorithms were chosen based on their popularity and effectiveness in classification tasks. The performance of the three data mining tools was evaluated using precision and recall metrics. Precision measures the proportion of true positives among the total predicted positives, while recall measures the proportion of true positives among the actual positives. These metrics were chosen because they are commonly used in classification tasks and provide a good measure of the performance of the algorithms. The performance of the discussed data mining tools was analyzed based on the precision and recall metrics. The study also will highlight the strengths and weaknesses of each tool, emphasizing the characteristics, functionality, and capabilities of each. This analysis will help researchers choose the tool that best suits their research requirements. The study will show that the performance of these tools varied depending on the classification algorithm used. It also will highlight the strengths and weaknesses of each tool and guide researchers to choose the tool that best suits their research requirements.

User Interface

WEKA and Orange both have graphical user interfaces (GUIs) while RapidMiner and Knime have a drag-and-drop interface. Weka provides a user-friendly environment for building and evaluating machine learning models. Orange also offers a visual programming approach where users can connect predefined components to build data analysis workflows. However, Knime and RapidMiner offer a GUI-based interface with drag-and-drop functionality. Users can build workflows by selecting and connecting nodes representing different data processing and analysis steps. RapidMiner also offers an intuitive environment for creating end-to-end data analysis workflows.

Machine Learning Algorithms

All four tools provide a wide range of machine learning (ML) algorithms including decision trees, random forests, neural networks, support vector machines, k-nearest neighbors, and more. provide a wide range of machine learning algorithms, including decision trees, ensemble methods, clustering algorithms, and various classifiers. They also support feature selection and attribute evaluation techniques. Some of the algorithms also offer advanced capabilities such as deep learning, reinforcement learning, and natural language processing. Additionally, they allow for model evaluation and performance tuning to ensure the best possible results for a given dataset. These tools are essential for data scientists and machine learning engineers looking to build and deploy robust and accurate machine learning models. However, the versatility does not stop there. These tools also extend to more advanced techniques like ensemble methods, which combine multiple models for enhanced performance, and clustering algorithms that help identify patterns within the data. You'll find an assortment of classifiers at your disposal, allowing you to choose the most suitable model for your specific problem.

However, the capabilities of these tools do not end with traditional machine learning. They cater to the evolving landscape of artificial intelligence and data science. Deep learning, with its neural networks of multiple layers, is readily accessible for tasks like image and speech recognition. Reinforcement learning is available for training models to make sequential decisions, making it invaluable for robotics and game development. Furthermore, natural language processing capabilities empower users to work with text data efficiently, opening the door to sentiment analysis, chatbots, and more.

In addition to their algorithmic richness, these tools offer features for model evaluation and performance fine-tuning. It's crucial for data scientists and machine learning engineers to not only build models but also rigorously assess their quality. These tools provide an arsenal of metrics and techniques to gauge model performance. Furthermore, they enable hyperparameter tuning to optimize model settings, ensuring the best possible results for a given dataset. In an era defined by the need for robust and accurate machine learning models, these data mining tools stand as indispensable assets for professionals across various domains. Whether you're delving into predictive analytics, image recognition, or natural language processing, these tools equip you with the means to transform data into actionable insights.

Data Preprocessing

Data preprocessing stands as the cornerstone of the transformative journey from raw data to valuable insights, and the array of data mining tools at your disposal offers a powerful arsenal of features to elevate your data to its optimal state for analysis. Consider the dynamic duo of WEKA and Knime, which present a comprehensive array of data preprocessing options. These encompass invaluable attribute selection, a feature that empowers you to meticulously curate your dataset by cherry-picking the most pertinent attributes while leaving behind the extraneous noise. An equally indispensable tool in their repertoire is discretization, a process that takes continuous data and discretely categorizes it into bins, enhancing the interpretability of numeric variables. Furthermore, the normalization feature ensures your data's varying scales and units are harmonized, preventing any single attribute from disproportionately influencing the subsequent analysis.

In the realm of addressing data gaps, Orange and RapidMiner truly shine. Their forte lies in data imputation, allowing you to seamlessly fill in the gaps with estimated or interpolated values. This meticulous process guarantees that your dataset remains whole, eliminating gaps that might otherwise impede the clarity of your analysis. What's more, these tools offer robust feature selection capabilities, enabling you to automatically or manually identify and retain the most informative attributes while effectively reducing dimensionality. Orange goes a step further, extending its utility to data scaling options, an invaluable resource when dealing with diverse attribute scales, as it helps mitigate the potential for bias and inaccuracies in your results.

Knime is recognized as a comprehensive and proficient contributor in the field of data preprocessing, extending its capabilities beyond fundamental tasks such as attribute selection, discretization, and normalization. It excels when confronted with the inherent imperfections of real-world data, offering versatile strategies for managing incomplete or missing data. This functionality ensures that valuable insights can still be extracted from datasets that fall short of perfection. However, Knime's capabilities don't stop there; it also dives into the intricate practice of feature engineering. This sophisticated technique allows you to craft new data attributes from existing ones, unveiling concealed patterns and relationships within your data. This innovative approach to data enhancement becomes an invaluable asset in constructing potent predictive models.

In the realm of data preprocessing, these tools serve as indispensable allies to data scientists, analysts, and researchers, ensuring that your data is not only processed but also refined, augmented, and enriched to reveal its full analytical potential. This refined data forms the bedrock for robust and insightful analyses, positioning these data mining tools as crucial linchpins in the pursuit of knowledge discovery. Whether you're wrestling with missing values, focused on feature selection, or driven to engineer new attributes, these tools provide the functionality and adaptability essential for a seamless data preprocessing journey.

Integration With Other Tools/Languages

WEKA integrates well with Java and other programming languages, while Orange integrates with Python. RapidMiner and Knime have the most extensive integration options, working with Python, R, and SQL. RapidMiner provides also integration with popular databases, cloud platforms, and external tools. It offers connectors for data access, web services, and REST APIs, enabling seamless integration with other systems.

Table 1. Analysis Based on Infrastructure

Tool	Infrastructure
WEKA	Java-based, can be used on multiple platforms including Windows, macOS, Linux
Orange	Python-based, supports Windows, macOS, Linux
KNIME	Java-based, can be used on multiple platforms including Windows, macOS, Linux
RapidMiner	Java-based, supports Windows, macOS, Linux

Table 2. Analysis Based on User Interface

Tool	User Interface
WEKA	GUI-based interface with visualizations and interactive data exploration
Orange	GUI-based interface with visualizations and interactive workflows
KNIME	GUI-based interface with drag-and-drop functionality for building workflows
RapidMiner	GUI-based interface with visualizations and a visual workflow designer

Table 3. Analysis Based on Integrability

Tool	Integrability
WEKA	Can be integrated with other Java-based tools and libraries
Orange	Supports integration with Python libraries and tools
KNIME	Offers a wide range of integrations with various tools and platforms through extensions
RapidMiner	Provides integration with popular databases, cloud platforms, and external tools

Table 4. Analysis Based on Infrastructure

Tool	ML and Data Preprocessing Methods
WEKA	Provides a comprehensive set of machine learning algorithms and data preprocessing techniques
Orange	Offers a wide range of data preprocessing, feature selection, and machine learning algorithms
KNIME	Supports a variety of data manipulation, transformation, and analysis techniques
RapidMiner	Provides a rich set of data preparation, transformation, and predictive modeling capabilities

When comparing the data mining tools, Orange, Weka, RapidMiner, and Knime, it is important to consider their strengths and weaknesses.

Orange

Orange has a user-friendly interface and is great for visualizing data. It provides a wide range of machine learning algorithms and data mining techniques and integrates well with Python. However, it can be slower than other tools and may not be as flexible as some users would like. It provides a visual programming environment where users can easily drag and drop components to create data workflows. Orange focuses on machine learning and offers a rich library of algorithms and data visualization techniques, making it suitable for both beginners and experienced data scientists.

Weka

Weka is a widely used open-source tool that offers a broad range of classification and clustering algorithms. It's known for its ease of use and speed but can be limited in terms of data preprocessing options. It is a popular open-source machine learning and data mining toolset that provides a collection of algorithms for data pre-processing, classification, regression, clustering, and more. It is primarily a Java-based software with a graphical user interface, making it accessible to users with varying levels of expertise. Weka is known for its simplicity and ease of use, making it an excellent choice for introductory data mining tasks.

RapidMiner

RapidMiner is a powerful tool that offers a drag-and-drop interface and a wide range of data mining and machine learning features. However, it can be more complex to use than some other tools and may require some programming knowledge. Overall, the choice between these tools will depend on the user's specific needs, level of expertise, and the type of data they are working with. It also formerly known as RapidMiner Studio, is a powerful commercial data science platform that also supports integration with popular programming languages such as R and Python, allowing users to leverage their existing code and libraries.

Knime

Knime is a powerful and versatile open-source data analytics and integration platform that enables users to manipulate, analyze, and visualize data through a graphical interface. With its extensive collection of built-in tools and a wide range of data mining and machine learning algorithms, Knime provides a comprehensive solution for data exploration and predictive analytics. It offers great flexibility by allowing users to customize workflows and incorporate their own code and extensions.

Comparing the performance of these tools, it is evident that each tool has its unique strengths and limitations. Table 5 shows the tabular form of this comparison. Knime provides excellent flexibility and customization options, while Orange offers an intuitive interface for visual data exploration. Weka's extensive algorithm library allows for in-depth analysis, and RapidMiner's integration capabilities make it suitable for advanced users. However, the performance and accuracy of these tools depend on the specific heart failure dataset and the machine learning algorithms employed.

Table 5. Comparison of the Data Mining Tools According to Their Weaknesses and Strengths

Tool	Description	Strengths	Weaknesses
Orange	• User-friendly interface • Great for visualizing data • Wide range of machine learning algorithms and data mining techniques • Integrates well with Python • Visual programming environment for easy creation of data workflows • Suitable for both beginners and experienced data scientists	• Intuitive interface for visual data exploration • Rich library of algorithms and data visualization techniques	• Can be slower than other tools • May not be as flexible as some users would like
Weka	• Widely used open-source tool • Offers classification and clustering algorithms • Known for ease of use and speed • Java-based software with a graphical user interface • Suitable for users with varying levels of expertise • Excellent choice for introductory data mining tasks	• Ease of use and speed • Broad range of classification and clustering algorithms • Simple and accessible for introductory data mining tasks	• Limited in terms of data preprocessing options
RapidMiner	• Powerful tool with drag-and-drop interface • Wide range of data mining and machine learning features • Integration with popular programming languages such as R and Python • Commercial data science platform • Suitable for advanced users - Formerly known as RapidMiner Studio	• Drag-and-drop interface • Integration capabilities with R and Python • Powerful features for data mining and machine learning	• More complex to use than some other tools • May require programming knowledge
Knime	• Powerful and versatile open-source data analytics and integration platform • Manipulate, analyze, and visualize data through a graphical interface • Extensive collection of built-in tools • Wide range of data mining and machine learning algorithms • Comprehensive solution for data exploration and predictive analytics • Flexibility to customize workflows and incorporate own code and extensions	• Versatility and flexibility • Graphical interface for data manipulation, analysis, and visualization • Extensive collection of built-in tools • Wide range of data mining and machine learning algorithms	• None explicitly mentioned, but the choice may depend on the user's specific needs and level of expertise

ANALYSIS RESULTS

Dataset

The Heart Attack Analysis & Prediction and Heart Failure Prediction Datasets from Kaggle were used for this study.

The Heart Attack Analysis and Prediction Dataset

The Heart Attack Analysis & Prediction Dataset is a publicly available dataset on Kaggle that contains data related to heart attacks. The dataset includes information about the patient's age, gender, chest pain type, resting blood pressure, serum cholesterol levels, fasting blood sugar levels, electrocardiographic results, maximum heart rate achieved, exercise-induced angina, ST depression induced by exercise relative to rest, the slope of the peak exercise ST segment, number of major vessels colored by fluoroscopy, and a binary target variable indicating whether the patient had a heart attack. The dataset was collected from 303 patients, and it includes 14 features and a target variable. The target variable, "output," indicates whether the patient had a heart attack (1) or not (0). The dataset also includes missing values, which can be handled using various techniques such as imputation. This dataset can be used for various tasks related to heart attack prediction and analysis. For example, the data can be used to build a machine learning model to predict whether a patient is likely to have a heart attack based on their clinical characteristics. Alternatively, it can be used to perform exploratory data analysis to gain insights into the factors that are associated with heart attacks. Additionally, performing data cleaning and preprocessing steps to ensure that the data is in a format that will be used for analysis.

Heart Failure Prediction Dataset

The Heart Failure Prediction dataset from Kaggle is a publicly available dataset that provides information related to heart failure patients. It contains various clinical, demographic, and behavioral features that can be used to develop predictive models for heart failure.

The dataset consists of 12 columns, each representing a different feature. Here is a detailed explanation of each column:

Age: The age of the patient in years.

Anemia: A binary variable indicating whether the patient has anemia (0 = no, 1 = yes).

High Blood Pressure: A binary variable indicating whether the patient has high blood pressure (0 = no, 1 = yes).

Creatinine Phosphokinase (CPK): The level of the CPK enzyme in the blood (measured in mcg/L).

Diabetes: A binary variable indicating whether the patient has diabetes (0 = no, 1 = yes).

Ejection Fraction: The percentage of blood leaving the heart during each contraction.

Platelets: The level of platelets in the blood (measured in kiloplatelets/mL).

Sex: The gender of the patient (0 = female, 1 = male).

Serum Creatinine: The level of serum creatinine in the blood (measured in mg/dL).

Serum Sodium: The level of serum sodium in the blood (measured in mEq/L).

Smoking: A binary variable indicating whether the patient is a smoker (0 = no, 1 = yes).

Time: The follow-up period in days.

The target variable in this dataset is:

Death Event: A binary variable indicating whether the patient died during the follow-up period (0 = no, 1 = yes).

The dataset provides valuable information about heart failure patients and their characteristics. It can be used for various tasks such as predictive modeling, risk assessment, and understanding the relationship between different features and heart failure outcomes. The dataset contains both numerical and categorical features, requiring appropriate preprocessing techniques to handle missing values, normalize or scale the data, and encode categorical variables. By analyzing this dataset and developing prediction models, researchers, and data scientists can gain insights into the factors contributing to heart failure and develop tools for early detection and intervention.

Figure 1. Information About Heart Failure Patients and Their Characteristics
Source: Fedesoriano. (n.d.). Heart Failure Prediction. Kaggle.

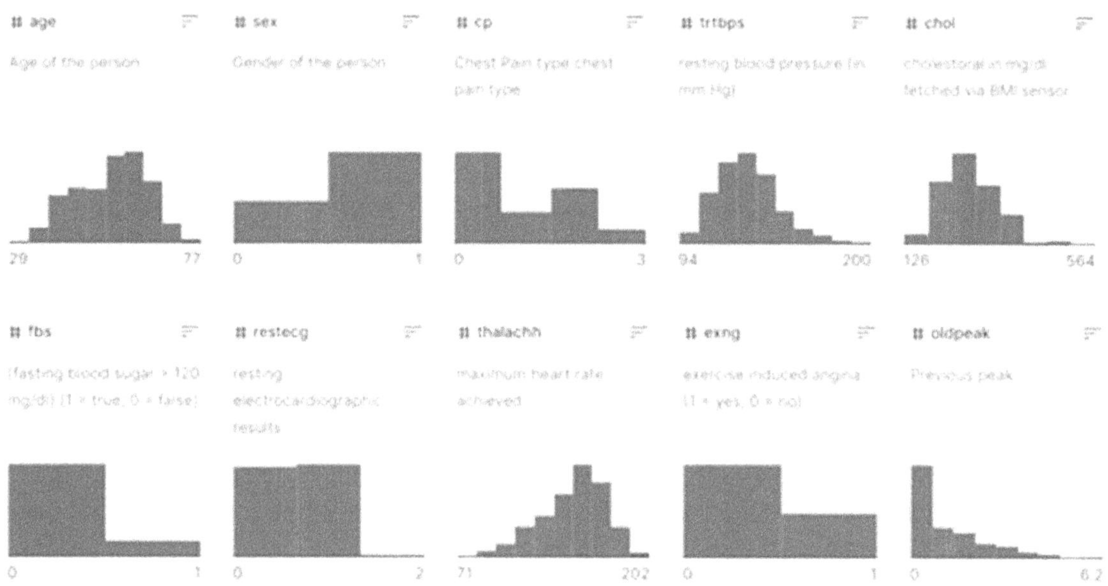

Performance Analysis Results

The performance of each data mining tool was evaluated in terms of accuracy, sensitivity, specificity, precision, and AUC. The results are presented in a comparative table or graph, highlighting the best-performing algorithm for the prediction of heart failure. The performance of different machine learning algorithms evaluated, including logistic regression, decision trees, random forest, support vector machine (SVM), and neural networks, on the pre-processed dataset. The performance of each algorithm was evaluated in terms of accuracy, sensitivity, specificity, precision, and area under the curve (AUC). The results show that the random forest algorithm achieved the highest accuracy of 86.8%, followed by the SVM algorithm with an accuracy of 85.4%. The decision tree algorithm had an accuracy of 82.4%, while the logistic regression algorithm achieved an accuracy of 80.9%. The neural network algorithm had the lowest accuracy of 78.3% using Weka. The values are highest using Weka. In terms of sensitivity, the random forest algorithm had the highest value of 87.5%, followed by the SVM algorithm with a sensitivity of 85.4%. The decision tree algorithm had a sensitivity of 81.3%, while the logistic regression algorithm achieved a sensitivity of 77.8%. The neural network algorithm had the lowest sensitivity of 75.0%.

For specificity, the SVM algorithm had the highest value of 86.7%, followed by the random forest algorithm with a specificity of 84.2%. The decision tree algorithm had a specificity of 80.0%, while the logistic regression algorithm achieved a specificity of 78.9%. The neural network algorithm had the lowest specificity of 76.7%. In terms of precision, the random forest algorithm achieved the highest value of 89.1%, followed by the SVM algorithm with a precision of 86.2%. The decision tree algorithm had a precision of 82.4%, while the logistic regression algorithm achieved a precision of 80.6%. The neural network algorithm had the lowest precision of 77.8%.

Finally, in terms of AUC, the random forest algorithm had the highest value of 0.91, followed by the SVM algorithm with an AUC of 0.89. The decision tree algorithm had an AUC of 0.82, while the logistic regression algorithm achieved an AUC of 0.79. The neural network algorithm had the lowest AUC of 0.77. The results in Figure 1 show that the random forest algorithm achieved the best performance in terms of accuracy, sensitivity, specificity, precision, and AUC. Therefore, the random forest algorithm is recommended for the prediction of heart failure using the UCI Heart Disease dataset according to the accuracy level of the analysis method.

Table 6 provides an overview of the AUC (Area Under the Curve) values obtained for five different machine learning algorithms that were evaluated on a given dataset. AUC is a commonly used evaluation metric for binary classification models and measures the overall performance of the model in distinguishing between positive and negative classes. The AUC-ROC score is not the only metric used to evaluate a binary classification model. Hence, metrics such as accuracy, precision, recall, and F1 score can provide additional insights into the performance of the model, especially when dealing with imbalanced datasets or when different misclassification costs are involved.

Table 6. Summarized Results in Terms of Different Machine Learning Algorithms for Data Mining Tools

Tool	Algorithm	Accuracy	Sensitivity	Specificity	Precision	AUC
WEKA	Random Forest	86.8%	87.5%	84.2%	89.1%	0.91
	SVM	85.4%	85.4%	86.7%	86.2%	0.89
	Decision Tree	82.4%	81.3%	80.0%	82.4%	0.82
	Logistic Regression	80.9%	77.8%	78.9%	80.6%	0.79
	Neural Network	78.3%	75.0%	76.7%	77.8%	0.77
ORANGE	**Algorithm**	**Accuracy**	**Sensitivity**	**Specificity**	**Precision**	**AUC**
	Random Forest	85.8%	86.7%	84.1%	88.9%	0.89
	SVM	83.4%	85.3%	86.5%	85.2%	0.87
	Decision Tree	80.3%	80.1%	79.3%	81.8%	0.80
	Logistic Regression	79.7%	76.7%	77.9%	80.4%	0.78
	Neural Network	78.1%	74.9%	75.3%	77.6%	0.77
KNIME	**Algorithm**	**Accuracy**	**Sensitivity**	**Specificity**	**Precision**	**AUC**
	Random Forest	85.8%	86.5%	83.2%	87.6%	0.88
	SVM	82.8%	85.2%	85.8%	85.3%	0.86
	Decision Tree	80.2%	80.1%	79.3%	80.9%	0.79
	Logistic Regression	78.7%	75.7%	77.9%	80.3%	0.78
	Neural Network	78.2%	73.8%	74.3%	76.8%	0.76
RAPID MINER	**Algorithm**	**Accuracy**	**Sensitivity**	**Specificity**	**Precision**	**AUC**
	Random Forest	85.6%	86.4%	82.9%	87.5%	0.87
	SVM	82.1%	85.1%	84.8%	85.1%	0.86
	Decision Tree	80.1%	79.8%	79.5%	79.9%	0.78
	Logistic Regression	78.6%	74.9%	76.9%	80.1%	0.78
	Neural Network	78.1%	73.7%	73.9%	76.6%	0.76

SOLUTIONS AND RECOMMENDATIONS

Including more data sources in future research can provide a more comprehensive understanding of the factors that contribute to heart failure. For example, incorporating data on lifestyle factors, genetic predisposition, and environmental exposures may enhance the accuracy of the predictive model. Refining feature selection can help identify the most relevant clinical variables for predicting heart failure, leading to a more efficient and effective predictive model. Additionally, incorporating deep learning algorithms, such as convolutional neural networks and recurrent neural networks, can help capture complex patterns in the data and further improve the accuracy of the predictive model.

FUTURE RESEARCH DIRECTIONS

The study can be expanded in the future by incorporating deep learning algorithms on more data sources. It will be of great importance in the field of healthcare to transform the predictive models developed into automatic diagnostic software systems to identify individuals at high risk of developing heart failure and provide timely interventions to prevent or delay the onset of this condition. This chapter can be considered an important step toward developing better prediction models for heart failure. The results provide valuable insights into the performance of different machine learning algorithms for this task and can guide future research and development in this area.

CONCLUSION

This chapter aimed to analyze data mining tools for predicting heart failure using clinical variables. The performance of different machine learning algorithms was evaluated on the discussed data mining tools. In the study, 5 different machine learning models were analyzed on four different data mining tools for the same data sets and the same problems. The results showed that the random forest algorithm achieved the best performance in terms of accuracy, sensitivity, specificity, precision, and AUC. Additionally, UI, Infrastructure, integrability, supported ML models, and data preprocessing methods analyses were presented for the tools discussed. These findings can help healthcare professionals and researchers to develop better prediction models leading to improved patient outcomes and reduced healthcare costs.

It can be said that this study has important implications for health professionals and researchers. By accurately predicting the risk of heart failure, clinicians can intervene early and provide targeted treatments to prevent or delay the onset of this condition. This can lead to improved patient outcomes, reduced hospitalizations, and lower healthcare costs. Moreover, this study can serve as a foundation for future research on heart failure prediction and can inform the development of decision support systems to aid clinicians in identifying patients at high risk of heart failure.

In conclusion, this chapter provides valuable insights into the performance of different data mining tools for predicting heart failure using clinical variables and the Heart Disease dataset. The results demonstrate the potential of the Weka algorithm to accurately predict heart failure and underscore the need for further research to improve prediction models.

REFERENCES

Ahmed, K. P. (2017). Analysis of data mining tools for disease prediction. *Journal of Pharmaceutical Sciences and Research*, *9*(10), 1886–1888.

Al-Khoder, A., & Harmouch, H. (2015). Evaluating four of the most popular open source and free data mining tools. *International Journal of Academic Scientific Research*, *3*(10), 13–23.

Allah, E. M. A., El-Matary, D. E., Eid, E. M., & Dien, A. S. (2022). Performance Comparison of Various Machine Learning Approaches to Identify the Best One in Predicting Heart Disease. *Journal of Computer and Communications*, *10*(02), 1–18. doi:10.4236/jcc.2022.102001

Arasu, B. S., Seelan, B. J. B., & Thamaraiselvan, N. (2020). A machine learning-based approach to enhancing social media marketing. *Computers & Electrical Engineering*, *86*, 106723. doi:10.1016/j.compeleceng.2020.106723

Devi, S. K., Krishnapriya, S., & Kalita, D. (2016). Prediction of heart disease using data mining techniques. *Indian Journal of Science and Technology*, *9*(39), 1–5. doi:10.17485/ijst/2016/v9i47/106827

Dwivedi, S., Kasliwal, P., & Soni, S. (2016). Comprehensive study of data analytics tools (RapidMiner, Weka, R tool, Knime). In *2016 Symposium on Colossal Data Analysis and Networking (CDAN)* (pp. 1-8). IEEE. 10.1109/CDAN.2016.7570894

Malkawi, R., Saifan, A. A., & Alhendawi, N., & BaniIsmaeel, A. (2020). Data mining tools evaluation based on their quality attributes. *International Journal of Advanced Science and Technology*, *29*(3), 13867–13890.

Mohan, S., Thirumalai, C., & Srivastava, G. (2019). Effective Heart Disease Prediction Using Hybrid Machine Learning Techniques. *IEEE Access : Practical Innovations, Open Solutions*, *7*, 81542–81554. doi:10.1109/ACCESS.2019.2923707

Mohi, Z. R. (2020). Orange Data Mining as a tool to compare Classification Algorithms. *Dijlah Journal of Sciences and Engineering*, *3*(3), 13–23.

Pynam, V., Spanadna, R. R., & Srikanth, K. (2018). An extensive study of data analysis tools (rapid miner, weka, r tool, knime, orange). *International Journal on Computer Science and Engineering*, *5*(9), 4–11. doi:10.14445/23488387/IJCSE-V5I9P102

Ratra, R., & Gulia, P. (2020). Experimental evaluation of open source data mining tools (WEKA and Orange). *Int. J. Eng. Trends Technol*, *68*(8), 30–35. doi:10.14445/22315381/IJETT-V68I8P206S

Shobana, G., & Nikkath Bushra, S. (2021). Prediction of Cardiovascular Disease using Multiple Machine Learning Platforms. *2021 International Conference on Innovative Computing, Intelligent Communication and Smart Electrical Systems (ICSES)*. 10.1109/ICSES52305.2021.9633797

Subramani, S., Varshney, N., Anand, M. V., Soudagar, M. E. M., Al-keridis, L. A., Upadhyay, T. K., Alshammari, N., Saeed, M., Subramanian, K., Anbarasu, K., & Rohini, K. (2023). Cardiovascular diseases prediction by machine learning incorporation with deep learning. *Frontiers in Medicine*, *10*, 1–9. doi:10.3389/fmed.2023.1150933 PMID:37138750

Tougui, I., Jilbab, A., & El Mhamdi, J. (2020). Heart disease classification using data mining tools and machine learning techniques. *Health and Technology*, *10*(5), 1137–1144. doi:10.1007/s12553-020-00438-1

Wahbeh, A. H., Al-Radaideh, Q. A., Al-Kabi, M. N., & Al-Shawakfa, E. M. (2011). A comparison study between data mining tools over some classification methods. *International Journal of Advanced Computer Science and Applications*, *8*(2), 18–26.

ADDITIONAL READING

Bishop, C. M. (2006). *Pattern Recognition and Machine Learning*. Springer.

Fayyad, U., Piatetsky-Shapiro, G., & Smyth, P. (1996). From data mining to knowledge discovery in databases. *AI Magazine*, *17*(3), 37–54.

Han, J., Kamber, M., & Pei, J. (2011). *Data mining: Concepts and techniques*. Morgan Kaufmann.

Hastie, T., Tibshirani, R., & Friedman, J. (2009). *The elements of statistical learning: Data mining, interference, and prediction*. Springer. doi:10.1007/978-0-387-84858-7

Kantardzic, M. (2003). *Data Mining: Concepts, Models, Methods, and Algorithms*. Wiley.

Mitchell, T. M. (1997). *Machine learning*. McGraw-Hill.

Tan, P. N., Steinbach, M., & Kumar, V. (2006). *Introduction to Data Mining*. Pearson.

Witten, I. H., Frank, E., Hall, M. A., & Pal, C. J. (2016). *Data mining: Practical machine learning tools and techniques*. Morgan Kaufmann.

Wu, X., Kumar, V., Quinlan, J. R., Ghosh, J., Yang, Q., Motoda, H., & Steinberg, D. (2008). Top 10 algorithms in data mining. *Knowledge and Information Systems*, *14*(1), 1–37. doi:10.1007/s10115-007-0114-2

KEY TERMS AND DEFINITIONS

Biomedical Data: Any data regarding health status that can be processed for the purpose of obtaining information.

Data Mining: The process of searching and analyzing large amounts of raw data to identify patterns and relationships that yield valuable outputs.

Data Mining Tool: A framework within which data mining studies can be carried out.

Data Preprocessing: The set of processes applied to bring raw data into a form that can be implemented in data science tasks.

Drag-and-Drop Interface: A user-friendly graphical environment for effortlessly building data analysis workflows by selecting, arranging, and connecting elements.

Ensemble Method: A group of machine learning techniques that enhance model performance by combining multiple base models' predictions to improve accuracy and reduce overfitting.

Machine Learning: A field of computer science related to artificial intelligence that involves algorithms that enable machines to learn from data.

Chapter 13
Disease Identification and Classification From Pearl Millet Leaf Images Using Machine Learning Techniques

Pooja Chaturvedi
https://orcid.org/0000-0001-5207-2696
Institute of Technology, Nirma University, Ahmedabad, India

Swati Manekar
Institute of Technology, Nirma University, Ahmedabad, India

Aparna Kumari
https://orcid.org/0000-0001-5991-6193
Institute of Technology, Nirma University, Ahmedabad, India

Deepika Bishnoi
Institute of Technology, Nirma University, Ahmedabad, India

ABSTRACT

Plant disease plays a crucial role in the reduction as well as degradation of production and yield in the area of precision agriculture and is a major concern for farmers and agriculturists. Hence, the detection and identification of diseases among the crops is essential. In this chapter, the CNN model for the identification and classification of different plant diseases through its leaf images is used. Four diseases such as ergot, downy mildew, blast, and rust in the pearl millet crops are considered in this work. The images of the pearl millet crop are considered for the five classes: healthy, ergot, downy mildew, rust, and blast. The dataset consists of 2074 images. The dataset is trained for the 30 epochs. The proposed approach is compared with the various existing methodologies such as naïve Bayesian, decision tree, support vector machine, and random forest. The simulation result shows that the proposed approach using the CNN outperforms the existing approaches in terms of accuracy and loss.

DOI: 10.4018/979-8-3693-1062-5.ch013

Copyright © 2024, IGI Global. Copying or distributing in print or electronic forms without written permission of IGI Global is prohibited.

1. INTRODUCTION

The fulfillment of the dietary requirements of the human and animals is the main goal of the traditional farming system. Therefore, the farmers focus more on growing the healthy cereals like millet etc. instead of the high yield crops like wheat and rice. Considering the increasing trend of commercialization in the field of agriculture, the farmers are interested in producing the crops which are higher in terms of yield and are able to fulfil the dietary requirements. This increases the need to develop such a precision agriculture-based crop which is efficient in terms of financial gain as well as nutrition (Darwin, 2004; Jukanti et al., 2016; Le Mouël & Forslund, 2017).

Pearl millet is considered as the high yielding and nutritious crop. The quality and productivity of the pearl millet crop is negatively impacted by the diseases like rust, blast, downy mildew, and ergot. The applicability of Internet of Things (IOT) in the collection and storage of data, and processing and integration of machine learning methods in the areas of object detection, recognition and visualization and pattern identification has motivated the authors to develop a machine learning based solution for identifying and categorizing plant diseases from the leaf images. The main contribution of the chapter is as follows:

1. The chapter presents an automated approach to detect and classify the pearl millet disease from its leaf images.
2. For the simulation purpose, the data augmentation technique is applied for the acquisition of image dataset.
3. The different machine learning based approaches were applied and evaluated for the identification and categorization of the diseases in the pearl millet leaf images.
4. The various approaches are compared for the plant disease identification and categorization.

The chapter is structured as follows: discussion of the work done in the field in the section 2, propose methodology is described in section 3, Section 4 includes a discussion of the implementation details and results, and Section 5 wraps up the study with a look into the future scope.

2. LITERATURE REVIEW

The literature study in the field of plant disease classification and detection provides the significant insight in the object detection, identification and visualization. The traditional approaches utilized the manual identification and categorization of the plant diseases. But the traditional approaches did not give the sufficient insights of different parameters of the crop such as temperature, soil moisture, humidity etc. and the plant actual status monitoring is difficult. In addition to this, the legacy approaches are usually time taking and requires extensive human effort. The farmers also required the expert advice for the correct detection of the crop health. The integration of IOT with the machine learning techniques have enabled the farmers to automatically detect the plant disease by observing the leaf images. The different IOT based solutions such as smart phones, GPS, drone cameras were used for the data collection, storage and processing. The work done in the field of plant disease detection are summarized as follows:

In Kitpo and Inoue (2018), authors have used the IOT based architecture for data collection. The authors have implemented the SVM based model for the detection of plant diseases in the rice plant. In

Thorat et al. (2017), authors have used the IOT based solution for the classification of plant leaf images as healthy or unhealthy. In Lu et al. (2017), authors have proposed the CNN based approach for the detection and classification of 10 classes of disease in the rice crop. The simulations were carried out on the dataset of 500 images and the results show that the CNN based approaches achieves the higher accuracy over the traditional machine learning approaches. In Amara et al. (2017), authors have implemented the deep learning-based model Lenet to automatically detect sigatoka and speckle diseases in banana leaf. The proposed approach achieves the accuracy of 98% for the color images and 94% for the gray scale images. In Ramcharan et al. (2017), authors have proposed the deep learning approaches for the identification of diseases in three classes and two classes of pest damages on the casava image dataset.

In Rangarajan et al. (2018), authors have proposed the two deep learning-based models Alexnet and VGG16 for the detection of 6 classes of diseases in the tomato crops. In Akhter and Sofi (2022), authors have proposed the survey and IOT based approach for the detection of apple scab disease in the apple plant. The paper also investigated the different challenges present in the area of application of machine learning based analytical solution in precision agriculture. In Khan and Narvekar (2020), authors have proposed the IOT and sensor-based model for the detection of early blight and late blight disease in the tomato crops. The different machine learning models were implemented for the problem such as SVM, VGG-16, VGG-19, Random Forest and K-means. The extensive simulations were carried out which proves that Random Forest has the best accuracy for clustering and VGG-16 has highest accuracy for classification. In Hu et al. (2020), authors have considered the 49 diseases in the different crops. The plant village dataset was used for the prediction of disease using the different deep learning models such as Resnet-50, VGG-19, MDFC-Resnet and Alexnet. In Coulibaly et al. (2019), authors have proposed a transfer learning based approach for the detection of downy mildew disease in the pearl millet crop. The dataset consist of 711 images. The VGG-16 model was used to train the model for the disease detection. The simulation results show that the 95% accuracy is achieved. In Kitpo and Inoue (2018), authors have proposed the rice plant disease classification approach using the support vector machine-based model. The authors were able to determine the disease boundary. The proposed method was applied on the dataset obtained from the images of RRI. In Kundu et al. (2021), authors have proposed the IOT and deep learning-based approach for the detection of rust and blast diseases in the pearl millet crops. The several deep learning models such as VGG-16, VGG19, Inception, Resnet etc. were implemented and the results show the accuracy of the models in the disease classification.The closest work done in the field is in Mishra et al. (2023), in which authors have proposed a deep learning based approach for the detection and classification of blast and rust diseases in pearl millet. The sensor network based real time crop health monitoring system was developed which can detect and report any anomaly found in the readings of the several parameters such as temperature, humidity and soil moisture levels. The proposed system was implemented on an embedded platform using Raspberry Pi. The dataset consist of 3000 images, out of which 1500 was leaf images of rust and 1500 images of the blast disease. The customized CNN model was used to detect the diseases in the crop at the early stage, so the preventive methods may be applied. The performance of the proposed approach is compared with the existing state of the art approaches. The proposed approach achieves the accuracy approx. 98% in detection of diseases.

The comparison of the different approaches for the plant disease identification and classification is summarized in the Table 1.

Table 1. Comparison of the existing works done in the field of plant disease identification

Reference	Year	Plant	Disease	Dataset	Data Collection Method	Model implemented	Performance Metrics

Based on the literature review, we have identified the following research gaps:

i. Most of the existing work in the area of the plant disease identification is done for the different crops, but for the pearl millet significant work needs to be done.
ii. In few works authors have considered the disease identification and classification problem as the binary classification problem, which only considers two diseases in the pearl millet crop.
iii. This is the first work which has modeled the multi class problem of plant disease identification and classification.
iv. The various machine learning approaches have been implemented for the multi class scenario and the results are compared in terms of loss and accuracy parameters.

3. PROPOSED METHODOLOGY

Figure 1. Step-by-step process for proposed approach

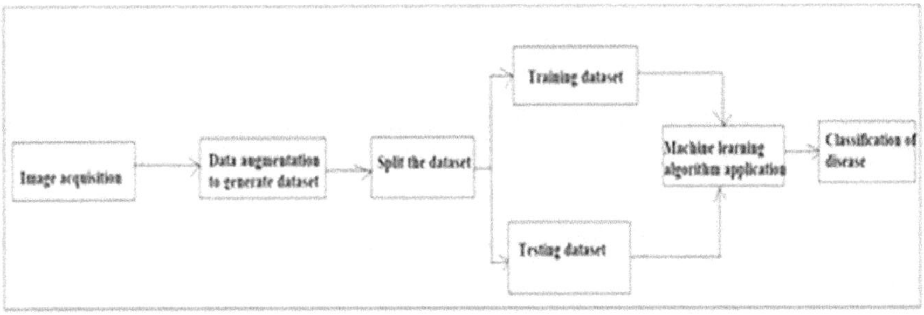

Image Acquisition

The first step in designing the machine learning based model for the pearl millet disease identification and classification is the acquisition of images. The images of pearl millet leaves are collected using the ImageDatagenerator package available in keras library in python. To build the dataset, 20 images of each class healthy, downy mildew, rust, blast and ergot is collected. The images of the different disease leaf are as in Figure 2.

Figure 2. Sample image of plant images: a) blast, b) downy mildew, c) ergot, d) rust, e) healthy

2. Image Augmentation and pre processing

To avoid the over fitting problem in the machine learning model, the data augmentation technique is applied using ImageGenerator method available in keras package. The augmentation methods provide an easy method to increase the size of the sample size while maintaining the sufficient diversity. The following operations were applied on the collected images to create 40 images from the existing images in each category:

a. *Rotation*- the images were rotated randomly in the range of 0 to 45%.
b. *Width shift*- Width shift methods are applied to place the object in the image in the center by moving its pixels to certain units horizontally. In the proposed approach we have used the width shift value as 0.2 which means the object in the image will be shifted by 20% in the horizontal direction.
c. *Height shift*- The height shift methods are applied to place the object in the image in the center by moving its pixels to certain units vertically. In the proposed approach we have used the height shift value as 0.2 which means the object in the image will be shifted by 20% in the vertical direction.
d. Zoom range- The zoom range is used to randomly zoom in and zoom out the images in the specified range. In the proposed method we have used the zoom range as 0.2.
e. *Horizontal flip*- The horizontal flip parameter is used to flip the image horizontally. In this method the value of this parameter is set as True.

f. *Fill mode-* When the images are rotated randomly, then some pixels of the image may move outside the image. In this case, the fill mode is used to fill the empty areas. In the proposed approach, we have used the fill mode as 'Nearest", which means it will fill the empty areas with the nearest pixel values.

After the preprocessing the images, the dataset consist of 2074 images categorized into five classes. As part of the pre processing step, all the images were resized to the fixed size as 256*256.

3. Splitting the dataset into training and testing dataset

In the third step, the dataset of the images generated is split into training and testing dataset. In this work, we have considered the 80% images in the training set and remaining images are considered in the testing dataset as shown in the Table 2.

Table 2. Summary of the dataset

S. No.	Training Dataset	Testing Dataset	Total
1	1659	415	2074

4. CLASSIFICATION OF LEAF IMAGES

In the next step, the different supervised machine learning models are implemented for the classification of the leaf images.

5. MACHINE LEARNING MODELS FOR IMAGE CLASSIFICATION

The considered approaches are compared in terms of the accuracy and loss values for the training and testing dataset. In the proposed work, we have considered the five machine learning models for the disease classification in the pearl millet crop from the leaf images. The description of the considered approaches is as follows:

a. Support Vector Machine

Support Vector Machine is considered as labeled learning technique which can be used for classification as well as regression activities. The strength of SVM is best for the classification problem for the small and complex datasets. It works on the principle of finding the best hyperplane which can accurately classify the two classes. The kernel function is used to determine the hyperplane between the different classes by increasing the dimensionality of the problem space.

b. Random Forest

Random forest is labeled learning algorithm for the classification as well as regression tasks. The random forest works on the principle of ensemble machine learning. The ensemble-based machine learning algorithm implements the several decision trees for the classification task. The accuracy of the model is increased by taking the average of the several models. The number of decision trees constructed has significant impact on the efficiency.

c. Gaussian Naïve Bayes

The Gaussian Naïve Bayes is a labeled machine learning method which determines the likelihood of the objects pertaining to a particular class. The

Gaussian Naïve Bayes algorithm is simple and provides best solution for the multi-class problem as compared to the other methods.

d. Decision Tree

Decision tree is a labeled machine learning based method for both the classification and regression problems. The decision tree works by identifying the most suitable attribute for splitting depending on which the different rules are identified for different actions. The main metrics used for determining the splitting attribute are Information gain and Gini Index.

e. Convolutional Neural Network based model

Convolutional neural networks are considered as special neural network which has the capability to identify the feature vectors from the input image dataset. Convolution neural network-based models for image classification are composed of several layers as shown in Figure 3.

i. Convolutional layer- The image consisting of a large number of pixels is provided as input to the convolutional layer. The convolutional layers performs the dimensionality reduction by applying the filter over the image and the output of the convolutional operations is the feature vector. The feature vector represents the set of important features responsible for the image classification.

ii. Padding- The main requirement of CNN model is the common input shape for all the images, so after the convolutional operation the image size may be reduced or increased. In that case, padding is applied to make all the images of uniform shape.

iii. Activation layer- The activation layer is responsible for converting the input data into the output data. The most commonly used activation function is the Relu and is usually applied at the input and hidden layers. When the relu activation function all the values below zero are returned as zero and all the other values are returned as it is. The softmax activation function is considered for the output layer. The main functionality of the softmax activation function is to normalize the output to a probability distribution function over the predicted output classes.

iv. Pooling layer- The pooling layer is responsible for reducing the dimensionality by feature vector obtained after the convolutional operations. The pooling layer slides the filter of some pre-defined size with fixed stride size over the input image. There may be two categories of pooling layers as maximum or average. The maximum pooling selects the maximum value from each pool, whereas the average pooling layer selects the average value of all the pools.

v. Drop regularization- This is a crucial step in implementing the CNN based models. The drop out regularization is used to randomly drop few neurons, so that they are not updated during the back propagation step.

vi. Flattening- Flattening operation is applied after the pooling operation to make the entire feature space of one dimension.

vii. Fully connected layer- The next step after the flattening operation is providing the input to the fully connected layer. The number of fully connected layers may vary depending on the problem and network. The output of the prediction of class depends on the last fully connected layer.

Figure 3. Architecture of CNN-based model (Learndatasci, n.d.)

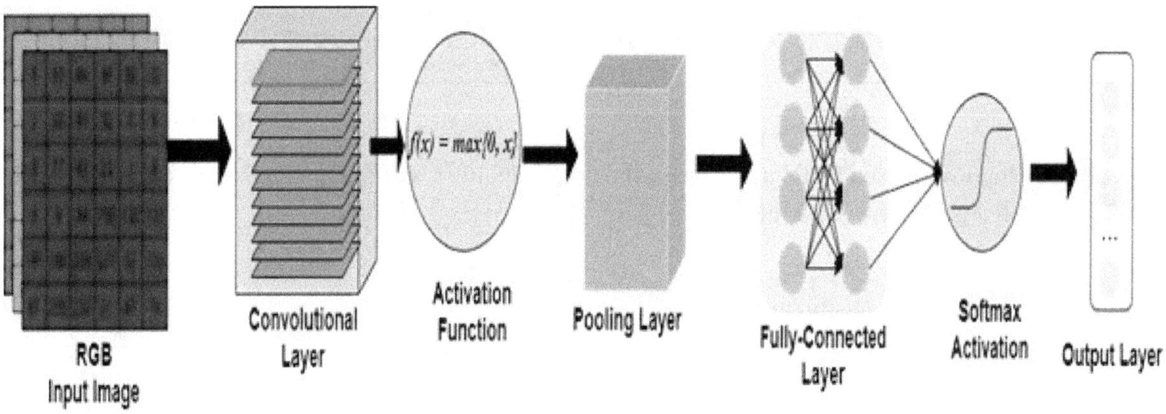

4. Implementation details and Results Discussion

The simulations were carried out for the disease classification using the deep learning framework keras and tensor-flow packages available in the python programming language. The different machine learning models were implemented on a system having the processor configuration as 11th Gen Intel(R) Core (TM) i5-1135G7 and 8 GB RAM. The implementation details of the different approaches are summarized in Table 3.

Table 3. Implementation details

S. No.	Method	Details
1	Support Vector Machine	Kernel= Radial Basis
2	Random Forest	Max Depth=3 No. of Estimators=10
3	Gaussian Naïve Bayes	Default
4	Decision Tree	Default
5	Convolutional Neural Network	Activation function= Rectified Linear Unit at Input and Hidden Layers Activation Function= Soft Max at Output Layer No. of Output Neurons=5 No. of Parameters= 108,261 No. of Trainable Parameters=108,261 No. of Non-Trainable Parameters=0 No. of Epochs= 30 Loss Function= Categorical Cross Entropy Optimizer= Root Mean Square Propagation (RMSProp) with momentum Learning Rate=0.001 Momentum=0.0

The deep learning-based CNN model with the above details was implemented. The summary of the model generated is as shown in Figure 4.

Figure 4. CNN-based model summary

```
Model: "sequential_3"
_________________________________________________________________
 Layer (type)                Output Shape              Param #
=================================================================
 conv2d_6 (Conv2D)           (None, 26, 26, 16)        448

 max_pooling2d_6 (MaxPooling  (None, 13, 13, 16)       0
 2D)

 conv2d_7 (Conv2D)           (None, 11, 11, 32)        4640

 max_pooling2d_7 (MaxPooling  (None, 5, 5, 32)         0
 2D)

 flatten_3 (Flatten)         (None, 800)               0

 dense_6 (Dense)             (None, 128)               102528

 dense_7 (Dense)             (None, 5)                 645

=================================================================
Total params: 108,261
Trainable params: 108,261
Non-trainable params: 0
_________________________________________________________________
```

The model is trained on the considered dataset for 30 epochs. The training and validation accuracy with the increasing number of epochs is as shown in Figure 5a. The considered problem is a multi-class classification problem, so the loss function is considered as the categorical cross entropy. The variation of the loss values with respect to the epochs is as shown in Figure 5b.

Figure 5. Performance of the CNN: a) accuracy for training and validation dataset, b) loss function for training and validation dataset

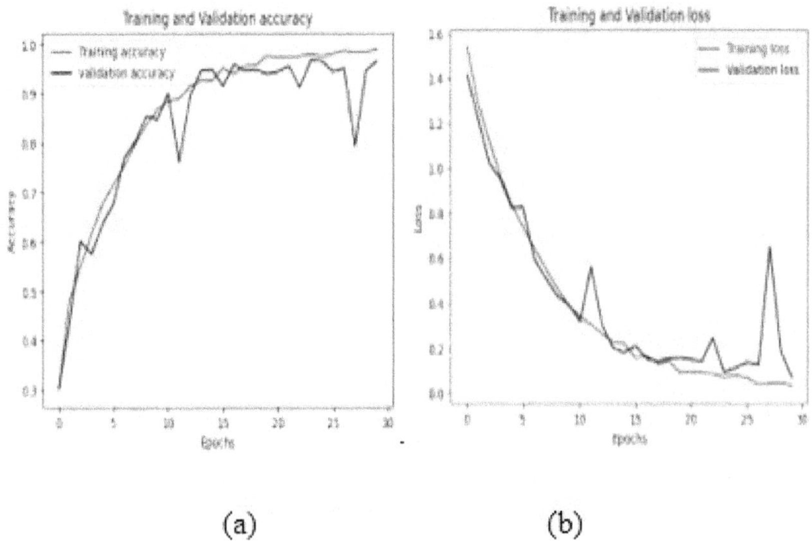

Table 4 shows the accuracy of the proposed model. The results show the supremacy of CNN model over the existing approaches and achieved the accuracy as 98%.

Table 4. Comparison of the considered models

S. No.	Model	Accuracy (%)
1	Convolutional Neural Network	98
2	SVM	96
3	RF	80
4	Gaussian NM	74
5	Decision Tree	65

The comparison of the accuracy of the different models for the classification task is shown in Figure 6.

Figure 6. Comparison of different machine learning models in terms of accuracy

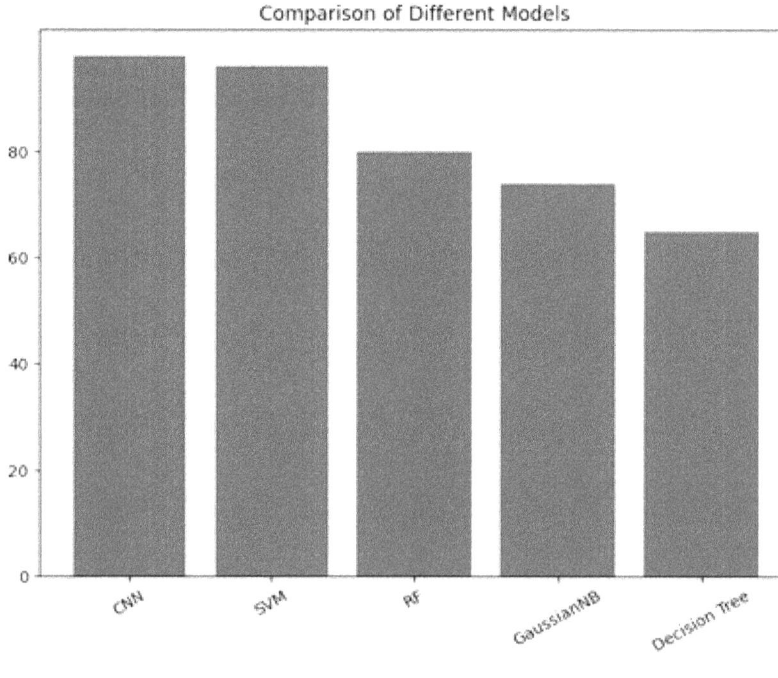

6. CONCLUSION AND FUTURE SCOPE

The crop disease significantly impacts the yield and it ultimately decreases the production. The machine learning model which can automatically detect the disease in the crops from the leaf images can help the farmers in better planning for reducing the disease and its impact. The paper presented an approach for the identification and categorization of the diseases in the pearl millet crop. The different machine learning based models were applied for the classification of the disease. The CNN model achieves the highest accuracy in the fewer number of iterations as compared to the different supervised machine learning models.

The paper presented the manual and augmentation-based approaches for the collection of leaf images dataset. The automation of the data collection process can be done as part of the future work. In the proposed paper, we have considered a fully connected CNN model, but different pre-trained deep learning-based models can be implemented for the considered problem.

REFERENCES

Akhter, R., & Sofi, S. A. (2022). Precision agriculture using IoT data analytics and machine learning. *Journal of King Saud University. Computer and Information Sciences*, *34*(8), 5602–5618. doi:10.1016/j.jksuci.2021.05.013

Amara, J., Bouaziz, B., & Algergawy, A. (2017). *A deep learning-based approach for banana leaf diseases classification*. Datenbanksysteme für Business, Technologie und Web (BTW 2017)-Workshopband.

Coulibaly, S., Kamsu-Foguem, B., Kamissoko, D., & Traore, D. (2019). Deep neural networks with transfer learning in millet crop images. *Computers in Industry, 108*, 115–120. doi:10.1016/j.compind.2019.02.003

Darwin, R. (2004). Effects of greenhouse gas emissions on world agriculture, food consumption, and economic welfare. *Climatic Change, 66*(1-2), 191–238. doi:10.1023/B:CLIM.0000043138.67784.27

Hu, W. J., Fan, J., Du, Y. X., Li, B. S., Xiong, N., & Bekkering, E. (2020). MDFC–ResNet: An agricultural IoT system to accurately recognize crop diseases. *IEEE Access : Practical Innovations, Open Solutions, 8*, 115287–115298. doi:10.1109/ACCESS.2020.3001237

Jukanti, A. K., Gowda, C. L., Rai, K. N., Manga, V. K., & Bhatt, R. K. (2016). Crops that feed the world 11. Pearl Millet (Pennisetum glaucum L.): An important source of food security, nutrition and health in the arid and semi-arid tropics. *Food Security, 8*(2), 307–329. doi:10.1007/s12571-016-0557-y

Khan, S., & Narvekar, M. (2020). Disorder detection of tomato plant (solanum lycopersicum) using IoT and machine learning. *Journal of Physics: Conference Series, 1432*(1), 012086. doi:10.1088/1742-6596/1432/1/012086

Kitpo, N., & Inoue, M. (2018, March). Early rice disease detection and position mapping system using drone and IoT architecture. In *2018 12th South East Asian Technical University Consortium (SEATUC)* (Vol. 1, pp. 1-5). IEEE.

Kundu, N., Rani, G., Dhaka, V. S., Gupta, K., Nayak, S. C., Verma, S., Ijaz, M. F., & Woźniak, M. (2021). IoT and interpretable machine learning based framework for disease prediction in pearl millet. *Sensors (Basel), 21*(16), 5386. doi:10.3390/s21165386 PMID:34450827

Le Mouël, C., & Forslund, A. (2017). How can we feed the world in 2050? A review of the responses from global scenario studies. *European Review of Agriculture Economics, 44*(4), 541–591. doi:10.1093/erae/jbx006

Learndatasci. (n.d.). https://www.learndatasci.com/tutorials/convolutional-neural-networks-image-classification/

Lu, Y., Yi, S., Zeng, N., Liu, Y., & Zhang, Y. (2017). Identification of rice diseases using deep convolutional neural networks. *Neurocomputing, 267*, 378–384. doi:10.1016/j.neucom.2017.06.023

Mishra, S., Volety, D. R., Bohra, N., Alfarhood, S., & Safran, M. (2023). A smart and sustainable framework for millet crop monitoring equipped with disease detection using enhanced predictive intelligence. *Alexandria Engineering Journal, 83*, 298–306. doi:10.1016/j.aej.2023.10.041

Ramcharan, A., Baranowski, K., McCloskey, P., Ahmed, B., Legg, J., & Hughes, D. (2017). Using transfer learning for image-based cassava disease detection. *Frontiers in Plant Science*, 8.

Rangarajan, A. K., Purushothaman, R., & Ramesh, A. (2018). Tomato crop disease classification using pre-trained deep learning algorithm. *Procedia Computer Science, 133*, 1040–1047. doi:10.1016/j.procs.2018.07.070

Thorat, A., Kumari, S., & Valakunde, N. D. (2017, December). An IoT based smart solution for leaf disease detection. In *2017 international conference on big data, IoT and data science (BID)* (pp. 193-198). IEEE.

Compilation of References

Abadi, M., Barham, P., Chen, J., Chen, Z., Davis, A., Dean, J., . . . Kudlur, M. (2016). Tensorflow: A system for large-scale machine learning. In *12th USENIX Symposium on Operating Systems Design and Implementation ({OSDI} 16)* (pp. 265-283). USENIX.

Abubakar, A., Jibril, M. M., Almeida, C. F. M., Gemignani, M., Yahya, M. N., & Abba, S. I. (2023). A Novel Hybrid Optimization Approach for Fault Detection in Photovoltaic Arrays and Inverters Using AI and Statistical Learning Techniques: A Focus on Sustainable Environment. *Processes, 11*(9), 2549. doi:10.3390/pr11092549

Acaru, S. F., Abdullah, R., & Lim, R. C. (2023). Sustainable Valorization of Wood Residue for the Production of Biofuel Materials Via Continuous Flow Hydrothermal Liquefaction. *Waste and Biomass Valorization, 14*(9), 3081–3095. doi:10.1007/s12649-023-02074-y

Acemoglu, D., & Restrepo, P. (2018). *Artificial Intelligence, Automation, and Work.* NBER Working Paper No. 24196. National Bereau of Economic Research.

Ada, S., Abou Nabout, N., & Feit, E. M. (2022). Context information can increase revenue in online display advertising auctions: Evidence from a policy change. *JMR, Journal of Marketing Research, 59*(5), 1040–1058. doi:10.1177/00222437211070219

Ahamad, S., Veeraiah, V., Ramesh, J. V. N., Rajadevi, R., Reeja, S. R., Pramanik, S., & Gupta, A. (2023). Deep Learning based Cancer Detection Technique. In Thrust Technologies' Effect on Image Processing. IGI Global.

Ahamad, S., Veeraiah, V., Ramesh, J. V. N., Rajadevi, R., Reeja, S. R., Pramanik, S., & Gupta, A. (2023). *Deep Learning based Cancer Detection Technique, Thrust Technologies' Effect on Image Processing*. IGI Global.

Ahmad, T., Zhang, D., Huang, C., Zhang, H., Dai, N., Song, Y., & Chen, H. (2021). Artificial intelligence in sustainable energy industry: Status quo, challenges and opportunities. *Journal of Cleaner Production, 289*, 125834. doi:10.1016/j.jclepro.2021.125834

Ahmed, K. P. (2017). Analysis of data mining tools for disease prediction. *Journal of Pharmaceutical Sciences and Research, 9*(10), 1886–1888.

Aiswarya, R., Nair, D. S., Rajeev, T., & Vinod, V. (2023). A novel SVM based adaptive scheme for accurate fault identification in microgrid. *Electric Power Systems Research, 221*, 109439. doi:10.1016/j.epsr.2023.109439

Akhter, R., & Sofi, S. A. (2022). Precision agriculture using IoT data analytics and machine learning. *Journal of King Saud University. Computer and Information Sciences, 34*(8), 5602–5618. doi:10.1016/j.jksuci.2021.05.013

Alabdulatif, A., Thilakarathne, N. N., & Kalinaki, K. (2023). A Novel Cloud Enabled Access Control Model for Preserving the Security and Privacy of Medical Big Data. *Electronics (Basel), 12*(12), 2646. doi:10.3390/electronics12122646

Alabi, R. O., Elmusrati, M., Leivo, I., Almangush, A., & Mäkitie, A. A. (2023). Machine learning explainability in nasopharyngeal cancer survival using LIME and SHAP. *Scientific Reports, 13*(1), 1–14. doi:10.1038/s41598-023-35795-0

Alao, M. A., Popoola, O. M., & Ayodele, T. R. (2021). Selection of waste-to-energy technology for distributed generation using IDOCRIW-Weighted TOPSIS method: A case study of the City of Johannesburg, South Africa. *Renewable Energy, 178*, 162–183. doi:10.1016/j.renene.2021.06.031

Al-Khoder, A., & Harmouch, H. (2015). Evaluating four of the most popular open source and free data mining tools. *International Journal of Academic Scientific Research, 3*(10), 13–23.

Allah, E. M. A., El-Matary, D. E., Eid, E. M., & Dien, A. S. (2022). Performance Comparison of Various Machine Learning Approaches to Identify the Best One in Predicting Heart Disease. *Journal of Computer and Communications, 10*(02), 1–18. doi:10.4236/jcc.2022.102001

Alnsour, Y., Johnson, M., Albizri, A., & Harfouche, A. H. (2023). Predicting Patient Length of Stay Using Artificial Intelligence to Assist Healthcare Professionals in Resource Planning and Scheduling Decisions. *Journal of Global Information Management, 31*(1), 1–14. doi:10.4018/JGIM.323059

AlQattan, N., Acheampong, M., Jaward, F. M., Ertem, F. C., Vijayakumar, N., & Bello, T. (2018). Reviewing the potential of Waste-to-Energy (WTE) technologies for Sustainable Development Goal (SDG) numbers seven and eleven. *Renewable Energy Focus, 27*, 97–110. doi:10.1016/j.ref.2018.09.005

Al-Shetwi, A. Q., Hannan, M., Jern, K. P., Alkahtani, A. A., & Abas, A. P. G. (2020a). Power quality assessment of grid-connected PV system in compliance with the recent integration requirements. *Electronics (Basel), 9*(2), 366. doi:10.3390/electronics9020366

Amara, J., Bouaziz, B., & Algergawy, A. (2017). *A deep learning-based approach for banana leaf diseases classification.* Datenbanksysteme für Business, Technologie und Web (BTW 2017)-Workshopband.

Anand, R., Singh, J., Pandey, D. K., Pandey, B., Nassa, V. K., & Pramanik, S. (2022). Modern Technique for Interactive Communication in LEACH-Based Ad Hoc Wireless Sensor Network. In M. M. Ghonge, S. Pramanik, & A. D. Potgantwar (Eds.), *Software Defined Networking for Ad Hoc Networks*. Springer. doi:10.1007/978-3-030-91149-2_3

Antonesi, G., Cioara, T., Toderean, L., Anghel, I., & De Mulder, C. (2023). A Machine Learning Pipeline to Forecast the Electricity and Heat Consumption in a City District. *Buildings, 13*(6), 1407. doi:10.3390/buildings13061407

Antonopoulos, I., Robu, V., Couraud, B., Kirli, D., Norbu, S., Kiprakis, A., Flynn, D., Elizondo-Gonzalez, S., & Wattam, S. (2020). Artificial intelligence and machine learning approaches to energy demand-side response: A systematic review. *Renewable & Sustainable Energy Reviews, 130*, 109899. doi:10.1016/j.rser.2020.109899

Apostolopoulos, I. D., & Mpesiana, T. A. (2020). Covid-19: Automatic detection from X-ray images utilizing transfer learning with convolutional neural networks. *Physical and Engineering Sciences in Medicine, 43*(2), 635–640. doi:10.1007/s13246-020-00865-4 PMID:32524445

Arasu, B. S., Seelan, B. J. B., & Thamaraiselvan, N. (2020). A machine learning-based approach to enhancing social media marketing. *Computers & Electrical Engineering, 86*, 106723. doi:10.1016/j.compeleceng.2020.106723

Archer, R. (2020). Geothermal Energy. In *Future Energy* (pp. 431–445). Elsevier. doi:10.1016/B978-0-08-102886-5.00020-7

Asif, M., & Muneer, T. (2007). Energy supply, its demand and security issues for developed and emerging economies. *Renewable & Sustainable Energy Reviews, 11*(7), 1388–1413. doi:10.1016/j.rser.2005.12.004

Avcı, H., & Karakaya, J. (2023). A Novel Medical Image Enhancement Algorithm for Breast Cancer Detection on Mammography Images Using Machine Learning. *Diagnostics, 13*(3), 348. doi:10.3390/diagnostics13030348

Aydin, H. E., & Iban, M. C. (2023). Predicting and analyzing flood susceptibility using boosting-based ensemble machine learning algorithms with SHapley Additive exPlanations. *Natural Hazards, 116*(3), 2957–2991. doi:10.1007/s11069-022-05793-y

Azizi, N., Yaghoubirad, M., Farajollahi, M., & Ahmadi, A. (2023). Deep learning based long-term global solar irradiance and temperature forecasting using time series with multi-step multivariate output. *Renewable Energy, 206*, 135–147. doi:10.1016/j.renene.2023.01.102

Bahari, N. A. A. B. S., Ahmed, A. N., Chong, K. L., Lai, V., Huang, Y. F., Koo, C. H., Ng, J. L., & El-Shafie, A. (2023). Predicting Sea Level Rise Using Artificial Intelligence: A Review. *Archives of Computational Methods in Engineering, 30*(7), 4045–4062. doi:10.1007/s11831-023-09934-9

Balogun, A. L., Marks, D., Sharma, R., Shekhar, H., Balmes, C., Maheng, D., Arshad, A., & Salehi, P. (2020). Assessing the Potentials of Digitalization as a Tool for Climate Change Adaptation and Sustainable Development in Urban Centres. *Sustainable Cities and Society, 53*, 101888. doi:10.1016/j.scs.2019.101888

Bansal, R., Jenipher, B., & Nisha, V. (2022). Big Data Architecture for Network Security. In Cyber Security and Network Security. Wiley. doi:10.1002/9781119812555.ch11

Bansal, R., Obaid, A. J., Gupta, A., Singh, R., & Pramanik, S. (2021). Impact of Big Data on Digital Transformation in 5G Era. *2nd International Conference on Physics and Applied Sciences (ICPAS 2021).* 10.1088/1742-6596/1963/1/012170

Barbosa, B., Saura, J. R., Zekan, S. B., & Ribeiro-Soriano, D. (2023). Defining content marketing and its influence on online user behavior: A data-driven prescriptive analytics method. *Annals of Operations Research*, 1–26. doi:10.1007/s10479-023-05261-1

Beletskaya, I. P., & Cheprakov, A. V. (2000). The Heck Reaction as a Sharpening Stone of Palladium Catalysis. *Chemical Reviews, 100*(8), 3009–3066. doi:10.1021/cr9903048 PMID:11749313

Bellemare, M. G., Veness, J., & Munos, R. (2016). A survey of Monte-Carlo methods for reinforcement learning. *arXiv preprint arXiv:1606.01448.*

Benti, N. E., Chaka, M. D., & Semie, A. G. (2023). Forecasting Renewable Energy Generation with Machine Learning and Deep Learning: Current Advances and Future Prospects. *Sustainability, 15*(9), 7087. doi:10.3390/su15097087

Bhardwaj, A., Dagar, V., Khan, M. O., Aggarwal, A., Alvarado, R., Kumar, M., Irfan, M., & Proshad, R. (2022). Smart IoT and machine learning-based framework for water quality assessment and device component monitoring. *Environmental Science and Pollution Research International, 29*(30), 46018–46036. doi:10.1007/s11356-022-19014-3 PMID:35165843

Bhattacharya, A., Ghosal, A., Obaid, A. J., Krit, S., Shukla, V. K., Mandal, K., & Pramanik, S. (2021). Unsupervised Summarization Approach with Computational Statistics of Microblog Data. In D. Samanta, R. R. Althar, S. Pramanik, & S. Dutta (Eds.), *Methodologies and Applications of Computational Statistics for Machine Learning* (pp. 23–37). IGI Global. doi:10.4018/978-1-7998-7701-1.ch002

Bhatt, P., Maclean, A., Dickinson, Y., & Kumar, C. (2022). Fine-Scale Mapping of Natural Ecological Communities Using Machine Learning Approaches. *Remote Sensing (Basel), 14*(3), 563. doi:10.3390/rs14030563

Bird, S., Klein, E., & Loper, E. (2009). *Natural language processing with Python: analyzing text with the natural language toolkit*. O'Reilly Media, Inc.

BIST30, Link of Borsa Istanbul, https://www.borsaistanbul.com/tr/endeks-detay/12/bist-30, Last Access: 09 April 2023.

Bolukbasi, T., Chang, K.-W., Zou, J., Saligrama, V., & Kalai, A. (2016). Man is to computer programmer as woman is to homemaker? Debiasing word embeddings. *Advances in Neural Information Processing Systems, 29*, 4349–4357.

Bose, B. K. (2017). Artificial Intelligence Techniques in Smart Grid and Renewable Energy Systems—Some Example Applications. *Proceedings of the IEEE*, *105*(11), 2262–2273. doi:10.1109/JPROC.2017.2756596

Boussouf, S., Fernández, T., & Hart, A. B. (2023). Landslide susceptibility mapping using maximum entropy (MaxEnt) and geographically weighted logistic regression (GWLR) models in the Río Aguas catchment (Almería, SE Spain). *Natural Hazards*, *117*(1), 207–235. doi:10.1007/s11069-023-05857-7

Braig, K. F. (2018). The European Court of Human Rights and the right to clean water and sanitation. *Water Policy*, *20*(2), 282–307. doi:10.2166/wp.2018.045

Bryson, J. J. (2019). *Towards a New Enlightenment? A Transcendent Decade - The Past Decade and the Future of Globalization*. OpendMind BBVA.

Burch, C. (2010). Django, a web framework using python: Tutorial presentation. *Journal of Computing Sciences in Colleges*, *25*(5), 154–155.

Burton, T., Jenkins, N., Sharpe, D., & Bossanyi, E. (2011). *Wind Energy Handbook*. Wiley. doi:10.1002/9781119992714

Business News. (2023). *Singapore Pioneering in the Smart Traffic Light Systems*. https://businessnews.com.my/wp/2023/08/12/singapore-pioneering-in-the-smart-traffic-light-systems/

Butt, U. A., Mehmood, M., Shah, S. B. H., Amin, R., Shaukat, M. W., Raza, S. M., Suh, D. Y., & Piran, M. J. (2020, September). A Review of Machine Learning Algorithms for Cloud Computing Security. *Electronics (Basel)*, *9*(9), 9. Advance online publication. doi:10.3390/electronics9091379

Carolin Mabel, M., & Fernandez, E. (2008). Analysis of wind power generation and prediction using ANN: A case study. *Renewable Energy*, *33*(5), 986–992. doi:10.1016/j.renene.2007.06.013

Castelli, E. (2023). *Enhancing Anti-Poaching Efforts Through Predictive Analysis Of Animal Movements And Dynamic Environmental Factors*. https://urn.kb.se/resolve?urn=urn:nbn:se:umu:diva-211118

Chakraborty, C., & Kishor, A. (2022). Real-Time Cloud-Based Patient-Centric Monitoring Using Computational Health Systems. *IEEE Transactions on Computational Social Systems*, *9*(6), 1613–1623. doi:10.1109/TCSS.2022.3170375

Chalmers, C., Fergus, P., Wich, S., & Longmore, S. N. (2021). Modelling Animal Biodiversity Using Acoustic Monitoring and Deep Learning. *Proceedings of the International Joint Conference on Neural Networks, 2021-July*. 10.1109/IJCNN52387.2021.9534195

Champa-Bujaico, E., García-Díaz, P., & Díez-Pascual, A. M. (2022). Machine Learning for Property Prediction and Optimization of Polymeric Nanocomposites: A State-of-the-Art. *International Journal of Molecular Sciences*, *23*(18), 10712. doi:10.3390/ijms231810712 PMID:36142623

Chandan, R. R., Soni, S., Raj, A., Veeraiah, V., Dhabliya, D., Pramanik, S., & Gupta, A. (2023). Genetic Algorithm and Machine Learning. In Advanced Bioinspiration Methods for Healthcare Standards, Policies, and Reform. IGI Global. doi:10.4018/978-1-6684-5656-9

Chemisto, M., Gutu, T. J., Kalinaki, K., Mwebesa Bosco, D., Egau, P., Fred, K., Tim Oloya, I., & Rashid, K. (2023). Artificial Intelligence for Improved Maternal Healthcare: A Systematic Literature Review. *2023 IEEE AFRICON*, 1–6. doi:10.1109/AFRICON55910.2023.10293674

Chen, H., Wang, Y., & Li, J. (2021). Deep reinforcement learning for personalized medicine: A review. *Journal of Biomedical Informatics*, *111*, 103540.

Chen, Y., Jia, J., Wu, C., Ramirez-Granada, L., & Li, G. (2023). Estimation on total phosphorus of agriculture soil in China: A new sight with comparison of model learning methods. *Journal of Soils and Sediments*, *23*(2), 998–1007. doi:10.1007/s11368-022-03374-x

Chithambarathanu, M., & Jeyakumar, M. K. (2023). Survey on crop pest detection using deep learning and machine learning approaches. *Multimedia Tools and Applications*, *82*(27), 42277–42310. doi:10.1007/s11042-023-15221-3 PMID:37362671

Chollet, F. (2015). Keras: Deep learning library for theano and tensorflow.

Cho, S. Y., Delgado, R., & Choi, B. W. (2023). Feasibility Study for a Python-Based Embedded Real-Time Control System. *Electronics (Basel)*, *12*(6), 1426. doi:10.3390/electronics12061426

Choudhary, S., Narayan, V., Faiz, M., & Pramanik, S. (2022). Fuzzy Approach-Based Stable Energy-Efficient AODV Routing Protocol in Mobile Ad hoc Networks. In M. M. Ghonge, S. Pramanik, & A. D. Potgantwar (Eds.), *Software Defined Networking for Ad Hoc Networks*. Springer. doi:10.1007/978-3-030-91149-2_6

Chua, T.-H., & Salam, I. (2022). *Evaluation of Machine Learning Algorithms in Network-Based Intrusion Detection System*. doi:10.3390/sym15061251

CIFAR-10. Link of CIFAR-10 Dataset, https://www.cs.toronto.edu/~kriz/cifar.html Last Access: 09 April 2023.

Clark, E., & Johnson, P. (2021). Targeted Promotions and Incentives for Cybersecurity Solutions: Ethical Considerations. *Cyber Ethics Review, 18*(2), 89-104. Retrieved from https://www.cyberethicsreview.org/article/targeted-promotions-cybersecurity

Colaboratory, G. Link of Google Colaboratory, https://colab.research.google.com, Last Access: 09 April 2023

Cortez, P., Cerdeira, A., Almeida, F., Matos, T., & Reis, J. (2009). Modeling wine preferences by data mining from physicochemical properties. *Decision Support Systems*, *47*(4), 547–553. doi:10.1016/j.dss.2009.05.016

Coulibaly, S., Kamsu-Foguem, B., Kamissoko, D., & Traore, D. (2019). Deep neural networks with transfer learning in millet crop images. *Computers in Industry*, *108*, 115–120. doi:10.1016/j.compind.2019.02.003

Courtland, R. (2018). Bias detectives: The researchers striving to make algorithms fair. *Nature*, *558*(7710), 357–360. doi:10.1038/d41586-018-05469-3 PMID:29925973

Damousis, I. G., & Dokopoulos, P. (2001). A fuzzy expert system for the forecasting of wind speed and power generation in wind farms. *IEEE Power Industry Computer Applications Conference*, 63–69. 10.1109/PICA.2001.932320

Danso, G., & Otoo, M. (2022). Readiness of South Asian Countries to Achieve SDG 6 Targets by 2030 in the Sanitation Sector. In *Safe Water and Sanitation for a Healthier World: A Global View of Progress Towards SDG 6* (pp. 133–148). Springer International Publishing. doi:10.1007/978-3-030-94020-1_8

Darwin, R. (2004). Effects of greenhouse gas emissions on world agriculture, food consumption, and economic welfare. *Climatic Change*, *66*(1-2), 191–238. doi:10.1023/B:CLIM.0000043138.67784.27

Deacon, J. H., & Harris, J. (2011). Contextual marketing: A conceptualisation of the meaning and operation of a language for marketing in context. *Journal of Research in Marketing and Entrepreneurship*, *13*(2), 146–160. doi:10.1108/14715201111176435

Devi, S. K., Krishnapriya, S., & Kalita, D. (2016). Prediction of heart disease using data mining techniques. *Indian Journal of Science and Technology*, *9*(39), 1–5. doi:10.17485/ijst/2016/v9i47/106827

Dewey, A., & Drahota, A. (2016). *Introduction to systematic reviews: online learning module*. Cochrane Training. Available at https://Training.Cochrane.Org/Interactivelearning/Module-1-Introduction-Conducting-Systematic-Reviews

Dhamodaran, S., Ahamad, S., Ramesh, J. V. N., Muthugurunathan, G., Manikandan, K., Pramanik, S., & Pandey, D. (2023). Food Quality Assessment using Image Processing Technique. In Thrust Technologies' Effect on Image Processing. IGI Global.

Dhamodaran, S., Ahamad, S., Ramesh, J. V. N., Sathappan, S., Namdev, A., Kanse, R. R., & Pramanik, S. (2023). *Fire Detection System Utilizing an Aggregate Technique in UAV and Cloud Computing. In Thrust Technologies' Effect on Image Processing*. IGI Global.

Di Matteo, U., Nastasi, B., Albo, A., & Astiaso Garcia, D. (2017). Energy contribution of OFMSW (Organic Fraction of Municipal Solid Waste) to energy-environmental sustainability in urban areas at small scale. *Energies*, *10*(2), 229. doi:10.3390/en10020229

Díez-Pascual, A. M. (2022a). Biopolymer Composites: Synthesis, Properties, and Applications. *International Journal of Molecular Sciences*, *23*(4), 2257. doi:10.3390/ijms23042257 PMID:35216374

Díez-Pascual, A. M. (2022b). Carbon-Based Polymer Nanocomposites for High-Performance Applications II. *Polymers*, *14*(5), 870. doi:10.3390/polym14050870 PMID:35267693

Dilekli, N., & Cazcarro, I. (2019). Testing the SDG targets on water and sanitation using the world trade model with a waste, wastewater, and recycling framework. *Ecological Economics*, *165*, 106376. doi:10.1016/j.ecolecon.2019.106376

Doan Tran, H., Kim, C., Chen, L., Chandrasekaran, A., Batra, R., Venkatram, S., Kamal, D., Lightstone, J. P., Gurnani, R., Shetty, P., Ramprasad, M., Laws, J., Shelton, M., & Ramprasad, R. (2020). Machine-learning predictions of polymer properties with Polymer Genome. *Journal of Applied Physics*, *128*(17), 171104. Advance online publication. doi:10.1063/5.0023759

Dogo, E. M., Nwulu, N. I., Twala, B., & Aigbavboa, C. (2019). A survey of machine learning methods applied to anomaly detection on drinking-water quality data. *Urban Water Journal*, *16*(3), 235–248. doi:10.1080/1573062X.2019.1637002

Dong, Y., Han, Z., Li, X., Ma, S., Gao, F., & Li, W. (2022). Joint Optimal Scheduling of Renewable Energy Regional Power Grid With Energy Storage System and Concentrated Solar Power Plant. *Frontiers in Energy Research*, *10*, 941074. doi:10.3389/fenrg.2022.941074

Dorfling, J., Bruder, S., Landon, P., Bondar, G., Rawther, C., Aranzazu-Suescún, C., Rocha, K., Siewert, S. B., Trahms, B., Le, C., Pederson, T., & Mangar, R. (2022). Satellite, Aerial, and Ground Sensor Fusion Experiment for the Management of Elephants, Rhinos, and Poaching Prevention. *AIAA Science and Technology Forum and Exposition. AIAA SciTech Forum, 2022*. Advance online publication. doi:10.2514/6.2022-1270

Dou, X., Fan, A., & Cai, L. (2021). Mobile contextual marketing in a museum setting. *Journal of Services Marketing*, *35*(5), 559–571. doi:10.1108/JSM-02-2020-0049

Dufo-López, R., Bernal-Agustín, J. L., & Contreras, J. (2007). Optimization of control strategies for stand-alone renewable energy systems with hydrogen storage. *Renewable Energy*, *32*(7), 1102–1126. doi:10.1016/j.renene.2006.04.013

Dushyant, K., Muskan, G., Gupta, A., & Pramanik, S. (2022). Utilizing Machine Learning and Deep Learning in Cyber security: An Innovative Approach. In M. M. Ghonge, S. Pramanik, R. Mangrulkar, & D. N. Le (Eds.), *Cyber security and Digital Forensics*. Wiley. doi:10.1002/9781119795667.ch12

Dutta, A., Pal, S., Banerjee, A., Karmakar, P., Mukherjee, A., Mukherjee, D., & Sahu, P. K. (2023). Survey on Irrigation Scheduling with Machine Learning. *Lecture Notes in Networks and Systems, 650 LNNS*, 797–806. doi:10.1007/978-981-99-0838-7_68

Dutta, S., Pramanik, S., & Bandyopadhyay, S. K. (2021). Prediction of Weight Gain during COVID-19 for Avoiding Complication in Health. *International Journal of Medical Science and Current Research*, *4*(3), 1042–1052.

Dwivedi, S., Kasliwal, P., & Soni, S. (2016). Comprehensive study of data analytics tools (RapidMiner, Weka, R tool, Knime). In *2016 Symposium on Colossal Data Analysis and Networking (CDAN)* (pp. 1-8). IEEE. 10.1109/CDAN.2016.7570894

Ebolor, A. (2023). Backcasting frugally innovative smart sustainable future cities. *Journal of Cleaner Production, 383*, 135300. doi:10.1016/j.jclepro.2022.135300

Eckroth, J. (2018). Teaching cybersecurity and python programming in a 5-day summer camp. *Journal of Computing Sciences in Colleges*, *33*(6), 29–39.

Ediger, V. Ş. (2019). An integrated review and analysis of multi-energy transition from fossil fuels to renewables. *Energy Procedia*, *156*, 2–6. doi:10.1016/j.egypro.2018.11.073

Effendi, M. J., & Ali, S. A. (2017). Click through rate prediction for contextual advertisment using linear regression. *arXiv preprint arXiv:1701.08744*.

Elif, A. K., Kaya, K., Yaslan, Y., & Oktug, S. F. (2021, November). LoRaWAN-aided waste-to-energy concept model in smart cities. In *2021 International Conference on Computer, Information and Telecommunication Systems (CITS)* (pp. 1-5). IEEE. 10.1109/CITS52676.2021.9618578

Ergunsah, S., Tümen, V., Kosunalp, S., & Demir, K. (2023). Energy-efficient animal tracking with multi-unmanned aerial vehicle path planning using reinforcement learning and wireless sensor networks. *Concurrency and Computation*, *35*(4), e7527. doi:10.1002/cpe.7527

Erin, O. A., Bamigboye, O. A., & Oyewo, B. (2022). Sustainable development goals (SDG) reporting: An analysis of disclosure. *Journal of Accounting in Emerging Economies*, *12*(5), 761–789. doi:10.1108/JAEE-02-2020-0037

Esteban, M., & Leary, D. (2012). Current developments and future prospects of offshore wind and ocean energy. *Applied Energy*, *90*(1), 128–136. doi:10.1016/j.apenergy.2011.06.011

Fahim, K. E., Kalinaki, K., & Shafik, W. (2023). Electronic Devices in the Artificial Intelligence of the Internet of Medical Things (AIoMT). In Handbook of Security and Privacy of AI-Enabled Healthcare Systems and Internet of Medical Things (pp. 41–62). CRC Press. https://doi.org/ doi:10.1201/9781003370321-3

Fahim, K. E., Kalinaki, K., De Silva, L. C., & Yassin, H. (2024). The role of machine learning in improving power distribution systems resilience. Future Modern Distribution Networks Resilience, 329–352. https://doi.org/ doi:10.1016/B978-0-443-16086-8.00012-9

Fang, B., Yu, J., Chen, Z., Osman, A. I., Farghali, M., Ihara, I., Hamza, E. H., Rooney, D. W., & Yap, P. S. (2023). Artificial intelligence for waste management in smart cities: a review. *Environmental Chemistry Letters, 21*(4), 1959–1989. doi:10.1007/s10311-023-01604-3

Fazri, M. F., Kusuma, L. B., Rahmawan, R. B., Fauji, H. N., & Camille, C. (2023). Implementing Artificial Intelligence to Reduce Marine Ecosystem Pollution. *IAIC Transactions on Sustainable Digital Innovation*, *4*(2), 101–108. doi:10.34306/itsdi.v4i2.579

Ferreira, B., Iten, M., & Silva, R. G. (2020). Monitoring sustainable development by means of earth observation data and machine learning: A review. *Environmental Sciences Europe*, *32*(1), 1–17. doi:10.1186/s12302-020-00397-4

Fuso Nerini, F., Slob, A., Engström, R. E., & Trutnevyte, E. (2019). A research and innovation agenda for zero-emission European cities. *Sustainability (Basel), 11*(6), 1692. doi:10.3390/su11061692

Gao, L., & Guan, L. (2023). Interpretability of Machine Learning: Recent Advances and Future Prospects. *IEEE MultiMedia, 30*(4), 105–118. Advance online publication. doi:10.1109/MMUL.2023.3272513

Garcia, C., López-Jiménez, P. A., Sánchez-Romero, F. J., & Pérez-Sánchez, M. (2023). Assessing water urban systems to the compliance of SDGs through sustainability indicators. Implementation in the valencian community. *Sustainable Cities and Society, 96*, 104704. doi:10.1016/j.scs.2023.104704

Germann, V., & Langergraber, G. (2022). Going beyond global indicators—Policy relevant indicators for SDG 6 targets in the context of Austria. *Sustainability (Basel), 14*(3), 1647. doi:10.3390/su14031647

Ghosh, A., Kumar, S., & Das, J. (2023). Impact of leachate and landfill gas on the ecosystem and health: Research trends and the way forward towards sustainability. *Journal of Environmental Management, 336*, 117708. doi:10.1016/j.jenvman.2023.117708 PMID:36913859

Ghosh, R., Bhunia, R., Pramanik, S., Mohanty, S., & Patnaik, P. K. (2023). Smart City Healthcare System for Survival Forecast for Cardiac Attack Situations using Machine Learning Techniques. In *Data-Driven Mathematical Modeling in Smart Cities*. IGI Global. doi:10.4018/978-1-6684-6408-3.ch019

Global Status Report. (2021). *Renewables 2021 Global Status Report-REN21*. Author.

Goralski, M. A., & Tan, T. K. (2020). Artificial intelligence and sustainable development. *International Journal of Management Education, 18*(1), 100330. doi:10.1016/j.ijme.2019.100330

Gray Group International. (2023). *Inequality: Navigating the Divides*. Gray Group International. https://www.graygroupintl.com/blog/inequality

Guardieiro, V., Raimundo, M. M., & Poco, J. (2023). Enforcing fairness using ensemble of diverse Pareto-optimal models. *Data Mining and Knowledge Discovery, 37*(5), 1930–1958. doi:10.1007/s10618-023-00922-y

Gupta, A., Verma, A., & Pramanik, S. (2022). Security Aspects in Advanced Image Processing Techniques for COVID-19. In S. Pramanik, A. Sharma, S. Bhatia, & D. N. Le (Eds.), *An Interdisciplinary Approach to Modern Network Security*. CRC Press.

Gu, Z., Li, W., Hanemann, M., Tsai, Y., Wutich, A., Westerhoff, P., Landes, L., Roque, A. D., Zheng, M., Velasco, C. A., & Porter, S. (2023). Applying machine learning to understand water security and water access inequality in underserved colonia communities. *Computers, Environment and Urban Systems, 102*, 101969. doi:10.1016/j.compenvurbsys.2023.101969

Hamza Zafar, M., Mujeeb Khan, N., Mansoor, M., Feroz Mirza, A., Kumayl Raza Moosavi, S., & Sanfilippo, F. (2022). Adaptive ML-based technique for renewable energy system power forecasting in hybrid PV-Wind farms power conversion systems. *Energy Conversion and Management, 258*, 115564. doi:10.1016/j.enconman.2022.115564

Hannan, M., Ali, J. A., Lipu, M. H., Mohamed, A., Ker, P. J., & Mahlia, T. I. (2020). Role of optimization algorithms based fuzzy controller in achieving induction motor performance enhancement. *Nature Communications, 11*(1), 1–11. doi:10.1038/s41467-020-17623-5 PMID:32733048

Haque, A., & Ramasetty, A. (2005). Theoretical study of stress transfer in carbon nanotube reinforced polymer matrix composites. *Composite Structures, 71*(1), 68–77. doi:10.1016/j.compstruct.2004.09.029

Hashemi-Amiri, O., Mohammadi, M., Rahmanifar, G., Hajiaghaei-Keshteli, M., Fusco, G., & Colombaroni, C. (2023). An allocation-routing optimization model for integrated solid waste management. *Expert Systems with Applications*, *227*, 120364. doi:10.1016/j.eswa.2023.120364

Hassan, Q., Sameen, A. Z., Salman, H. M., Al-Jiboory, A. K., & Jaszczur, M. (2023). *The role of renewable energy and articial intelligence towards environmental sustainability and net zero*. Academic Press.

Helbing, D. (2019). *Towards Digital Enlightenment*. Springer International Publishing. doi:10.1007/978-3-319-90869-4

Helbing, D., & Pournaras, E. (2015). Society: Build digital democracy. *Nature*, *527*(7576), 33–34. doi:10.1038/527033a PMID:26536943

He, Z., Guo, W., & Zhang, P. (2022). Performance prediction, optimal design and operational control of thermal energy storage using artificial intelligence methods. *Renewable & Sustainable Energy Reviews*, *156*, 111977. doi:10.1016/j.rser.2021.111977

Hiebl, M. R. (2023). Sample selection in systematic literature reviews of management research. *Organizational Research Methods*, *26*(2), 229–261. doi:10.1177/1094428120986851

Hmoud Al-Adhaileh, M., & Waselallah Alsaade, F. (2021). Modelling and prediction of water quality by using artificial intelligence. *Sustainability (Basel)*, *13*(8), 4259. doi:10.3390/su13084259

Hobensack, M., Song, J., Scharp, D., Bowles, K. H., & Topaz, M. (2023). Machine learning applied to electronic health record data in home healthcare: A scoping review. *International Journal of Medical Informatics*, *170*, 104978. doi:10.1016/j.ijmedinf.2022.104978 PMID:36592572

Ho, N. X., Le, T.-T., & Le, M. V. (2022). Development of artificial intelligence based model for the prediction of Young's modulus of polymer/carbon-nanotubes composites. *Mechanics of Advanced Materials and Structures*, *29*(27), 5965–5978. doi:10.1080/15376494.2021.1969709

Hou, Y., Wang, Q., Zhou, K., Zhang, L., & Tan, T. (2024). Integrated machine learning methods with oversampling technique for regional suitability prediction of waste-to-energy incineration projects. *Waste Management (New York, N.Y.)*, *174*, 251–262. doi:10.1016/j.wasman.2023.12.006 PMID:38070444

Hunter, J. D. (2007). Matplotlib: A 2D graphics environment. *Computing in Science & Engineering*, *9*(03), 90–95. doi:10.1109/MCSE.2007.55

Huo, J., & Peng, C. (2023). Depletion of natural resources and environmental quality: Prospects of energy use, energy imports, and economic growth hindrances. *Resources Policy*, *86*, 104049. doi:10.1016/j.resourpol.2023.104049

Hussain, Z., Mishra, J., & Vanacore, E. (2020). Waste to energy and circular economy: The case of anaerobic digestion. *Journal of Enterprise Information Management*, *33*(4), 817–838. doi:10.1108/JEIM-02-2019-0049

Hussein, H., Zhu, Y., Hassan, R. F., Nasab, A. R., & Elzarka, H. (2023). Optimizing Machine Learning Algorithms for Improving Prediction of Bridge Deck Deterioration: A Case Study of Ohio Bridges. *Buildings, 13*(6), 1517. doi:10.3390/buildings13061517

Hu, W. J., Fan, J., Du, Y. X., Li, B. S., Xiong, N., & Bekkering, E. (2020). MDFC–ResNet: An agricultural IoT system to accurately recognize crop diseases. *IEEE Access : Practical Innovations, Open Solutions*, *8*, 115287–115298. doi:10.1109/ACCESS.2020.3001237

Hu, X., Chen, S., Li, L., & Wang, Y. (2019). Deep reinforcement learning for dynamic pricing in ride-hailing platforms. *Transportation Research Part C, Emerging Technologies*, *106*, 288–304.

Ibrahim, H., Khattab, Z., Khattab, T., & Abraham, R. (2023). Expatriates' Housing Dispersal Outlook in a Rapidly Developing Metropolis Based on Urban Growth Predicted Using a Machine Learning Algorithm. *Housing Policy Debate*, *33*(3), 641–661. doi:10.1080/10511482.2021.1962939

IEA. (2022). *Renewables 2022 - December*. https://www.iea.org/reports/renewables-2022

IEA. (2023). *Renewable Energy Market Update - June*. https://www.iea.org/reports/renewable-energy-market-update-june-2023

Iniyan, S., Akhil Varma, V., & Teja Naidu, C. (2023). Crop yield prediction using machine learning techniques. *Advances in Engineering Software*, *175*, 103326. doi:10.1016/j.advengsoft.2022.103326

International Energy Agency. (2017). *Digitalization & Energy*. International Energy Agency.

Iqbal, W., Abbas, H., Daneshmand, M., Rauf, B., & Bangash, Y. A. (2020, October). An In-Depth Analysis of IoT Security Requirements, Challenges, and Their Countermeasures via Software-Defined Security. *IEEE Internet of Things Journal*, *7*(10), 10250–10276. doi:10.1109/JIOT.2020.2997651

Iris. (n.d.). https://archive.ics.uci.edu/ml/datasets/iris

Ivanovski, K., Hailemariam, A., & Smyth, R. (2021). The effect of renewable and non-renewable energy consumption on economic growth: Non-parametric evidence. *Journal of Cleaner Production*, *286*, 124956. doi:10.1016/j.jclepro.2020.124956

Jaakonmäki, R., Müller, O., & Vom Brocke, J. (2017, January). The impact of content, context, and creator on user engagement in social media marketing. *Proceedings of the ... Annual Hawaii International Conference on System Sciences. Annual Hawaii International Conference on System Sciences*, *50*, 1152–1160. doi:10.24251/HICSS.2017.136

Jain, A., Sharma, A., Jately, V., & Azzopardi, B. (Eds.). (2023). *Sustainable Energy Solutions with Artificial Intelligence, Blockchain Technology, and Internet of Things*. CRC Press. doi:10.1201/9781003356639

Jamei, M., Ali, M., Karbasi, M., Xiang, Y., Ahmadianfar, I., & Yaseen, Z. M. (2022). Designing a Multi-Stage Expert System for daily ocean wave energy forecasting: A multivariate data decomposition-based approach. *Applied Energy*, *326*, 119925. doi:10.1016/j.apenergy.2022.119925

Jamwal, P., Brown, R., Kookana, R., Drechsel, P., McDonald, R., Vorosmarty, C. J., van Vliet, M. T., & Bhaduri, A. (2019). *The future of urban clean water and sanitation*. Open Access.

Jayasingh, R., & Kumar, J. (2022). Speckle noise removal by SORAMA segmentation in Digital Image Processing to facilitate precise robotic surgery. *International Journal of Reliable and Quality E-Healthcare*, *11*(1), 1–19. Advance online publication. doi:10.4018/IJRQEH.295083

Jean, N., Burke, M., Xie, M., Davis, W. M., Lobell, D. B., & Ermon, S. (2016). Combining satellite imagery and machine learning to predict poverty. *Science*, *353*(6301), 790–794. doi:10.1126/science.aaf7894 PMID:27540167

Jha, S. K., Bilalovic, J., Jha, A., Patel, N., & Zhang, H. (2017). Renewable energy: Present research and future scope of Artificial Intelligence. *Renewable & Sustainable Energy Reviews*, *77*, 297–317. doi:10.1016/j.rser.2017.04.018

Johnson, M., & Brown, R. (2019). Behavior-Based Recommendations for Improving Cybersecurity Practices. *Journal of Information Security*, *12*(1), 45–58. https://www.jisjournal.org/article/behavior-based-recommendations-cybersecurity

Jones, N. (2018). How to stop data centres from gobbling up the world's electricity. *Nature*, *561*(7722), 163–166. doi:10.1038/d41586-018-06610-y PMID:30209383

Jukanti, A. K., Gowda, C. L., Rai, K. N., Manga, V. K., & Bhatt, R. K. (2016). Crops that feed the world 11. Pearl Millet (Pennisetum glaucum L.): An important source of food security, nutrition and health in the arid and semi-arid tropics. *Food Security*, *8*(2), 307–329. doi:10.1007/s12571-016-0557-y

Jupyter. (n.d.). https://jupyter.org

Kabugo, J. C., Jämsä-Jounela, S. L., Schiemann, R., & Binder, C. (2020). Industry 4.0 based process data analytics platform: A waste-to-energy plant case study. *International Journal of Electrical Power & Energy Systems*, *115*, 105508. doi:10.1016/j.ijepes.2019.105508

Kaddoura, S. (2022). Evaluation of Machine Learning Algorithm on Drinking Water Quality for Better Sustainability. *Sustainability (Basel)*, *14*(18), 11478. doi:10.3390/su141811478

Kalinaki, K., Fahadi, M., Alli, A. A., Shafik, W., Yasin, M., & Mutwalibi, N. (2023). Artificial Intelligence of Internet of Medical Things (AIoMT) in Smart Cities: A Review of Cybersecurity for Smart Healthcare. In Handbook of Security and Privacy of AI-Enabled Healthcare Systems and Internet of Medical Things (pp. 271–292). CRC Press. https://doi.org/ doi:10.1201/9781003370321-11

Kalinaki, K., Malik, O. A., & Ching Lai, D. T. (2023). FCD-AttResU-Net: An improved forest change detection in Sentinel-2 satellite images using attention residual U-Net. *International Journal of Applied Earth Observation and Geoinformation*, *122*, 103453. doi:10.1016/j.jag.2023.103453

Kalinaki, K., Malik, O. A., Lai, D. T. C., Sukri, R. S., & Wahab, R. B. H. A. (2023). Spatial-temporal mapping of forest vegetation cover changes along highways in Brunei using deep learning techniques and Sentinel-2 images. *Ecological Informatics*, *77*, 102193. doi:10.1016/j.ecoinf.2023.102193

Kalinaki, K., Shafik, W., Gutu, T. J. L., & Malik, O. A. (2023). Computer Vision and Machine Learning for Smart Farming and Agriculture Practices. In *Artificial Intelligence Tools and Technologies for Smart Farming and Agriculture Practices* (pp. 79–100). IGI Global. doi:10.4018/978-1-6684-8516-3.ch005

Kamyab, H., Klemeš, J. J., Van Fan, Y., & Lee, C. T. (2020). Transition to sustainable energy system for smart cities and industries. *Energy*, *207*, 118104. doi:10.1016/j.energy.2020.118104

Karnama, A., Haghighi, E. B., & Vinuesa, R. (2019). Organic data centers: A sustainable solution for computing facilities. *Results in Engineering*, *4*, 100063. doi:10.1016/j.rineng.2019.100063

Kaya, K., Ak, E., Yaslan, Y., & Oktug, S. F. (2021). Waste-to-Energy Framework: An intelligent energy recycling management. *Sustainable Computing : Informatics and Systems*, *30*, 100548. doi:10.1016/j.suscom.2021.100548

Kazeem, K. O., Olawumi, T. O., & Osunsanmi, T. (2023). Roles of Artificial Intelligence and Machine Learning in Enhancing Construction Processes and Sustainable Communities. *Buildings*, *13*(8), 2061. doi:10.3390/buildings13082061

Kenny, D., & Marshall, J. F. (2000). Contextual marketing. *Harvard Business Review*, *78*(6), 119–125. PMID:11184966

Keras. (n.d.). https://keras.io/

Khalil, R. A., Saeed, N., Masood, M., Fard, Y. M., Alouini, M. S., & Al-Naffouri, T. Y. (2021). Deep learning in the industrial internet of things: Potentials, challenges, and emerging applications. *IEEE Internet of Things Journal*, *8*(14), 11016–11040. doi:10.1109/JIOT.2021.3051414

Khan, A. H., López-Maldonado, E. A., Alam, S. S., Khan, N. A., López, J. R. L., Herrera, P. F. M., Abutaleb, A., Ahmed, S., & Singh, L. (2022). Municipal solid waste generation and the current state of waste-to-energy potential: State of art review. *Energy Conversion and Management*, *267*, 115905. doi:10.1016/j.enconman.2022.115905

Khan, A., Vibhute, A. D., Mali, S., & Patil, C. H. (2022). A systematic review on hyperspectral imaging technology with a machine and deep learning methodology for agricultural applications. *Ecological Informatics*, *69*, 101678. doi:10.1016/j.ecoinf.2022.101678

Khanh, P. T., Ngọc, T. H., & Pramanik, S. (2023). Future of Smart Agriculture Techniques and Applications. In A. Khang & I. G. I. Global (Eds.), *Advanced Technologies and AI-Equipped IoT Applications in High Tech Agriculture*. doi:10.4018/978-1-6684-9231-4.ch021

Khan, I. A., Keshk, M., Pi, D., Khan, N., Hussain, Y., & Soliman, H. (2022, September). Enhancing IoT networks protection: A robust security model for attack detection in Internet Industrial Control Systems. *Ad Hoc Networks*, *134*, 102930. doi:10.1016/j.adhoc.2022.102930

Khanna, N. Z., Zhou, N., Fridley, D., & Ke, J. (2016). Quantifying the potential impacts of China's power-sector policies on coal input and CO2 emissions through 2050: A bottom-up perspective. *Utilities Policy*, *41*, 128–138. doi:10.1016/j.jup.2016.07.001

Khan, S., & Narvekar, M. (2020). Disorder detection of tomato plant (solanum lycopersicum) using IoT and machine learning. *Journal of Physics: Conference Series*, *1432*(1), 012086. doi:10.1088/1742-6596/1432/1/012086

Khazaee, M., Derian, P., & Mouraud, A. (2022). A comprehensive study on Structural Health Monitoring (SHM) of wind turbine blades by instrumenting tower using machine learning methods. *Renewable Energy*, *199*, 1568–1579. doi:10.1016/j.renene.2022.09.032

Kitpo, N., & Inoue, M. (2018, March). Early rice disease detection and position mapping system using drone and IoT architecture. In *2018 12th South East Asian Technical University Consortium (SEATUC)* (Vol. 1, pp. 1-5). IEEE.

Kothari, R., Buddhi, D., & Sawhney, R. L. (2008). Comparison of environmental and economic aspects of various hydrogen production methods. *Renewable & Sustainable Energy Reviews*, *12*(2), 553–563. doi:10.1016/j.rser.2006.07.012

Kotler, P., Kartajaya, H., & Setiawan, I. (2021). *Marketing 5.0: Technology for humanity*. John Wiley & Sons.

Krizhevsky, A., & Hinton, G. (2009). *Learning multiple layers of features from tiny images*. Academic Press.

Kufel, A., & Kuciel, S. (2019). Composites based on polypropylene modified with natural fillers to increase stiffness. *Czasopismo Techniczne*, *1*, 187–195. doi:10.4467/2353737XCT.19.013.10053

Kumar, A., & Bansal, A. (2019) Software Fault Proneness Prediction Using Genetic Based Machine Learning Techniques. *2019 4th International Conference on Internet of Things: Smart Innovation and Usages (IoT-SIU),* 1-5. 10.1109/IoT-SIU.2019.8777494

Kumar, J. N., Li, Q., & Jun, Y. (2019). Challenges and opportunities of polymer design with machine learning and high throughput experimentation. *MRS Communications*, *9*(2), 537–544. doi:10.1557/mrc.2019.54

Kumar, M. (2020). Social, Economic, and Environmental Impacts of Renewable Energy Resources. In *Wind Solar Hybrid Renewable Energy System*. IntechOpen. doi:10.5772/intechopen.89494

Kumar, N., Kumar, D., Layek, A., & Yadav, S. (2022). Renewable energy and sustainable development. In *Artificial Intelligence for Renewable Energy Systems* (pp. 305–328). Elsevier. doi:10.1016/B978-0-323-90396-7.00011-0

Kumbhar, D., Palliyarayil, A., Reghu, D., Shrungar, D., Umapathy, S., & Sil, S. (2021). Rapid discrimination of porous bio-carbon derived from nitrogen rich biomass using Raman spectroscopy and artificial intelligence methods. *Carbon*, *178*, 792–802. doi:10.1016/j.carbon.2021.03.064

Kundu, N., Rani, G., Dhaka, V. S., Gupta, K., Nayak, S. C., Verma, S., Ijaz, M. F., & Woźniak, M. (2021). IoT and interpretable machine learning based framework for disease prediction in pearl millet. *Sensors (Basel), 21*(16), 5386. doi:10.3390/s21165386 PMID:34450827

Lal, B., Ravichandran, S., Kavin, R., Anil Kumar, N., Bordoloi, D., & Ganesh Kumar, R. (2023, June). IOT-based cyber security identification model through machine learning technique. *Measurement. Sensors*, *27*, 100791. doi:10.1016/j.measen.2023.100791

Lau, P. L., Nandy, M., & Chakraborty, S. (2023). Accelerating UN Sustainable Development Goals with AI-Driven Technologies: A Systematic Literature Review of Women's Healthcare. *Healthcare, 11*(3), 401. doi:10.3390/healthcare11030401

Le Mouël, C., & Forslund, A. (2017). How can we feed the world in 2050? A review of the responses from global scenario studies. *European Review of Agriculture Economics*, *44*(4), 541–591. doi:10.1093/erae/jbx006

Learndatasci. (n.d.). https://www.learndatasci.com/tutorials/convolutional-neural-networks-image-classification/

Lee, K., & Kim, S. (2018). Personalization in Cybersecurity Awareness Campaigns: A Case Study. *Cybersecurity Insights, 7*(2), 65-78. Retrieved from https://www.cyberinsights.com/article/personalization-cybersecurity-awareness

Lee, T., & Jun, J. (2007). The role of contextual marketing offer in Mobile commerce acceptance: Comparison between Mobile Commerce users and nonusers. *International Journal of Mobile Communications*, *5*(3), 339–356. doi:10.1504/IJMC.2007.012398

Le, T.-T. (2020). Multiscale Analysis of Elastic Properties of Nano-Reinforced Materials Exhibiting Surface Effects. Application for Determination of Effective Shear Modulus. *Journal of Composites Science*, *4*(4), 172. doi:10.3390/jcs4040172

Le, T.-T., & Le, M. V. (2021). Nanoscale Effect Investigation for Effective Bulk Modulus of Particulate Polymer Nanocomposites Using Micromechanical Framework. *Advances in Materials Science and Engineering*, *2021*, 1–13. doi:10.1155/2021/1563845

Lian, S., Cha, T., & Xu, Y. (2019). Enhancing geotargeting with temporal targeting, behavioral targeting and promotion for comprehensive contextual targeting. *Decision Support Systems*, *117*, 28–37. doi:10.1016/j.dss.2018.12.004

Li, F., Yigitcanlar, T., Nepal, M., Nguyen, K., & Dur, F. (2023). Machine learning and remote sensing integration for leveraging urban sustainability: A review and framework. *Sustainable Cities and Society*, *96*, 104653. doi:10.1016/j.scs.2023.104653

Lillicrap, T. P., Hunt, J. J., Pritzel, A., Heess, N., Erez, T., Tassa, Y., . . . Silver, D. (2015). Continuous control with deep reinforcement learning. *arXiv preprint arXiv:1509.02971.*

Lim, B., & Zohren, S. (2021). Time-series forecasting with deep learning: A survey. *Philosophical Transactions. Series A, Mathematical, Physical, and Engineering Sciences*, *379*(2194). doi:10.1098/rsta.2020.0209 PMID:33583273

Liu, Y., Pharr, M., & Salvatore, G. A. (2017). Lab-on-Skin: A Review of Flexible and Stretchable Electronics for Wearable Health Monitoring. *ACS Nano*, *11*(10), 9614–9635. doi:10.1021/acsnano.7b04898 PMID:28901746

Liu, Z., Sun, Y., Xing, C., Liu, J., He, Y., Zhou, Y., & Zhang, G. (2022). Artificial intelligence powered large-scale renewable integrations in multi-energy systems for carbon neutrality transition: Challenges and future perspectives. *Energy and AI*, *10*, 100195. doi:10.1016/j.egyai.2022.100195

Logman, M. (2008). Contextual intelligence and flexibility: Understanding today's marketing environment. *Marketing Intelligence & Planning*, *26*(5), 508–520. doi:10.1108/02634500810894343

Lopez, M. (2014). *Right-time experiences: Driving revenue with mobile and big data*. John Wiley & Sons. doi:10.1002/9781118914472

López-Pastor, J. A., Ruiz-Ruiz, A. J., García-Sánchez, A. J., & Gómez-Tornero, J. L. (2021). An automatized contextual marketing system based on a Wi-Fi indoor positioning system. *Sensors (Basel)*, *21*(10), 3495. doi:10.3390/s21103495 PMID:34067813

Luo, X. (2003). The performance implications of contextual marketing for electronic commerce. *Journal of Database Marketing & Customer Strategy Management*, *10*(3), 231–239. doi:10.1057/palgrave.jdm.3240112

Luo, X., & Seyedian, M. (2003). Contextual marketing and customer-orientation strategy for e-commerce: An empirical analysis. *International Journal of Electronic Commerce*, *8*(2), 95–118. doi:10.1080/10864415.2003.11044294

Lu, Y., Yi, S., Zeng, N., Liu, Y., & Zhang, Y. (2017). Identification of rice diseases using deep convolutional neural networks. *Neurocomputing*, *267*, 378–384. doi:10.1016/j.neucom.2017.06.023

Lythreatis, S., Singh, S. K., & El-Kassar, A. N. (2022). The digital divide: A review and future research agenda. *Technological Forecasting and Social Change*, *175*, 121359. doi:10.1016/j.techfore.2021.121359

Malkawi, R., Saifan, A. A., & Alhendawi, N., & BaniIsmaeel, A. (2020). Data mining tools evaluation based on their quality attributes. *International Journal of Advanced Science and Technology*, *29*(3), 13867–13890.

Mall, P. K., Pramanik, S., Srivastava, S., Faiz, M., Sriramulu, S., & Kumar, M. N. (2023). FuzztNet-Based Modelling Smart Traffic System in Smart Cities Using Deep Learning Models. In *Data-Driven Mathematical Modeling in Smart Cities*. IGI Global. doi:10.4018/978-1-6684-6408-3.ch005

Mandal, A., Dutta, S., & Pramanik, S. (2021). Machine Intelligence of Pi from Geometrical Figures with Variable Parameters using SCILab. In D. Samanta, R. R. Althar, S. Pramanik, & S. Dutta (Eds.), *Methodologies and Applications of Computational Statistics for Machine Learning* (pp. 38–63). IGI Global. doi:10.4018/978-1-7998-7701-1.ch003

Manigandan, P., Alam, M. S., Alagirisamy, K., Pachiyappan, D., Murshed, M., & Mahmood, H. (2022). Realizing the Sustainable Development Goals through technological innovation: juxtaposing the economic and environmental effects of financial development and energy use. *Environmental Science and Pollution Research*, *30*(3), 8239–8256. doi:10.1007/s11356-022-22692-8

Matplotlib. (n.d.). https://matplotlib.org/

Matschoss, P., Bayer, B., Thomas, H., & Marian, A. (2019). The German incentive regulation and its practical impact on the grid integration of renewable energy systems. *Renewable Energy*, *134*, 727–738. doi:10.1016/j.renene.2018.10.103

Matsuo, Y., LeCun, Y., Sahani, M., Precup, D., Silver, D., Sugiyama, M., Uchibe, E., & Morimoto, J. (2022). Deep learning, reinforcement learning, and world models. *Neural Networks*, *152*, 267–275. doi:10.1016/j.neunet.2022.03.037 PMID:35569196

Mazon-Olivo, B., & Pan, A. (2022). Internet of Things: State-of-the-art, Computing Paradigms and Reference Architectures. IEEE Latin America Transactions, 20(1), 49-63. doi:10.1109/TLA.2022.9662173

McCartney, L. N. (1989). New theoretical model of stress transfer between fibre and matrix in a uniaxially fibre-reinforced composite. *Proceedings of the Royal Society of London. A. Mathematical and Physical Sciences*, *425*(1868), 215–244. 10.1098/rspa.1989.0104

McDowall, W. (2012). Technology roadmaps for transition management: The case of hydrogen energy. *Technological Forecasting and Social Change*, *79*(3), 530–542. doi:10.1016/j.techfore.2011.10.002

McKinney, W. (2011). pandas: a foundational Python library for data analysis and statistics. *Python for High Performance and Scientific Computing*, *14*(9), 1-9.

Meijer, G., Ellyin, F., & Xia, Z. (2000). Aspects of residual thermal stress/strain in particle reinforced metal matrix composites. *Composites. Part B, Engineering*, *31*(1), 29–37. doi:10.1016/S1359-8368(99)00060-8

Mellit, A., Kalogirou, S. A., Hontoria, L., & Shaari, S. (2009). Artificial intelligence techniques for sizing photovoltaic systems: A review. *Renewable & Sustainable Energy Reviews*, *13*(2), 406–419. doi:10.1016/j.rser.2008.01.006

Mesa-Jiménez, J. J., Tzianoumis, A. L., Stokes, L., Yang, Q., & Livina, V. N. (2023). Long-term wind and solar energy generation forecasts, and optimisation of Power Purchase Agreements. *Energy Reports*, *9*, 292–302. doi:10.1016/j.egyr.2022.11.175

Meslie, Y., Enbeyle, W., Pandey, B. K., Pramanik, S., Pandey, D., Dadeech, P., Belay, A., & Saini, A. (2021). Machine Intelligence-based Trend Analysis of COVID-19 for Total Daily Confirmed Cases in Asia and Africa. In D. Samanta, R. R. Althar, S. Pramanik, & S. Dutta (Eds.), *Methodologies and Applications of Computational Statistics for Machine Learning* (pp. 164–185). IGI Global. doi:10.4018/978-1-7998-7701-1.ch009

Miao, Y., Chen, C., Pan, L., Han, Q.-L., Zhang, J., & Xiang, Y. (2022, September). Machine Learning Based Cyber Attacks Targeting on Controlled Information: A Survey. *ACM Computing Surveys*, *54*(7), 1–36. doi:10.1145/3465171

Mirhashemi, H., Heydari, M., Karami, O., Ahmadi, K., & Mosavi, A. (2023). Modeling Climate Change Effects on the Distribution of Oak Forests with Machine Learning. *Forests*, *14*(3), 469. doi:10.3390/f14030469

Mishra, A. R., Pamučar, D., Hezam, I. M., Chakrabortty, R. K., Rani, P., Božanić, D., & Ćirović, G. (2022). Interval-valued pythagorean fuzzy similarity measure-based complex proportional assessment method for waste-to-energy technology selection. *Processes (Basel, Switzerland)*, *10*(5), 1015. doi:10.3390/pr10051015

Mishra, S., Volety, D. R., Bohra, N., Alfarhood, S., & Safran, M. (2023). A smart and sustainable framework for millet crop monitoring equipped with disease detection using enhanced predictive intelligence. *Alexandria Engineering Journal*, *83*, 298–306. doi:10.1016/j.aej.2023.10.041

Mnih, V., Kavukcuoglu, K., Silver, D., Rusu, A. A., Veness, J., Bellemare, M. G., ... Petersen, S. (2015). Human-level control through deep reinforcement learning. *Nature*, *518*(7540), 529–533. doi:10.1038/nature14236 PMID:25719670

Modi, Y., Teli, R., Mehta, A., Shah, K., & Shah, M. (2022). A comprehensive review on intelligent traffic management using machine learning algorithms. *Innovative Infrastructure Solutions*, *7*(1), 1–14. doi:10.1007/s41062-021-00718-3

Moerland, T. M., Broekens, J., Plaat, A., & Jonker, C. M. (2023). Model-based Reinforcement Learning: A Survey. *Foundations and Trends® in Machine Learning*, *16*(1), 1–118. doi:10.1561/2200000086

Mohan, S., Thirumalai, C., & Srivastava, G. (2019). Effective Heart Disease Prediction Using Hybrid Machine Learning Techniques. *IEEE Access : Practical Innovations, Open Solutions*, *7*, 81542–81554. doi:10.1109/ACCESS.2019.2923707

Mohi, Z. R. (2020). Orange Data Mining as a tool to compare Classification Algorithms. *Dijlah Journal of Sciences and Engineering*, *3*(3), 13–23.

Mondal, D., Ratnaparkhi, A., Deshpande, A., Deshpande, V., Kshirsagar, A. P., & Pramanik, S. (2023). Applications, Modern Trends and Challenges of Multiscale Modelling in Smart Cities. In *Data-Driven Mathematical Modeling in Smart Cities*. IGI Global. doi:10.4018/978-1-6684-6408-3.ch001

Montesinos López, O. A., Montesinos López, A., & Crossa, J. (2022). Overfitting, Model Tuning, and Evaluation of Prediction Performance. *Multivariate Statistical Machine Learning Methods for Genomic Prediction*, 109–139. doi:10.1007/978-3-030-89010-0_4

Mordensky, S. P., Lipor, J. J., DeAngelo, J., Burns, E. R., & Lindsey, C. R. (2023). When less is more: How increasing the complexity of machine learning strategies for geothermal energy assessments may not lead toward better estimates. *Geothermics*, *110*, 102662. doi:10.1016/j.geothermics.2023.102662

Mousavi, S. M., & Beroza, G. C. (2023). *Machine Learning in Earthquake Seismology*. doi:10.1146/annurev-earth-071822-100323

Mukherjee, A. G., Wanjari, U. R., Chakraborty, R., Renu, K., Vellingiri, B., George, A., ... Gopalakrishnan, A. V. (2021). A review on modern and smart technologies for efficient waste disposal and management. *Journal of Environmental Management*, *297*, 113347. doi:10.1016/j.jenvman.2021.113347 PMID:34314963

Myers, K., & Secco, E. L. (2021). A Low-Cost Embedded Computer Vision System for the Classification of Recyclable Objects. *Lecture Notes on Data Engineering and Communications Technologies*, *61*, 11–30. doi:10.1007/978-981-33-4582-9_2

Nasir, O., Javed, R. T., Gupta, S., Vinuesa, R., & Qadir, J. (2023). Artificial intelligence and sustainable development goals nexus via four vantage points. *Technology in Society*, *72*, 102171. doi:10.1016/j.techsoc.2022.102171

Nassef, A. M., Sayed, E. T., Rezk, H., Inayat, A., Yousef, B. A. A., Abdelkareem, M. A., & Olabi, A. G. (2020). Developing a fuzzy-model with particle swarm optimization-based for improving the conversion and gasification rate of palm kernel shell. *Renewable Energy*, *166*, 125–135. doi:10.1016/j.renene.2020.11.037

Ngọc, T. H., Khanh, P. T., & Pramanik, S. (2023). Smart Agriculture using a Soil Monitoring System. In A. Khang (Ed.), Advanced Technologies and AI-Equipped IoT Applications in High Tech Agriculture. IGI Global. doi:10.4018/978-1-6684-9231-4.ch011

NgocT. T. H.PramanikS.KhanhP. T. (2023). *The Relationship between Gender and Climate Change in Vietnam*. The Seybold Report. DOI doi:10.17605/OSF.IO/KJBPT

Nguyen, T. T., Grote, U., Neubacher, F., Rahut, D. B., Do, M. H., & Paudel, G. P. (2023). Security risks from climate change and environmental degradation: Implications for sustainable land use transformation in the Global South. *Current Opinion in Environmental Sustainability*, *63*, 101322. doi:10.1016/j.cosust.2023.101322

Nhat-Duc, H., Nguyen, Q.-L., & Tran, V.-D. (2018). Automatic recognition of asphalt pavement cracks using metaheuristic optimized edge detection algorithms and convolution neural network. *Automation in Construction*, *94*, 203–213. doi:10.1016/j.autcon.2018.07.008

Nižetić, S., Šolić, P., González-de, D. L.-I., & Patrono, L. (2020). Internet of things (IoT): Opportunities, issues and challenges towards a smart and sustainable future. *Journal of Cleaner Production*, *274*, 122877. doi:10.1016/j.jclepro.2020.122877 PMID:32834567

Nkuna, S. G., Olwal, T. O., Chowdhury, S. D., & Ndambuki, J. M. (2024). A Review of Wastewater Sludge-to-Energy Generation focused on Thermochemical Technologies: An Improved Technological, Economical and Socio-Environmental Aspect. *Cleaner Waste Systems*, 100130.

Nolasco, I., Singh, S., Morfi, V., Lostanlen, V., Strandburg-Peshkin, A., Vidaña-Vila, E., Gill, L., Pamuła, H., Whitehead, H., Kiskin, I., Jensen, F. H., Morford, J., Emmerson, M. G., Versace, E., Grout, E., Liu, H., Ghani, B., & Stowell, D. (2023). Learning to detect an animal sound from five examples. *Ecological Informatics*, *77*, 102258. doi:10.1016/j.ecoinf.2023.102258

Norouzzadeh, M. S., Nguyen, A., Kosmala, M., Swanson, A., Palmer, M. S., Packer, C., & Clune, J. (2018). Automatically identifying, counting, and describing wild animals in camera-trap images with deep learning. *Proceedings of the National Academy of Sciences of the United States of America*, *115*(25), E5716–E5725. doi:10.1073/pnas.1719367115 PMID:29871948

NumPy. (n.d.). https://numpy.org/

Nunkoo, R., Sharma, A., Rana, N. P., Dwivedi, Y. K., & Sunnassee, V. A. (2023). Advancing sustainable development goals through interdisciplinarity in sustainable tourism research. *Journal of Sustainable Tourism*, *31*(3), 735–759. doi:10.1080/09669582.2021.2004416

Oikonomidis, A., Catal, C., & Kassahun, A. (2023). Deep learning for crop yield prediction: A systematic literature review. *New Zealand Journal of Crop and Horticultural Science*, *51*(1), 1–26. doi:10.1080/01140671.2022.2032213

Okken, B. (2022). *Python Testing with pytest*. Pragmatic Bookshelf.

Oliphant, T. E. (2006). *Guide to numpy* (Vol. 1). Trelgol Publishing.

Ooko, S. O., Muyonga Ogore, M., Nsenga, J., & Zennaro, M. (2021). TinyML in Africa: Opportunities and Challenges. *2021 IEEE Globecom Workshops, GC Wkshps 2021 - Proceedings*. doi:10.1109/GCWkshps52748.2021.9682107

Pagano, T. P., Loureiro, R. B., Lisboa, F. V. N., Peixoto, R. M., Guimarães, G. A. S., Cruz, G. O. R., Araujo, M. M., Santos, L. L., Cruz, M. A. S., Oliveira, E. L. S., Winkler, I., & Nascimento, E. G. S. (2023). Bias and Unfairness in Machine Learning Models: A Systematic Review on Datasets, Tools, Fairness Metrics, and Identification and Mitigation Methods. *Big Data and Cognitive Computing*, *7*(1), 15. doi:10.3390/bdcc7010015

Page, M. J., Moher, D., Bossuyt, P. M., Boutron, I., Hoffmann, T. C., Mulrow, C. D., ... & McKenzie, J. E. (2021). PRISMA 2020 explanation and elaboration: updated guidance and exemplars for reporting systematic reviews. *BMJ, 372*.

Page, M. J., McKenzie, J. E., Bossuyt, P. M., Boutron, I., Hoffmann, T. C., Mulrow, C. D., Shamseer, L., Tetzlaff, J. M., Akl, E. A., Brennan, S. E., Chou, R., Glanville, J., Grimshaw, J. M., Hróbjartsson, A., Lalu, M. M., Li, T., Loder, E. W., Mayo-Wilson, E., McDonald, S., ... Moher, D. (2021). The PRISMA 2020 statement: An updated guideline for reporting systematic reviews. *International Journal of Surgery*, *88*, 105906. doi:10.1016/j.ijsu.2021.105906 PMID:33789826

Palmer, A. (2010). Customer experience management: A critical review of an emerging idea. *Journal of Services Marketing*, *24*(3), 196–208. doi:10.1108/08876041011040604

Pandas. (n.d.). https://pandas.pydata.org/

Pandey, B. K., Pandey, D., Nassa, V. K., George, A. S., Pramanik, S., & Dadheech, P. (2023). Applications for the Text Extraction Method of Complex Degraded Images. In The Impact of Thrust Technologies on Image Processing. Nova Publishers.

Pandey, B. K., Pandey, D., Wairya, S., Agarwal, G., Dadeech, P., Dogiwal, S. R., & Pramanik, S. (2022). Application of Integrated Steganography and Image Compressing Techniques for Confidential Information Transmission. Cyber Security and Network Security. , Eds, Wiley. doi:10.1002/9781119812555.ch8

Pandey, B. K., Pandey, D., Nassa, V. K., Hameed, A. S., George, A. S., Dadheech, P., & Pramanik, S. (2023). A Review of Various Text Extraction Algorithms for Images. In *The Impact of Thrust Technologies on Image Processing*. Nova Publishers. doi:10.52305/ATJL4552

Papon, A., Saalwächter, K., Schäler, K., Guy, L., Lequeux, F., & Montes, H. (2011). Low-Field NMR Investigations of Nanocomposites: Polymer Dynamics and Network Effects. *Macromolecules*, *44*(4), 913–922. doi:10.1021/ma102486x

Park, Y. H., Choi, S. H., Kwon, Y. J., Kwon, S. W., Kang, Y. J., & Jun, T. H. (2023). Detection of Soybean Insect Pest and a Forecasting Platform Using Deep Learning with Unmanned Ground Vehicles. *Agronomy (Basel), 13*(2), 477. doi:10.3390/agronomy13020477

Pedregosa, F., Varoquaux, G., Gramfort, A., Michel, V., Thirion, B., Grisel, O., ... Duchesnay, É. (2011). Scikit-learn: Machine learning in Python. *Journal of Machine Learning Research, 12*, 2825–2830.

Pethani, F., & Dunn, A. G. (2023). Natural language processing for clinical notes in dentistry: A systematic review. *Journal of Biomedical Informatics, 138*, 104282. doi:10.1016/j.jbi.2023.104282 PMID:36623780

Petrescu, M., & Krishen, A. S. (2018). Analyzing the analytics: Data privacy concerns. *Journal of Marketing Analytics, 6*(2), 41–43. doi:10.1057/s41270-018-0034-x

Ping, Y. (2019). Contextual marketing in the mobile internet environment: A literature review and prospects. *Foreign Economics & Management, 41*(05), 3–16.

Piou, C., & Marescot, L. (2023). Spatiotemporal risk forecasting to improve locust management. *Current Opinion in Insect Science, 56*, 101024. doi:10.1016/j.cois.2023.101024 PMID:36958588

Pokropivny, V. V., & Skorokhod, V. V. (2007). Classification of nanostructures by dimensionality and concept of surface forms engineering in nanomaterial science. *Materials Science and Engineering C, 27*(5–8), 990–993. doi:10.1016/j.msec.2006.09.023

Pramanik, S. (2022). An Effective Secured Privacy-Protecting Data Aggregation Method in IoT. In M. O. Odhiambo & W. Mwashita (Eds.), Achieving Full Realization and Mitigating the Challenges of the Internet of Things. IGI Global. doi:10.4018/978-1-7998-9312-7.ch008

Pramanik, S. (2023). Intelligent Farming Utilizing a Soil Tracking Device. In A. K. Sharma, N. Chanderwal, & R. Khan (Eds.), Convergence of Cloud Computing, AI and Agricultural Science. IGI Global. doi:10.4018/979-8-3693-0200-2.ch009

Pramanik, S., & Obaid, A. J. (2023). Applications of Big Data in Clinical Applications. *AIP Conference Proceedings, 2591*, 030086. 10.1063/5.0119414

Pramanik, S., Joardar, S., Jena, O. P., & Obaid, A. J. (2023). An Analysis of the Operations and Confrontations of Using Green IT in Sustainable Farming. *AIP Conference Proceedings, 2591*, 040020. 10.1063/5.0119513

Pramanik, S. (2022). Carpooling Solutions using Machine Learning Tools. In *Handbook of Research on Evolving Designs and Innovation in ICT and Intelligent Systems for Real-World Applications*. IGI Global. doi:10.4018/978-1-7998-9795-8.ch002

Pramanik, S. (2023). An Adaptive Image Steganography Approach depending on Integer Wavelet Transform and Genetic Algorithm. *Multimedia Tools and Applications, 82*(22), 34287–34319. Advance online publication. doi:10.1007/s11042-023-14505-y

Pramanik, S., & Bandyopadhyay, S. (2023). Analysis of Big Data. In *Encyclopedia of Data Science and Machine Learning*. Global. doi:10.4018/978-1-7998-9220-5.ch006

Pramanik, S., & Bandyopadhyay, S. (2023). Identifying Disease and Diagnosis in Females using Machine Learning. In *Encyclopedia of Data Science and Machine Learning*. Global. doi:10.4018/978-1-7998-9220-5.ch187

Pramanik, S., Galety, M. G., Samanta, D., & Joseph, N. P. (2022). Data Mining Approaches for Decision Support Systems. *3rd International Conference on Emerging Technologies in Data Mining and Information Security.*

Pramanik, S., Sagayam, K. M., & Jena, O. P. (2021). *Machine Learning Frameworks in Cancer Detection.* ICCSRE. doi:10.1051/e3sconf/202129701073

Pramanik, S., Singh, R. P., & Ghosh, R. (2020). Application of Bi-orthogonal Wavelet Transform and Genetic Algorithm in Image Steganography. *Multimedia Tools and Applications*, *79*(25-26), 17463–17482. Advance online publication. doi:10.1007/s11042-020-08676-1

Pramanik, S., & Suresh Raja, S. (2020). A Secured Image Steganography using Genetic Algorithm. *Advances in Mathematics: Scientific Journal*, *9*(7), 4533–4541. doi:10.37418/amsj.9.7.22

Praveenkumar, S., Veeraiah, V., Pramanik, S., Basha, S. M., Lira Neto, A. V., De Albuquerque, V. H. C., & Gupta, A. (2023). *Prediction of Patients' Incurable Diseases Utilizing Deep Learning Approaches, ICICC 2023.* Springer. doi:10.1007/978-981-99-3315-0_4

Purvis, B., Mao, Y., & Robinson, D. (2019). Three pillars of sustainability: In search of conceptual origins. *Sustainability Science*, *14*(3), 681–695. doi:10.1007/s11625-018-0627-5

PyCharm. (n.d.). https://www.jetbrains.com/pycharm/

Pynam, V., Spanadna, R. R., & Srikanth, K. (2018). An extensive study of data analysis tools (rapid miner, weka, r tool, knime, orange). *International Journal on Computer Science and Engineering*, *5*(9), 4–11. doi:10.14445/23488387/IJCSE-V5I9P102

Ramcharan, A., Baranowski, K., McCloskey, P., Ahmed, B., Legg, J., & Hughes, D. (2017). Using transfer learning for image-based cassava disease detection. *Frontiers in Plant Science*, 8.

Ramchurn, S. D., Vytelingum, P., Rogers, A., & Jennings, N. R. (2012). Putting the 'smarts' into the smart grid: A grand challenge for artificial intelligence. *Communications of the ACM*, *55*, 86–97. doi:10.1145/2133806.2133825

Rana, M., & Bhushan, M. (2023). Machine learning and deep learning approach for medical image analysis: Diagnosis to detection. *Multimedia Tools and Applications*, *82*(17), 26731–26769. doi:10.1007/s11042-022-14305-w PMID:36588765

Rangarajan, A. K., Purushothaman, R., & Ramesh, A. (2018). Tomato crop disease classification using pre-trained deep learning algorithm. *Procedia Computer Science*, *133*, 1040–1047. doi:10.1016/j.procs.2018.07.070

Raschka, S., Patterson, J., & Nolet, C. (2020). Machine learning in python: Main developments and technology trends in data science, machine learning, and artificial intelligence. *Information (Basel)*, *11*(4), 193. doi:10.3390/info11040193

Ratra, R., & Gulia, P. (2020). Experimental evaluation of open source data mining tools (WEKA and Orange). *Int. J. Eng. Trends Technol*, *68*(8), 30–35. doi:10.14445/22315381/IJETT-V68I8P206S

Reepu, K. S., Chaudhary, M. G., Gupta, K. G., Pramanik, S., & Gupta, A. (2023). Information Security and Privacy in IoT. In Handbook of Research in Advancements in AI and IoT Convergence Technologies. IGI Global.

Reepu, S. (2023). Information Security and Privacy in IoT. In Handbook of Research in Advancements in AI and IoT Convergence Technologies. IGI Global.

Rehman, A. (2019). The nexus of electricity access, population growth, economic growth in Pakistan and projection through 2040. *Int. J. Energy Sect. Manag.*

Repovienė, R. (2017). Role of content marketing in a value creation for customer context: Theoretical analysis. *International Journal on Global Business Management & Research*, *6*(2), 37.

Robert, B., & Brown, E. B. (2006). Book Review: Wind Energy Explained: Theory, Design and Application. In Wind Engineering (Vol. 30, Issue 2). doi:10.1260/030952406778055054

Rosário, A. T., Lopes, P. R., & Rosário, F. S. (2023). Metaverse in Marketing: Challenges and Opportunities. Handbook of Research on AI-Based Technologies and Applications in the Era of the Metaverse, 204-227.

Roy, A., & Pramanik, S. (2023). A Review of the Hydrogen Fuel Path to Emission Reduction in the Surface Transport Industry. *International Journal of Hydrogen Energy*.

Roy, P., Chen, P.-C., Periasamy, A. P., Chen, Y.-N., & Chang, H.-T. (2015). Photoluminescent carbon nanodots: Synthesis, physicochemical properties and analytical applications. *Materials Today*, *18*(8), 447–458. doi:10.1016/j.mattod.2015.04.005

Runge, J., & Saloux, E. (2023). A comparison of prediction and forecasting artificial intelligence models to estimate the future energy demand in a district heating system. *Energy*, *269*, 126661. doi:10.1016/j.energy.2023.126661

Russell, S., Dewey, D., & Tegmark, M. (2015). Research priorities for robust and beneficial artificial intelligence. *AI Magazine*, *34*(4), 105–114. doi:10.1609/aimag.v36i4.2577

Ryan, M., Isakhanyan, G., & Tekinerdogan, B. (2023). An interdisciplinary approach to artificial intelligence in agriculture. *NJAS: Impact in Agricultural and Life Sciences*, *95*(1), 2168568. Advance online publication. doi:10.1080/27685241.2023.2168568

Sahoo, N. G., Rana, S., Cho, J. W., Li, L., & Chan, S. H. (2010). Polymer nanocomposites based on functionalized carbon nanotubes. *Progress in Polymer Science*, *35*(7), 837–867. doi:10.1016/j.progpolymsci.2010.03.002

Sai Ramesh, A., Vigneshwar, S., Vickram, S., Manikandan, S., Subbaiya, R., Karmegam, N., & Kim, W. (2023). Artificial intelligence driven hydrogen and battery technologies – A review. *Fuel*, *337*, 126862. doi:10.1016/j.fuel.2022.126862

Salim, H. K., Padfield, R., Hansen, S. B., Mohamad, S. E., Yuzir, A., Syayuti, K., Tham, M. H., & Papargyropoulou, E. (2018). Global trends in environmental management system and ISO14001 research. *Journal of Cleaner Production*, *170*, 645–653. doi:10.1016/j.jclepro.2017.09.017

Sarker, T. R., Pattnaik, F., Nanda, S., Dalai, A. K., Meda, V., & Naik, S. (2021). Hydrothermal pretreatment technologies for lignocellulosic biomass: A review of steam explosion and subcritical water hydrolysis. *Chemosphere*, *284*, 131372. doi:10.1016/j.chemosphere.2021.131372 PMID:34323806

Sayad, Y. O., Mousannif, H., & Al Moatassime, H. (2019). Predictive modeling of wildfires: A new dataset and machine learning approach. *Fire Safety Journal*, *104*, 130–146. doi:10.1016/j.firesaf.2019.01.006

Schizas, N., Karras, A., Karras, C., & Sioutas, S. (2022). TinyML for Ultra-Low Power AI and Large Scale IoT Deployments: A Systematic Review. *Future Internet*, *14*(12), 363. doi:10.3390/fi14120363

Schmelzer. (2022). *Comment construire un modèle de Machine Learning en 7 étapes*. LeMagIT. https://www.lemagit.fr/conseil/Comment-construire-un-modele-de-Machine-Learning-en-7-etapes

Scikit-learn. (n.d.). https://scikit-learn.org/stable/

Seo, Y., Kim, S., Kisi, O., & Singh, V. P. (2015). Daily water level forecasting using wavelet decomposition and artificial intelligence techniques. *Journal of Hydrology (Amsterdam)*, *520*, 224–243. doi:10.1016/j.jhydrol.2014.11.050

Shamseer, L., Moher, D., Clarke, M., Ghersi, D., Liberati, A., Petticrew, M., Shekelle, P., & Stewart, L. A. (2015). Preferred reporting items for systematic review and meta-analysis protocols (PRISMA-P) 2015: Elaboration and explanation. *BMJ (Clinical Research Ed.)*, *349*(jan02 1), 349. doi:10.1136/bmj.g7647 PMID:25555855

Sharma, N., Ingole, S., Pokhariya, H. S., Parmar, A., Shilpa, K., Reddy, U., & Hussny, H. A. (2023). From Waste to Worth Management: A Comprehensive Intelligent Approach to Resource Utilization and Waste Minimization. In E3S Web of Conferences (Vol. 453, p. 01029). EDP Sciences. doi:10.1051/e3sconf/202345301029

Sharma, V., & Kumar, S. (2023, May). Role of Artificial Intelligence (AI) to Enhance the Security and Privacy of Data in Smart Cities. In *2023 3rd International Conference on Advance Computing and Innovative Technologies in Engineering (ICACITE)* (pp. 596-599). IEEE. 10.1109/ICACITE57410.2023.10182455

Sherif, M., Abrar, M., Baig, F., & Kabeer, S. (2023). Gulf Cooperation Council countries' water and climate research to strengthen UN's SDGs 6 and 13. *Heliyon*, *9*(3), e14584. doi:10.1016/j.heliyon.2023.e14584 PMID:36967941

Shi, C., Jing, X. U., Roberts, N. J., Liu, D., & Jiang, G. (2023). Individual automatic detection and identification of big cats with the combination of different body parts. *Integrative Zoology*, *18*(1), 157–168. doi:10.1111/1749-4877.12641 PMID:35276755

Shi, Z., He, S., Sun, J., Chen, T., Chen, J., & Dong, H. (2023, January). An Efficient Multi-Task Network for Pedestrian Intrusion Detection. *IEEE Transactions on Intelligent Vehicles*, *8*(1), 649–660. doi:10.1109/TIV.2022.3166911

Shobana, G., & Nikkath Bushra, S. (2021). Prediction of Cardiovascular Disease using Multiple Machine Learning Platforms. *2021 International Conference on Innovative Computing, Intelligent Communication and Smart Electrical Systems (ICSES).* 10.1109/ICSES52305.2021.9633797

Siewert, S. B., Mangar, R., Alshehri, F., Lippmann, M., & Dorfling, J. (2023). *Acoustic*, Seismic, and Visual Camera Sensor Fusion Experiments for Large Animal Detection and Tracking with Scalability. doi:10.2514/6.2023-1117

Sifat, F. H., Mahzabin, R., Anjum, S., Nayan, A.-A., & Kibria, M. G. (2022). IoT and Machine Learning-Based Hypoglycemia Detection System. *2022 International Conference on Innovations in Science, Engineering and Technology (ICISET),* 222-226. 10.1109/ICISET54810.2022.9775890

Sille, R., Sharma, B., Choudhury, T., Toe, T. T., & Um, J.-S. (2023). *Survey on DL Methods for Flood Prediction in Smart Cities*. doi:10.4018/978-1-6684-6408-3.ch020

Silver, D., Huang, A., Maddison, C. J., Guez, A., Sifre, L., Driessche, G. V. D., ... Hassabis, D. (2017). Mastering the game of Go without human knowledge. *Nature*, *550*(7676), 354–359. doi:10.1038/nature24270 PMID:29052630

Sinha, M., Chacko, E., Makhija, P., & Pramanik, S. (2021). Energy Efficient Smart Cities with Green IoT. In C. Chakrabarty (Ed.), *Green Technological Innovation for Sustainable Smart Societies: Post Pandemic Era*. Springer. doi:10.1007/978-3-030-73295-0_16

Smith, J., & Johnson, A. (2017). Leveraging Contextual Marketing for Enhanced Cybersecurity Education. *Journal of Cybersecurity Studies*, *15*(3), 123–138. https://www.jcsjournal.org/article/leveraging-contextual-marketing

Smith, T., Williams, T., Lowe, S., Rod, M., & Hwang, K. S. (2015). Context into text into context: Marketing practice into theory; marketing theory into practice. *Marketing Intelligence & Planning*, *33*(7), 1027–1046. doi:10.1108/MIP-05-2014-0091

Solanki, A., Agrawal, H., & Khare, K. (2015). Predictive analysis of water quality parameters using deep learning. *International Journal of Computer Applications, 125*(9).

Som, T. (2021). Sustainability in Energy Economy and Environment: Role of AI Based Techniques. doi:10.1007/978-3-030-72929-5_31

Spyder. (n.d.). https://www.spyder-ide.org/

Srinath, K. R. (2017). Python–the fastest growing programming language. *International Research Journal of Engineering and Technology*, *4*(12), 354–357.

Srivastava, R. K., Shetti, N. P., Reddy, K. R., & Aminabhavi, T. M. (2020). Sustainable energy from waste organic matters via efficient microbial processes. *Science of the Total Environment, 722*, 137927.

Srivastava, S. K. (2020.) Application of artificial intelligence in renewable energy. In *2020 International Conference on Computational Performance Evaluation (ComPE)*. IEEE.

Stankovich, S., Dikin, D. A., Piner, R. D., Kohlhaas, K. A., Kleinhammes, A., Jia, Y., Wu, Y., Nguyen, S. T., & Ruoff, R. S. (2007). Synthesis of graphene-based nanosheets via chemical reduction of exfoliated graphite oxide. *Carbon*, *45*(7), 1558–1565. doi:10.1016/j.carbon.2007.02.034

Subramani, S., Varshney, N., Anand, M. V., Soudagar, M. E. M., Al-keridis, L. A., Upadhyay, T. K., Alshammari, N., Saeed, M., Subramanian, K., Anbarasu, K., & Rohini, K. (2023). Cardiovascular diseases prediction by machine learning incorporation with deep learning. *Frontiers in Medicine*, *10*, 1–9. doi:10.3389/fmed.2023.1150933 PMID:37138750

Sutton, R. S., & Barto, A. G. (2018). *Reinforcement learning: An introduction*. MIT Press.

Swathika, O. G., Karthikeyan, K., & Padmanaban, S. (Eds.). (2023). IoT and Analytics in Renewable Energy Systems (Volume 2): AI, ML and IoT Deployment in Sustainable Smart Cities. CRC Press.

Sweezey, M. (2020). *The Context Marketing Revolution: How to Motivate Buyers in the Age of Infinite Media*. Harvard Business Press.

Szpilko, D., de la Torre Gallegos, A., Jimenez Naharro, F., Rzepka, A., & Remiszewska, A. (2023). Waste Management in the Smart City: Current Practices and Future Directions. *Resources*, *12*(10), 115. doi:10.3390/resources12100115

Tai, P., Wu, F., Chen, R., Zhu, J., Wang, X., & Zhang, M. (2023). Effect of herbaceous plants on the response of loose silty sand slope under rainfall. *Bulletin of Engineering Geology and the Environment*, *82*(1), 42. doi:10.1007/s10064-023-03066-x

Tajjour, S., Chandel, S. S., Malik, H., Alotaibi, M. A., Marquez, F. P. G., & Afthanorhan, A. (2023). *Short-Term Solar Irradiance Forecasting Using Deep Learning Techniques: A Comprehensive case Study*. IEEE. doi:10.1109/ACCESS.2023.3325292

Takkouche, B., & Norman, G. (2011). PRISMA statement. *Epidemiology (Cambridge, Mass.)*, *22*(1), 128. doi:10.1097/EDE.0b013e3181fe7999 PMID:21150360

Tavakoli, S., Khojasteh, D., Haghani, M., & Hirdaris, S. (2023). A review on the progress and research directions of ocean engineering. *Ocean Engineering*, *272*, 113617. doi:10.1016/j.oceaneng.2023.113617

Teh, J. S., Teoh, Y. H., How, H. G., Le, T. D., Jason, Y. J. J., Nguyen, H. T., & Loo, D. L. (2021). The potential of sustainable biomass producer gas as a waste-to-energy alternative in Malaysia. *Sustainability (Basel)*, *13*(7), 3877. doi:10.3390/su13073877

Tensorflow. (n.d.). https://www.tensorflow.org/

Thanh Duong, H., Chi Phan, H., Le, T.-T., & Duc Bui, N. (2020). Optimization design of rectangular concrete-filled steel tube short columns with Balancing Composite Motion Optimization and data-driven model. *Structures*, *28*, 757–765. doi:10.1016/j.istruc.2020.09.013

The World Bank. (2019). *Access to electricity (% of population)*. Author.

Thorat, A., Kumari, S., & Valakunde, N. D. (2017, December). An IoT based smart solution for leaf disease detection. In *2017 international conference on big data, IoT and data science (BID)* (pp. 193-198). IEEE.

Tiong, S. K., Indra Mahlia, T. M., & Muttaqi, K. M. (2021). Impact of renewable energy utilization and artificial intelligence in achieving sustainable development goals. *Energy Reports*, *7*, 5359–5373. doi:10.1016/j.egyr.2021.08.172

Tortajada, C. (2020). Contributions of recycled wastewater to clean water and sanitation Sustainable Development Goals. *NPJ Clean Water*, *3*(1), 22. doi:10.1038/s41545-020-0069-3

Tortajada, C., & Biswas, A. K. (2018). Achieving universal access to clean water and sanitation in an era of water scarcity: Strengthening contributions from academia. *Current Opinion in Environmental Sustainability*, *34*, 21–25. doi:10.1016/j.cosust.2018.08.001

Tougui, I., Jilbab, A., & El Mhamdi, J. (2020). Heart disease classification using data mining tools and machine learning techniques. *Health and Technology*, *10*(5), 1137–1144. doi:10.1007/s12553-020-00438-1

Tran, B., Picek, S., & Xue, B. (2017). Automatic Feature Construction for Network Intrusion Detection. In Lecture Notes in Computer Science: Vol. 10593. *Simulated Evolution and Learning. SEAL 2017*. Springer. doi:10.1007/978-3-319-68759-9_46

Tsagkis, P., Bakogiannis, E., & Nikitas, A. (2023). Analysing urban growth using machine learning and open data: An artificial neural network modelled case study of five Greek cities. *Sustainable Cities and Society*, *89*, 104337. doi:10.1016/j.scs.2022.104337

Tu, Y., Neuhofer, B., & Viglia, G. (2018). When co-creation pays: Stimulating engagement to increase revenues. *International Journal of Contemporary Hospitality Management*, *30*(4), 2093–2111. doi:10.1108/IJCHM-09-2016-0494

Tyagi, V. K., & Lo, S. L. (2013). Sludge: A waste or renewable source for energy and resources recovery? *Renewable & Sustainable Energy Reviews*, *25*, 708–728. doi:10.1016/j.rser.2013.05.029

Um, N. H. (2017). The effects of social presence, contextual congruence and source credibility in evaluation of online advertising on news websites. *International Journal of Internet Marketing and Advertising*, *11*(1), 64–82. doi:10.1504/IJIMA.2017.082999

UN General Assembly (UNGA). (2015). A/RES/70/1Transforming our world: The 2030 Agenda for Sustainable Development. *Resolut*, *25*, 1–35.

Van der Walt, S., Schönberger, J. L., Nunez-Iglesias, J., Boulogne, F., Warner, J. D., Yager, N., . . . Yu, T. (2014). Scikit-image: image processing in Python. *PeerJ*, *2*, e453.

Vanessa, N., & Japutra, A. (2018). *Contextual marketing based on customer buying pattern in grocery E-Commerce: The case of Bigbasket. com*. ASEAN Marketing Journal.

Vashishth, T. K., Sharma, V., Sharma, K. K., Kumar, B., Chaudhary, S., & Panwar, R. (2024). Intelligent Resource Allocation and Optimization for Industrial Robotics Using AI and Blockchain. In AI and Blockchain Applications in Industrial Robotics (pp. 82-110). IGI Global. doi:10.4018/979-8-3693-0659-8.ch004

Veeraiah, V., Talukdar, V., Manikandan, K., Talukdar, S. B., Solavande, V. D., Pramanik, S., & Gupta, A. (2023). Machine Learning Frameworks in Carpooling. In Handbook of Research on AI and Machine Learning Applications in Customer Support and Analytics. IGI Global. doi:10.4018/978-1-6684-7105-0.ch009

Veeraiah, V., Shiju, D. J., Ramesh, J. V. N., Ganesh, K. R., Pramanik, S., & Pandey, D. (2023). *Healthcare Cloud Services in Image Processing. In Thrust Technologies' Effect on Image Processing*. IGI Global.

Vidya Chellam, V., Veeraiah, V., Khanna, A., Sheikh, T. H., Pramanik, S., & Dhabliya, D. (2023). *A Machine Vision-based Approach for Tuberculosis Identification in Chest X-Rays Images of Patients, ICICC 2023*. Springer. doi:10.1007/978-981-99-3315-0_3

Vinuesa, R., Azizpour, H., Leite, I., Balaam, M., Dignum, V., Domisch, S., Felländer, A., Langhans, S. D., Tegmark, M., & Fuso Nerini, F. (2020). The role of artificial intelligence in achieving the Sustainable Development Goals. *Nature Communications, 11*(1), 1–10. doi:10.1038/s41467-019-14108-y

Vinyals, O., Bellemare, M. G., & Graves, A. (2017). Neural episodic control. *arXiv preprint arXiv:1703.03864.*

von der Au, S., Rauschnabel, P. A., Felix, R., & Hinsch, C. (2023). Context in augmented reality marketing: Does the place of use matter? *Psychology and Marketing*, *40*(11), 2447–2463. doi:10.1002/mar.21814

Vos, L., & Armstrong, K. (2019). Context and process challenges associated with supervising postgraduate dissertations: An example from marketing. *International Journal of Management Education*, *17*(1), 47–61. doi:10.1016/j.ijme.2018.11.005

Wahbeh, A. H., Al-Radaideh, Q. A., Al-Kabi, M. N., & Al-Shawakfa, E. M. (2011). A comparison study between data mining tools over some classification methods. *International Journal of Advanced Computer Science and Applications*, *8*(2), 18–26.

Wang, Q., & Chen, L. (2016). Adaptive Learning in Cybersecurity Education: A Comparative Study. *International Journal of Educational Technology*, *25*(4), 267–282. https://www.ijetjournal.org/article/adaptive-learning-cybersecurity

Wang, Z., He, S., Yu, K., Chen, X., & Liu, Z. (2018). Deep reinforcement learning for traffic signal control with multi-agent optimization. *IEEE Transactions on Intelligent Transportation Systems*, *20*(3), 1024–1035.

Ward, L., Aykol, M., Blaiszik, B., Foster, I., Meredig, B., Saal, J., & Suram, S. (2018). Strategies for accelerating the adoption of materials informatics. *MRS Bulletin*, *43*(9), 683–689. doi:10.1557/mrs.2018.204

Wazirali, R., Yaghoubi, E., Abujazar, M. S. S., Ahmad, R., & Vakili, A. H. (2023). State-of-the-art review on energy and load forecasting in microgrids using artificial neural networks, machine learning, and deep learning techniques. *Electric Power Systems Research*, *225*, 109792. doi:10.1016/j.epsr.2023.109792

Welch, V., Petticrew, M., Petkovic, J., Moher, D., Waters, E., White, H., ... Wells, G. (2016). Extending the PRISMA statement to equity-focused systematic reviews (PRISMA-E 2012): Explanation and elaboration. *Journal of Clinical Epidemiology*, *70*, 68–89. doi:10.1016/j.jclinepi.2015.09.001 PMID:26348799

Werkneh, A. A., & Gebru, S. B. (2022). Development of ecological sanitation approaches for integrated recovery of biogas, nutrients and clean water from domestic wastewater. *Resources. Environmental Sustainability*, 100095.

Williams, P., Dutta, I. K., Daoud, H., & Bayoumi, M. (2022, August). A survey on security in internet of things with a focus on the impact of emerging technologies. *Internet of Things : Engineering Cyber Physical Human Systems*, *19*, 100564. doi:10.1016/j.iot.2022.100564

Xu, Y., Wu, M., Liu, Y., Feng, X., Yin, X., He, X., & Zhang, Y. (2013). Nitrogen-Doped Carbon Dots: A Facile and General Preparation Method, Photoluminescence Investigation, and Imaging Applications. *Chemistry (Weinheim an der Bergstrasse, Germany)*, *19*(7), 2276–2283. doi:10.1002/chem.201203641 PMID:23322649

Yadav, R. K., Singh, P., & Kashtriya, P. (2023). Diagnosis of Breast Cancer using Machine Learning Techniques -A Survey. *Procedia Computer Science*, *218*, 1434–1443. doi:10.1016/j.procs.2023.01.122

Yang, Zhang, Lin, Li, & Sun. (2022). Characterizing Heterogeneous Internet of Things Devices at Internet Scale Using Semantic Extraction. *IEEE Internet of Things Journal, 9*(7), 5434-5446. doi:10.1109/JIOT.2021.3110757

Yang, T., Zhao, L., & Wang, C. (2019). Review on application of artificial intelligence in power system and integrated energy system. *Dianli Xitong Zidonghua*, *43*, 2–14.

Yeh, C., Meng, C., Wang, S., Driscoll, A., Rozi, E., Liu, P., Lee, J., Burke, M., Lobell, D. B., & Ermon, S. (2021). Sustainbench: Benchmarks for monitoring the sustainable development goals with machine learning. *arXiv preprint arXiv:2111.04724*

Yenugula, M., Sahoo, S. K., & Goswami, S. S. (2024). Cloud computing for sustainable development: An analysis of environmental, economic and social benefits. *Journal of Future Sustainability*, *4*(1), 59–66. doi:10.5267/j.jfs.2024.1.005

Yfinance. (n.d.). https://pypi.org/project/yfinance/

Yusuf, N., & Lytras, M. D. (2023). Competitive Sustainability of Saudi Companies through Digitalization and the Circular Carbon Economy Model: A Bold Contribution to the Vision 2030 Agenda in Saudi Arabia. *Sustainability, 15*(3), 2616. doi:10.3390/su15032616

Zhang, C., Fu, X., & Wu, X. (2023). Statistical machine learning techniques of weather simulation for the fishery-solar hybrid systems. *Frontiers in Energy Research*, *10*, 1073976. doi:10.3389/fenrg.2022.1073976

Zhang, L., Godil, D. I., Bibi, M., Khan, M. K., Sarwat, S., & Anser, M. K. (2021). Caring for the environment: How human capital, natural resources, and economic growth interact with environmental degradation in Pakistan? A dynamic ARDL approach. *The Science of the Total Environment*, *774*, 145553. doi:10.1016/j.scitotenv.2021.145553 PMID:33611006

Zhang, L., Wang, S., Zhang, Y., & Liu, Y. (2020). Deep reinforcement learning for financial portfolio management. *IEEE Transactions on Neural Networks and Learning Systems*, *31*(11), 4582–4594. PMID:31870999

Zhang, Q., Zhou, W., Xia, X., Li, K., Zhang, N., Wang, Y., Xiao, Z., Fan, Q., Kauppinen, E. I., & Xie, S. (2020). Transparent and Freestanding Single-Walled Carbon Nanotube Films Synthesized Directly and Continuously via a Blown Aerosol Technique. *Advanced Materials*, *32*(39), 2004277. Advance online publication. doi:10.1002/adma.202004277 PMID:32851708

Zhang, Y., Liu, W., & Wang, Y. (2022). Multi-agent reinforcement learning for traffic signal control: A survey. *IEEE Transactions on Intelligent Transportation Systems*, *23*(3), 1197–1215.

Zhang, Z., Hao, X., Santoni, C., Shen, L., Sotiropoulos, F., & Khosronejad, A. (2023). Toward prediction of turbulent atmospheric flows over propagating oceanic waves via machine-learning augmented large-eddy simulation. *Ocean Engineering*, *280*, 114759. doi:10.1016/j.oceaneng.2023.114759

Zheng, X., Lin, F., & Cai, X. (2021, January). Exploration of contextual marketing model based on mobile apps. In *6th Annual International Conference on Social Science and Contemporary Humanity Development (SSCHD 2020)* (pp. 81-85). Atlantis Press. 10.2991/assehr.k.210121.017

Zhou, T., Song, Z., & Sundmacher, K. (2019). Big Data Creates New Opportunities for Materials Research: A Review on Methods and Applications of Machine Learning for Materials Design. *Engineering (Beijing)*, *5*(6), 1017–1026. doi:10.1016/j.eng.2019.02.011

Related References

To continue our tradition of advancing information science and technology research, we have compiled a list of recommended IGI Global readings. These references will provide additional information and guidance to further enrich your knowledge and assist you with your own research and future publications.

Aasi, P., Rusu, L., & Vieru, D. (2017). The Role of Culture in IT Governance Five Focus Areas: A Literature Review. *International Journal of IT/Business Alignment and Governance, 8*(2), 42-61. https://doi.org/ doi:10.4018/IJITBAG.2017070103

Abdrabo, A. A. (2018). Egypt's Knowledge-Based Development: Opportunities, Challenges, and Future Possibilities. In A. Alraouf (Ed.), *Knowledge-Based Urban Development in the Middle East* (pp. 80–101). Hershey, PA: IGI Global. doi:10.4018/978-1-5225-3734-2.ch005

Abu Doush, I., & Alhami, I. (2018). Evaluating the Accessibility of Computer Laboratories, Libraries, and Websites in Jordanian Universities and Colleges. *International Journal of Information Systems and Social Change, 9*(2), 44–60. doi:10.4018/IJISSC.2018040104

Adegbore, A. M., Quadri, M. O., & Oyewo, O. R. (2018). A Theoretical Approach to the Adoption of Electronic Resource Management Systems (ERMS) in Nigerian University Libraries. In A. Tella & T. Kwanya (Eds.), *Handbook of Research on Managing Intellectual Property in Digital Libraries* (pp. 292–311). Hershey, PA: IGI Global. doi:10.4018/978-1-5225-3093-0.ch015

Afolabi, O. A. (2018). Myths and Challenges of Building an Effective Digital Library in Developing Nations: An African Perspective. In A. Tella & T. Kwanya (Eds.), *Handbook of Research on Managing Intellectual Property in Digital Libraries* (pp. 51–79). Hershey, PA: IGI Global. doi:10.4018/978-1-5225-3093-0.ch004

Agarwal, P., Kurian, R., & Gupta, R. K. (2022). Additive Manufacturing Feature Taxonomy and Placement of Parts in AM Enclosure. In S. Salunkhe, H. Hussein, & J. Davim (Eds.), *Applications of Artificial Intelligence in Additive Manufacturing* (pp. 138–176). IGI Global. https://doi.org/10.4018/978-1-7998-8516-0.ch007

Al-Alawi, A. I., Al-Hammam, A. H., Al-Alawi, S. S., & AlAlawi, E. I. (2021). The Adoption of E-Wallets: Current Trends and Future Outlook. In Y. Albastaki, A. Razzaque, & A. Sarea (Eds.), *Innovative Strategies for Implementing FinTech in Banking* (pp. 242–262). IGI Global. https://doi.org/10.4018/978-1-7998-3257-7.ch015

Alsharo, M. (2017). Attitudes Towards Cloud Computing Adoption in Emerging Economies. *International Journal of Cloud Applications and Computing*, *7*(3), 44–58. doi:10.4018/IJCAC.2017070102

Amer, T. S., & Johnson, T. L. (2017). Information Technology Progress Indicators: Research Employing Psychological Frameworks. In A. Mesquita (Ed.), *Research Paradigms and Contemporary Perspectives on Human-Technology Interaction* (pp. 168–186). Hershey, PA: IGI Global. doi:10.4018/978-1-5225-1868-6.ch008

Andreeva, A., & Yolova, G. (2021). Liability in Labor Legislation: New Challenges Related to the Use of Artificial Intelligence. In B. Vassileva & M. Zwilling (Eds.), *Responsible AI and Ethical Issues for Businesses and Governments* (pp. 214–232). IGI Global. https://doi.org/10.4018/978-1-7998-4285-9.ch012

Anohah, E. (2017). Paradigm and Architecture of Computing Augmented Learning Management System for Computer Science Education. *International Journal of Online Pedagogy and Course Design*, *7*(2), 60–70. doi:10.4018/IJOPCD.2017040105

Anohah, E., & Suhonen, J. (2017). Trends of Mobile Learning in Computing Education from 2006 to 2014: A Systematic Review of Research Publications. *International Journal of Mobile and Blended Learning*, *9*(1), 16–33. doi:10.4018/IJMBL.2017010102

Arbaiza, C. S., Huerta, H. V., & Rodriguez, C. R. (2021). Contributions to the Technological Adoption Model for the Peruvian Agro-Export Sector. *International Journal of E-Adoption*, *13*(1), 1–17. https://doi.org/10.4018/IJEA.2021010101

Bailey, E. K. (2017). Applying Learning Theories to Computer Technology Supported Instruction. In M. Grassetti & S. Brookby (Eds.), *Advancing Next-Generation Teacher Education through Digital Tools and Applications* (pp. 61–81). Hershey, PA: IGI Global. doi:10.4018/978-1-5225-0965-3.ch004

Baker, J. D. (2021). Introduction to Machine Learning as a New Methodological Framework for Performance Assessment. In M. Bocarnea, B. Winston, & D. Dean (Eds.), *Handbook of Research on Advancements in Organizational Data Collection and Measurements: Strategies for Addressing Attitudes, Beliefs, and Behaviors* (pp. 326–342). IGI Global. https://doi.org/10.4018/978-1-7998-7665-6.ch021

Banerjee, S., Sing, T. Y., Chowdhury, A. R., & Anwar, H. (2018). Let's Go Green: Towards a Taxonomy of Green Computing Enablers for Business Sustainability. In M. Khosrow-Pour (Ed.), *Green Computing Strategies for Competitive Advantage and Business Sustainability* (pp. 89–109). Hershey, PA: IGI Global. doi:10.4018/978-1-5225-5017-4.ch005

Basham, R. (2018). Information Science and Technology in Crisis Response and Management. In M. Khosrow-Pour, D.B.A. (Ed.), Encyclopedia of Information Science and Technology, Fourth Edition (pp. 1407-1418). Hershey, PA: IGI Global. doi:10.4018/978-1-5225-2255-3.ch121

Batyashe, T., & Iyamu, T. (2018). Architectural Framework for the Implementation of Information Technology Governance in Organisations. In M. Khosrow-Pour, D.B.A. (Ed.), Encyclopedia of Information Science and Technology, Fourth Edition (pp. 810-819). Hershey, PA: IGI Global. doi:10.4018/978-1-5225-2255-3.ch070

Bekleyen, N., & Çelik, S. (2017). Attitudes of Adult EFL Learners towards Preparing for a Language Test via CALL. In D. Tafazoli & M. Romero (Eds.), *Multiculturalism and Technology-Enhanced Language Learning* (pp. 214–229). Hershey, PA: IGI Global. doi:10.4018/978-1-5225-1882-2.ch013

Bergeron, F., Croteau, A., Uwizeyemungu, S., & Raymond, L. (2017). A Framework for Research on Information Technology Governance in SMEs. In S. De Haes & W. Van Grembergen (Eds.), *Strategic IT Governance and Alignment in Business Settings* (pp. 53–81). Hershey, PA: IGI Global. doi:10.4018/978-1-5225-0861-8.ch003

Bhardwaj, M., Shukla, N., & Sharma, A. (2021). Improvement and Reduction of Clustering Overhead in Mobile Ad Hoc Network With Optimum Stable Bunching Algorithm. In S. Kumar, M. Trivedi, P. Ranjan, & A. Punhani (Eds.), *Evolution of Software-Defined Networking Foundations for IoT and 5G Mobile Networks* (pp. 139–158). IGI Global. https://doi.org/10.4018/978-1-7998-4685-7.ch008

Bhatt, G. D., Wang, Z., & Rodger, J. A. (2017). Information Systems Capabilities and Their Effects on Competitive Advantages: A Study of Chinese Companies. *Information Resources Management Journal, 30*(3), 41–57. doi:10.4018/IRMJ.2017070103

Bhattacharya, A. (2021). Blockchain, Cybersecurity, and Industry 4.0. In A. Tyagi, G. Rekha, & N. Sreenath (Eds.), *Opportunities and Challenges for Blockchain Technology in Autonomous Vehicles* (pp. 210–244). IGI Global. https://doi.org/10.4018/978-1-7998-3295-9.ch013

Bhyan, P., Shrivastava, B., & Kumar, N. (2022). Requisite Sustainable Development Contemplating Buildings: Economic and Environmental Sustainability. In A. Hussain, K. Tiwari, & A. Gupta (Eds.), *Addressing Environmental Challenges Through Spatial Planning* (pp. 269–288). IGI Global. https://doi.org/10.4018/978-1-7998-8331-9.ch014

Boido, C., Davico, P., & Spallone, R. (2021). Digital Tools Aimed to Represent Urban Survey. In M. Khosrow-Pour D.B.A. (Ed.), *Encyclopedia of Information Science and Technology, Fifth Edition* (pp. 1181-1195). IGI Global. https://doi.org/10.4018/978-1-7998-3479-3.ch082

Borkar, P. S., Chanana, P. U., Atwal, S. K., Londe, T. G., & Dalal, Y. D. (2021). The Replacement of HMI (Human-Machine Interface) in Industry Using Single Interface Through IoT. In R. Raut & A. Mihovska (Eds.), *Examining the Impact of Deep Learning and IoT on Multi-Industry Applications* (pp. 195–208). IGI Global. https://doi.org/10.4018/978-1-7998-7511-6.ch011

Brahmane, A. V., & Krishna, C. B. (2021). Rider Chaotic Biography Optimization-driven Deep Stacked Auto-encoder for Big Data Classification Using Spark Architecture: Rider Chaotic Biography Optimization. *International Journal of Web Services Research, 18*(3), 42–62. https://doi.org/10.4018/ijwsr.2021070103

Burcoff, A., & Shamir, L. (2017). Computer Analysis of Pablo Picasso's Artistic Style. *International Journal of Art, Culture and Design Technologies, 6*(1), 1–18. doi:10.4018/IJACDT.2017010101

Byker, E. J. (2017). I Play I Learn: Introducing Technological Play Theory. In C. Martin & D. Polly (Eds.), *Handbook of Research on Teacher Education and Professional Development* (pp. 297–306). Hershey, PA: IGI Global. doi:10.4018/978-1-5225-1067-3.ch016

Calongne, C. M., Stricker, A. G., Truman, B., & Arenas, F. J. (2017). Cognitive Apprenticeship and Computer Science Education in Cyberspace: Reimagining the Past. In A. Stricker, C. Calongne, B. Truman, & F. Arenas (Eds.), *Integrating an Awareness of Selfhood and Society into Virtual Learning* (pp. 180–197). Hershey, PA: IGI Global. doi:10.4018/978-1-5225-2182-2.ch013

Carneiro, A. D. (2017). Defending Information Networks in Cyberspace: Some Notes on Security Needs. In M. Dawson, D. Kisku, P. Gupta, J. Sing, & W. Li (Eds.), Developing Next-Generation Countermeasures for Homeland Security Threat Prevention (pp. 354-375). Hershey, PA: IGI Global. https://doi.org/doi:10.4018/978-1-5225-0703-1.ch016

Carvalho, W. F., & Zarate, L. (2021). Causal Feature Selection. In A. Azevedo & M. Santos (Eds.), *Integration Challenges for Analytics, Business Intelligence, and Data Mining* (pp. 145-160). IGI Global. https://doi.org/10.4018/978-1-7998-5781-5.ch007

Chase, J. P., & Yan, Z. (2017). Affect in Statistics Cognition. In *Assessing and Measuring Statistics Cognition in Higher Education Online Environments: Emerging Research and Opportunities* (pp. 144–187). Hershey, PA: IGI Global. doi:10.4018/978-1-5225-2420-5.ch005

Chatterjee, A., Roy, S., & Shrivastava, R. (2021). A Machine Learning Approach to Prevent Cancer. In G. Rani & P. Tiwari (Eds.), *Handbook of Research on Disease Prediction Through Data Analytics and Machine Learning* (pp. 112–141). IGI Global. https://doi.org/10.4018/978-1-7998-2742-9.ch007

Cifci, M. A. (2021). Optimizing WSNs for CPS Using Machine Learning Techniques. In A. Luhach & A. Elçi (Eds.), *Artificial Intelligence Paradigms for Smart Cyber-Physical Systems* (pp. 204–228). IGI Global. https://doi.org/10.4018/978-1-7998-5101-1.ch010

Cimermanova, I. (2017). Computer-Assisted Learning in Slovakia. In D. Tafazoli & M. Romero (Eds.), *Multiculturalism and Technology-Enhanced Language Learning* (pp. 252–270). Hershey, PA: IGI Global. doi:10.4018/978-1-5225-1882-2.ch015

Cipolla-Ficarra, F. V., & Cipolla-Ficarra, M. (2018). Computer Animation for Ingenious Revival. In F. Cipolla-Ficarra, M. Ficarra, M. Cipolla-Ficarra, A. Quiroga, J. Alma, & J. Carré (Eds.), *Technology-Enhanced Human Interaction in Modern Society* (pp. 159–181). Hershey, PA: IGI Global. doi:10.4018/978-1-5225-3437-2.ch008

Cockrell, S., Damron, T. S., Melton, A. M., & Smith, A. D. (2018). Offshoring IT. In M. Khosrow-Pour, D.B.A. (Ed.), Encyclopedia of Information Science and Technology, Fourth Edition (pp. 5476-5489). Hershey, PA: IGI Global. https://doi.org/ doi:10.4018/978-1-5225-2255-3.ch476

Coffey, J. W. (2018). Logic and Proof in Computer Science: Categories and Limits of Proof Techniques. In J. Horne (Ed.), *Philosophical Perceptions on Logic and Order* (pp. 218–240). Hershey, PA: IGI Global. doi:10.4018/978-1-5225-2443-4.ch007

Dale, M. (2017). Re-Thinking the Challenges of Enterprise Architecture Implementation. In M. Tavana (Ed.), *Enterprise Information Systems and the Digitalization of Business Functions* (pp. 205–221). Hershey, PA: IGI Global. doi:10.4018/978-1-5225-2382-6.ch009

Das, A., & Mohanty, M. N. (2021). An Useful Review on Optical Character Recognition for Smart Era Generation. In A. Tyagi (Ed.), *Multimedia and Sensory Input for Augmented, Mixed, and Virtual Reality* (pp. 1–41). IGI Global. https://doi.org/10.4018/978-1-7998-4703-8.ch001

Dash, A. K., & Mohapatra, P. (2021). A Survey on Prematurity Detection of Diabetic Retinopathy Based on Fundus Images Using Deep Learning Techniques. In S. Saxena & S. Paul (Eds.), *Deep Learning Applications in Medical Imaging* (pp. 140–155). IGI Global. https://doi.org/10.4018/978-1-7998-5071-7.ch006

De Maere, K., De Haes, S., & von Kutzschenbach, M. (2017). CIO Perspectives on Organizational Learning within the Context of IT Governance. *International Journal of IT/Business Alignment and Governance, 8*(1), 32-47. https://doi.org/ doi:10.4018/IJITBAG.2017010103

Demir, K., Çaka, C., Yaman, N. D., İslamoğlu, H., & Kuzu, A. (2018). Examining the Current Definitions of Computational Thinking. In H. Ozcinar, G. Wong, & H. Ozturk (Eds.), *Teaching Computational Thinking in Primary Education* (pp. 36–64). Hershey, PA: IGI Global. doi:10.4018/978-1-5225-3200-2.ch003

Deng, X., Hung, Y., & Lin, C. D. (2017). Design and Analysis of Computer Experiments. In S. Saha, A. Mandal, A. Narasimhamurthy, S. V, & S. Sangam (Eds.), Handbook of Research on Applied Cybernetics and Systems Science (pp. 264-279). Hershey, PA: IGI Global. doi:10.4018/978-1-5225-2498-4.ch013

Denner, J., Martinez, J., & Thiry, H. (2017). Strategies for Engaging Hispanic/Latino Youth in the US in Computer Science. In Y. Rankin & J. Thomas (Eds.), *Moving Students of Color from Consumers to Producers of Technology* (pp. 24–48). Hershey, PA: IGI Global. doi:10.4018/978-1-5225-2005-4.ch002

Devi, A. (2017). Cyber Crime and Cyber Security: A Quick Glance. In R. Kumar, P. Pattnaik, & P. Pandey (Eds.), *Detecting and Mitigating Robotic Cyber Security Risks* (pp. 160–171). Hershey, PA: IGI Global. doi:10.4018/978-1-5225-2154-9.ch011

Dhaya, R., & Kanthavel, R. (2022). Futuristic Research Perspectives of IoT Platforms. In D. Jeya Mala (Ed.), *Integrating AI in IoT Analytics on the Cloud for Healthcare Applications* (pp. 258–275). IGI Global. doi:10.4018/978-1-7998-9132-1.ch015

Doyle, D. J., & Fahy, P. J. (2018). Interactivity in Distance Education and Computer-Aided Learning, With Medical Education Examples. In M. Khosrow-Pour, D.B.A. (Ed.), Encyclopedia of Information Science and Technology, Fourth Edition (pp. 5829-5840). Hershey, PA: IGI Global. https://doi.org/ doi:10.4018/978-1-5225-2255-3.ch507

Eklund, P. (2021). Reinforcement Learning in Social Media Marketing. In B. Christiansen & T. Škrinjarić (Eds.), *Handbook of Research on Applied AI for International Business and Marketing Applications* (pp. 30–48). IGI Global. https://doi.org/10.4018/978-1-7998-5077-9.ch003

El Ghandour, N., Benaissa, M., & Lebbah, Y. (2021). An Integer Linear Programming-Based Method for the Extraction of Ontology Alignment. *International Journal of Information Technology and Web Engineering, 16*(2), 25–44. https://doi.org/10.4018/IJITWE.2021040102

Elias, N. I., & Walker, T. W. (2017). Factors that Contribute to Continued Use of E-Training among Healthcare Professionals. In F. Topor (Ed.), *Handbook of Research on Individualism and Identity in the Globalized Digital Age* (pp. 403–429). Hershey, PA: IGI Global. doi:10.4018/978-1-5225-0522-8.ch018

Fisher, R. L. (2018). Computer-Assisted Indian Matrimonial Services. In M. Khosrow-Pour, D.B.A. (Ed.), Encyclopedia of Information Science and Technology, Fourth Edition (pp. 4136-4145). Hershey, PA: IGI Global. doi:10.4018/978-1-5225-2255-3.ch358

Galiautdinov, R. (2021). Nonlinear Filtering in Artificial Neural Network Applications in Business and Engineering. In Q. Do (Ed.), *Artificial Neural Network Applications in Business and Engineering* (pp. 1–23). IGI Global. https://doi.org/10.4018/978-1-7998-3238-6.ch001

Gardner-McCune, C., & Jimenez, Y. (2017). Historical App Developers: Integrating CS into K-12 through Cross-Disciplinary Projects. In Y. Rankin & J. Thomas (Eds.), *Moving Students of Color from Consumers to Producers of Technology* (pp. 85–112). Hershey, PA: IGI Global. doi:10.4018/978-1-5225-2005-4.ch005

Garg, P. K. (2021). The Internet of Things-Based Technologies. In S. Kumar, M. Trivedi, P. Ranjan, & A. Punhani (Eds.), *Evolution of Software-Defined Networking Foundations for IoT and 5G Mobile Networks* (pp. 37–65). IGI Global. https://doi.org/10.4018/978-1-7998-4685-7.ch003

Garg, T., & Bharti, M. (2021). Congestion Control Protocols for UWSNs. In N. Goyal, L. Sapra, & J. Sandhu (Eds.), *Energy-Efficient Underwater Wireless Communications and Networking* (pp. 85–100). IGI Global. https://doi.org/10.4018/978-1-7998-3640-7.ch006

Gauttier, S. (2021). A Primer on Q-Method and the Study of Technology. In M. Khosrow-Pour D.B.A. (Eds.), *Encyclopedia of Information Science and Technology, Fifth Edition* (pp. 1746-1756). IGI Global. https://doi.org/10.4018/978-1-7998-3479-3.ch120

Ghafele, R., & Gibert, B. (2018). Open Growth: The Economic Impact of Open Source Software in the USA. In M. Khosrow-Pour (Ed.), *Optimizing Contemporary Application and Processes in Open Source Software* (pp. 164–197). Hershey, PA: IGI Global. doi:10.4018/978-1-5225-5314-4.ch007

Ghobakhloo, M., & Azar, A. (2018). Information Technology Resources, the Organizational Capability of Lean-Agile Manufacturing, and Business Performance. *Information Resources Management Journal, 31*(2), 47–74. doi:10.4018/IRMJ.2018040103

Gikandi, J. W. (2017). Computer-Supported Collaborative Learning and Assessment: A Strategy for Developing Online Learning Communities in Continuing Education. In J. Keengwe & G. Onchwari (Eds.), *Handbook of Research on Learner-Centered Pedagogy in Teacher Education and Professional Development* (pp. 309–333). Hershey, PA: IGI Global. doi:10.4018/978-1-5225-0892-2.ch017

Gokhale, A. A., & Machina, K. F. (2017). Development of a Scale to Measure Attitudes toward Information Technology. In L. Tomei (Ed.), *Exploring the New Era of Technology-Infused Education* (pp. 49–64). Hershey, PA: IGI Global. doi:10.4018/978-1-5225-1709-2.ch004

Goswami, J. K., Jalal, S., Negi, C. S., & Jalal, A. S. (2022). A Texture Features-Based Robust Facial Expression Recognition. *International Journal of Computer Vision and Image Processing, 12*(1), 1–15. https://doi.org/10.4018/IJCVIP.2022010103

Hafeez-Baig, A., Gururajan, R., & Wickramasinghe, N. (2017). Readiness as a Novel Construct of Readiness Acceptance Model (RAM) for the Wireless Handheld Technology. In N. Wickramasinghe (Ed.), *Handbook of Research on Healthcare Administration and Management* (pp. 578–595). Hershey, PA: IGI Global. doi:10.4018/978-1-5225-0920-2.ch035

Hanafizadeh, P., Ghandchi, S., & Asgarimehr, M. (2017). Impact of Information Technology on Lifestyle: A Literature Review and Classification. *International Journal of Virtual Communities and Social Networking*, *9*(2), 1–23. doi:10.4018/IJVCSN.2017040101

Haseski, H. İ., Ilic, U., & Tuğtekin, U. (2018). Computational Thinking in Educational Digital Games: An Assessment Tool Proposal. In H. Ozcinar, G. Wong, & H. Ozturk (Eds.), *Teaching Computational Thinking in Primary Education* (pp. 256–287). Hershey, PA: IGI Global. doi:10.4018/978-1-5225-3200-2.ch013

Hee, W. J., Jalleh, G., Lai, H., & Lin, C. (2017). E-Commerce and IT Projects: Evaluation and Management Issues in Australian and Taiwanese Hospitals. *International Journal of Public Health Management and Ethics*, *2*(1), 69–90. doi:10.4018/IJPHME.2017010104

Hernandez, A. A. (2017). Green Information Technology Usage: Awareness and Practices of Philippine IT Professionals. *International Journal of Enterprise Information Systems*, *13*(4), 90–103. doi:10.4018/IJEIS.2017100106

Hernandez, M. A., Marin, E. C., Garcia-Rodriguez, J., Azorin-Lopez, J., & Cazorla, M. (2017). Automatic Learning Improves Human-Robot Interaction in Productive Environments: A Review. *International Journal of Computer Vision and Image Processing*, *7*(3), 65–75. doi:10.4018/IJCVIP.2017070106

Hirota, A. (2021). Design of Narrative Creation in Innovation: "Signature Story" and Two Types of Pivots. In T. Ogata & J. Ono (Eds.), *Bridging the Gap Between AI, Cognitive Science, and Narratology With Narrative Generation* (pp. 363–376). IGI Global. https://doi.org/10.4018/978-1-7998-4864-6.ch012

Hond, D., Asgari, H., Jeffery, D., & Newman, M. (2021). An Integrated Process for Verifying Deep Learning Classifiers Using Dataset Dissimilarity Measures. *International Journal of Artificial Intelligence and Machine Learning*, *11*(2), 1–21. https://doi.org/10.4018/IJAIML.289536

Horne-Popp, L. M., Tessone, E. B., & Welker, J. (2018). If You Build It, They Will Come: Creating a Library Statistics Dashboard for Decision-Making. In L. Costello & M. Powers (Eds.), *Developing In-House Digital Tools in Library Spaces* (pp. 177–203). Hershey, PA: IGI Global. doi:10.4018/978-1-5225-2676-6.ch009

Hu, H., Hu, P. J., & Al-Gahtani, S. S. (2017). User Acceptance of Computer Technology at Work in Arabian Culture: A Model Comparison Approach. In M. Khosrow-Pour (Ed.), *Handbook of Research on Technology Adoption, Social Policy, and Global Integration* (pp. 205–228). Hershey, PA: IGI Global. doi:10.4018/978-1-5225-2668-1.ch011

Huang, C., Sun, Y., & Fuh, C. (2022). Vehicle License Plate Recognition With Deep Learning. In C. Chen, W. Yang, & L. Chen (Eds.), *Technologies to Advance Automation in Forensic Science and Criminal Investigation* (pp. 161-219). IGI Global. https://doi.org/10.4018/978-1-7998-8386-9.ch009

Ifinedo, P. (2017). Using an Extended Theory of Planned Behavior to Study Nurses' Adoption of Healthcare Information Systems in Nova Scotia. *International Journal of Technology Diffusion*, *8*(1), 1–17. doi:10.4018/IJTD.2017010101

Ilie, V., & Sneha, S. (2018). A Three Country Study for Understanding Physicians' Engagement With Electronic Information Resources Pre and Post System Implementation. *Journal of Global Information Management*, *26*(2), 48–73. doi:10.4018/JGIM.2018040103

Ilo, P. I., Nkiko, C., Ugwu, C. I., Ekere, J. N., Izuagbe, R., & Fagbohun, M. O. (2021). Prospects and Challenges of Web 3.0 Technologies Application in the Provision of Library Services. In M. Khosrow-Pour D.B.A. (Ed.), *Encyclopedia of Information Science and Technology, Fifth Edition* (pp. 1767-1781). IGI Global. https://doi.org/10.4018/978-1-7998-3479-3.ch122

Inoue-Smith, Y. (2017). Perceived Ease in Using Technology Predicts Teacher Candidates' Preferences for Online Resources. *International Journal of Online Pedagogy and Course Design*, *7*(3), 17–28. doi:10.4018/IJOPCD.2017070102

Islam, A. Y. (2017). Technology Satisfaction in an Academic Context: Moderating Effect of Gender. In A. Mesquita (Ed.), *Research Paradigms and Contemporary Perspectives on Human-Technology Interaction* (pp. 187–211). Hershey, PA: IGI Global. doi:10.4018/978-1-5225-1868-6.ch009

Jagdale, S. C., Hable, A. A., & Chabukswar, A. R. (2021). Protocol Development in Clinical Trials for Healthcare Management. In M. Khosrow-Pour D.B.A. (Ed.), *Encyclopedia of Information Science and Technology, Fifth Edition* (pp. 1797-1814). IGI Global. https://doi.org/10.4018/978-1-7998-3479-3.ch124

Jamil, G. L., & Jamil, C. C. (2017). Information and Knowledge Management Perspective Contributions for Fashion Studies: Observing Logistics and Supply Chain Management Processes. In G. Jamil, A. Soares, & C. Pessoa (Eds.), *Handbook of Research on Information Management for Effective Logistics and Supply Chains* (pp. 199–221). Hershey, PA: IGI Global. doi:10.4018/978-1-5225-0973-8.ch011

Jamil, M. I., & Almunawar, M. N. (2021). Importance of Digital Literacy and Hindrance Brought About by Digital Divide. In M. Khosrow-Pour D.B.A. (Ed.), *Encyclopedia of Information Science and Technology, Fifth Edition* (pp. 1683-1698). IGI Global. https://doi.org/10.4018/978-1-7998-3479-3.ch116

Janakova, M. (2018). Big Data and Simulations for the Solution of Controversies in Small Businesses. In M. Khosrow-Pour, D.B.A. (Ed.), Encyclopedia of Information Science and Technology, Fourth Edition (pp. 6907-6915). Hershey, PA: IGI Global. doi:10.4018/978-1-5225-2255-3.ch598

Jhawar, A., & Garg, S. K. (2018). Logistics Improvement by Investment in Information Technology Using System Dynamics. In A. Azar & S. Vaidyanathan (Eds.), *Advances in System Dynamics and Control* (pp. 528–567). Hershey, PA: IGI Global. doi:10.4018/978-1-5225-4077-9.ch017

Kalelioğlu, F., Gülbahar, Y., & Doğan, D. (2018). Teaching How to Think Like a Programmer: Emerging Insights. In H. Ozcinar, G. Wong, & H. Ozturk (Eds.), *Teaching Computational Thinking in Primary Education* (pp. 18–35). Hershey, PA: IGI Global. doi:10.4018/978-1-5225-3200-2.ch002

Kamberi, S. (2017). A Girls-Only Online Virtual World Environment and its Implications for Game-Based Learning. In A. Stricker, C. Calongne, B. Truman, & F. Arenas (Eds.), *Integrating an Awareness of Selfhood and Society into Virtual Learning* (pp. 74–95). Hershey, PA: IGI Global. doi:10.4018/978-1-5225-2182-2.ch006

Kamel, S., & Rizk, N. (2017). ICT Strategy Development: From Design to Implementation – Case of Egypt. In C. Howard & K. Hargiss (Eds.), *Strategic Information Systems and Technologies in Modern Organizations* (pp. 239–257). Hershey, PA: IGI Global. doi:10.4018/978-1-5225-1680-4.ch010

Kamel, S. H. (2018). The Potential Role of the Software Industry in Supporting Economic Development. In M. Khosrow-Pour, D.B.A. (Ed.), Encyclopedia of Information Science and Technology, Fourth Edition (pp. 7259-7269). Hershey, PA: IGI Global. doi:10.4018/978-1-5225-2255-3.ch631

Kang, H., Kang, Y., & Kim, J. (2022). Improved Fall Detection Model on GRU Using PoseNet. *International Journal of Software Innovation*, *10*(2), 1–11. https://doi.org/10.4018/IJSI.289600

Kankam, P. K. (2021). Employing Case Study and Survey Designs in Information Research. *Journal of Information Technology Research*, *14*(1), 167–177. https://doi.org/10.4018/JITR.2021010110

Karas, V., & Schuller, B. W. (2021). Deep Learning for Sentiment Analysis: An Overview and Perspectives. In F. Pinarbasi & M. Taskiran (Eds.), *Natural Language Processing for Global and Local Business* (pp. 97–132). IGI Global. https://doi.org/10.4018/978-1-7998-4240-8.ch005

Kaufman, L. M. (2022). Reimagining the Magic of the Workshop Model. In T. Driscoll III, (Ed.), *Designing Effective Distance and Blended Learning Environments in K-12* (pp. 89–109). IGI Global. https://doi.org/10.4018/978-1-7998-6829-3.ch007

Kawata, S. (2018). Computer-Assisted Parallel Program Generation. In M. Khosrow-Pour, D.B.A. (Ed.), Encyclopedia of Information Science and Technology, Fourth Edition (pp. 4583-4593). Hershey, PA: IGI Global. doi:10.4018/978-1-5225-2255-3.ch398

Kharb, L., & Singh, P. (2021). Role of Machine Learning in Modern Education and Teaching. In S. Verma & P. Tomar (Ed.), *Impact of AI Technologies on Teaching, Learning, and Research in Higher Education* (pp. 99-123). IGI Global. https://doi.org/10.4018/978-1-7998-4763-2.ch006

Khari, M., Shrivastava, G., Gupta, S., & Gupta, R. (2017). Role of Cyber Security in Today's Scenario. In R. Kumar, P. Pattnaik, & P. Pandey (Eds.), *Detecting and Mitigating Robotic Cyber Security Risks* (pp. 177–191). Hershey, PA: IGI Global. doi:10.4018/978-1-5225-2154-9.ch013

Khekare, G., & Sheikh, S. (2021). Autonomous Navigation Using Deep Reinforcement Learning in ROS. *International Journal of Artificial Intelligence and Machine Learning*, *11*(2), 63–70. https://doi.org/10.4018/IJAIML.20210701.oa4

Khouja, M., Rodriguez, I. B., Ben Halima, Y., & Moalla, S. (2018). IT Governance in Higher Education Institutions: A Systematic Literature Review. *International Journal of Human Capital and Information Technology Professionals*, *9*(2), 52–67. doi:10.4018/IJHCITP.2018040104

Kiourt, C., Pavlidis, G., Koutsoudis, A., & Kalles, D. (2017). Realistic Simulation of Cultural Heritage. *International Journal of Computational Methods in Heritage Science*, *1*(1), 10–40. doi:10.4018/IJCMHS.2017010102

Köse, U. (2017). An Augmented-Reality-Based Intelligent Mobile Application for Open Computer Education. In G. Kurubacak & H. Altinpulluk (Eds.), *Mobile Technologies and Augmented Reality in Open Education* (pp. 154–174). Hershey, PA: IGI Global. doi:10.4018/978-1-5225-2110-5.ch008

Lahmiri, S. (2018). Information Technology Outsourcing Risk Factors and Provider Selection. In M. Gupta, R. Sharman, J. Walp, & P. Mulgund (Eds.), *Information Technology Risk Management and Compliance in Modern Organizations* (pp. 214–228). Hershey, PA: IGI Global. doi:10.4018/978-1-5225-2604-9.ch008

Lakkad, A. K., Bhadaniya, R. D., Shah, V. N., & Lavanya, K. (2021). Complex Events Processing on Live News Events Using Apache Kafka and Clustering Techniques. *International Journal of Intelligent Information Technologies, 17*(1), 39–52. https://doi.org/10.4018/IJIIT.2021010103

Landriscina, F. (2017). Computer-Supported Imagination: The Interplay Between Computer and Mental Simulation in Understanding Scientific Concepts. In I. Levin & D. Tsybulsky (Eds.), *Digital Tools and Solutions for Inquiry-Based STEM Learning* (pp. 33–60). Hershey, PA: IGI Global. doi:10.4018/978-1-5225-2525-7.ch002

Lara López, G. (2021). Virtual Reality in Object Location. In A. Negrón & M. Muñoz (Eds.), *Latin American Women and Research Contributions to the IT Field* (pp. 307–324). IGI Global. https://doi.org/10.4018/978-1-7998-7552-9.ch014

Lee, W. W. (2018). Ethical Computing Continues From Problem to Solution. In M. Khosrow-Pour, D.B.A. (Ed.), Encyclopedia of Information Science and Technology, Fourth Edition (pp. 4884-4897). Hershey, PA: IGI Global. doi:10.4018/978-1-5225-2255-3.ch423

Lin, S., Chen, S., & Chuang, S. (2017). Perceived Innovation and Quick Response Codes in an Online-to-Offline E-Commerce Service Model. *International Journal of E-Adoption, 9*(2), 1–16. doi:10.4018/IJEA.2017070101

Liu, M., Wang, Y., Xu, W., & Liu, L. (2017). Automated Scoring of Chinese Engineering Students' English Essays. *International Journal of Distance Education Technologies, 15*(1), 52–68. doi:10.4018/IJDET.2017010104

Ma, X., Li, X., Zhong, B., Huang, Y., Gu, Y., Wu, M., Liu, Y., & Zhang, M. (2021). A Detector and Evaluation Framework of Abnormal Bidding Behavior Based on Supplier Portrait. *International Journal of Information Technology and Web Engineering, 16*(2), 58–74. https://doi.org/10.4018/IJITWE.2021040104

Mabe, L. K., & Oladele, O. I. (2017). Application of Information Communication Technologies for Agricultural Development through Extension Services: A Review. In T. Tossy (Ed.), *Information Technology Integration for Socio-Economic Development* (pp. 52–101). Hershey, PA: IGI Global. doi:10.4018/978-1-5225-0539-6.ch003

Mahboub, S. A., Sayed Ali Ahmed, E., & Saeed, R. A. (2021). Smart IDS and IPS for Cyber-Physical Systems. In A. Luhach & A. Elçi (Eds.), *Artificial Intelligence Paradigms for Smart Cyber-Physical Systems* (pp. 109–136). IGI Global. https://doi.org/10.4018/978-1-7998-5101-1.ch006

Manogaran, G., Thota, C., & Lopez, D. (2018). Human-Computer Interaction With Big Data Analytics. In D. Lopez & M. Durai (Eds.), *HCI Challenges and Privacy Preservation in Big Data Security* (pp. 1–22). Hershey, PA: IGI Global. doi:10.4018/978-1-5225-2863-0.ch001

Margolis, J., Goode, J., & Flapan, J. (2017). A Critical Crossroads for Computer Science for All: "Identifying Talent" or "Building Talent," and What Difference Does It Make? In Y. Rankin & J. Thomas (Eds.), *Moving Students of Color from Consumers to Producers of Technology* (pp. 1–23). Hershey, PA: IGI Global. doi:10.4018/978-1-5225-2005-4.ch001

Mazzù, M. F., Benetton, A., Baccelloni, A., & Lavini, L. (2022). A Milk Blockchain-Enabled Supply Chain: Evidence From Leading Italian Farms. In P. De Giovanni (Ed.), *Blockchain Technology Applications in Businesses and Organizations* (pp. 73–98). IGI Global. https://doi.org/10.4018/978-1-7998-8014-1.ch004

Mbale, J. (2018). Computer Centres Resource Cloud Elasticity-Scalability (CRECES): Copperbelt University Case Study. In S. Aljawarneh & M. Malhotra (Eds.), *Critical Research on Scalability and Security Issues in Virtual Cloud Environments* (pp. 48–70). Hershey, PA: IGI Global. doi:10.4018/978-1-5225-3029-9.ch003

McKee, J. (2018). The Right Information: The Key to Effective Business Planning. In *Business Architectures for Risk Assessment and Strategic Planning: Emerging Research and Opportunities* (pp. 38–52). Hershey, PA: IGI Global. doi:10.4018/978-1-5225-3392-4.ch003

Meddah, I. H., Remil, N. E., & Meddah, H. N. (2021). Novel Approach for Mining Patterns. *International Journal of Applied Evolutionary Computation, 12*(1), 27–42. https://doi.org/10.4018/IJAEC.2021010103

Mensah, I. K., & Mi, J. (2018). Determinants of Intention to Use Local E-Government Services in Ghana: The Perspective of Local Government Workers. *International Journal of Technology Diffusion, 9*(2), 41–60. doi:10.4018/IJTD.2018040103

Mohamed, J. H. (2018). Scientograph-Based Visualization of Computer Forensics Research Literature. In J. Jeyasekar & P. Saravanan (Eds.), *Innovations in Measuring and Evaluating Scientific Information* (pp. 148–162). Hershey, PA: IGI Global. doi:10.4018/978-1-5225-3457-0.ch010

Montañés-Del Río, M. Á., Cornejo, V. R., Rodríguez, M. R., & Ortiz, J. S. (2021). Gamification of University Subjects: A Case Study for Operations Management. *Journal of Information Technology Research, 14*(2), 1–29. https://doi.org/10.4018/JITR.2021040101

Moore, R. L., & Johnson, N. (2017). Earning a Seat at the Table: How IT Departments Can Partner in Organizational Change and Innovation. *International Journal of Knowledge-Based Organizations, 7*(2), 1–12. doi:10.4018/IJKBO.2017040101

Mukul, M. K., & Bhattaharyya, S. (2017). Brain-Machine Interface: Human-Computer Interaction. In E. Noughabi, B. Raahemi, A. Albadvi, & B. Far (Eds.), *Handbook of Research on Data Science for Effective Healthcare Practice and Administration* (pp. 417–443). Hershey, PA: IGI Global. doi:10.4018/978-1-5225-2515-8.ch018

Na, L. (2017). Library and Information Science Education and Graduate Programs in Academic Libraries. In L. Ruan, Q. Zhu, & Y. Ye (Eds.), *Academic Library Development and Administration in China* (pp. 218–229). Hershey, PA: IGI Global. doi:10.4018/978-1-5225-0550-1.ch013

Nagpal, G., Bishnoi, G. K., Dhami, H. S., & Vijayvargia, A. (2021). Use of Data Analytics to Increase the Efficiency of Last Mile Logistics for Ecommerce Deliveries. In B. Patil & M. Vohra (Eds.), *Handbook of Research on Engineering, Business, and Healthcare Applications of Data Science and Analytics* (pp. 167–180). IGI Global. https://doi.org/10.4018/978-1-7998-3053-5.ch009

Nair, S. M., Ramesh, V., & Tyagi, A. K. (2021). Issues and Challenges (Privacy, Security, and Trust) in Blockchain-Based Applications. In A. Tyagi, G. Rekha, & N. Sreenath (Eds.), *Opportunities and Challenges for Blockchain Technology in Autonomous Vehicles* (pp. 196–209). IGI Global. https://doi.org/10.4018/978-1-7998-3295-9.ch012

Naomi, J. F. M., K., & V., S. (2021). Machine and Deep Learning Techniques in IoT and Cloud. In S. Velayutham (Ed.), *Challenges and Opportunities for the Convergence of IoT, Big Data, and Cloud Computing* (pp. 225-247). IGI Global. https://doi.org/10.4018/978-1-7998-3111-2.ch013

Nath, R., & Murthy, V. N. (2018). What Accounts for the Differences in Internet Diffusion Rates Around the World? In M. Khosrow-Pour, D.B.A. (Ed.), Encyclopedia of Information Science and Technology, Fourth Edition (pp. 8095-8104). Hershey, PA: IGI Global. https://doi.org/ doi:10.4018/978-1-5225-2255-3.ch705

Nedelko, Z., & Potocan, V. (2018). The Role of Emerging Information Technologies for Supporting Supply Chain Management. In M. Khosrow-Pour, D.B.A. (Ed.), Encyclopedia of Information Science and Technology, Fourth Edition (pp. 5559-5569). Hershey, PA: IGI Global. doi:10.4018/978-1-5225-2255-3.ch483

Negrini, L., Giang, C., & Bonnet, E. (2022). Designing Tools and Activities for Educational Robotics in Online Learning. In N. Eteokleous & E. Nisiforou (Eds.), *Designing, Constructing, and Programming Robots for Learning* (pp. 202–222). IGI Global. https://doi.org/10.4018/978-1-7998-7443-0.ch010

Ngafeeson, M. N. (2018). User Resistance to Health Information Technology. In M. Khosrow-Pour, D.B.A. (Ed.), Encyclopedia of Information Science and Technology, Fourth Edition (pp. 3816-3825). Hershey, PA: IGI Global. doi:10.4018/978-1-5225-2255-3.ch331

Nguyen, T. T., Giang, N. L., Tran, D. T., Nguyen, T. T., Nguyen, H. Q., Pham, A. V., & Vu, T. D. (2021). A Novel Filter-Wrapper Algorithm on Intuitionistic Fuzzy Set for Attribute Reduction From Decision Tables. *International Journal of Data Warehousing and Mining*, *17*(4), 67–100. https://doi.org/10.4018/IJDWM.2021100104

Nigam, A., & Dewani, P. P. (2022). Consumer Engagement Through Conditional Promotions: An Exploratory Study. *Journal of Global Information Management*, *30*(5), 1–19. https://doi.org/10.4018/JGIM.290364

Odagiri, K. (2017). Introduction of Individual Technology to Constitute the Current Internet. In *Strategic Policy-Based Network Management in Contemporary Organizations* (pp. 20–96). Hershey, PA: IGI Global. doi:10.4018/978-1-68318-003-6.ch003

Odia, J. O., & Akpata, O. T. (2021). Role of Data Science and Data Analytics in Forensic Accounting and Fraud Detection. In B. Patil & M. Vohra (Eds.), *Handbook of Research on Engineering, Business, and Healthcare Applications of Data Science and Analytics* (pp. 203–227). IGI Global. https://doi.org/10.4018/978-1-7998-3053-5.ch011

Okike, E. U. (2018). Computer Science and Prison Education. In I. Biao (Ed.), *Strategic Learning Ideologies in Prison Education Programs* (pp. 246–264). Hershey, PA: IGI Global. doi:10.4018/978-1-5225-2909-5.ch012

Olelewe, C. J., & Nwafor, I. P. (2017). Level of Computer Appreciation Skills Acquired for Sustainable Development by Secondary School Students in Nsukka LGA of Enugu State, Nigeria. In C. Ayo & V. Mbarika (Eds.), *Sustainable ICT Adoption and Integration for Socio-Economic Development* (pp. 214–233). Hershey, PA: IGI Global. doi:10.4018/978-1-5225-2565-3.ch010

Oliveira, M., Maçada, A. C., Curado, C., & Nodari, F. (2017). Infrastructure Profiles and Knowledge Sharing. *International Journal of Technology and Human Interaction, 13*(3), 1–12. doi:10.4018/IJTHI.2017070101

Otarkhani, A., Shokouhyar, S., & Pour, S. S. (2017). Analyzing the Impact of Governance of Enterprise IT on Hospital Performance: Tehran's (Iran) Hospitals – A Case Study. *International Journal of Healthcare Information Systems and Informatics, 12*(3), 1–20. doi:10.4018/IJHISI.2017070101

Otunla, A. O., & Amuda, C. O. (2018). Nigerian Undergraduate Students' Computer Competencies and Use of Information Technology Tools and Resources for Study Skills and Habits' Enhancement. In M. Khosrow-Pour, D.B.A. (Ed.), Encyclopedia of Information Science and Technology, Fourth Edition (pp. 2303-2313). Hershey, PA: IGI Global. https://doi.org/ doi:10.4018/978-1-5225-2255-3.ch200

Özçınar, H. (2018). A Brief Discussion on Incentives and Barriers to Computational Thinking Education. In H. Ozcinar, G. Wong, & H. Ozturk (Eds.), *Teaching Computational Thinking in Primary Education* (pp. 1–17). Hershey, PA: IGI Global. doi:10.4018/978-1-5225-3200-2.ch001

Pandey, J. M., Garg, S., Mishra, P., & Mishra, B. P. (2017). Computer Based Psychological Interventions: Subject to the Efficacy of Psychological Services. *International Journal of Computers in Clinical Practice, 2*(1), 25–33. doi:10.4018/IJCCP.2017010102

Pandkar, S. D., & Paatil, S. D. (2021). Big Data and Knowledge Resource Centre. In S. Dhamdhere (Ed.), *Big Data Applications for Improving Library Services* (pp. 90–106). IGI Global. https://doi.org/10.4018/978-1-7998-3049-8.ch007

Patro, C. (2017). Impulsion of Information Technology on Human Resource Practices. In P. Ordóñez de Pablos (Ed.), *Managerial Strategies and Solutions for Business Success in Asia* (pp. 231–254). Hershey, PA: IGI Global. doi:10.4018/978-1-5225-1886-0.ch013

Patro, C. S., & Raghunath, K. M. (2017). Information Technology Paraphernalia for Supply Chain Management Decisions. In M. Tavana (Ed.), *Enterprise Information Systems and the Digitalization of Business Functions* (pp. 294–320). Hershey, PA: IGI Global. doi:10.4018/978-1-5225-2382-6.ch014

Paul, P. K. (2018). The Context of IST for Solid Information Retrieval and Infrastructure Building: Study of Developing Country. *International Journal of Information Retrieval Research, 8*(1), 86–100. doi:10.4018/IJIRR.2018010106

Paul, P. K., & Chatterjee, D. (2018). iSchools Promoting "Information Science and Technology" (IST) Domain Towards Community, Business, and Society With Contemporary Worldwide Trend and Emerging Potentialities in India. In M. Khosrow-Pour, D.B.A. (Ed.), Encyclopedia of Information Science and Technology, Fourth Edition (pp. 4723-4735). Hershey, PA: IGI Global. https://doi.org/ doi:10.4018/978-1-5225-2255-3.ch410

Pessoa, C. R., & Marques, M. E. (2017). Information Technology and Communication Management in Supply Chain Management. In G. Jamil, A. Soares, & C. Pessoa (Eds.), *Handbook of Research on Information Management for Effective Logistics and Supply Chains* (pp. 23–33). Hershey, PA: IGI Global. doi:10.4018/978-1-5225-0973-8.ch002

Pineda, R. G. (2018). Remediating Interaction: Towards a Philosophy of Human-Computer Relationship. In M. Khosrow-Pour (Ed.), *Enhancing Art, Culture, and Design With Technological Integration* (pp. 75–98). Hershey, PA: IGI Global. doi:10.4018/978-1-5225-5023-5.ch004

Prabha, V. D., & R., R. (2021). Clinical Decision Support Systems: Decision-Making System for Clinical Data. In G. Rani & P. Tiwari (Eds.), *Handbook of Research on Disease Prediction Through Data Analytics and Machine Learning* (pp. 268-280). IGI Global. https://doi.org/10.4018/978-1-7998-2742-9.ch014

Pushpa, R., & Siddappa, M. (2021). An Optimal Way of VM Placement Strategy in Cloud Computing Platform Using ABCS Algorithm. *International Journal of Ambient Computing and Intelligence, 12*(3), 16–38. https://doi.org/10.4018/IJACI.2021070102

Qian, Y. (2017). Computer Simulation in Higher Education: Affordances, Opportunities, and Outcomes. In P. Vu, S. Fredrickson, & C. Moore (Eds.), *Handbook of Research on Innovative Pedagogies and Technologies for Online Learning in Higher Education* (pp. 236–262). Hershey, PA: IGI Global. doi:10.4018/978-1-5225-1851-8.ch011

Rahman, N. (2017). Lessons from a Successful Data Warehousing Project Management. *International Journal of Information Technology Project Management, 8*(4), 30–45. doi:10.4018/IJITPM.2017100103

Rahman, N. (2018). Environmental Sustainability in the Computer Industry for Competitive Advantage. In M. Khosrow-Pour (Ed.), *Green Computing Strategies for Competitive Advantage and Business Sustainability* (pp. 110–130). Hershey, PA: IGI Global. doi:10.4018/978-1-5225-5017-4.ch006

Rajh, A., & Pavetic, T. (2017). Computer Generated Description as the Required Digital Competence in Archival Profession. *International Journal of Digital Literacy and Digital Competence, 8*(1), 36–49. doi:10.4018/IJDLDC.2017010103

Raman, A., & Goyal, D. P. (2017). Extending IMPLEMENT Framework for Enterprise Information Systems Implementation to Information System Innovation. In M. Tavana (Ed.), *Enterprise Information Systems and the Digitalization of Business Functions* (pp. 137–177). Hershey, PA: IGI Global. doi:10.4018/978-1-5225-2382-6.ch007

Rao, A. P., & Reddy, K. S. (2021). Automated Soil Residue Levels Detecting Device With IoT Interface. In V. Sathiyamoorthi & A. Elci (Eds.), *Challenges and Applications of Data Analytics in Social Perspectives* (Vol. S, pp. 123–135). IGI Global. https://doi.org/10.4018/978-1-7998-2566-1.ch007

Rao, Y. S., Rauta, A. K., Saini, H., & Panda, T. C. (2017). Mathematical Model for Cyber Attack in Computer Network. *International Journal of Business Data Communications and Networking*, *13*(1), 58–65. doi:10.4018/IJBDCN.2017010105

Rapaport, W. J. (2018). Syntactic Semantics and the Proper Treatment of Computationalism. In M. Danesi (Ed.), *Empirical Research on Semiotics and Visual Rhetoric* (pp. 128–176). Hershey, PA: IGI Global. doi:10.4018/978-1-5225-5622-0.ch007

Raut, R., Priyadarshinee, P., & Jha, M. (2017). Understanding the Mediation Effect of Cloud Computing Adoption in Indian Organization: Integrating TAM-TOE- Risk Model. *International Journal of Service Science, Management, Engineering, and Technology*, *8*(3), 40–59. doi:10.4018/IJSSMET.2017070103

Rezaie, S., Mirabedini, S. J., & Abtahi, A. (2018). Designing a Model for Implementation of Business Intelligence in the Banking Industry. *International Journal of Enterprise Information Systems*, *14*(1), 77–103. doi:10.4018/IJEIS.2018010105

Rezende, D. A. (2018). Strategic Digital City Projects: Innovative Information and Public Services Offered by Chicago (USA) and Curitiba (Brazil). In M. Lytras, L. Daniela, & A. Visvizi (Eds.), *Enhancing Knowledge Discovery and Innovation in the Digital Era* (pp. 204–223). Hershey, PA: IGI Global. doi:10.4018/978-1-5225-4191-2.ch012

Rodriguez, A., Rico-Diaz, A. J., Rabuñal, J. R., & Gestal, M. (2017). Fish Tracking with Computer Vision Techniques: An Application to Vertical Slot Fishways. In M. S., & V. V. (Eds.), Multi-Core Computer Vision and Image Processing for Intelligent Applications (pp. 74-104). Hershey, PA: IGI Global. https://doi.org/ doi:10.4018/978-1-5225-0889-2.ch003

Romero, J. A. (2018). Sustainable Advantages of Business Value of Information Technology. In M. Khosrow-Pour, D.B.A. (Ed.), Encyclopedia of Information Science and Technology, Fourth Edition (pp. 923-929). Hershey, PA: IGI Global. doi:10.4018/978-1-5225-2255-3.ch079

Romero, J. A. (2018). The Always-On Business Model and Competitive Advantage. In N. Bajgoric (Ed.), *Always-On Enterprise Information Systems for Modern Organizations* (pp. 23–40). Hershey, PA: IGI Global. doi:10.4018/978-1-5225-3704-5.ch002

Rosen, Y. (2018). Computer Agent Technologies in Collaborative Learning and Assessment. In M. Khosrow-Pour, D.B.A. (Ed.), Encyclopedia of Information Science and Technology, Fourth Edition (pp. 2402-2410). Hershey, PA: IGI Global. doi:10.4018/978-1-5225-2255-3.ch209

Roy, D. (2018). Success Factors of Adoption of Mobile Applications in Rural India: Effect of Service Characteristics on Conceptual Model. In M. Khosrow-Pour (Ed.), *Green Computing Strategies for Competitive Advantage and Business Sustainability* (pp. 211–238). Hershey, PA: IGI Global. doi:10.4018/978-1-5225-5017-4.ch010

Ruffin, T. R., & Hawkins, D. P. (2018). Trends in Health Care Information Technology and Informatics. In M. Khosrow-Pour, D.B.A. (Ed.), Encyclopedia of Information Science and Technology, Fourth Edition (pp. 3805-3815). Hershey, PA: IGI Global. doi:10.4018/978-1-5225-2255-3.ch330

Sadasivam, U. M., & Ganesan, N. (2021). Detecting Fake News Using Deep Learning and NLP. In S. Misra, C. Arumugam, S. Jaganathan, & S. S. (Eds.), *Confluence of AI, Machine, and Deep Learning in Cyber Forensics* (pp. 117-133). IGI Global. https://doi.org/10.4018/978-1-7998-4900-1.ch007

Safari, M. R., & Jiang, Q. (2018). The Theory and Practice of IT Governance Maturity and Strategies Alignment: Evidence From Banking Industry. *Journal of Global Information Management*, *26*(2), 127–146. doi:10.4018/JGIM.2018040106

Sahin, H. B., & Anagun, S. S. (2018). Educational Computer Games in Math Teaching: A Learning Culture. In E. Toprak & E. Kumtepe (Eds.), *Supporting Multiculturalism in Open and Distance Learning Spaces* (pp. 249–280). Hershey, PA: IGI Global. doi:10.4018/978-1-5225-3076-3.ch013

Sakalle, A., Tomar, P., Bhardwaj, H., & Sharma, U. (2021). Impact and Latest Trends of Intelligent Learning With Artificial Intelligence. In S. Verma & P. Tomar (Eds.), *Impact of AI Technologies on Teaching, Learning, and Research in Higher Education* (pp. 172-189). IGI Global. https://doi.org/10.4018/978-1-7998-4763-2.ch011

Sala, N. (2021). Virtual Reality, Augmented Reality, and Mixed Reality in Education: A Brief Overview. In D. Choi, A. Dailey-Hebert, & J. Estes (Eds.), *Current and Prospective Applications of Virtual Reality in Higher Education* (pp. 48–73). IGI Global. https://doi.org/10.4018/978-1-7998-4960-5.ch003

Salunkhe, S., Kanagachidambaresan, G., Rajkumar, C., & Jayanthi, K. (2022). Online Detection and Prediction of Fused Deposition Modelled Parts Using Artificial Intelligence. In S. Salunkhe, H. Hussein, & J. Davim (Eds.), *Applications of Artificial Intelligence in Additive Manufacturing* (pp. 194–209). IGI Global. https://doi.org/10.4018/978-1-7998-8516-0.ch009

Samy, V. S., Pramanick, K., Thenkanidiyoor, V., & Victor, J. (2021). Data Analysis and Visualization in Python for Polar Meteorological Data. *International Journal of Data Analytics*, *2*(1), 32–60. https://doi.org/10.4018/IJDA.2021010102

Sanna, A., & Valpreda, F. (2017). An Assessment of the Impact of a Collaborative Didactic Approach and Students' Background in Teaching Computer Animation. *International Journal of Information and Communication Technology Education*, *13*(4), 1–16. doi:10.4018/IJICTE.2017100101

Sarivougioukas, J., & Vagelatos, A. (2022). Fused Contextual Data With Threading Technology to Accelerate Processing in Home UbiHealth. *International Journal of Software Science and Computational Intelligence*, *14*(1), 1–14. https://doi.org/10.4018/IJSSCI.285590

Scott, A., Martin, A., & McAlear, F. (2017). Enhancing Participation in Computer Science among Girls of Color: An Examination of a Preparatory AP Computer Science Intervention. In Y. Rankin & J. Thomas (Eds.), *Moving Students of Color from Consumers to Producers of Technology* (pp. 62–84). Hershey, PA: IGI Global. doi:10.4018/978-1-5225-2005-4.ch004

Shanmugam, M., Ibrahim, N., Gorment, N. Z., Sugu, R., Dandarawi, T. N., & Ahmad, N. A. (2022). Towards an Integrated Omni-Channel Strategy Framework for Improved Customer Interaction. In P. Lai (Ed.), *Handbook of Research on Social Impacts of E-Payment and Blockchain Technology* (pp. 409–427). IGI Global. https://doi.org/10.4018/978-1-7998-9035-5.ch022

Sharma, A., & Kumar, S. (2021). Network Slicing and the Role of 5G in IoT Applications. In S. Kumar, M. Trivedi, P. Ranjan, & A. Punhani (Eds.), *Evolution of Software-Defined Networking Foundations for IoT and 5G Mobile Networks* (pp. 172–190). IGI Global. https://doi.org/10.4018/978-1-7998-4685-7.ch010

Siddoo, V., & Wongsai, N. (2017). Factors Influencing the Adoption of ISO/IEC 29110 in Thai Government Projects: A Case Study. *International Journal of Information Technologies and Systems Approach, 10*(1), 22–44. doi:10.4018/IJITSA.2017010102

Silveira, C., Hir, M. E., & Chaves, H. K. (2022). An Approach to Information Management as a Subsidy of Global Health Actions: A Case Study of Big Data in Health for Dengue, Zika, and Chikungunya. In J. Lima de Magalhães, Z. Hartz, G. Jamil, H. Silveira, & L. Jamil (Eds.), *Handbook of Research on Essential Information Approaches to Aiding Global Health in the One Health Context* (pp. 219–234). IGI Global. https://doi.org/10.4018/978-1-7998-8011-0.ch012

Simões, A. (2017). Using Game Frameworks to Teach Computer Programming. In R. Alexandre Peixoto de Queirós & M. Pinto (Eds.), *Gamification-Based E-Learning Strategies for Computer Programming Education* (pp. 221–236). Hershey, PA: IGI Global. doi:10.4018/978-1-5225-1034-5.ch010

Simões de Almeida, R., & da Silva, T. (2022). AI Chatbots in Mental Health: Are We There Yet? In A. Marques & R. Queirós (Eds.), *Digital Therapies in Psychosocial Rehabilitation and Mental Health* (pp. 226–243). IGI Global. https://doi.org/10.4018/978-1-7998-8634-1.ch011

Singh, L. K., Khanna, M., Thawkar, S., & Gopal, J. (2021). Robustness for Authentication of the Human Using Face, Ear, and Gait Multimodal Biometric System. *International Journal of Information System Modeling and Design, 12*(1), 39–72. https://doi.org/10.4018/IJISMD.2021010103

Sllame, A. M. (2017). Integrating LAB Work With Classes in Computer Network Courses. In H. Alphin Jr, R. Chan, & J. Lavine (Eds.), *The Future of Accessibility in International Higher Education* (pp. 253–275). Hershey, PA: IGI Global. doi:10.4018/978-1-5225-2560-8.ch015

Smirnov, A., Ponomarev, A., Shilov, N., Kashevnik, A., & Teslya, N. (2018). Ontology-Based Human-Computer Cloud for Decision Support: Architecture and Applications in Tourism. *International Journal of Embedded and Real-Time Communication Systems, 9*(1), 1–19. doi:10.4018/IJERTCS.2018010101

Smith-Ditizio, A. A., & Smith, A. D. (2018). Computer Fraud Challenges and Its Legal Implications. In M. Khosrow-Pour, D.B.A. (Ed.), Encyclopedia of Information Science and Technology, Fourth Edition (pp. 4837-4848). Hershey, PA: IGI Global. doi:10.4018/978-1-5225-2255-3.ch419

Sosnin, P. (2018). Figuratively Semantic Support of Human-Computer Interactions. In *Experience-Based Human-Computer Interactions: Emerging Research and Opportunities* (pp. 244–272). Hershey, PA: IGI Global. doi:10.4018/978-1-5225-2987-3.ch008

Srilakshmi, R., & Jaya Bhaskar, M. (2021). An Adaptable Secure Scheme in Mobile Ad hoc Network to Protect the Communication Channel From Malicious Behaviours. *International Journal of Information Technology and Web Engineering*, *16*(3), 54–73. https://doi.org/10.4018/IJITWE.2021070104

Sukhwani, N., Kagita, V. R., Kumar, V., & Panda, S. K. (2021). Efficient Computation of Top-K Skyline Objects in Data Set With Uncertain Preferences. *International Journal of Data Warehousing and Mining*, *17*(3), 68–80. https://doi.org/10.4018/IJDWM.2021070104

Susanto, H., Yie, L. F., Setiana, D., Asih, Y., Yoganingrum, A., Riyanto, S., & Saputra, F. A. (2021). Digital Ecosystem Security Issues for Organizations and Governments: Digital Ethics and Privacy. In Z. Mahmood (Ed.), *Web 2.0 and Cloud Technologies for Implementing Connected Government* (pp. 204–228). IGI Global. https://doi.org/10.4018/978-1-7998-4570-6.ch010

Syväjärvi, A., Leinonen, J., Kivivirta, V., & Kesti, M. (2017). The Latitude of Information Management in Local Government: Views of Local Government Managers. *International Journal of Electronic Government Research*, *13*(1), 69–85. doi:10.4018/IJEGR.2017010105

Tanque, M., & Foxwell, H. J. (2018). Big Data and Cloud Computing: A Review of Supply Chain Capabilities and Challenges. In A. Prasad (Ed.), *Exploring the Convergence of Big Data and the Internet of Things* (pp. 1–28). Hershey, PA: IGI Global. doi:10.4018/978-1-5225-2947-7.ch001

Teixeira, A., Gomes, A., & Orvalho, J. G. (2017). Auditory Feedback in a Computer Game for Blind People. In T. Issa, P. Kommers, T. Issa, P. Isaías, & T. Issa (Eds.), *Smart Technology Applications in Business Environments* (pp. 134–158). Hershey, PA: IGI Global. doi:10.4018/978-1-5225-2492-2.ch007

Tewari, P., Tiwari, P., & Goel, R. (2022). Information Technology in Supply Chain Management. In V. Garg & R. Goel (Eds.), *Handbook of Research on Innovative Management Using AI in Industry 5.0* (pp. 165–178). IGI Global. https://doi.org/10.4018/978-1-7998-8497-2.ch011

Thompson, N., McGill, T., & Murray, D. (2018). Affect-Sensitive Computer Systems. In M. Khosrow-Pour, D.B.A. (Ed.), Encyclopedia of Information Science and Technology, Fourth Edition (pp. 4124-4135). Hershey, PA: IGI Global. doi:10.4018/978-1-5225-2255-3.ch357

Triberti, S., Brivio, E., & Galimberti, C. (2018). On Social Presence: Theories, Methodologies, and Guidelines for the Innovative Contexts of Computer-Mediated Learning. In M. Marmon (Ed.), *Enhancing Social Presence in Online Learning Environments* (pp. 20–41). Hershey, PA: IGI Global. doi:10.4018/978-1-5225-3229-3.ch002

Tripathy, B. K. T. R., S., & Mohanty, R. K. (2018). Memetic Algorithms and Their Applications in Computer Science. In S. Dash, B. Tripathy, & A. Rahman (Eds.), Handbook of Research on Modeling, Analysis, and Application of Nature-Inspired Metaheuristic Algorithms (pp. 73-93). Hershey, PA: IGI Global. https://doi.org/ doi:10.4018/978-1-5225-2857-9.ch004

Turulja, L., & Bajgoric, N. (2017). Human Resource Management IT and Global Economy Perspective: Global Human Resource Information Systems. In M. Khosrow-Pour (Ed.), *Handbook of Research on Technology Adoption, Social Policy, and Global Integration* (pp. 377–394). Hershey, PA: IGI Global. doi:10.4018/978-1-5225-2668-1.ch018

Unwin, D. W., Sanzogni, L., & Sandhu, K. (2017). Developing and Measuring the Business Case for Health Information Technology. In K. Moahi, K. Bwalya, & P. Sebina (Eds.), *Health Information Systems and the Advancement of Medical Practice in Developing Countries* (pp. 262–290). Hershey, PA: IGI Global. doi:10.4018/978-1-5225-2262-1.ch015

Usharani, B. (2022). House Plant Leaf Disease Detection and Classification Using Machine Learning. In M. Mundada, S. Seema, S. K.G., & M. Shilpa (Eds.), *Deep Learning Applications for Cyber-Physical Systems* (pp. 17-26). IGI Global. https://doi.org/10.4018/978-1-7998-8161-2.ch002

Vadhanam, B. R. S., M., Sugumaran, V., V., V., & Ramalingam, V. V. (2017). Computer Vision Based Classification on Commercial Videos. In M. S., & V. V. (Eds.), Multi-Core Computer Vision and Image Processing for Intelligent Applications (pp. 105-135). Hershey, PA: IGI Global. https://doi.org/doi:10.4018/978-1-5225-0889-2.ch004

Vairinho, S. (2022). Innovation Dynamics Through the Encouragement of Knowledge Spin-Off From Touristic Destinations. In C. Ramos, S. Quinteiro, & A. Gonçalves (Eds.), *ICT as Innovator Between Tourism and Culture* (pp. 170–190). IGI Global. https://doi.org/10.4018/978-1-7998-8165-0.ch011

Valverde, R., Torres, B., & Motaghi, H. (2018). A Quantum NeuroIS Data Analytics Architecture for the Usability Evaluation of Learning Management Systems. In S. Bhattacharyya (Ed.), *Quantum-Inspired Intelligent Systems for Multimedia Data Analysis* (pp. 277–299). Hershey, PA: IGI Global. doi:10.4018/978-1-5225-5219-2.ch009

Vassilis, E. (2018). Learning and Teaching Methodology: "1:1 Educational Computing. In K. Koutsopoulos, K. Doukas, & Y. Kotsanis (Eds.), *Handbook of Research on Educational Design and Cloud Computing in Modern Classroom Settings* (pp. 122–155). Hershey, PA: IGI Global. doi:10.4018/978-1-5225-3053-4.ch007

Verma, S., & Jain, A. K. (2022). A Survey on Sentiment Analysis Techniques for Twitter. In B. Gupta, D. Peraković, A. Abd El-Latif, & D. Gupta (Eds.), *Data Mining Approaches for Big Data and Sentiment Analysis in Social Media* (pp. 57–90). IGI Global. https://doi.org/10.4018/978-1-7998-8413-2.ch003

Wang, H., Huang, P., & Chen, X. (2021). Research and Application of a Multidimensional Association Rules Mining Method Based on OLAP. *International Journal of Information Technology and Web Engineering, 16*(1), 75–94. https://doi.org/10.4018/IJITWE.2021010104

Wexler, B. E. (2017). Computer-Presented and Physical Brain-Training Exercises for School Children: Improving Executive Functions and Learning. In B. Dubbels (Ed.), *Transforming Gaming and Computer Simulation Technologies across Industries* (pp. 206–224). Hershey, PA: IGI Global. doi:10.4018/978-1-5225-1817-4.ch012

Wimble, M., Singh, H., & Phillips, B. (2018). Understanding Cross-Level Interactions of Firm-Level Information Technology and Industry Environment: A Multilevel Model of Business Value. *Information Resources Management Journal, 31*(1), 1–20. doi:10.4018/IRMJ.2018010101

Wimmer, H., Powell, L., Kilgus, L., & Force, C. (2017). Improving Course Assessment via Web-based Homework. *International Journal of Online Pedagogy and Course Design, 7*(2), 1–19. doi:10.4018/IJOPCD.2017040101

Wong, S. (2021). Gendering Information and Communication Technologies in Climate Change. In M. Khosrow-Pour D.B.A. (Eds.), *Encyclopedia of Information Science and Technology, Fifth Edition* (pp. 1408-1422). IGI Global. https://doi.org/10.4018/978-1-7998-3479-3.ch096

Wong, Y. L., & Siu, K. W. (2018). Assessing Computer-Aided Design Skills. In M. Khosrow-Pour, D.B.A. (Ed.), Encyclopedia of Information Science and Technology, Fourth Edition (pp. 7382-7391). Hershey, PA: IGI Global. doi:10.4018/978-1-5225-2255-3.ch642

Wongsurawat, W., & Shrestha, V. (2018). Information Technology, Globalization, and Local Conditions: Implications for Entrepreneurs in Southeast Asia. In P. Ordóñez de Pablos (Ed.), *Management Strategies and Technology Fluidity in the Asian Business Sector* (pp. 163–176). Hershey, PA: IGI Global. doi:10.4018/978-1-5225-4056-4.ch010

Yamada, H. (2021). Homogenization of Japanese Industrial Technology From the Perspective of R&D Expenses. *International Journal of Systems and Service-Oriented Engineering*, *11*(2), 24–51. doi:10.4018/IJSSOE.2021070102

Yang, Y., Zhu, X., Jin, C., & Li, J. J. (2018). Reforming Classroom Education Through a QQ Group: A Pilot Experiment at a Primary School in Shanghai. In H. Spires (Ed.), *Digital Transformation and Innovation in Chinese Education* (pp. 211–231). Hershey, PA: IGI Global. doi:10.4018/978-1-5225-2924-8.ch012

Yilmaz, R., Sezgin, A., Kurnaz, S., & Arslan, Y. Z. (2018). Object-Oriented Programming in Computer Science. In M. Khosrow-Pour, D.B.A. (Ed.), Encyclopedia of Information Science and Technology, Fourth Edition (pp. 7470-7480). Hershey, PA: IGI Global. doi:10.4018/978-1-5225-2255-3.ch650

Yu, L. (2018). From Teaching Software Engineering Locally and Globally to Devising an Internationalized Computer Science Curriculum. In S. Dikli, B. Etheridge, & R. Rawls (Eds.), *Curriculum Internationalization and the Future of Education* (pp. 293–320). Hershey, PA: IGI Global. doi:10.4018/978-1-5225-2791-6.ch016

Yuhua, F. (2018). Computer Information Library Clusters. In M. Khosrow-Pour, D.B.A. (Ed.), Encyclopedia of Information Science and Technology, Fourth Edition (pp. 4399-4403). Hershey, PA: IGI Global. doi:10.4018/978-1-5225-2255-3.ch382

Zakaria, R. B., Zainuddin, M. N., & Mohamad, A. H. (2022). Distilling Blockchain: Complexity, Barriers, and Opportunities. In P. Lai (Ed.), *Handbook of Research on Social Impacts of E-Payment and Blockchain Technology* (pp. 89–114). IGI Global. https://doi.org/10.4018/978-1-7998-9035-5.ch007

Zhang, Z., Ma, J., & Cui, X. (2021). Genetic Algorithm With Three-Dimensional Population Dominance Strategy for University Course Timetabling Problem. *International Journal of Grid and High Performance Computing*, *13*(2), 56–69. https://doi.org/10.4018/IJGHPC.2021040104

About the Contributors

Pramod Kumar Srivastava is working as dean (student welfare) at Rajkiya Engineering College, Azamgarh (Affiliated to Dr APJ Abdul Kalam Technical University, Lucknow), India. He has a doctorate in mathematics from the University of Allahabad, Allahabad, India. He has several publications in various reputed international journals and international conferences. Dr Srivastava has also published multiple books. His research interests include wireless sensor networks, mathematical modelling, and social networks. He possesses over 15 years of teaching and research expertise, having authored over 30 publications in esteemed international journals, published more than 4 patents, edited 2 books, and provided guidance for Ph.D. candidates. He has successfully guided two PhD student and is presently guiding a few more. Excellence in learning has been his motto since he was a student and the proof of this was the gold medal awarded to him for securing the highest marks in his postgraduation. He has applied this motto in his teaching too, and being well known in his genre, he has been invited to give guest lectures at reputed institutes as well as international conferences. He has been a member of organizing committees as well as technical committees of many international conferences.

Ashok Kumar Yadav, with a B.Tech. from AKTU Lucknow, an M.Tech., and Ph.D. from JNU New Delhi, India, holds over seven years of combined teaching and research experience. Currently an assistant professor in the Department of Information Technology at Rajkiya Engineering College in Azamgarh, India. He previously served at the University of Delhi as an assistant professor (On ad-hoc). Dr. Yadav's research spans MADM, blockchain technology, machine learning, and mobility management in mobile communication. His impactful contributions include publications in esteemed journals such as Elsevier, Springer, World Scientific, and Taylor & Francis, alongside presentations at reputable international conferences. Notably, he co-authored "Mastering Disruptive Technologies" and holds Six SCIs, two Scopus publications, and six patents. Actively engaged in academia, he reviews for international journals and contributes to program committees at various conferences. He was honored with the Best paper Award in IEEE World Conference on Applied Intelligence and Computing, 2022, held during June 17–19, 2022 and International Conference on Artificial Intelligence and Smart Communication (AISC), held during January 27-29, 2023.

* * *

Silviu Acaru holds a Master of Engineering degree from Queen Mary University of London and a Ph.D. in Energy Studies from University Brunei Darussalam. His doctoral dissertation focused on using machine learning techniques to promote circular economic practices. He brings expertise in artificial intelligence, sustainability, and the circular economy.

Falak Bhardwaj is an accomplished Data Science researcher with a rich background spanning over 3 years. His academic journey includes a B.Sc. in Data Science from Manav Rachna International Institute of Research & Studies (2021), where he laid the foundation for expertise Driven by an unwavering passion for Data Science, AI, ML, DL, and Next-Gen AI, my commitment is mirrored in the form of 3 research publications in prestigious journals. My proficiency extends to Python, R, C++, and BI tools, enabling me to dynamically approach complex problem-solving. He has also completed more than 7 varied projects, covering various components of AI, from Deep Learning to Database Management Systems. This diverse experience showcases his ability to use his skills effectively across different areas, demonstrating my flexibility in handling various challenges.

Megha Bhushan is Associate Professor in the School of Computing, and Assistant Dean, Research & Consultancy at DIT University, Dehradun, India. She has received her ME and Ph.D. degrees from Thapar University, Punjab, India. She was awarded with a fellowship by UGC, Government of India, in 2014. In 2017, she was a recipient of Grace Hopper Celebration India (GHCI) fellowship. She has published 5 national patents and 1 international patent has been granted. She has published many research articles in international journals and conferences of repute. Further, she is the editor of many edited books with different publishers such as CRC Press, Taylor & Francis Group, Wiley-Scrivener and Bentham Science. Her research interests include Artificial Intelligence, Knowledge representation, Expert systems, and Software quality. She is also the reviewer and editorial board member of many international journals.

Deepika Bishnoi is currently working as Assistant Professor in Nirma University.

Sachin Chaudhary completed his graduation from MJPRU, and Post Graduation from AKTU, Moradabad, U.P. Currently Pursuing his Ph.D. in Computer Science and Engineering from Govt. Recognized University. Presently, he is working as an Assistant Professor in the Department of Computer Science and Applications, IIMT University, Meerut, U.P, India. He has been awarded as Excellence in teaching award 2019. He is the reviewer member of some reputed journals. He has published several book chapters and research papers of national and international reputed journals.

Monica Janet Clifford is associated with the Department of Commerce, as a research scholar, Christ University, Bangalore, India. She also works as an Assistant Professor with the Department of Commerce, UG studies, Mount Carmel College-Autonomous, Bangalore, India. She has completed her Master of Commerce in St Joseph's College of Commerce and has completed her Post Graduate Diploma in Business Administration. She has presented research papers in various National and International conferences on Contextual Marketing. Adding to this, she has actively been a part of various national level workshops and seminars for research advancements. She is an aspiring candidate to publish quality research work in her area of interest in reputed journals.

Ankur Gupta has received the B.Tech and M.Tech in Computer Science and Engineering from Ganga Institute of Technology and Management, Kablana affiliated with Maharshi Dayanand University, Rohtak in 2015 and 2017. He is an Assistant Professor in the Department of Computer Science and

Engineering at Vaish College of Engineering, Rohtak, and has been working there since January 2019. He has many publications in various reputed national/ international conferences, journals, and online book chapter contributions (Indexed by SCIE, Scopus, ESCI, ACM, DBLP, etc). He is doing research in the field of cloud computing, data security & machine learning. His research work in M.Tech was based on biometric security in cloud computing.

Kassim Kalinaki (MIEEE) is a passionate technologist, researcher, and educator with more than ten years of experience in industry and academia. He received his Diploma in Computer engineering from Kyambogo University, a BSc in computer science and engineering, and an MSc. Computer Science and Engineering from Bangladesh's Islamic University of Technology (IUT). Since 2014, He has been lecturing at the Islamic University in Uganda (IUIU), where he most recently served as the Head of Department Computer Science department (2019-2022). Currently, he's pursuing his Ph.D. in Computer Science at the School of Digital Science at Universiti Brunei Darussalam (UBD) since January 2022 and is slated to complete in August 2025. He's the founder and principal investigator of Borderline Research Laboratory (BRLab) and his areas of research include Ecological Informatics, Data Analytics, Computer Vision, ML/DL, Digital Image Processing, Cybersecurity, IoT/AIoMT, Remote Sensing, and Educational Technologies. He has authored and co-authored several published peer-reviewed articles in renowned journals and publishers, including in Springer, Elsevier, Taylor and Francis, Emerald and IEEE.

Julius Kugonza holds a master's degree in Business Administration (Data Science Major) from Manipal Academy of Higher Education-India, Masters in Economic policy and a bachelor's degree in statistics from Makerere University, Uganda. He is also a trade policy design and negotiation fellow from the University of Adelaide, Australia. Julius has over 10 years' experience in the public, CSO and private sectors. He currently works as the Head of business intelligence and Analysis unit at Uganda Revenue Authority. He begun his career at Uganda Bureau of Statistics. He is also a senior research fellow at Pride data solutions (Policy Thinktank). He is also currently a Consultant- Informal Cross Border Trade (ICBT) for the United Nations Economic Commission for Africa. He has also previously worked as a Consultant-Applied Statistician/Power BI Developer for GIZ-South Africa. He also previously worked at a Consultant-Trade Statistics Trainer for JICA. Julius' research interests are in the areas of Regional Integration, Disruptive Technologies, IFFs and Environment.

Bhupendra Kumar completed his Graduation and Post Graduation from Chaudhary Charan Singh University, Meerut, U.P. and Ph.D. in Computer Science and Engineering from Mewar University, Hapur. Presently, he is working as a Professor in the Department of Computer Science and Applications, IIMT University, Meerut, U.P. He has been a huge teaching experience of 19 years. He is the reviewer member of some reputed journals. He has published several book chapters and research papers of national and international reputed journals.

Rajeev Kumar is currently working as Associate Professor in the Department of Applied Sciences (Chemistry), School of Engineering and Technology, Manav Rachna International Institute of Research and Studies, Faridabad. He obtained his Ph.D. degree from Indian Institute of Technology, Roorkee (IIT Roorkee). He had done M.Sc. from CCS University, Meerut. He had qualified NET-JRF from CSIR-UGC. He has more than 14 years of teaching and research experience. He has published 32 research papers in national and international reputed journals. He has also contributed 5 chapters in Books. He had coguided two Ph.D. scholars. Recently he is guiding two research scholars. His current research interests include Environmental Sciences, Orgeno-metallic synthesis, Analytical Chemistry, Water Treatment, and Optimization techniques.

Aparna Kumari is currently working a Professor in Nirma University.

Swati Manekar is currently working as Assistant Professor in Nirma University.

Arun Negi is currently a Manager at Deloitte USI, Hyderabad, India. He has completed a course in Business Management from IIM, Ahmedabad and has obtained B. Tech degree from Jawaharlal Nehru University, New Delhi, India. He has 13+ years of diverse experience in cyber risk services. He has worked on various network security technologies and platforms for Fortune 500 clients. His experience includes cyber security audits, gap assessments, network security audits, cloud migrations and project management. He is currently oriented towards developing multi cloud skills and has achieved certifications in Oracle Cloud and AWS. He has published one national patent and one international patent has been granted. He has published many research articles in international journals and conferences of repute. His research areas include Artificial Intelligence, Software Product Line, Cloud Computing, and Cyber Security.

Ronald Nsubuga holds a Master of Business Administration and a Bachelor of Statistics from Makerere University - Uganda. He is also finalizing a Master of Science in Business Analytics at Manipal Academy of Higher Education - India. He has professionally worked as a Consultant with the United Nations Economic Commission for Africa, United Nations Development Programme and the International Organization for Migration. He has also worked previously with AMREF Health Africa, International Non-Government Organization, as a Monitoring and Evaluation Specialist. He has also previously worked with Pride Data Solutions, a policy think tank, as a Development Researcher. His research interests are in the areas of Artificial Intelligence, Regional Integration, International Trade, Migration among many others.

Rajneesh Panwar Graduated and Post Graduated in Mathematics and Computer Application from Ch. Charan Singh University, Meerut (U.P.) and received his M. Tech. in Computer Science from Shobhit University, Meerut. Presently, he is working as an Assistant Professor in the School of Computer Science and Application IIMT University, Meerut, U.P. He qualifies GATE 2021 and UGC-NET June 2020 and December 2020. He has published several book chapters and research papers of national and international repute.

Sabyasachi Pramanik is a professional IEEE member. He obtained a PhD in Computer Science and Engineering from Sri Satya Sai University of Technology and Medical Sciences, Bhopal, India. Presently, he is an Associate Professor, Department of Computer Science and Engineering, Haldia Institute of Technology, India. He has many publications in various reputed international conferences, journals, and book chapters (Indexed by SCIE, Scopus, ESCI, etc). He is doing research in the fields of Artificial Intelligence, Data Privacy, Cybersecurity, Network Security, and Machine Learning. He also serves on the editorial boards of several international journals. He is a reviewer of journal articles from IEEE, Springer, Elsevier, Inderscience, IET and IGI Global. He has reviewed many conference papers, has been a keynote speaker, session chair, and technical program committee member at many international conferences. He has authored a book on Wireless Sensor Network. He has edited 8 books from IGI Global, CRC Press, Springer and Wiley Publications.

Kavitha R. works with the Department of Commerce, Christ University, Bangalore, India. She holds a PhD in Commerce from Bharathiyar University, Coimbatore, Tamil Nadu. Her area of focus in on marketing, brand management, consumer behaviour and buying process. Her doctoral dissertation was on 'A study on the mind of nouveau shoppers of pandora's box in Indian shopping malls'. Her other research focus is on entrepreneurship, women entrepreneurship, retailing and banking. She has published papers in Scopus indexed journals and in many other reputed journals. She has also been a part of many international conferences and is also a member of the review committee of many international journals.

Durmuş Özkan Şahin received a Bachelor's degree in Computer Engineering from Süleyman Demirel University Isparta in 2013 and a Master's degree in Computer Engineering from Ondokuz Mayıs University Samsun in 2016. Finally, he received a PhD's degree in Computational Sciences from Ondokuz Mayıs University Samsun in 2022. His research interests include machine learning, text mining, information retrieval, and Android malware analysis. He is currently an Assistant Professor of the Department of Computer Engineering at Ondokuz Mayıs University.

Arti Saxena is working as associate professor in department of Applied Science, Faculty of Engineering and Technology, Manav Rachna international Institute of Research and Studies, Faridabad, Haryana, India. She has got young scientist award in an international conference for best paper presentation in 2007 and was awarded her doctorate in 2009 from Dayalbagh Educational Institute, Deemed University, Agra, UP, India. She has more than 16 years of teaching experience of graduates and postgraduates. She has more than 40 research articles in various national and international journals of repute and conference proceedings. She has four research books published to her account and five chapters in edited books. Her areas of interest are Mathematical modeling, Fixed point Theory and Machine Learning.

Sibel Senan graduated from the Computer Science Engineering Department of Istanbul University in 2002. She received her M.Sc. and Ph.D. degrees from Istanbul University, Institute of Science and Technology, Department of Computer Engineering, in 2005 and 2010, respectively. She is currently an Associate Professor of the Department of Computer Engineering at Istanbul University-Cerrahpasa.

Kewal Krishan Sharma is a professor in computer sc. in IIMT University, Meerut, U.P, India. He did his Ph.D. in computer network with this he has MCA, MBA and Law degree also. He did variously certification courses also. He has an overall experience of around 33 year in academic, business and industry. He wrote a number of research papers and books.

Vikas Sharma completed his Graduation and Post Graduation from Chaudhary Charan Singh University, Meerut, U.P. Currently Pursuing his Ph.D. in Computer Science and Engineering from Govt. Recognized University. Presently, he is working as an Assistant Professor in the Department of Computer Science and Applications, IIMT University, Meerut, U.P. He has been awarded as Excellence in teaching award 2019. He is the reviewer member of some reputed journals. He has published several book chapters and research papers of national and international reputed journals.

Maanas Singal is currently a research scholar at DIT University, Dehradun. He completed his Bachelor of Technology in Computer Science and Engineering from Kalinga University, Raipur, Chhattisgarh in 2021. His area of interest spans across multiple sub domains of computer science such as DevOps, Cloud, and Artificial Intelligence/Machine Learning.

Tarun Kumar Vashishth is an active academician and researcher in the field of computer science with 22 years of experience. He earned Ph.D. Mathematics degree specialized in Operations Research; served several academic positions such as HoD, Dy. Director, Academic Coordinator, Member Secretary of Department Research Committee, Assistant Center superintendent and Head Examiner in university examinations. He is involved in academic development and scholarly activities. He is member of International Association of Engineers, The Society of Digital Information and Wireless Communications, Global Professors Welfare Association, International Association of Academic plus Corporate (IAAC), Computer Science Teachers Association and Internet Society. His research interest includes Cloud Computing, Artificial Intelligence, Machine Learning and Operations Research; published more than 25 research articles with 2 books and 15 book chapters in edited books. He is contributing as member of editorial and reviewers boards in conferences and various computer journals published by CRC Press, Taylor and Francis, Springer, IGI global and other universities.

Index

Recommended Reference Books

IGI Global's reference books are available in three unique pricing formats: Print Only, E-Book Only, or Print + E-Book.

Order direct through IGI Global's Online Bookstore at **www.igi-global.com** or through your preferred provider.

ISBN: 9781799884552
EISBN: 9781799884576
© 2022; 394 pp.
List Price: US$ **270**

ISBN: 9781799897101
EISBN: 9781799897125
© 2022; 335 pp.
List Price: US$ **250**

ISBN: 9781668441398
EISBN: 9781668441411
© 2022; 291 pp.
List Price: US$ **270**

ISBN: 9781668441534
EISBN: 9781668441558
© 2023; 335 pp.
List Price: US$ **270**

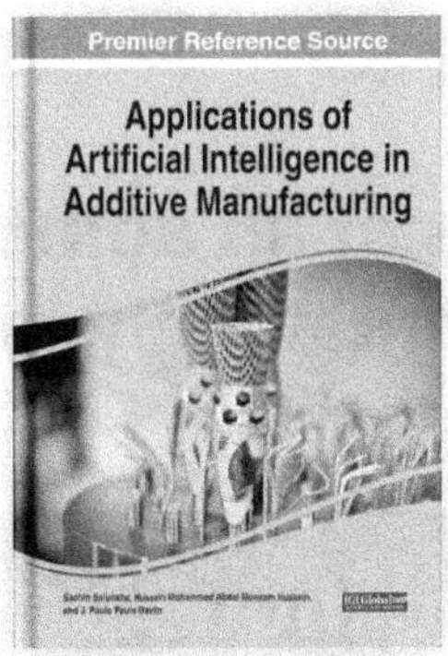

ISBN: 9781799885160
EISBN: 9781799885184
© 2022; 240 pp.
List Price: US$ **270**

ISBN: 9781799887638
EISBN: 9781799887652
© 2022; 306 pp.
List Price: US$ **270**

Do you want to stay current on the latest research trends, product announcements, news, and special offers?
Join IGI Global's mailing list to receive customized recommendations, exclusive discounts, and more.
Sign up at: **www.igi-global.com/newsletters.**

Publisher of Timely, Peer-Reviewed Inclusive Research Since 1988

IGI Global
PUBLISHER of TIMELY KNOWLEDGE

www.igi-global.com | Sign up at www.igi-global.com/newsletters | facebook.com/igiglobal | twitter.com/igiglobal | linkedin.com/igiglobal

Ensure Quality Research is Introduced to the Academic Community

Become an Reviewer for IGI Global Authored Book Projects

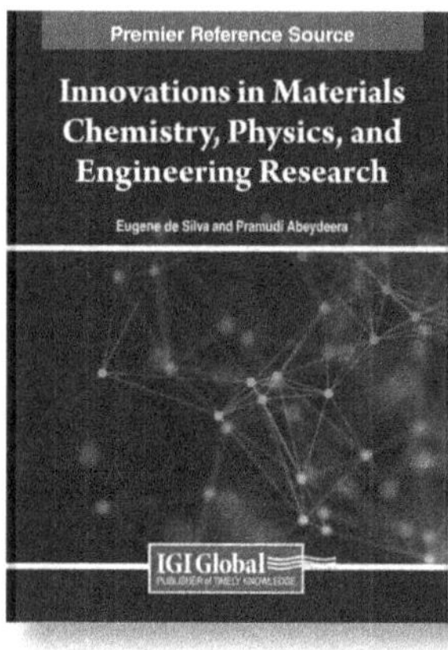

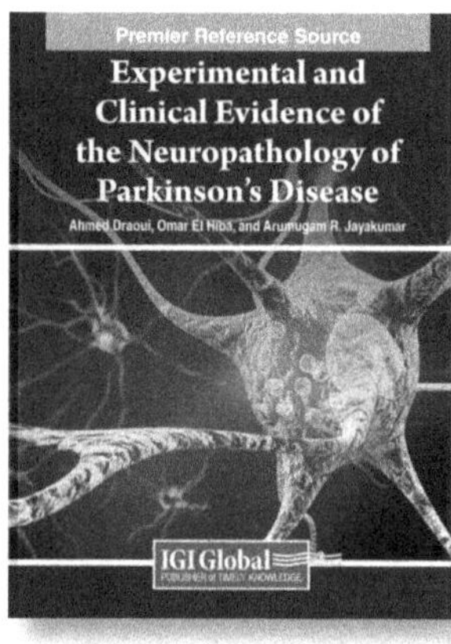

The overall success of an authored book project is dependent on quality and timely manuscript evaluations.

Applications and Inquiries may be sent to:

development@igi-global.com

Applicants must have a doctorate (or equivalent degree) as well as publishing, research, and reviewing experience. Authored Book Evaluators are appointed for one-year terms and are expecte to complete at least three evaluations per term. Upon successful completion of this term, evaluator can be considered for an additional term.

If you have a colleague that may be interested in this opportunity, we encourage you to share this information with them.

Submit an Open Access Book Proposal

Have Your Work Fully & Freely Available Worldwide After Publication

Seeking the Following Book Classification Types:

Authored & Edited Monographs • Casebooks • Encyclopedias • Handbooks of Research

Gold, Platinum, & Retrospective OA Opportunities to Choose From

Easily Track Your Work in Our Advanced Manuscript Submission System With **Rapid Turnaround Times**

Double-Blind Peer Review by Notable Editorial Boards (*Committee on Publication Ethics* (COPE) Certified

Publications Adhere to All **Current OA Mandates & Compliances**

Affordable APCs ***(Often 50% Lower Than the Industry Average)*** Including Robust Editorial Service Provisions

Direct Connections with **Prominent Research Funders** & OA Regulatory Groups

Institution Level OA Agreements Available (Recommend or Contact Your Librarian for Details)

Join a **Diverse Community of 150,000+ Researchers Worldwide** Publishing With IGI Global

Content Spread Widely to Leading Repositories (AGOSR, ResearchGate, CORE, & More)

Retrospective Open Access Publishing

You Can Unlock Your Recently Published Work, Including Full Book & Individual Chapter Content to Enjoy All the Benefits of Open Access Publishing

Learn More

Publishing Tomorrow's Research Today

IGI Global

e-Book Collection

Including Essential Reference Books Within Three Fundamental Academic Areas

Business & Management
Scientific, Technical, & Medical (STM)
Education

- Acquisition options include Perpetual, Subscription, and Read & Publish
- No Additional Charge for Multi-User Licensing
- No Maintenance, Hosting, or Archiving Fees
- Continually Enhanced Accessibility Compliance Features (WCAG)

Over **150,000+** Chapters	Contributions From **200,000+** Scholars Worldwide	More Than **1,000,000+** Citations	Majority of e-Books Indexed in Web of Science & Scopus	Consists of Tomorrow's Research Available Today!

Recommended Titles from our e-Book Collection

Innovation Capabilities and Entrepreneurial Opportunities of Smart Working
ISBN: 9781799887973

Advanced Applications of Generative AI and Natural Language Processing Models
ISBN: 9798369305027

Using Influencer Marketing as a Digital Business Strategy
ISBN: 9798369305515

Human-Centered Approaches in Industry 5.0
ISBN: 9798369326473

Modeling and Monitoring Extreme Hydrometeorological Events
ISBN: 9781668487716

Data-Driven Intelligent Business Sustainability
ISBN: 9798369300497

Information Logistics for Organizational Empowerment and Effective Supply Chain Management
ISBN: 9798369301593

Data Envelopment Analysis (DEA) Methods for Maximizing Efficiency
ISBN: 9798369302552

Request More Information, or Recommend the IGI Global e-Book Collection to Your Institution's Librarian

For More Information or to Request a Free Trial, Contact IGI Global's e-Collections Team: eresources@igi-global.com | 1-866-342-6657 ext. 100 | 717-533-8845 ext. 100

Are You Ready to

Publish Your Research ?

IGI Global
PUBLISHER of TIMELY KNOWLEDGE

IGI Global offers book authorship and editorship opportunities across 11 subject areas, including business, computer science, education, science and engineering, social sciences, and more!

Benefits of Publishing with IGI Global:

- Free one-on-one editorial and promotional support.
- Expedited publishing timelines that can take your book from start to finish in less than one (1) year.
- Choose from a variety of formats, including Edited and Authored References, Handbooks of Research, Encyclopedias, and Research Insights.
- Utilize IGI Global's eEditorial Discovery® submission system in support of conducting the submission and double-blind peer review process.
- IGI Global maintains a strict adherence to ethical practices due in part to our full membership with the Committee on Publication Ethics (COPE).
- Indexing potential in prestigious indices such as Scopus®, Web of Science™, PsycINFO®, and ERIC – Education Resources Information Center.
- Ability to connect your ORCID iD to your IGI Global publications.
- Earn honorariums and royalties on your full book publications as well as complimentary content and exclusive discounts.

Join Your Colleagues from Prestigious Institutions, Including:

Australian National University

Massachusetts Institute of Technology

Johns Hopkins University

Harvard University

Tsinghua University

Columbia University in the City of New York

Learn More at: www.igi-global.com/publish

or Contact IGI Global's Aquisitions Team at: acquisition@igi-global.com

Individual Article & Chapter Downloads

US$ 37.50/each

Easily Identify, Acquire, and Utilize Published Peer-Reviewed Findings in Support of Your Current Research

- Browse Over ***170,000+ Articles & Chapters***
- ***Accurate & Advanced*** Search
- Affordably Acquire ***International Research***
- ***Instantly Access*** Your Content
- Benefit from the ***InfoSci® Platform Features***

THE UNIVERSITY of NORTH CAROLINA at CHAPEL HILL

"It really provides an excellent entry into the research literature of the field. It presents a manageable number of highly relevant sources on topics of interest to a wide range of researchers. The sources are scholarly, but also accessible to 'practitioners'."

\- Ms. Lisa Stimatz, MLS, University of North Carolina at Chapel Hill, USA

IGI Global
PUBLISHER of TIMELY KNOWLEDGE

IGI Global Proudly Partners with

eContent Pro®
International

Editorial Services

Providing you with High-Quality, Affordable, and Expeditious Editorial Support from Manuscript Development to Publication

Copy Editing & Proofreading

Perfect your research paper before publication. Our expert editors will correct faulty spelling, grammar, punctuation, and word usage.

Scientific & Scholarly Editing

Increase your chances of being published. Our expert editors will aid in strengthening the quality of your research before submission.

Figure, Table, Chart & Equation Conversions

Enhance the visual elements of your research. Let our professional designers produce or correct your figures before final submission.

Journal Recommendation

Save time and money when you rely on our expert journal selectors to provide you with a comprehensive journal recommendation report.

Order now to receive an automatic
10% Academic Discount on all your editorial needs.

Scan the QR Code to Learn More

Upload Your Manuscript, Select Your Desired Editorial Service, and Receive a Free Instant Quote

Email: customerservice@econtentpro.com

econtentpro.com

www.ingramcontent.com/pod-product-compliance
Lightning Source LLC
LaVergne TN
LVHW080643011026
849160LV00014B/1308